Praise for Moving Beyond Icebreakers

Moving Beyond Icebreakers goes far beyond activities and games. Part I explores the fears, hopes, and anxieties that leaders may have about using "activities" in meetings and groups. It is the clearest, most coherent explanation of why, how, and when to use activities that I have ever read. Part II is a creative conglomeration of interactive possibilities to help group members bond in effective ways—but there should be a "lock" on this part until you've read Part I. For practitioners in teaching, social work, administrative, and community settings, this book will be a terrific addition to your personal and professional library.

Susan Rice, DSW
Department of Social Work
California State University at Long Beach

Mr. Pollack has written a comprehensive manual for designing, conducting and evaluating interactive meetings, classes, and group exercises. This book is packed with ideas, examples, advice, and how-to-do-it guidelines for group facilitators. *Moving Beyond Icebreakers* is an invaluable resource for more participatory, spirited and productive meetings.

Lee Staples
Clinical Professor of Social Work
Boston University

Moving Beyond Icebreakers is the encyclopedia of interactive group activities. But it is much more than that. Nothing wastes the power and kills the will of the community more insidiously than endless deadly, unproductive meetings. This book raises expectations for what meetings should do and feel like, and then provides the means to fulfill them.

Charles Deutsch
Senior Research Scientist
Harvard School of Public Health

Moving Beyond Icebreakers offers an approach to gathering information in ways that provide a variety of vantage points as a group engages in interactions that are centered on a common purpose. The approach grows out of Stanley Pollack's longstanding experience in developing city youth into masterful facilitators. The lessons from his experience with young people are definitely worth learning.

Janice Jackson
Boston College Lynch School of Education
Former Deputy Superintendent of the Boston Public Schools

Moving Beyond Icebreakers

An Innovative Approach to Group Facilitation, Learning, and Action

Stanley Pollack
with Mary Fusoni

The Center for Teen Empowerment, Inc.
Boston, MA

384 warren Street, 3rd Floor
Boston, MA 02119
(617) 536-4266
www.teenempowerment.org
www.movingbeyondicebreakers.org

Design by Nick Jehlen
Illustrations by Nick Thorkelson

Printed in Canada

Publisher's Cataloging-in-Publication
(Provided by Quality Books, Inc.)

Fusoni, Mary.
Moving beyond icebreakers : an innovative approach to group facilitation, learning, and action / Mary Fusoni and Stanley Pollack.
p. cm.
Includes index.
ISBN 978-0-9766658-0-9

1. Group facilitation. 2. Communication in social action. 3. Conversation--Social aspects. 4. Group counseling for teenagers. I. Pollack, Stanley. II. Title.

HM751.F87 2005 302.3'46
QBI05-800233

Part I: A Methodology for Interactive Meetings

Acknowledgements

This book is the result of over 30 years of work in group facilitation and represents the collective wisdom of many talented and dedicated people. In the early 1970's I was just starting out as a youth worker in Somerville, MA. Through my work I came to realize the importance of involving young people as partners in solving the city's serious problems with youth crime. This analysis led to the development of the Teen Empowerment Model®, which includes processes for selecting youth leaders, training youth to take action for positive change, and using a behavior change system that helps youth, including high risk youth, to reach their highest potential. An essential element of this strategy is the innovative use of interactive group methods, which is applicable in both youth and adult settings and is the subject of this book.

I gained my initial understanding of the importance of interactive methods through a class called "Training for Trainers" taught by an inspiring trainer and facilitator, Pat Papernow. Over the many weeks of the course, I went from a rudimentary understanding of running groups to an appreciation of how interactive methods can work to bring people together in new and powerful ways. As I incorporated what I had learned into meetings of the Somerville Youth Council, the program's effectiveness grew dramatically, and I have spent the three decades since expanding and refining the methodology. Thanks to Pat for opening my eyes to the power of interaction.

Along the way, many other people have contributed insight, hard work, further inspiration, and more ideas to shape the contents of this book. Mary Fusoni, who is both my professional and life partner, turned my hurried and headlong prose into a clear and readable volume, and for that I owe her an enormous debt of gratitude. In addition, she has patiently documented each exercise and variation, shaping them into a standardized and highly usable format. Without her, this book would most definitely not exist.

Mary and I would like to acknowledge how much the love of our daughters, Andrea and Jana Pollack, sustains us in life and in our work. We also want to express our love and our gratitude for their ongoing support to Mary's sisters, Ann Palmer and Eleanor Fusoni.

Since the founding of the Center for Teen Empowerment in 1992, TE staff have used the Interactive Meeting Format with skill and enthusiasm, and through this process we have all learned how to run groups more effectively. In particular I want to thank the following past or present TE staff members for their work and their contributions:

- Stella Repetto Downie, who contributed material to this book's precursor, *The Art of Group Facilitation*. Stella wrote several of the scenarios that have carried over to this book and supplied documentation for approximately 50 interactive exercises.
- Doug Ackley, who has been with Teen Empowerment since 1993 and has been my collaborative partner in every aspect of the program. He created and documented many of the exercise variations in this book.
- Sara Jo Slate, who wrote and researched the first draft of chapter 7, "The Engaged Learner: Interactive Methods in the Classroom." Nearly everything from that draft is in the book.
- Emily Silas, who reviewed "The Engaged Learner" chapter and provided helpful suggestions from the perspective of a teacher in a Boston public high school.
- Wendy Jebens, who reviewed drafts and provided many good ideas, including the concept of outlining intermediate steps that developed into chapter 2, "Working into Interaction."

Thanks, also, to these current and former TE staff members whose contributions of scenarios, agendas, lesson plans, exercises, enthusiasm, and thoughtful awareness have helped shape the contents of the book: Shirronda Almeida, Jennifer Banister, Sheri Bridgeman, Frenia Cuff, Steven Godfrey, Andy Haydu, LaTia King, Lauren Lapat, Craig McClay, Susan McDonald, Kim Molle, Sapna Padte, and Nick Richardson. Other TE staff have worked on book production and marketing and taken on numerous tasks that needed doing so that Mary and I could concentrate on this project. Thanks to Stephanie Berkowitz, Alex Ocasio, Carol Orme-Johnson, and Porche Viarruel. Teen Empowerment has a most remarkable staff. Others who work every day to build and sustain the program are José Carrera, Demetrius Jackson, Natacha Montina, Marlon Ramdehal, Robert Ricks, Nicole Rodriguez, Gina San Inocencio, and Marquis Tucker. I am grateful to them all.

I also want to thank the many hundreds of youth who have worked as TE youth organizers over the years, as well as those youth who have volunteered their time to TE projects. These young people's thoughtfulness, creativity, leadership, hard work, and dedication to creating positive change in their schools and communities have been a continual source of inspiration. And thanks to the teachers, police officers, youth workers, social workers, and others who, through their participation in TE trainings and workshops, have helped us to develop and refine the methods and exercises found in the book.

I am deeply grateful to three skilled professionals whose contributions to this finished product are beyond adequate expressions of thanks:

- Nick Jehlen, for his clear and attractive design, as well as his accessibility and patience.
- Nick Thorkelson, whose cartoons and illustrations have kept us laughing and captured in images what I struggled to convey in words.
- Michelle Kwitkin-Close for her intelligent, careful, and nuanced editing.

To all three I say thank you not only for your skills, but also for your hard work and understanding throughout a lengthy process. Thanks also to Jim O'Brien for creating the book's finishing touch, its index.

In 1999, we decided it was past time to capture in print the interactive methodology in use every day at Teen Empowerment. The result was a book called *The Art of Group Facilitation*. Its audience was narrowly defined as our own staff and those who used TE consulting services, but the book achieved word of mouth reputation and, with no advertising, we sold more than 500 copies. In addition, we were increasingly doing training and consulting with adult groups and discovering a broad range of applications for our approach. We had also fine-tuned the methodology and created many exercises and variations that had not yet been documented. Therefore, in 2002 we hired Wellspring Consulting, LLC, to study the feasibility of publishing an expanded version of the book. Thanks to Christopher Keevil and his associates at Wellspring for their guidance.

As part of the feasibility study, several people agreed to read *The Art of Group Facilitation* and give us their suggestions for the new book. Thanks to the following reviewers, whose insights we have tried to incorporate into *Moving Beyond Icebreakers*: Dr. Lauren Abramson, Matt Brown, Shari Churwin, Emily Gill, Nancy Haydu, Caitlin Hollister, Randy Nelson, and Elizabeth Olson. Special thanks to Bill Ryan, who read the earlier book and gave us detailed feedback, and to Mary Phillips and Tatum Nolan, who reviewed early drafts of this book. I also want to thank Michele Scaramozza of Partners for Youth with

Disabilities for talking with us about making interactive work broadly accessible.

Teen Empowerment is a nonprofit agency that depends on foundation support to fulfill our mission. Several members of the foundation world have believed steadfastly in Teen Empowerment's work to create this book and to bring this aspect of our approach to a wider audience. I am particularly grateful to:

- The late Polly Germeshausen and her daughter, Nancy Klavans, whose support of Teen Empowerment through the Germeshausen Foundation has been visionary and unwavering.
- Martin S. Kaplan, whose work for good throughout the world has been important to so many people. I particularly appreciate his attention to quality in the work of nonprofits and his commitment to the youth he has met through Teen Empowerment.
- Pamela L. Trefler, who has dedicated herself to improving urban education and encouraged TE's work in Boston schools.
- Melinda Marble of the Paul and Phyllis Fireman Charitable Trust, who has consistently provided us with helpful advice and wise counsel.

The growth and continued existence of Teen Empowerment would not be possible without the many foundations that have supported us over the years. Thank you to the John W. Alden Trust, the Andrus Family Fund, the Arthur M. Blank Family Foundation, the Boston Foundation, the Boston Globe Foundation, the J.E. and Z. B. Butler Foundation, the Church Home Society, the Cricket Island Foundation, the Mary W. B. Curtis Trust, EdVestors, the Paul and Phyllis Fireman Charitable Trust, the Charles Hayden Foundation, the Roy A. Hunt Foundation, the Hyams Foundation, Inc., Mellon New England, the Frank Reed and Margaret Jane Peters Memorial Fund, the Mabel Louise Riley Foundation, the Rochester Area Community Foundation, the Rowland Foundation, Sovereign Bank New England, State Street Bank Global Philanthropy, the Surdna Foundation, the Trefler Foundation, Wilmer Cutler Pickering Hale and Dorr LLP, the Wilson Foundation, and the Yawkey Foundation.

Thanks are due, also, to the many individual contributors whose donations help Teen Empowerment to thrive.

Finally, my deepest gratitude to Teen Empowerment's board of directors, who give their time and energy to ensure the stability and growth of our organization: Dennis Maguire, Kevin Lee Hepner, Joe Jackson, Alice Andrus, Lia DeMarderosian, Stella Repetto Downie, Martha Frost, Lauren Lapat, Elsa Martinez, Debra McLaughlin, Bobbette Morrison, Danyella Myers, José Rodriguez-Villalobos, Helen Soussou, and Pamela Trefler. Without their aid and support, Teen Empowerment could not carry on its work.

Part I: A Methodology for Interactive Meetings

Introduction

- Who Is This Book for?
- Beyond Icebreakers: The Interactive Meeting Format
- Does This Work with Adults?

Who Is This Book for?

This book is for anyone who runs groups, meetings, or classes, large or small, with participants of any age or demographic makeup. If you facilitate groups (teaching, organizing, leading others toward productive goals), this book is for you—that is, if you want the sessions you run to be lively, creative, interactive, and effective.

What Is a "Group"?
By "group" we mean any gathering of people who come together to achieve a goal.

What Is a "Meeting"?
We use the word "meeting" to describe many different kinds of gatherings. When we say "meeting," we are referring to all of the following:

- a class, with students from elementary school through adult education.
- a group session of any kind, from a book club to a therapy group to a community organization.
- a staff meeting or other kind of business meeting.
- any gathering of six or more people who have come together for a common purpose.

Some of the advice and instructions in this book will be more or less appropriate for different kinds of meetings, but if you keep an open mind and are willing to experiment, you'll be amazed at the techniques that will work in unexpected circumstances.

It's a safe bet that everyone reading these words has been to a meeting that was boring, tedious, and unproductive. Maybe it was even an infuriating waste of your precious time and life's energy. Maybe you have sat through many meetings like that. This book is dedicated to the proposition that such meetings are against human nature and need not exist upon the earth. We are dedicated to replacing boring, unproductive meetings with meetings that are, at the very least, interesting and productive. But first, let's visit the bad-meeting world that we all have experienced:

Tap this page if you've been to a meeting

- that did not accomplish any of its goals.
- that did not have any discernable goals.
- where you had something to contribute but couldn't get a word in.
- where you came thinking you were interested in the topic, but left convinced you weren't.
- where you came not knowing anyone and left not knowing anyone—after two hours in the

same small room.
- where you learned people's names only by chance.
- that had no agenda.
- that had an agenda, but the leader didn't follow it.
- that was hijacked by someone who had their own agenda.
- that was so boring you were fighting to keep your eyes open.
- where you longed for movement, longed for laughter, longed for human connection.

Cover your eyes and groan if you've ever led such a meeting. (But please don't feel guilty. You're in good company, including the company of the authors.)

Wave your arms in the air if you want to run meetings that are lively and creative, accomplish their goals, and involve all participants. Then put your arms down and keep turning these pages.

Beyond Icebreakers: The Interactive Meeting Format

Most people who pick up this book will do so at first because they want ideas for more "icebreakers." The book is full of ideas, and you could just skip ahead and find an exercise to do at the next meeting that you run. But to limit your use of the book in that way would be a mistake. We strongly urge you to take the next step as a group facilitator: to have the courage to move beyond icebreakers.

Most of us think of an icebreaker as an exercise that might help people relax and get to know each other at the beginning of a meeting. You will see that in this book we never talk about "icebreakers," because we believe that icebreakers are only the smallest beginning steps toward running effective meetings. The book describes a methodology that is more than a beginning and has effects far beyond helping people to relax. It is a comprehensive approach that:

- provides an interactive structure from the beginning to the end of a meeting,
- extends throughout the life of a group, and
- has the power to fundamentally transform the way a group functions and heighten the effectiveness of the group's work together.

This book describes only one aspect of the Teen Empowerment Model, which is a comprehensive methodology for working with groups that has wide-ranging applications in both youth and adult settings. Teen Empowerment plans to publish additional materials explaining how to work with other parts of the model.

For information about Teen Empowerment—the model, our history, our programs, and more—see our website, www.teenempowerment.org.

Moving Beyond Icebreakers talks about "interactive exercises" and the context in which they are most effective—the Interactive Meeting Format, described in chapter 4. This book will show you how to move in your thinking and your action beyond the limits implied by the word "icebreaker" into a greatly expanded understanding of the power of group interaction. This approach to group facilitation will real-

ly "bring everyone to the table" (not drag them there in chains, like these poor folks) so that their ideas and feelings are expressed and heard and the group's goals will be more readily accomplished. Consistent and thoughtful use of the Interactive Meeting Format will transform your world of meetings.

Does This Work with Adults?

This book outlines an approach to working with groups of all ages for a variety of purposes. While a great deal of our experience has involved working with inner-city teens, we have also used the Interactive Meeting Format extensively with people of all ages. Over a 30-year period, we've used the format in countless training sessions with teachers, administrators, police officers, agency board members, and other adults working in various capacities. We've used it in classrooms, staff meetings, board meetings, action-oriented groups, therapy groups, recreational groups, and training sessions of all kinds.

We have learned that most of the principles and practices that are effective in engaging teens in important work are also effective with adults. Both youth and adults want to be heard, to feel valued, and to have meaningful input into the decisions that affect their professional and personal lives. Both youth and adults have a need for community and for being connected to the people around them in more than superficial ways. Both youth and adults far too often find themselves at meetings where they feel disconnected, undervalued, isolated, and bored by the monotonous practices that are the norm for most group work situations.

The difference is that while many teenagers in alienating situations will act out their alienation in ways that cannot be ignored, most adults have learned to hide their feelings. Teens may put their heads down on a desk, get a blank look in their eyes, or begin talking with friends in a way that disrupts the group. And if they are required to come to boring or directionless meetings over and over again, some

may decide not to come at all. Adults, on the other hand, will try to maintain their focus and look interested. If the meeting seems to be going nowhere and decisions are not being made, if there is no clear agenda and seemingly no point to the discussion, or if the meeting is driving toward a goal but a few people dominate the discussion while others are silent, most adults will nevertheless pay attention if they can, or maintain the appearance of paying attention if they can't.

However, even though adults have learned to adapt to the bad-meeting world, we have found repeatedly that people welcome the Interactive Meeting Format, which opens up the process to everyone's thoughts and creativity while maintaining structure and focus. We have seen how dramatically levels of productivity are increased through the consistent use of the format. We hope that you will read on, and learn how this new approach to meetings, groups, and classes can help your group or organization develop more productive working relationships, learn important information, and come up with creative ways of overcoming problems.

Some of the exercises in this book are in common use, some were created by Teen Empowerment staff, and some were brought into our practice by TE staff from other sources. We have adapted the exercises to fit a variety of settings, always with a consciousness about how each exercise can further the development of active, cohesive, and productive working groups.

A Note about Pronouns

In order to avoid awkward constructions such as "his or her," which would occur with great frequency in this text, we have chosen to use the third person plural in sentences such as, "Have each person say their name."

Chapter 1

Why Use Interactive Methods?

If you were to look in on a staff meeting of our organization, you would certainly wonder what was going on. You might see 18 adults walking backwards within a circle of chairs, crisscrossing and weaving around each other, apparently trying simultaneously to tag someone and to avoid being tagged. There's a general sense of confusion, and a couple of people may be laughing too hard to concentrate on tagging. In the few moments before the facilitator calls an end to the exercise, you might be thinking, "Don't these people have important work to do? Why are they wasting time with this silly game?"

Working up to It
This chapter shows people working with the Interactive Meeting Format in its entirety, but we know that many readers will need to build up gradually to that level. Find out how in chapter 2, "Working into Interaction."

Then people take their seats, pulling the chairs into a closer circle. The facilitator asks for reactions to the exercise. Someone observes that doing the exercise backwards makes it even crazier than usual. People share their experiences with the exercise and strategies they used to deal with this new challenge. The facilitator draws the parallels between this exercise (BACKWARDS STOP TAG, p. 273) and a situation the group is currently facing: they are planning an event that they "backed into," without fully understanding the ramifications, and now everyone has to work extra hard to make it successful. They also discuss how important it is for everyone to take responsibility for their own tasks, rather than trying to "tag" other people and pass off their jobs.

The exercise, together with the discussion ("processing") that followed, have brought the group in less than ten minutes to a point where they are focused on their common goal of organizing a successful event and aware of some of the dynamics they must deal with to achieve their goal. They have had an in-the-body experience that illustrates some of the intangible issues confronting the group. Energized by the exercise, the group comes up with a variety of creative strategies as they work through their agenda.

This meeting presents a bright contrast to a "normal" meeting. It's safe to say that every day millions of people leave meetings feeling that they have wasted their time, or that their potential contributions have not been allowed to emerge. Vast numbers of people regularly sit through meetings that are alienating and unfocused, that fail to produce forward movement toward the group's goals, or that produce such movement with input from only a minority of the meetings' participants. Even meetings with the avowed purpose of seeking new approaches often are mired in old, ineffective methods—such as:

a workshop entitled "Using Interactive Teaching Methods" that consists of a lecture and a question-and-answer period, or a conference about the importance of relationship-building for effective learning that does no relationship-building among participants and contains no practical information about how to build relationships within a group.

This book invites you to break out of these static and largely unproductive traditional meeting formats and to take on the challenge of the *Moving Beyond Icebreakers* approach. With this approach, you will learn how to create a dynamic group context where the norms are excellent communication, strong and positive motivation, and creative problem solving. Its many benefits can be summarized under four headings:

1. Building Relationships and Bringing a Group to Life

Groups exist for people to be in relationship, and meetings exist for people to come together and create something through their interaction that could not otherwise have been created. If you accept this view, then you will surely agree that building relationships is central to the purpose of any meeting. Yet people often leave group meetings knowing little to nothing about those they've met with. If any relationship-building occurred, it may have happened despite the meeting structure, not because of it.

An interactive approach, on the other hand, begins with the need felt by people of all ages for connection and for active engagement in the world around them. It always includes mechanisms both to ensure that group members are awake and engaged and to build relationships and trust as a basis for the work that lies ahead. A meeting, workshop, or classroom where everyone has the opportunity to move, laugh, speak, and share their ideas is going to be much more interesting and productive than a traditional lecture/question-and-answer format where very few people speak and even fewer people really listen. The skillful use of interactive methods creates a context in which group members get to know each other and have opportunities to participate actively in the group's work.

2. Increasing the Group's Understanding of and Investment in Its Mission

When a group faces challenges, as every group does when it is engaged in meaningful work, a strong understanding of the group's goals and a belief in those goals will keep people involved in the task at hand. For a group to function most effectively, people need to be consistently aware of their common purpose. Often, groups begin meeting without clearly stating or discussing their mission, or they discuss their mission only at an initial meeting and then do not revisit it. As time passes and people struggle to accomplish their tasks, they may lose sight of the purpose that brought them into the group in the first place. They may find that they are facing difficult and overwhelming tasks without a conscious awareness of the importance of their work.

Interactive methods provide the mechanisms to enable group members to explore, on a regular basis, the reasons they are doing their work and why it is important. They provide people with opportunities to consider and share the experiences, understandings, and commitments that brought them to the group. Being in touch with these fundamental elements is critically important if group members are to be invested in the group's work and motivated to make difficult decisions, resolve disagreements, and apply energy and focus to their work. Scenario 1 is an example of how interactive exercises can help a group stay connected to its mission.

Scenario 1: Connecting to the Mission

Julie was a teacher in a middle school in which teachers and students were organized into clusters. Her cluster had a number of students with difficult behavior issues and learning problems, and the school year thus far had not been going well. Teachers in the cluster had tried several strategies with minimal success. Some were feeling frustrated and were beginning to adopt a "just get through the year" attitude. Julie volunteered to run the next teachers' meeting for the cluster, at which the teachers would try find a new approach to dealing with these problems.

She felt it was important as they got started to restore people's sense of confidence in themselves as effective teachers and to combat the sense of hopelessness that was beginning to take hold. Therefore, after a brief introduction, she asked the group to answer a Warm-up Question (chapter 10): Tell us about a difficult student you remember from your teaching career whom you were able to reach, and how you were able to reach that student.

As people recounted their successes, Julie could feel the pessimistic mood lifting. The exercise had several positive effects on the group:

- Individuals had the opportunity to remember and rethink strategies that had worked for them in the past.
- Each story sparked ideas in other group members about possible solutions to the current

situation.

- People were able to reconnect to the reasons they had become teachers in the first place.

Julie followed the Warm-up Question with an exercise called BAG TOSS (p. 302), in which people throw an increasing number of beanbags in a set pattern within the circle. After a chaotic round with many dropped bags (and a lot of laughter), she added the variation THINK AHEAD BAG TOSS (p.304); in this version, people think about strategies and set goals before they start throwing bags. Julie then took a few minutes to discuss ("process") the exercise. She pointed out that the first time they did the exercise, everyone felt overwhelmed, as students often do (and as the teachers were feeling at this point in the school year). She said that by working together thoughtfully, the group could find ways to strengthen the network among themselves so that no students would be "dropped."

The group then went on to do BRAINSTORMING (p.385) about possible solutions, and to discuss and prioritize their ideas. From the prioritized ideas, they created an action plan.

When they evaluated the meeting, the teachers expressed many positive feelings. They said they had made progress toward resolving the cluster's problems, they had a renewed sense of commitment to meeting these challenges, and they felt more unified in their approach and more aware that they were all in this together.

3. Surfacing Dissension and Building Strong Agreement for Effective Action

Agreement is intimately related to productivity. When people are truly behind a group's decisions, they act on those decisions with inspiration and dedication, allowing the group to achieve a great deal. Conversely, productivity and effectiveness suffer greatly when a group is not united behind its chosen course of action.

The tendency of most facilitators is to bring the group to agreement as quickly as possible, believing that this is the most efficient way to get through the decision-making process to the point where a group is ready to take action. They set the agenda and position the issues in ways that minimize dissension, and they do not seek to draw out doubts and questions. If no one in the group expresses disagreement, they assume the group is united behind the proposed course of action. However, these leaders fail to recognize that, in a typical group, some people are quiet because they are uncomfortable speaking up; others do not speak because they are unsure of their true feelings; and others may not feel that it is their right or responsibility to contribute their perspective.

While facilitators would prefer agreement, they are often satisfied with a lack of dissent. When a group is at the discussion stage, this approach seems efficient and productive. But its negative impact on productivity becomes apparent when the group tries to move into action. The people who silently disagree will be uninspired and unmotivated in their work. They may passively, or even actively, undermine the group's work. Meanwhile, the leadership may not be aware that disagreement exists, and may be puzzled or frustrated by the lack of energy and momentum in the work of the group.

Interactive techniques move a group toward authentic agreement by helping people to clarify and articulate their thoughts and feelings. Often people are surprised to find that an interactive exercise uncovers feelings they had not been conscious of about an issue, or prompts ideas about possible solu-

tions to problems that the group is working with. An interactive format combines this process of discovery with a comfortable environment for speaking up in a group. Interaction thus brings more voices into the discussion, increasing the opportunities for creative ideas and solutions to problems.

Without interaction, solid agreement about a group's goals and activities cannot be achieved because disagreements and doubts are likely to be invisible, at least among some members of the group. By skillful use of interactive techniques, facilitators can bring out people's opinions, feelings, and ideas, so that all members of the group are heard. The spirit of the group and its ability to achieve its mission are greatly enhanced by surfacing disagreements and encouraging all voices. By using interactive methods thoughtfully and consistently, you can bring individuals' feelings about the group and its projects to the surface of the group's daily life. Once surfaced, these issues can be acknowledged and worked through. This process makes it possible for the group to build real agreement about what it is doing and should be doing, and to set the stage for powerful and effective group action.

4. Surfacing and Resolving Dysfunctional Group Dynamics

Interactive techniques can be used to help a group define its own dynamics and its own problems—the first step in moving through the issues and toward the group's goals. When tension between people, general stress, or individuals' personal issues or behaviors are impeding a group's functioning, these can be dealt with most effectively when the group itself, rather than the leader, articulates the problems.

Picture a group that includes three people who are dysfunctional in the group context; perhaps they are unmotivated, unable to listen, unwilling to follow through on group decisions, disruptive, or always bringing up side issues. The group also includes six other people who are basically functional in terms of the group's work, on a continuum from highly to marginally motivated and involved. This group is working on a big project, but progress is stop-and-go. The facilitator decides that it's necessary to articulate the problems he or she sees: "This group isn't motivated. We have an important job to do and we are just not doing it. People are being irresponsible," etc. Instead of being motivated by this talk, however, most groups will respond in one of these ways:

- Individuals fuse together, creating a wall in opposition to the leadership. Now *everyone* is resistant to the work. The facilitator has defined the group as having problems, which tends to push everyone together, place people's varying degrees of motivation on the same level, and create a united and dysfunctional front against the facilitator's attempt to reinvigorate the group's efforts.

- Members of the group turn against each other and begin blaming one another for the group's difficulties. Now even those motivated to do the work are distracted by the need to uproot those who are letting the group down.

- Or, most likely of all, the group is simply unaffected by the facilitator's talk, which is not connected to the layers of feelings that are preventing some group members from being motivated and taking action.

A more effective approach is to come at the problem indirectly, giving the group the tools to help them recognize problems for themselves and articulate what they see. Interactive techniques have the power to surface what's going on in a group: agreement, disagreement, resistance, anger, enthusiasm, pessimism, or personal and interpersonal issues. By selecting techniques that address the group's issues in a subtle way, you can create a context for group members to see and talk about the dysfunctional group dynamics in ways that change these dynamics and allow the group to become more productive in achieving its mission.

Furthermore, problems that hinder the group's work can best be solved in an atmosphere and a format where everyone's voice is heard. Solutions to problems often lie in the authentic voices of group members, and interaction is the tool that can free those voices to speak.

If an issue outside the group (such as someone dealing with a family problem or other personal problem) is impeding the group's work, carefully chosen interactive techniques can bring the situation to the surface in an appropriate way. Once the issue is brought to light, understanding, empathy, and assistance may be available to help alleviate the problem, in contrast to the anger and frustration that group members might otherwise be feeling toward the dysfunctional person.

Even if the group cannot do anything to help, simply knowing the source of the problem will be helpful to the group's functioning. For example, if a group member is moody but no one knows why, each person in the group will form an opinion, and many of these opinions may be far from the truth of the situation. Some will take the moodiness personally ("He must be upset with me for some reason") and others will be angry about it ("What's her problem!"), whereas the moodiness may have nothing to do with anyone in the group and be a normal reaction to the person's situation. When the source of the problem is unknown and there are insufficient channels of communication between the moody person and the rest of the group, both the group and the individual will suffer. In the hands of a skilled facilitator, interactive techniques can help the person to see how their behavior is affecting the group and to take steps to remedy the dysfunction. In our example, if the moody person is given a supportive context to explain the problems that are causing them distress, or at least to explain that they have some things on their mind that don't have to do with the group, the dysfunctional impact of their moods will be greatly reduced. Furthermore, this communication may open up opportunities for group members to support this individual in a way that helps them to participate effectively in the group once again.

Scenario 2: Interaction Surfaces Group Issues

In Cody's group, there had been some problems getting everyone to participate on equal terms. Several group members complained of feeling left out all the time.

For the meeting at which the group was to begin planning its next project, Cody selected the exercise ALL ABOARD (p. 299). This exercise challenges the group to fit everyone into a small square marked off on the floor with tape. The activity is a metaphor for incorporating all of the differing opinions and skills of group members into the work of the group.

Melissa was the last person to get into the square. At first she didn't want to get in at all. She said that she wouldn't fit; there was no room for her. Finally, with a lot of encouragement from the group, she got in, and the group successfully completed the exercise.

In discussing ("processing") the exercise, Cody asked various group members about their experience of ALL ABOARD. He asked the person who got in the square first if he often took the lead in the group, and why. He asked Melissa if she was often the last person to join in. She admitted that she was, then with great hesitation explained that she didn't feel part of the group and worried that they would not appreciate her input or ideas. Other members of the group quickly responded that this wasn't true, that they wanted to get to know her and hear what she had to say. They pointed out that Melissa was always holding back, to the point where she would even walk behind the rest of the group when they were going somewhere together. They explained that it seemed Melissa had put up a wall between herself and the rest of the group.

Everyone in the group was changed at least a bit by this experience. Melissa began to open up more and to bring her thoughts and talents forward. Others felt more understanding of Melissa and began to reach out to her and more consciously include her in group activities and discussions. The exercise brought to the surface an important dynamic that was keeping the group from fully bonding and utilizing everyone's talents. If this issue had not been brought to the surface in a way that was caring and supportive of Melissa, she would have continued either to create unease and drain motivation from the group by her aloofness, or to pull away from the group until she left it completely.

Chapter 2

Working Into Interaction

- The Bare Minimum for Meetings
- Steps toward Interaction

There are certain elements, which we call the "Bare Minimum," that are essential for a well-run meeting. Facilitating meetings according to the Bare Minimum standards will immediately help to improve any group's productivity, and adhering to these standards is a great start on the road to a fully interactive approach.

Your personality and the nature of the meetings you facilitate are the prime determinants of how quickly and completely you implement the Interactive Meeting Format, described in chapter 4. If you are a fearless facilitator with a group that is open to a new approach, we urge you to plunge right in using the Bare Minimum plus all the elements of the format. Under other circumstances, you may prefer to concentrate on the Bare Minimum for a few meetings, then gradually take the "Steps toward Interaction" recommended in this chapter.

Whichever approach you take, the Bare Minimum standards should always be your baseline.

The Bare Minimum for Meetings

There is a lot involved in being a skilled group facilitator, but let's start with the absolute basics:

1. **An Agenda.** You need to come to the meeting with a coherent, written agenda that will move the group toward achieving its goals. During the meeting, work with the agenda in a thoughtful way—that is, assume that you will stay with the agenda, but if a topic or point of discussion comes up that clearly needs to be dealt with, be flexible enough to make room for it on the agenda. Ideally, you would go over the agenda at the beginning of the meeting; see p.37.

2. **For Action-oriented Meetings, a Note-taker**. Every day, people make decisions at meetings and volunteer for tasks, then leave the meetings with no record of what has occurred. When the group reconvenes, people may have different recollections of what was decided and no one may be able to remember exactly who was responsible for particular tasks. This is not the path to productivity. To set out on a different path, make it a priority to find someone (ideally someone you are sure has the capacity to do the job well) to take minutes, or at least to take notes about the group's decisions and individuals' responsibilities. This person should also be willing to make copies of their minutes (or notes) and distribute them to all group members, including those not in attendance at the meeting. If no one is willing to take on this task, write all decisions and responsibilities on the board or flip chart during the meeting, and bring this to the next meeting for reference.

3. **Introductions.** Beginning on p. 41, you can read about how knowing other people's names contributes to the success of a meeting. Even if you are not ready to ask the group to work on actually

learning names, the Bare Minimum calls for a go-around introduction, in which everyone introduces themselves to the group.

4. **A Speaking Order.** As facilitator of a meeting, you need to be active, alert, and focused in order to create an environment where everyone can be heard. Ask people to raise their hands when they wish to speak, and let them speak in order. If several people raise their hands at once, indicate the speaking order and stick to it. (For example, "Moving from left to right, first we'll hear from Joe, then Sonia, Gloria, and Ted.")

   To make the speaking order work, you need to be firm. People may not be used to having a speaking order at meetings; some may try to ignore the order and to jump in whenever they have something to say. It is essential that you enforce the order and not allow people to speak out of turn.

   Your own contributions to a discussion must also be part of the speaking order. You need to recognize yourself to speak in the same way that you recognize others, being careful not to violate the order in which group members have signaled their desire to speak.

   Keeping the speaking order is not easy in some groups, and you also must balance the speaking

order with the need to follow the agenda. If, for example, someone persistently brings up points unrelated to the subject at hand, you can gently insist that all comments be on topic. Tell the group that if someone wishes to speak about another topic, it can be placed on the agenda and dealt with later if there is time, or at a subsequent meeting if necessary.

In most meetings, there is at least one person who has something to contribute but finds it difficult to break into the discussion. Others, of course, have no such difficulty, and these are the people whose voices are typically heard. Without a speaking order, those who are the most assertive tend to dominate the conversation, while those with a quieter and sometimes more thoughtful approach tend to be silent, and may eventually become disengaged from the decision-making process. The effective use of a speaking order prevents any one person from dominating the conversation and allows everyone an equal chance to be heard.

At first it may appear to you that the speaking order is not having the desired effect; the quieter members of the group may not be raising their hands to speak and it may still seem that they do not have anything to contribute to the discussion. For people whose habit is to be silent, it may take several meetings before they gain enough trust in the new system and confidence in themselves to begin participating. If people continue not to participate after several meetings, rather than giving up on a speaking order you should move toward implementation of the Interactive Meeting Format. Thoughtfully chosen Warm-up Questions and Springboard Exercises can open people up and bring them in as fully participating members of the group.

Your job as facilitator is to make room for everyone in the conversation. This is not easy, but it is essential.

5. **A Clear Ending Time.** Be clear at the beginning about the time the meeting will end, and strive to complete the meeting by that time. If discussion is intense and more time is needed, check with the group to see if they wish to set a new ending time.

6. **A Summary of Next Steps.** As the meeting is concluding, summarize the meeting's accomplishments and the next steps toward achieving the group's goals. For an action-oriented group, ask the note-taker to recap the decisions made and responsibilities assigned.

These elements of good facilitation are not enough to make a meeting truly interactive, but they do set up a comprehensible environment in which people see how the group is going to make progress and they know what they have to do in order to contribute their ideas.

Everything you read about group facilitation in this book presumes that you are at least running meetings according to the Bare Minimum requirements. The rest of the book is about building an interactive structure on this solid platform.

Steps toward Interaction

If you have implemented the Bare Minimum standards and found your meetings much improved, you may be tempted to stay at that level and not move toward further interaction. This is a natural tendency, but you should not give in to it; these improvements represent only the beginning of what can be achieved through the thoughtful implementation of the *Moving Beyond Icebreakers* approach. Instead of resting on your initial accomplishments, take the next steps.

Use Warm-up Questions. With the Bare Minimum in place, the next step in moving your group toward interactive meetings is the Warm-up Question (unless your group is too large—see the table on p. 39). Chapter 10 lists more than 100 ideas for Warm-up Questions, and you can learn about the purposes and procedure starting on p. 39.

In the beginning, and especially if the group is likely to have a lot of resistance, you may want to start with questions that are directly related to the work of the meeting. Here are some examples:

- Say your name and one reason you think it's important to work on this issue.
- Say one thing you liked or didn't like about the story we read for today.
- Say a phrase to describe what you want to accomplish today.

Emphasize that everyone should keep their answers brief, and that there should be no discussion of people's answers until the appropriate time in the agenda. If you control the Warm-up Question and do not allow it to become too lengthy, people will be receptive to adding this element to the agenda.

Provocative or disturbing feelings or ideas may come to the surface during the Warm-up Question—for example, someone may express fundamental disagreement with some aspect of the group's work. While initially you may feel dismayed by this, you should recognize that surfacing true feelings is one of the reasons for doing interactive exercises. When negative feelings remain below the surface, they cannot be dealt with. If they come out during the Warm-up, you and the rest of the group can work with them. See chapter 1 for a further discussion of the importance of surfacing dissension.

Do BRAINSTORMING. Another aspect of interactive work that you can easily bring in to a meeting is BRAINSTORMING (p. 385). This is a familiar concept to many people and you will probably not encounter resistance when you design your agenda to include a Brainstorm. Be aware, however, that often facilitators use the term "Brainstorm," but they do not actually follow the procedure that makes BRAINSTORMING a powerful interactive technique. When you introduce BRAINSTORMING, be sure to enforce the rules, especially about not discussing ideas during the Brainstorm.

End with Evaluations. Finally, as you are easing your group into the Interactive Meeting Format, you can begin to include the Evaluation component (p. 48). Chapter 18 describes several evaluation techniques, but with most groups of up to 20 people, you can do a simple EVALUATION SCALE (p. 422) from 1 to 10.

Add More Elements. Once the group is accustomed to these elements of the format, you can begin to include a Springboard Exercise (see p. 43) and to do more of the work of the meeting by means of Work Exercises (see p. 45), as appropriate.

Deal with Resistance. At any point along the way, you may encounter resistance from others and from within yourself. Dealing with the resistance of the group and your own resistance is the most fundamental element of becoming an effective facilitator.

Please read chapter 3 so that you will be better prepared to deal with resistance when it arises. Above all, don't be discouraged as you begin to bring interactive methods into your group. What you are trying to accomplish won't always work according to your plan, and you may feel that your efforts to change the meeting culture are not yielding the results that you hoped for. If you give yourself time and remain consistent, the gains will come and will be a substantial reward for your hard work.

Chapter 3

Coping With Resistance and Fear of Failure

If you have ever tried to change a longstanding personal habit, you know that the force of habit is a powerful thing. Change inevitably meets with resistance, and you need courage, persistence, and belief in what you are doing to overcome it.

The kind of meeting we are all used to is like a longstanding habit. When you begin using interactive methods to create real change in the old structures, you will encounter resistance from all directions: from the group you're working with, from yourself, and from those who control your working environment. To use the methods in this book, you must be ready to face your own fears of change and the natural resistance that you will encounter from others.

From the Group

As you begin working with interactive methods, you will find that some group members will object to introducing themselves through a Name Exercise; they will complain that the Warm-up Question is unnecessary and a waste of time; they will participate only halfheartedly; they will insist that the group cannot afford five minutes to discuss an issue in PAIRING (see p. 237); or they will try to ignore the speaking order or the rules for BRAINSTORMING (p. 385). You may feel that the group members think what you're asking them to do is stupid, silly, and a waste of time. In fact, this is exactly what some will be thinking.

When people come together in a group, each person has their own set of fears and anxieties. While they want to be seen as intelligent and as valuable members of the group, they are fearful that other group members won't accept them or appreciate what they have to offer.

Interactive techniques ask people both to look inside themselves and to take a step toward others; they are vehicles for opening people up, for surfacing feelings, and for moving past inhibitions. Most people want to experience this opening, but they are fearful and ambivalent about it. Therefore, they aim those negative feelings toward the safest target they can find, which is usually the facilitator.

In addition, there are a few people who actually thrive on dysfunctional meetings. People who are more aggressive and outgoing and have no problem speaking their minds are usually able to dominate the action and impose their own will on the outcome of a group process. Some of these people may be highly resistant to an interactive meeting structure that brings in everyone's voices.

Also, people's past experiences with "icebreakers" may be a significant source of the resistance that you encounter. Some may have enjoyed doing this type of exercise and are willing to try the interactive approach. Others, however, may feel they had been forced to do things that made them feel silly, and they don't know why the exercises were done or what anyone gained from doing them. When the group leader has not connected the exercises to the group's work, some people conclude that all experiences of this type are a waste of time. Furthermore, meetings that begin with "icebreakers" often raise people's expectations that everyone's ideas will be welcomed; when these meetings then proceed in a top-down style with no further opportunities for interaction or participation, some people develop a cynical dislike of all interactive exercises.

These are legitimate reactions to situations where the group facilitation was heavy-handed, the purpose of the exercise was not clear, or the purpose was to provide a false sense of camaraderie. These experiences have left a meeting landscape littered with people who have a knee-jerk, hostile reaction to the idea of "icebreakers." However, the *Moving Beyond Icebreakers* approach is completely different from these experiences because:

- The exercises are not pointless. They grow out of the goals of the meeting and are chosen to help the group meet its goals.
- The Interactive Meeting Format welcomes participation and input throughout the meeting, not just during the initial exercises.

Nevertheless, groups that are new to the interactive approach will assail you with various forms of resistance. In order to meet and counter the resistance, you need to be clear about your purpose, determined to build a structure in which everyone is heard, and well-grounded in the Interactive Meeting Format.

From Yourself

When the group is resistant, inexperienced facilitators often feel their resolve slipping away. They may react with nervousness and lack of conviction in explaining an exercise, a half-hearted implementation of the exercise, or abandonment of the interactive agenda and a speedy retreat to a more familiar format.

It is your first job, as you learn to be an effective facilitator of interactive meetings, to recognize and work through your own fears and resistance. If you do not do this, you will be unable to address the fears and resistance of those you are working with, and the many benefits of interactive work will be unavailable to your group.

It is not easy to work through your own resistance and then go on to work through the resistance of the group. In the beginning you may have to take it on faith that interactive techniques will bring great

benefits to the groups you work with. However, as you persevere in overcoming your resistance and as you acquire greater skill with interactive techniques, you will begin to see concrete results, including deep changes in individuals' behavior and significant increases in a group's ability to make decisions and work effectively together.

The willingness to take risks, ask questions, and make mistakes is a requirement for the development of expertise.[1] *Deborah Meier*

Nevertheless, you will find that the voice of resistance within yourself is persistent and full of ideas. Here is some of what the voice will whisper to you:

I shouldn't do this exercise because:

- Some members of the group are too old.
- Some members of the group are too young.
- I'll look foolish.
- We can't move the table out of the way.
- The room is set up wrong.

---

[1]Deborah Meier, *In Schools We Trust* (Boston, MA: Beacon Press, 2002), p. 14.

- It's too hot.
- It's too much trouble to move the chairs into place.
- Someone will get hurt.
- I'll look foolish.
- I don't know what to say.
- It will be easier to skip it and just move on with the agenda.
- People are feeling relaxed. They don't need to do interactives.
- This group already has a lot to say. They don't need to do interactives.
- This group is getting along very well. They don't need to do interactives.
- This exercise is too high-risk.
- This is the wrong exercise for right now.
- I'll look foolish.
- This exercise is too silly.
- The group will think this is childish.
- I'll do it next time.
- What if they won't do it?
- We don't have time.
- What if it takes too much time?
- I'm not prepared to process it well (lead a discussion).
- I'll look foolish.

Sometimes, of course, the voice will be raising a good point. You should always listen to your inner voice and examine its claim. Perhaps the exercise you've planned *is* too high-risk for this group, or perhaps there *is* reason to fear that someone could get hurt. The skill you need to develop is to distinguish between the voice of resistance and the voice of reason. You also need to remember that the group experience is not about your own comfort. (So what if you look foolish!) It's about creating an effective environment for the group to meet its goals.

From the Top

Interactive methods open up communication and give group members a real voice in problem-solving and decision-making. For those who believe that the best answers come from a process where everyone is heard, this is a welcome approach. However, it is difficult to implement an interactive decision-making process in an organization based on the belief that decisions are best made at the top.

Because interaction opens up dialogue and brings more voices into the discussion, it tends to bring out intense resistance from entrenched centers of power that seek to maintain control, even when the cost of that control is continued dysfunction and inability to meet the organization's mission. The greatest source of resistance to interactive methods comes from those who believe in authoritarian leadership and have an underlying agenda of maintaining their positions of power and control. Often this resistance will be cloaked in complaints about "no time for games" or "getting touchy-feely."

Chapter 1 describes how interactive methods contribute to a group's effectiveness and productivity. In order to achieve the benefits of a process in which everyone in a group is free to contribute their thoughts and ideas, those in leadership positions need to cede some of their power and control to the group. They need to be ready to let people speak, to hear what they say, and to act based on what they hear.

Scenario 3: Resistance from an Authority Figure

Sharon and Marcus, counselors at an urban high school, wanted to help students overcome the anxiety that was contributing to their poor performance on a high-stakes standardized test. They devised an interactive lesson plan for this purpose, which they conducted in each of the school's test-preparation classes. (See p. 118 for more on this lesson plan.) The first few times they ran these sessions, the agenda generated discussion, reflection, and focus from the participants, and the sessions were deemed successful by all.

In Ms. Smith's class, however, though the students were disciplined and seemed to be listening, they would not open up and participate. Throughout the session, students were nervous, tense, and not willing to talk more than necessary. In response to the Warm-up Question "How are you feeling right now?" students answered "Fine" or "OK." The Wordstorm on "success" failed to yield any real discussion, whereas students in earlier sessions had been passionate and engaged on this subject. The facilitators found themselves struggling to fill out the 80-minute period; in other classes they had come close to running out of time.

Sharon and Marcus soon realized that the problem lay with Ms. Smith; she was the only one of the test-prep teachers who had been negative about the idea of these sessions and had not wanted her class to participate. However, with ten minutes remaining in the session, Ms. Smith left the room to attend to some business. Sharon then asked the class if there was anything they wanted to say while the teacher was not present. The class opened up and began to discuss the conflicting emotions and high levels of stress that they were feeling around the test. With the powerful presence of a resistant authority figure removed, students were able to make some progress toward grappling with the anxieties that were hindering their motivation and holding them back from success on the test.

In this case, the force of the students' feelings was strong enough to eventually overcome the negativity of a resistant authority figure. In less charged circumstances, however, resistance from the top often wins the day entirely, pre-empting all dialogue and interactivity.

The Resistance Diagram

To deal with resistance successfully, it helps to be aware of some of the factors influencing the level of resistance you and the group experience, and to understand the dynamic relationship among these factors. The Resistance Diagram illustrates these relationships.

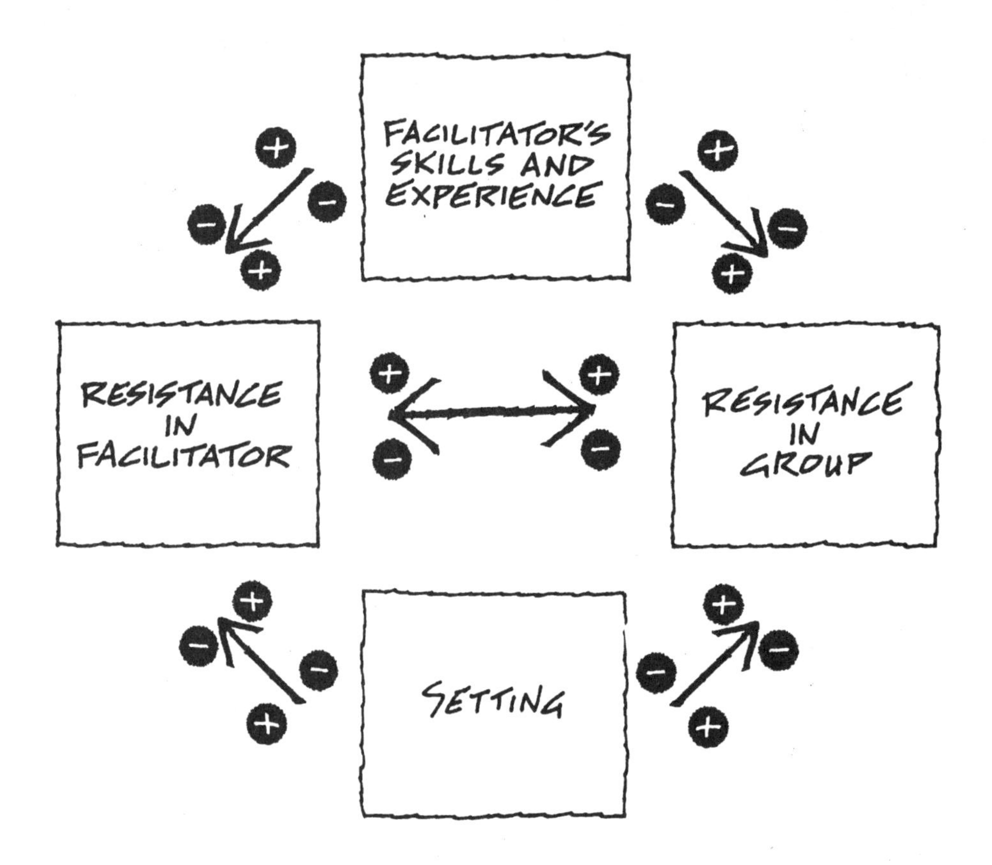

The Facilitator's Resistance and the Group's Resistance. When someone in the role of facilitator has a high level of resistance to the use of interactive methods, this feeds the group's own natural resistance. Increased resistance from the group, in turn, increases the level of resistance in the facilitator. If this is happening to you, you need to break the cycle by recognizing your growing resistance for what it is. If you don't do this, you may find that the group's resistance will reinforce your own resistance until you abandon the effort to learn this new skill and accept the notion that interactive methods are silly, stupid, and a waste of time. See scenario 4 for an example of how resistance breeds resistance.

On the other hand, someone coming to the role of facilitator with a high level of commitment to working interactively is much better able to overcome the resistance in the group. The ability to deal with resistance while maintaining an attitude of confidence in what you are doing is probably the largest factor in determining the degree to which interactive methods will be successful in your group.

Scenario 4: Resistance Breeds Resistance
Robin was a high school teacher and had just assumed the position of faculty advisor to the student government. For the first meeting of the 16 newly elected class officers, Robin created an agenda that began with learning names and helping people get to know each other before moving on to discussing the work of the student government.

After a brief introduction, Robin asked the group to do NAME CHANT AND MOTION (p. 135). In this exercise, everyone takes a turn saying their name while making a motion. The entire group then repeats that person's name and does their motion three times.

As Robin explained the exercise, she noticed questioning stares from group members. She started to feel self-conscious in her role as facilitator, and to doubt the appropriateness of the exercise. She tried to reassure herself and the group by giving an example of the kind of motion someone might make. But as she gave a brief demonstration, her face got red, she laughed nervously, and her embarrassment was evident. The group responded with nervous laughter of their own. Not surprisingly, when Robin asked who would like to go first, no one volunteered. Although she muddled her way through the rest of the exercise, it was a painful experience for everyone involved.

Robin's lack of confidence with using interactive techniques had undermined her ability to present the exercise as fun and non-threatening. She had responded to the initial resistance of the group by becoming overwhelmed with her own resistance and fear of looking foolish. Her body language clearly communicated to the group that she felt silly doing this, and that if they did it they would probably look and feel silly, too.

Robin has since become confident in her role as a facilitator and she is comfortable using interactive techniques with student groups and others. She has used NAME CHANT AND MOTION successfully in many different settings, and she has learned to break through a group's initial resistance by using humor and by modeling that the exercise is fun and safe.

There are two other important factors that influence the level of resistance in the group and the facilitator:

- **The Setting.** The more comfortable the setting, the fewer reasons anyone has to feel resistant. When people are at ease, when they know that the meeting space is private, and when other elements of an ideal setting are in place, everyone is more relaxed and willing to try new things. Conversely, when the meeting space is cramped, noisy, or lacking in privacy, these factors increase everyone's discomfort and make people more resistant to working interactively. See p. 53 for a discussion of the ideal setting and how to provide it.

- **The Facilitator's Skills and Experience.** The more experienced you are with interactive methods and the more confident you are in your skills, the more you are able to relax and to communicate a relaxed attitude to the group. This means, of course, that when you are new to interactive methods and unsure of your skills, you are more likely to feel resistant to trying out your new skills in public and more likely to communicate a sense of insecurity, which tends to foster resistance in the group.

The best antidote for inexperience in the short term is to be thoroughly familiar with the contents of this book, especially chapter 5. All the information and suggestions in that chapter will build your confidence, thereby decreasing your resistance. In particular, you will find it helpful to practice giving the instructions for the exercises in advance; if you are not worried about getting the information right, your comfort level will be dramatically increased, which will help put the group at ease.

In the long term, consistent use of the Interactive Meeting Format will dissolve the group's resistance both by honing your facilitation skills and by making the interactive approach familiar and comfortable to the group members. Using interaction sporadically or inconsistently actually serves to increase the group's resistance. Consistency is a major contributing factor to success.

Resistance is Forever

Resistance in the group and in yourself never goes away. Working interactively is not easy, and ingrained habits usually lurk inside us waiting for opportune moments to reassert their control. If you are committed to an interactive approach, you need to be continually aware of the need to confront and disperse resistance.

While it's impossible to predict when and where resistance will rise to the surface, some of the exercises in this book are more likely than others to call up resistance from the group, and some of these are noted with the "Resistance" icon.

Getting a grip on resistance, no matter what its source, will make it possible for you to run groups that serve their intended purposes and are vibrant, engaging, and productive.

Chapter 4

The Interactive Meeting Format

- A Note about Processing
- Preparation
- Format Overview
- The Sections in Detail
  - Table 1. The Six-part Interactive Meeting Format
  - 1. The Introduction
  - 2. The Names/Warm-up Section
    - Table 2. Guidelines for Designing the Names/Warm-up Section
    - Scenario 5: Processing a Warm-up Question
  - 3. The Springboard Section
    - Scenario 6: Balancing Tasks and Group Issues
  - 4. The Work Section
  - 5. The Summation
  - 6. The Evaluation

The six-part format described here is a time-tested approach to conducting meetings for both one-time groups and ongoing groups. In our work, we use this format in every possible setting where six or more people are coming together to accomplish a goal, including group meetings with youth and adults, staff meetings, meetings of our board of directors, and professional development sessions for police, teachers, and others.

This chapter includes:

- The steps to follow in preparing for a meeting
- An overview of the meeting format
- Detailed information about each of the six sections of the format.

Chapter 5 gives further information about how to work with the format, and chapter 6 has examples of agendas that use the format to reach specific goals.

A Note about Processing

Much of the power of the Interactive Meeting Format comes from the facilitator's skilled processing of the exercises. By "processing" we mean leading a discussion and/or making observations about a completed exercise in order to draw understanding from it. This chapter describes in general how to process particular sections of the meeting, and chapter 5, especially pp. 65-70, provides further guidance about how to use processing to help your group meet its goals.

Preparation

In addition to setting up the meeting space (see p. 53), here's what you need to do to prepare for an interactive meeting:

1. Define your goals for the meeting.
2. Construct an agenda based on those goals, following the Interactive Meeting Format. See chapter 5 for detailed information about how to choose the appropriate exercises.
3. Write a summary of the goals and an outline of the day's agenda on the flip chart.
4. Gather any materials you will need during the meeting.
5. Follow the preparation instructions for each interactive exercise that is on the agenda.
6. If you are working with an action-oriented group, prepare or update one or more timelines for the group's work.

You can draw a timeline as a grid, like a calendar, or you can simply draw horizontal lines to represent weeks, with each day marked by a vertical crosshatch. Fill in noteworthy deadlines, events, holidays, and so on. If the group is involved in a complex project or multiple projects, you may want to have separate timelines that display tasks and deadlines the group is working with.

Format Overview

The six-part meeting format is a cohesive system, with each section designed to lead in to the one that follows. Table 1 outlines the six parts of the format.

Section	Purposes	Procedures
Introduction	Clarify goals. Foreshadow the meeting. Calm and focus the group. For ongoing groups: Acknowledge those present and absent. Establish the meeting in time.	Goals Who's here, who's not Date and Timeline
Names/ Warm-up Section	Learn names and the importance of knowing names. Hear every voice. Help people feel comfortable. Create fun and energy. Assess how people are feeling. Establish "buy-in." Focus attention on the day's work. Connect to the group's mission.	One or more Name Exercises (see chapter 9) Warm-up Question, with names in some circumstances (see chapter 10)
Springboard Section	Establish a creative bridge to the Work Section. Surface group dynamics. Generate energy. Reflect group issues. (See chapter 8 for the many specific goals these exercises can help address.)	See chapters 11 through 16 for exercises.
Work Section	Fulfill the concrete purpose of the group. Focus on the group's "product."	Perform specific tasks. See chapter 17 for Work Exercises.
Summation	Summarize accomplishments. Make announcements. For ongoing groups: Connect one day with the next.	Review timeline and next steps. Address outstanding issues.
Evaluation	Gather evaluative information. "Package" the experience. Disperse negativity. Communicate group responsibility. Empower the group.	See chapter 18 for exercises.

Table 1. The Six-part Interactive Meeting Format

Groups come together for a purpose, and part 4 of the format, the Work Section, gives structure to that purpose. The three earlier sections—the Introduction, Names/Warm-up Section, and Springboard Section—are designed to bring the group to the Work Section emotionally and intellectually prepared to make that part of the meeting as productive as possible. When these early sections are designed with care and executed well, the group's level of productivity during the Work Section increases dramatically. Following the Work Section, a brief Summation and an Evaluation Exercise bring the meeting to a satisfactory conclusion in which everyone's input is included and valued.

The Sections in Detail

1. The Introduction

How to Do It

The Introduction is the short opening piece of the agenda (five minutes or less), during which you do the following:

- Welcome the group.
- Provide them with a brief overview of the meeting's goals.
- Briefly preview the agenda.
- State what time the meeting will conclude.

For ongoing groups, you should also:

- Acknowledge visitors or new people in the group.
- Acknowledge those who are missing and where they are (to the extent that you know).
- Review timelines as needed (for action-oriented groups).

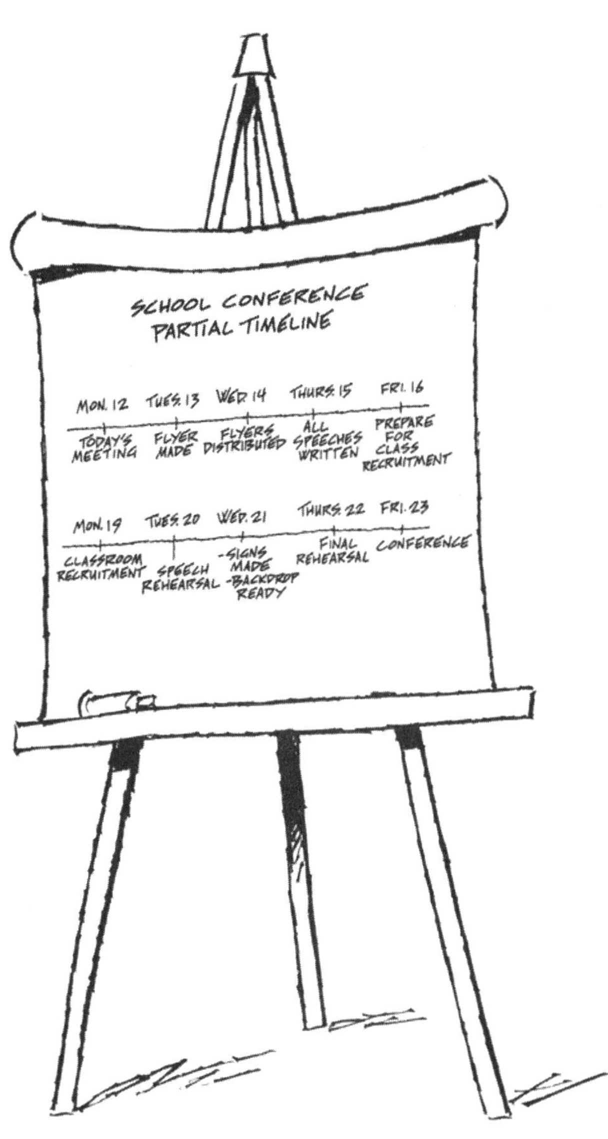

Why Do It

In just a few moments, the Introduction serves many purposes. As you are welcoming people, taking note of who is present and absent, and going over the goals and the agenda, you are also setting the tone of the meeting. In addition, this part of the meeting is designed to:

1. Give group members a few minutes to get settled. For this brief time, people don't have to do anything; they just need to sit quietly and listen.
2. Set the context for the day's work and activities by taking note of the meeting's setting in time. This is helpful and important for everyone, but it is especially useful for developing awareness in adolescents and children of the flow of time.
3. Gradually focus the group's attention on three important questions: What are we doing? Why are we doing it? How will we go about it?
4. Foreshadow and thus prepare the group for the kind of experience they will be having at this meeting. This is par-

ticularly helpful when the group will be facing some difficult issues. On such a day you might say something like, "Today we'll be doing some hard work and dealing with tough issues, but if we work together we'll get through them and set the stage for real progress." This will prepare people emotionally and give them a better chance of successfully navigating a potentially stressful meeting.

2. The Names/Warm-up Section

After the Introduction, the next section of the agenda uses Name Exercises and Warm-up Questions, either singly or in combination. A few minutes invested in these exercises can give a meeting a tremendous head start toward a productive working atmosphere.

How to Do It

Designing the Section. The group's purpose, its size, its stage of development, how often it meets, and the time you have available for the meeting will all determine how you design this section.

For most meetings, this section will take about ten minutes. However, it can take as little as two minutes (for example, in a large one-time group that does only the exercise NAME SHOUT) or as long as 30 minutes (for example, in the first meeting of an ongoing group in which learning names and getting to know each other are the primary goals of the meeting).

Table 2 gives general guidelines, but you are the best judge of how much emphasis to place on this part of the meeting. In some meetings you will do only a Name Exercise, in some only a Warm-up Question, in some a combination, and in some you will skip this component altogether. Here are examples of how facilitators might design this section:

- In a one-time, two-hour workshop of 35 people: Do NAME SHOUT (p. 142) or NAME RACE (p. 140).
- In a one-time, all-day workshop of 35 people: Begin with an exercise such as NAME CHANT AND MOTION (p. 135). When the workshop breaks up into small groups, include a Warm-up Question with names in the small-group agenda.
- In a bi-weekly staff meeting of 15-20 people: Begin with a Warm-up Question.
- In a class of 25 students meeting four times per week, in a large school where the students may not all know each other: Do a Name Exercise every day for the first week. In subsequent classes, you might then use a Warm-up Question from time to time. Also, if a new student joins the class, do Name Exercises for a few classes.
- In a class of 15 students meeting three times per week: Begin each class with a Warm-up Question that relates to and leads into the subject matter for the day.
- In a support group or therapy group with 20 participants: Begin each session with a Warm-up Question that focuses everyone's attention on the purpose of the group. Do Name Exercises in addition to Warm-up Questions until names have been learned.

For most Name Exercises and for all Warm-up Questions, the amount of time spent is directly related to the size of the group and the complexity of the question. In groups larger than 20 or so, Warm-up Questions are generally too time-consuming, though a question that asks for short responses may sometimes be appropriate.

Here are the general guidelines for designing this part of the agenda:

Type of Group	Group Size	Designing the Names/Warm-up Section
One-time group	20 or fewer	Name Exercise Warm-up Question with names
One-time group	Between 20 and 50	Name Exercise
One-time group	More than 50	Name Exercise for a large group (NAME SHOUT, NAME WHISPER, NAME RACE, NAME WAVE)
Ongoing group: first several meetings	20 or fewer	One or more Name Exercises Warm-up Question with names
Ongoing group: next few meetings	20 or fewer	Name Exercise to measure if everyone has learned names Warm-up Question
Ongoing group: subsequent meetings	20 or fewer	Warm-up Question
Ongoing group with a visitor or new person	20 or fewer	Warm-up Question with names Might also start with a Name Exercise
Ongoing group: first several meetings	20-35	Name Exercise

Table 2. Guidelines for Designing the Names/Warm-up Section

Name Exercises. Chapter 9 contains a variety of Name Exercises that suit different group situations.

In a small to mid-size group, there are several exercises you can do that will advance the primary goal of the Name Exercise, which is, of course, learning each other's names and how to pronounce them. Some exercises are geared toward helping the group members learn everyone's name by means of repetition, and some will assess how successful the group has been at learning names.

In a large group, Name Exercises acknowledge the importance of people naming themselves, while not expecting that everyone can learn all the other names. With a group of 40-50, you can give people a few seconds each to speak their names with the NAME RACE (p. 140). You can use NAME CHANT (p. 135) or NAME WAVE (p. 145) in a group of up to 80 people, and even in such a large group people will learn some names. In a group that is too large for each person to speak individually, you can nevertheless let people speak their names with the NAME SHOUT (p. 142) or NAME WHISPER exercise.

For a one-time group that will be working together for an hour or more, a Name Exercise combined with nametags will be extremely helpful in facilitating communication.

Warm-up Questions. Warm-up Questions simply involve each group member in turn answering a question that you pose. In some circumstances, people will also say their names as they answer the question. Chapter 10 has more than 180 questions and information about how to choose questions for particular situations.

Running the Exercise. Before you begin the exercise or question, state these guidelines (which apply to all except exercises for a large group, such as NAME SHOUT):

- Pay attention to the person whose turn it is.
- The group needs everyone's participation; however, a person can pass if they feel they must. When someone passes, they can ask to take their turn at the end.
- Even if someone passes, they need to give their name if that is being asked for.

Then follow this procedure:

- Ask for a volunteer to begin. This approach allows those who feel ready to go or have an answer in mind to set the tone, and it avoids putting someone in the spotlight who may not be ready for it.
- After the first person's turn, have the group proceed in order around the circle from the starting point, going in the direction that you indicate.
- All facilitators should participate in the exercise, and do so in a way that models the engagement, depth, humor, or thoughtfulness that they want group members to emulate.
- Be attentive during the exercise, both to absorb information about the group and to model positive behavior. It is helpful to jot down some notes about how people's responses and participation relate to the group's dynamics, the work for the day, or other important points that can be used for processing.

Follow these additional procedures for Warm-up Questions:

- Do not let others interrupt the person who is speaking, especially to ask questions or begin a discussion about what the person is saying.
- If someone raises a point that should be on the agenda, make a note of it, and after you've finished processing the Warm-up Question, add it to the written agenda for all to see.
- Do not let anyone speak for too long. Find a gentle or humorous way to suggest that the next person is waiting their turn.
- Allow people to interpret the question as they wish. For example, if the question is, "How do you feel about flying," people might talk about being in an airplane, flying in dreams or in daydreams, being on a roller coaster, or many other possible interpretations of "flying." Whatever people say can be used in your processing.

Processing. Processing of this section should be brief. Don't ask questions; simply make some comments based on what people said and did. Summarize the ideas that people expressed and any nonverbal cues they gave in a way that moves the group toward achieving its goals, taking note of the negative as well as the positive. Refer to your notes, if you have them, for dynamics in the group that might be useful to point out.

You can process each exercise and question separately, or you can process all the elements of the Names/Warm-up Section together.

If you have done a Name Exercise, mention how important it is to learn names if the group is going to work together productively. Also, some of the Name Exercises lend themselves to processing about the purpose of the group. For example, if a group's focus is on dealing with peer pressure, the exercise NAME CHANT AND MOTION (p.135) provides an illustration of people following a leader and doing what everyone else is doing.

For a Warm-up Question, it can be helpful to repeat back some of the answers you heard. However, don't focus too directly on any individual answer; people need to feel free to express themselves, and to be singled out might be inhibiting.

Scenario 5: Processing a Warm-up Question
Molly's group was organizing a community barbecue. At a meeting a week before the event, she used the Warm-up Question "Say a word that describes how you feel about the barbecue." Responses included words like "worried," "tired," "excited," "overwhelmed," and "fearful." Molly processed the question by saying, "People seem tired today and some of us seem to be scared of what might happen at the barbecue. To me, that points out how important it is for us to be prepared for what could be a really exciting event. We have a week to keep working, to keep doing publicity and outreach, making sure we're organized. Even though people are tired, I also hear a lot of motivation. We all want our project to be successful after all we've put into it. So let's move through what we have to do today, and let's be nice to each other along the way."

Why Do It

It is commonplace at meetings to go around and have everyone introduce themselves and perhaps say where they are from or why they came to the meeting. Some people may not like doing this, but most of us are glad to introduce ourselves and to place some aspect of who we are into the group context. We like getting to know something about the others in the meeting and we hope that these introductions will enhance communication and cooperation. What most of us do not realize is that this part of a meeting can yield so much more benefit.

The Names/Warm-up Section serves many purposes. These vary according to the size and duration of the group, but even with groups as large as 80 people these exercises will help your group to achieve its goals.

Learning Names. The first and most obvious purpose (for a small to mid-size group) is for people to learn each other's names. This is an indispensable first step in the formation of a functional working group. In an ongoing group, it is essential for everyone to know all the other participants' names and how to pronounce them properly. Even in a one-time group, people work together more effectively if they have had a chance to identify themselves and to learn the names of others.

Unless you are thoroughly familiar with everyone in a group, you should never assume that people know each other's names. Communication will be inhibited if even one person doesn't know how to directly address one other person. If your goal is to facilitate a group where everyone can communicate freely, you should plan on doing a Name Exercise.

Many facilitators handle names with the simple question, "Does everyone know each other?" Almost invariably, everyone will nod, and the facilitator will move to the next item on the agenda. These facilitators need to realize that no one wants to risk being the only person in the group to admit they don't know everyone else. If the facilitator makes the assumption that everyone knows everyone else, people tend to go along with the assumption, even if they know that it's untrue.

Here are two good reasons for focusing on learning names:

- People relate more easily to those whose names they are comfortable with. Conversely, people tend not to relate to those whose names they don't know or are unsure of. Particularly in a group with people from diverse cultural backgrounds, mastering the pronunciation of names can be challenging, and people may avoid speaking directly to someone with an unfamiliar name for fear of getting it wrong. A situation like this can lead to the development of serious tensions that reinforce the distance and suspicion that often exist among people from different cultures.

- It is difficult to ask a person for help or to initiate contact with someone if you don't know their name. For instance, there is a huge difference between, "Hey, can you give me a hand with this box?" and "Hey, Zuleika, can you help me out with this box?"

It takes time and repetition for everyone in a group to learn all the others' names. Some people pick up names and pronunciations quickly but others find it more difficult, and it's best to structure your agendas with awareness of those who have difficulty. Also, tell the group that if they cannot remember someone's name or how to pronounce it, even if they've heard it several times, it's better to ask politely for a name refresher than to avoid speaking to the person altogether.

In an ongoing group, you can use NAME, FOOD, AND REMEMBER (p. 138) or NAME CONTEST (p. 137) to check whether people are ready to stop using Name Exercises.

Establishing the Importance of Knowing Names. Even in a group that is too large for people to learn names, it is often a good idea to do a Name Exercise appropriate for the group's size. This allows you to make the point that knowing others' names is important to good working relationships, and it emphasizes the significance to the group of each individual's identity and investment in the work.

Hearing Every Voice. Even when the exercise gives each person only a few seconds to speak or act, those few seconds provide an opportunity for people to establish their identities, use their voices, and be heard by the group. This is particularly important for those who tend to be introverted. For someone who is generally quiet in meetings and goes along with whatever is happening, consistent participation in the Names/Warm-up Section can be the first step toward transformation into someone who speaks their mind and contributes their creative energies to this group and others. In an ongoing group, the Warm-up Question provides each person with regular practice in speaking in front of a group and helps people learn to be articulate and concise.

Helping People Feel Comfortable in the Group. Meetings usually begin with a certain amount of tension, as each person brings into the room their own concerns and a degree of self-consciousness. Hearing one another speak in an orderly way helps to put people at ease.

Creating Fun and Energy. Many of these exercises and questions give the group a chance to move around and to laugh together. This helps to wake people up, break down inhibitions, and generate energy that can be directed toward reaching the group's goals, and it can open up opportunities for creating positive relationships. (Some Warm-up Questions that make people laugh are: "If this group were a food, what would it be?" "What was a time that you felt foolish?" "If you could have any power, natural or supernatural, what power would you have and why would you choose to have it?")

Assessing How People Are Feeling. As people take turns doing Name Exercises and answering the Warm-up Question, each individual is providing you and other group members with information, by means of their body language and general way of responding, about how they are feeling and what kind of energy they are bringing to the group that day. The content of people's answers to the Warm-up Question can help everyone in the group understand each other's behavior on a deeper level (for example, see scenario 10, "Subtle Processing of a Warm-up Question," in chapter 5). You can also learn a lot about how the group as a whole is doing from the way people interact and pay attention to each other.

Establishing "Buy-in." The Warm-up Question gives each person a way to tell the group how much or how little they are invested in its success. Even if the question is not about the substance of the work, the degree to which each person is willing to participate signals their willingness at this time to contribute to the group—information that is extremely helpful to the facilitator.

Focusing on the Work of the Day. The Warm-up Question can be used to focus the group's attention on the work to be done that day and to begin generating ideas that can help to meet the group's goals. For example, on a day when the group has a lot to get done, you can ask, "What's the most important thing we need to accomplish today?" Not only will this focus everyone on the work, but it will also provide insight into different people's priorities and areas of interest.

Connecting the Group to Its Mission. An effective Warm-up Question can reinforce the vital link between the mission that underlies the group's existence and the work the group is currently engaged in, thereby increasing the group's investment in its work and in the ultimate success of its efforts. Here are some examples:

- For a drug rehabilitation group: "Who is someone you admire who's overcome drug abuse?"
- For a group of teachers meeting to discuss issues among their students: "Talk about a student who's doing well and one who's having difficulty."
- For a meeting to plan a publicity campaign: "Tell us about an ad you've seen recently that caught your attention."

3. The Springboard Section

The Springboard Section involves an activity that engages the group and gets people ready to do the work of the day. Generally this section consists of one exercise, but depending on time and your goals for the meeting, you might choose to do more than one.

The Springboard Exercises are contained in chapters 11 through 16. They vary widely in time (from one minute to more than 20 minutes) and in level of physical activity (from people talking in pairs to people hoisting each other over a barrier). Many work well in classrooms or conference rooms, while others require open floor space.

These exercises are designed to meet a wide spectrum of goals, and you can match your goals to various exercises in chapter 8. However, for an exercise to be effective in meeting the goals, you need to have:

- A solid understanding of why you chose that exercise. For information about how to choose an exercise read "Designing the Agenda" beginning on p. 55.
- A belief in its value to the group. Remember the lessons about resistance in chapter 3, to reinforce your belief that what you are doing will help your group to achieve its goals

- The ability to process the exercise effectively. Read "Processing the Exercises" beginning on p. 65.

If you are working with adults, it's likely that this part of the meeting format will stir up the most resistance, both in the group and in yourself. Often people have had experiences with Warm-up Questions, they can see the logic behind Name Exercises, they enjoy doing the work of the meeting in an interactive way, and they welcome the opportunity to evaluate. The Springboard Exercise, however, may appear to be nothing but the facilitator's time-wasting whim. Without effective processing to tie the activity to the day's work, the exercise may not, in the eyes of participants, serve any obvious purpose. It's important, therefore, to choose this exercise carefully. Be sure the risk level is appropriate to the group, remembering that adult groups inexperienced with the Interactive Meeting Format will regard almost any form of interaction as high-risk.

How to Do It

The general procedure for a Springboard Exercise consists of carefully giving the instructions for the chosen activity, conducting the activity, and then processing the information and dynamics that emerge.

Why Do It

Springboard Exercises serve one or more of the following purposes:

- Give the group an experience (frequently a creative or a body-centered experience) related to the tasks or issues they will be addressing in the Work Section, thus building a bridge to the work of the meeting.
- Surface group dynamics for discussion and provide group members with insights into how they work together.
- Provide the group with a chance to have fun, laugh together, and be energized to do the work of the day.
- Generate enthusiasm for being in the group and working together, or reflect the difficulties the group is having and help people understand what needs to be changed.

You might select a Springboard Exercise either to address group issues or to help the group understand their work for the day, but often it will end up serving both purposes. Whatever dynamics are present in the group will be present in the Springboard Exercise. A skilled facilitator will know which dynamics the group needs to address at this moment, and will struggle to balance the work the group needs to accomplish with the emotional health and well-being of the group.

Scenario 6: Balancing Tasks and Group Issues

Brian's group was preparing to host a teen gathering for the young people in their neighborhood, and they had many loose ends to take care of before the event the next evening. In preparing the meeting agenda, Brian planned for a quick Springboard Exercise that would allow him to make the point that the group needed to be focused and work hard to finish all their tasks so they would be ready for the gathering. He planned to dedicate most of the meeting to getting the tasks completed.

The exercise Brian chose was HANDS TOGETHER (p. 164), which involves everyone clapping at the same time. He planned to process the exercise by saying that they could create a powerful, unified sound when they all focused and clapped together, and that they could also create a powerful event for the community if they brought the same focus to their work on the teen gathering.

However, to Brian's surprise the group had a hard time getting through the exercise. Two people, Sam and Alison, persistently clapped out of time with the rest. Others got annoyed but insisted that everyone continue trying to do it right. Instead of moving on quickly to the Work Section, the group spent five minutes doing HANDS TOGETHER.

Mindful of the tasks that needed doing, Brian nevertheless recognized that his group needed to deal with some issues if they were going to work well together and be role models for appropriate behavior at their event. He knew that the group's state of mind was even more critical to their success than the completion of tasks; the group needed to spend some time processing the experience of HANDS TOGETHER and the feelings it brought up, rather than rushing on to the Work Section. In the processing discussion, it became clear that Sam had not been able to concentrate on the exercise due to an illness in his family. Once this came out, anger toward him dissipated and people offered him support instead. Also, the discussion brought out that Alison had been deliberately sabotaging the exercise because she knew it would annoy Taylor, with whom she had been arguing recently.

In light of all this, Brian was able to say, "There are some problems that are affecting the group, and it's important for us to know what's going on and to work things out, and not to be too hard on each other in the process. But for now, let's remember that all of us have said we want this event to go well. A lot of people are counting on us to create a safe space tomorrow night, and we all know that if we don't do a good job, people could get hurt. We'll need to spend some time soon dealing with the issues in the group, but right now we need to come together and support each other so that we have a safe and successful event. We only have a little time left, so let's work in a focused way to get done what needs to be done."

Some tasks had not been finished by the end of the meeting time, but the group left knowing that they would be able to count on each other at the gathering the next evening. If the group had skipped the Springboard Exercise and attempted to get straight to work, the dysfunction that came out in the exercise may well have come out instead in their work preparing for the event, and even during the event itself.

4. The Work Section

Why Do It

The Work Section fulfills the main purpose for which the group has come together, and its content is specific to the group. In a one-time group, the purpose might be to explore a specific issue or to gain some particular knowledge. An ongoing group might be working on exploring issues more extensively or planning and implementing an agenda for action. The work of the day in either of these cases might involve one or more of the following kinds of activities:

- Creating a vision for action.
- Hearing updates from subcommittees and determining next steps in several areas.
- Doing specific tasks (such as writing articles, making phone calls, creating posters, or gathering materials) to prepare for an activity the group is organizing.
- Learning about or reviewing a body of material (such as a period of history or a math concept).
- Discussing experiences or concepts.

- Working on dynamics within the group (so that the group can pursue its purpose more effectively).

Any of this work can be done in a variety of ways, some more productive than others.
For example, uninterrupted lecturing or top-down distribution of tasks may seem to be efficient approaches to a group's work. In the long run, however, these approaches are often ineffective because they fail to engage the group and make use of everyone's talents. Conversely, an interactive approach can help to bring the group's work alive and to ensure that everyone's input is welcome and that everyone is fully invested in the group's success.

How to Do It

The structure of the Work Section will vary depending on the purpose of the group and its stage of development. When planning the section, start with the goals for the meeting and think about how you can meet those goals with a lively approach that helps assure maximum engagement by group members. The specific methods you choose should be tailored to the goals and the tasks that the group needs to accomplish.

Chapter 17 contains several exercises for this part of the meeting. If you are familiar with these exercises, using them to work toward the group's goals will soon come naturally to you. A few of the exercises, such as BRAINSTORMING (p. 385) and WORDSTORMS (p. 413), are excellent techniques for almost any setting and can help groups to reach a variety of goals. In an ongoing group, you may want to use these exercises frequently. BRAINSTORMING, in particular, is a technique that helps all kinds of groups at any stage of their work to use the creative capacities of all their members. For example, you can use BRAINSTORMING to set goals, decide on actions to reach the goals, list the tasks needed for the actions, and anticipate problems that might come up.

Two of the Work Exercises—BRAINSTORMING and WORDSTORMS—are "Super Exercises," profiled and used in the agendas in chapter 6. Other Work Exercises, such as LIFE LINES (p. 401) or DIVERSITY IN MOTION (p. 391), are suitable for particular types of groups to reach specific goals; you would probably do them no more than once in the life of a group.

In an ongoing group, the Work Section must be structured coherently with clear connections from one meeting to the next over the life of the group. Maintaining this awareness of connection enables group members to see the logical progression in their work and to understand the work within the context of their long-term goals.

The Work Section can take place entirely in the whole group or it can be structured in a variety of other ways. It might contain large- and small-group activities as well as time for people to work on individual tasks, or it might consist entirely of people working on tasks individually or in pairs. Some work is better executed in the large group with everyone present. This is especially true if the work involves making decisions that the whole group needs to support, such as setting goals for an event or disseminating information that everyone needs. Work that is more task-oriented and discussions that require more personal disclosure are sometimes better in smaller groups where people can share tasks efficiently and more inclusive discussions can take place.

Structuring Small Groups. Most of the Work Exercises in chapter 17 are designed for groups of 20 or fewer. If you have a larger number, break into small groups. Be sure that each small group has the supplies it needs, such as flip chart paper and markers.

In some situations, division into small groups comes naturally—for example, if people have signed up for certain tasks or subcommittees based on their skills and interests. In other circumstances (for example, if you need to create small groups to do BRAINSTORMING), try to connect people with others who are not in their usual friendship circles. In an ongoing group, you can prepare the groupings ahead of time. If you want to create small groups according to where people are sitting ("The six people in this corner are one group," etc.), you can precede that with a Springboard Exercise such as THE WIND BLOWS (p. 377) that mixes people up around the room. There are also two exercises, PSYCHIC SHAKE (p. 175) and GROUP THE GROUP (p. 289), that are helpful in creating small groups.

Your preparation for the meeting should include specific agendas for the small groups to follow, with the level of detail necessary for them to complete the tasks they are given. In situations where those in the small groups may not know each other, you should start the small group agenda with a brief Warm-up Question that includes saying names; if people are to work together productively in their groups, it is essential that they be able to speak directly to each other. The groups could then go on to use BRAINSTORMING, WORDSTORMS, ROLE-PLAYS, or other Work Exercises or tasks.

Ideally, each small group would have a facilitator who knows how to work with the agenda. If there are not enough facilitators, you should keep the agendas simple. At a later stage in the group's development, when group members have worked with interactive techniques as participants, they can gain valuable experience as facilitators by leading Brainstorms and other exercises in small groups.

Report-backs. When the meeting includes small groups or individual tasks, set aside time at the end of the Work Section for reporting back to the whole group on what has been accomplished, decided, or discussed. Allow time also for others to ask questions and give input. Pay careful attention to the information that emerges during report-backs, because often it contains important issues that require the group's attention or approval, or that can be used to spark deeper exploration of issues. In addition, this process keeps the entire group informed and invested in the group's mission.

Note that the exercise FREEZE-FRAME REPORT-BACKS (p. 393) can be an interesting way for groups to report back from time to time.

5. The Summation

The last two sections of the meeting format are parallel to the first two. Like the Introduction, the Summation allows the group to relax for a few minutes; all people need to do is listen. The Evaluation then allows each person the opportunity to speak, as in the Names/Warm-up Section.

Why Do It

The Summation allows you to give people information, address concerns that you have observed, and preview the work or issues that the group will be focusing on in the future.

How to Do It

Ask everyone to settle down, then speak briefly about what has been accomplished and what is coming up for the group. Use this time for announcements or logistical concerns: assignments, reminder of the next meeting date, handouts to be picked up, etc.

The Summation is not always necessary. If there are no announcements or logistical issues, you may decide to move directly into the Evaluation.

6. The Evaluation

This last section of the Interactive Meeting Format is tremendously important for all kinds of groups.

How to Do It

Every meeting should conclude with an Evaluation. For a group of 20 or fewer, the most common form of Evaluation is simply to go around the group, with each person evaluating the meeting on a scale from 1 (worst) to 10 (best), and commenting on their rating. Chapter 18 describes this and some similar exercises. These Evaluations should take about five minutes. Evaluations are also important and useful for larger groups, and chapter 18 includes several evaluation techniques that you can use with groups of any size.

When introducing the Evaluation, give people the following information:

- The emphasis should be on evaluating the whole experience of the meeting, especially in terms of how well the meeting achieved its goals. You are not asking people to rate your performance or their own participation.
- Evaluations are extremely helpful to the group, but people can pass if they wish on all or part of their evaluation (for example, someone could pass entirely or they could give a number with no comment or a comment with no number). Make clear, however, that if someone does not feel comfortable sharing their opinions with the group, they will not be required to do so.

Ask for a volunteer to begin.

During the Evaluation, your role is to participate as a member of the group, to provide your own evaluation, and to listen respectfully. If an evaluation is negative, do not argue, become defensive, ask questions, or allow other group members to question or criticize the person who gave the evaluation.

You should never skip the Evaluation. If you see that time is running short, do not sacrifice the Evaluation as a way to end on time. For all the reasons stated below, the Evaluation is a critical component of the Interactive Meeting Format.

Processing. Observe the evaluations given for the meeting and then make some brief summary comments about what you heard. This is your opportunity to disperse any anxiety the group is experiencing and to acknowledge what went well and why, and what didn't go well and why. It is important for you to end the meeting in a way that reassures group members and sets a positive tone for the next meeting. Here are some examples:

- "Today was a really hard day and a lot of people are frustrated. But I think it helped that we got those issues out on the table. Let's everyone come in with an open attitude next time and we'll get through this as a group."
- "This was a good day. It seems like everyone got a lot done and enjoyed it. I'll see you next time."

Written Evaluations. Written evaluations are sometimes a valuable supplement to verbal evaluations because they allow you to gather detailed information in a permanent form. They are especially important in large groups, where individual verbal evaluations are not possible, and in one-time groups, where people may be reluctant to speak frankly in an unfamiliar setting. The evaluations should be anonymous, and you should encourage people to be candid.

See Appendix A for a sample evaluation form.

If you plan to ask for written evaluations, be sure to allow time in your agenda and to have enough pens or pencils available.

Why Do It

The Evaluation Section serves numerous purposes:

- It provides information on what went well, what didn't go well, what issues exist as a consequence of the day's work, and what changes need to be made in the group's operation. It gives you a fuller perspective on which to base future actions in the group and a much greater ability to prepare for a successful meeting next time.
- By allowing everyone an opportunity to express their opinion about the meeting, the Evaluation communicates that everyone's voice is important and that all participants share responsibility for what takes place in the group. Through this process, the Evaluation further empowers the individuals and helps to increase their investment in the success of the group.
- The fact that the Evaluation is done in the group means that everyone is aware of what the other members think of what took place during the meeting. This tends to bring a group together and to reduce the chance that misunderstandings will take root.

- The Evaluation creates a flow of information that may shed new light on group issues or dynamics. At times you may be surprised to learn that group members have a more positive view than you expect of a meeting or some aspect of a meeting.
- If the meeting did not go well, group members have the opportunity to voice their concerns and you are able gain insight into what the problems were. While it may be difficult to hear people's negative thoughts and feelings, it is important to realize that expressing them tends to disperse and release them, and thus allows the group to start fresh at the next session. When a facilitator avoids the Evaluation Section of a meeting that did not go well, the negativity remains present in a vague, unnamed, and diffuse form that can have a corrosive impact on the future functioning of the group.
- If the meeting went well, the Evaluation gives each participant the opportunity to testify to the value of the group and its positive qualities. This testimony creates a positive group identity that can help empower the group to accomplish challenging goals or help bring them through rough times that may lie ahead. Furthermore, the expression of the positive nature of the group tends to "package" the experience in a way that will last in people's memories, whereas without this expression the experience might soon be forgotten.
- The Evaluation brings the meeting full circle by once again allowing each member to have the attention of the entire group. Even in a large group that does an exercise such as GROUP SHOUT EVALUATION (p. 423), everyone has the chance to express their opinion, although not everyone can receive individual attention.

Chapter 5

Interactive Meetings: Making Them Work

To work effectively with interactive methods, you need to do several things. All of it will be worthwhile. You need to:

- First, overcome your own resistance. Then overcome the resistance of the group. You may also need to deal with resistance from supervisors or other authority figures. All of these are ongoing processes. This is so important that chapter 3 is all about it.
- Find or create a space that accommodates an interactive meeting.
- Design an interactive agenda.
- Implement the agenda with skill.
- "Process" the exercises effectively.
- Make it work for the long term.

Arranging the Setting

The physical setting for a group meeting has a direct impact on the level of cooperation or resistance that both the group and the facilitator will feel, and therefore has a powerful impact on the success of the meeting. If people are in an uncomfortable environment or one that presents some challenges, they are less able to relax and follow the agenda you've designed. Everything you can do to bring the space closer to the ideal will have a positive effect on the group experience.

If possible, become familiar with the meeting room before creating the agenda so that you can choose exercises the group can do in the space available. If you are not able to see the room beforehand, try to get a description of the layout and find out whether you can move furniture and whether the materials you need will be available.

The settings we describe here can range from living rooms to classrooms to boardrooms, and we are mainly thinking in terms of small to medium-size groups (between 6 and 30 people). Remember, however, that the Interactive Meeting Format can work with groups of up to 100, and can be implemented at some level for a group of any size.

The Ideal Setting

The ideal setting for an interactive meeting of a small to medium-size group is a quiet, private, and comfortable space where people can sit in a horseshoe shape—not around a table—and have some room to move around. The facilitator should have room to stand at the front of the horseshoe, with a board or flip chart to write on. (A flip chart is best because it allows you to keep a record of the group's work.) Having a clock is helpful, and if you plan to do BRAINSTORMING (p. 385), the rules can be posted.

For some meetings, having food available sets a welcoming atmosphere. If people may be arriving hungry, having food will help them be more focused. At other times, food may be a distraction that will hinder the progress of the meeting. Consider whether or not having food will help or hurt your meeting, and arrange for it if you think it will help.

The Less-than-Ideal Setting

If the space is crowded, dirty, too hot, or too cold, if there is noise, no open space to move around in, or a sense that someone might walk in at any moment, these conditions will have a negative impact on the group's ability to function effectively. You might not be able to control what room a group will meet in, but you should do whatever you can to arrange a setting that will help the group to succeed.

What to Do. If the meeting room is set up with chairs in rows or around a table, change the furniture arrangement if possible. Move tables or desks aside and pull the chairs into a circle. If the tables or desks can't be moved, perhaps you can bring the chairs into a circle in a corner of the room and post flip chart paper on the wall in that corner.

Also, do what you can before the meeting begins to make the room comfortable and free of distractions. Clean up any trash or items left over from other meetings. Post "Do Not Disturb" signs if necessary, and close the door when the meeting starts. Be sure you know how to regulate the temperature. Think ahead about materials needed for the group and be sure that arrangements have been made to provide these items.

Table in the Middle. The traditional meeting culture is centered on "bringing people to the table." This element is so well established that, in many settings, the table is actually bolted to the floor. The table, however, often functions as a barrier between people, allowing group members to hide from one another, and it can serve to mask inattention. Furthermore, many of the exercises in this book that work to energize and focus a group cannot be done with a table in the middle of the room.

If at all possible, get rid of the table, move it out of the way, or find a meeting room that does not have a table. As you practice the skills in this book, you will see the dramatic difference in energy, focus, and productivity between meetings that happen around a table and those that take place in a room with open floor space.

Recognizing, however, that not all settings are ideal, chapter 13 contains exercises that work with people seated at desks or tables or in an "audience-style" setting.

Be prepared for resistance related to removing the table; people will say, for example, that they need the table so they can take notes. This is only true if all they have to write on is loose paper, and you can anticipate and remove this issue by having clipboards, pads of paper, or books available to provide surfaces for writing.

Designing the Agenda

Chapter 4 describes the components of the Interactive Meeting Format in detail; this chapter explains the most important considerations when you are working with those components to design an agenda.

There are two ways to design an agenda based on the Interactive Meeting Format:

- Do it quickly, skimming the exercises in this book and choosing those that will fill up the time. Choose a Warm-up Question like "How was your day?" Pick a simple Springboard Exercise. Then plunge ahead into the "real work" of the meeting.
- Design the agenda carefully and thoughtfully, choosing exercises and activities that will help the group to meet its goals.

If you want your group to grow and change in positive ways and to be effective and productive in its tasks, choose the second way.

The ideal agenda anticipates and structures both the issues the group is facing and the work they need to accomplish on a given day. It shapes a coherent meeting in which the purposes are clear to participants and the elements build logically upon each other. The various pieces of the agenda should be connected thematically, and the themes should be a reflection of the meeting's goals. The pieces leading up to the Work Section should help the group to anticipate and perform their work effectively, while the Work Section can be structured to help the group deal with its issues as people accomplish other tasks.

There is a template at the end of this chapter that you can copy and use for creating agendas. We suggest that you keep a loose-leaf notebook holding both blank copies of the template and your meeting agendas, filed in chronological order for future reference.

Here are the guidelines for thoughtful agenda design.

Clearly Identify the Purposes of the Meeting
To begin, list the major goals for the meeting. For example, some goals might be:

- Helping people get to know each other in the first meeting of an ongoing group
- Presenting information to the group and engaging everyone in discussion, such as in a one-time drug-abuse prevention workshop
- Accomplishing tasks related to a work project or an event the group is planning
- Making a decision about the group's course of action
- Working with a complex emotional issue (such as trust, fear of failure, or lack of motivation) in a group that has been meeting for a while
- Dealing with dysfunctional group dynamics (such as cliques, a few people dominating the conversation, or people chronically arriving late).

Carefully consider which tasks and/or issues are calling for attention most urgently. Will the meeting be primarily task-oriented? Are there conflicts or group dynamics that need to be addressed or resolved before the group can accomplish its tasks? What are your goals in addressing these issues and tasks? What are the barriers to accomplishing your goals?

Be Aware of Individual and Group Dynamics
Successful agenda design for any group involves carefully considering individuals' feelings and the group dynamics. It is always important to take into consideration what may be happening below the surface.

In an unformed group, which can be either a one-time group or a new group, you will know little or nothing about individual participants and the dynamics among people will be undeveloped. Nevertheless, you can examine what you do know and think about how to work with it. For example, in a mandatory one-time teacher training session that is taking place after school, a facilitator could reasonably anticipate that:

- Some participants will be tired.
- Some may feel resentful at being required to attend the session.
- Some will have doubts regarding the facilitator's ability to offer useful information.

With this awareness, the facilitator can design an agenda that addresses these sensitivities. For example:

- In the Introduction, acknowledge the time of day and express appreciation for the effort that participants are making in attending the session.
- To surface the feelings and attitudes that people are bringing to the session, use a Warm-up

Question such as, "Say a word that describes what you were thinking about this session on your way here today."
- Use a Springboard Exercise that energizes people, and process it in a way that makes useful connections between the experience of the exercise and the work of the day.
- Plan a Work Section that builds on the strength and experience of the teachers involved.

In a formed group (that is, a group that has been together for a while), you will know a lot about the individuals and the dynamics that exist among people—alliances, tensions, attractions, etc. To design an effective agenda, you need to recognize a group's strengths and weaknesses and be able to anticipate the sensitivities of individuals. Before you plunge into the details of planning the meeting, think about the group and its members. The areas to think about will vary depending on the group and its purpose, but in general some questions to consider are:

- How committed are people to meeting the group's goals? If there is a wide range of commitment, how does the group handle this?
- How well is the group moving toward meeting its goals? In a classroom setting, how well are individuals learning the material?
- What are the varied skill levels of individuals for the tasks required? What are the coping mechanisms of those who appear to be less skilled? How does the whole group cope with disparity of skills?
- Are some people feeling overwhelmed by their tasks or afraid they will not be able to accomplish what is expected of them? If so, is this a source of dysfunction in the group?
- What issues are individuals dealing with in their lives outside of the group, and how are these situations affecting the group? Is anyone in the group facing a crisis?
- How are the members of the group getting along with one another?
- Is the group factionalized? What are the issues that divide people?
- Is someone in the group playing the role of scapegoat?
- Where are the tensions, attractions, alliances, or isolations present in the group?
- Which issues are on the surface and which are beneath the surface?

Depending on the purpose of the group, you may focus more on personal issues and less on group issues, or vice versa. Considering these questions will help you to create a design that moves the group forward through their issues into richer and more productive work.

Choose Appropriate Exercises

To make the best choices for your group, you should become familiar with a broad range of exercises and know how they can be processed. Then, with many interactive techniques to choose from, consider which will best address the dynamics of the group and help the group move toward the fulfillment of its goals. Once you have identified the dynamics or tasks that you want to address, there are a number of ways to select the appropriate approach.

- **Mirror the Dynamic.** You can choose an exercise that mirrors the dynamic you see in the group. For example, when you want to raise the issue of factions in the group, you could choose an exercise like AMOEBA TAG (p. 258), which breaks people up into small, competing groups.

- **Create the Opposite Dynamic.** Conversely, you can select an exercise that creates the dynamic you would like to foster in the group. For example, when you want to illustrate the importance of letting people speak without being interrupted, you might use GROUP COUNT (p. 221), which requires that group members not speak at the same time.

- **Inform the Group's Behavior.** You can select an exercise that gives the group a better understanding of their work for that day or a greater awareness of the importance of their group's mission. For example, for a group that is preparing to host a large-scale gathering and needs to practice making people feel comfortable, a good choice would be FILL THE SPACE, SHAKE THE HAND (p. 282), which requires people to reach out to each other and shake hands. For a group that is looking at the issue of homelessness, the facilitator might use the exercise THE WIND BLOWS (p. 377), which illustrates how it feels to be left out and stranded without a resource that most people have.

In any exercise you select (in fact, in any action a group takes), various dynamics will emerge. The key is to design a format that creates a context for the exploration of the issues, information, or dynamics that the group needs to explore in order to move toward the fulfillment of its goals.

Be Aware of Risk

Asking people to participate in an interactive exercise is asking them to take a risk with their self-esteem and their image in the group. The risk can be so small as to be almost nonexistent, as in the

case of a group that knows each other well and feels comfortable together. Or the risk can be great—for example, if members of the group do not know each other, want very much to be accepted by others, and are fearful that they will not be.

An exercise defeats its purpose if it presents too great a risk for too many people. If people are made uncomfortable and asked to share too much in a group that is not ready to support them, there is a danger that individuals will be hurt rather than helped by their participation in the group.

Determining what level of risk a group can handle involves forethought and consideration. For example, the Warm-up Question "What was your favorite class in high school?" is low-risk for a group of college graduates but high-risk for a group of people who did not finish high school.

The more you know about individuals in the group and their vulnerabilities, and about issues affecting the whole group at a given time, the better equipped you are to identify the appropriate level of risk. If the meeting you are planning is likely to include individuals you do not know, this automatically lowers the acceptable level of risk. If you do not know the group at all, you should keep the risk level very low.

However, while you want to avoid challenging a group beyond its capacity, this does not mean using only exercises that present little or no challenge. As a group develops and gets to know each other, there may be times when you want to push the level of risk higher in order to dig deeper into the issues facing the group. You are striving for a balance between challenge and safety, with the presumption that it is better to err, slightly, on the side of safety.

As you consider how much to ask of your group in terms of risk, be alert to the dynamic of your own resistance (see p. 26). If you think that the group is not ready for a certain level of risk, consider whether your own resistance may be clouding your understanding of how best to address the needs and goals of the group.

Be Subtle

If a group is to develop into a cohesive, functional unit, members must see with their own eyes and draw their own lessons. Your job is to hold a mirror up to the group. When the design and facilitation are subtle and insightful, the group sees itself in that mirror and people adjust their behavior according to what

they like and don't like about what they see. However, when subtlety is lacking, the group sees the intention of the facilitator rather than seeing itself, and the effectiveness of the exercise is diminished.

It is best if the group's issues and new perceptions and understandings are brought to the surface by group members themselves, rather than by the facilitator. You should strive, therefore, not to select exercises that broadcast to the group what you think the issues are.

For example: We frequently use a WORDSTORM (p. 413) to bring issues to a group's consciousness. This exercise involves putting a word on the flip chart and having the group call out related words that come to mind. Being subtle in choosing the central word is key to the success of the exercise. If a group is having problems trusting each other and you want to surface this issue, doing a WORDSTORM on "trust" may at first seem like a good idea. However, this will make it clear to the group that you think trust is an issue among them. Being thus labeled can make group members feel attacked and may cause some people to withdraw. Even worse, it may become a negative point of reference for the group and feed into a perception of themselves that is not helpful in moving forward. Instead of the too-direct word "trust," you could do a WORDSTORM on the word "friendship." This will not reveal your intentions, and the group will be more likely to participate undistracted by an awareness of your motives. With skilled processing, the issue of trust will come out of the word "friendship" spontaneously, originating from the group rather than from the facilitator.

The ability to be subtle is particularly important in ongoing groups whose dynamics are fully formed. The farther away you can get from the point you want to make while still getting back to that point, the more effective the exercise will be. The real learning, change, and growth take place for the group in the space between doing the exercise and the process of discovery that the group goes through in order to discern its meaning.

Keep Your Designs Fresh
With an ongoing group, overuse of an exercise will eventually flatten the experience; yet an exercise can be repeated many times and still remain fresh and unpredictable. Here are some ways to keep useful exercises working for your group.

- **Use the Same Exercise but Process It Differently.** An exercise used with a new group will often play out very differently with the same group later on when people know each other better. Group dynamics that were too high-risk to bring up in discussion the first time the group does an exercise may be ripe for surfacing another time. You may also be able to see and point out changes in the group through changes in the way they relate to the exercise. Each time you process a familiar exercise, you can focus on aspects that have not been raised previously.

- **Make Subtle Changes in the Exercise.** An exercise can be kept new and interesting by slightly altering the directions you give to the group. For example, consider the HUMAN KNOT (p. 332), an exercise in which a small group of people become knotted up and must get disentangled. You can significantly change the group's experience of the exercise by assigning one person as the leader and telling everyone else to follow their instructions, or by asking several of the participants to close their eyes during the exercise, or by setting the exercise up as a competition between two groups. With such variations, you can make a basic exercise more complex and higher risk. This book includes many variations that we suggest for the exercises. We encourage you to make thoughtful and purposeful variations of your own. Interactive exercises are tools to create a desired experience for your group. As long as you are clear about what it is you want to communicate through an exercise, feel free to adjust the exercise to suit your purpose. See scenario 7, "A Small Change Creates a Fresh Experience."

Scenario 7: A Small Change Creates a Fresh Experience

An ongoing group had used the exercise ZIP ZAP ZUP (p. 182) previously as a way to generate energy and illustrate the flow of energy in the group.

Annette, the group's facilitator, had just learned about a potential obstacle to the success of the group's current project, which had been fairly straightforward up to this point. Preparing for a meeting at which she planned to inform the group of this complication and brainstorm ways to cope with it, Annette thought about how the group's even flow of work was being disrupted. She remembered how the group had enjoyed getting into the rhythm of ZIP ZAP ZUP, and it occurred to her that a variation on this exercise might serve to illustrate their current situation and help them get focused on dealing with it. For the Springboard Exercise, therefore, she thought she might try ZIP ZAP ZUP WITH FOOT-STAMPING: each time someone said "Zup," they simultaneously had to stamp their foot.

Before deciding to use this variation, Annette tried it out with some family members; her guess that the foot-stamping requirement would make the exercise significantly more difficult proved to be correct. In the group, Annette introduced the exercise and said that anyone who made a mistake would be out. People were amazed at how hard it was to stay in the game with this extra step to remember. The exercise took very little time, because everyone was out in a matter of moments.

Processing focused on how the addition of this seemingly minor requirement had such a huge impact on their ability to succeed at the exercise. Annette asked if people had formulated any strategies to remember the extra step; some people felt that with more time and practice, they would have been able to do much better. Others talked about strategies they had used in other areas of their lives to change ingrained habits.

Later in the meeting, as the group discussed their project and what to do about the new situation confronting them, insights from the processing of ZIP ZAP ZUP cast some light on how the group might take on this additional challenge. Annette brought up some of the ideas that people had offered for coping with the necessity of change, and these ideas helped the group think more deeply about their current dilemma.

Create Your Own Exercises

There may be times when the issue you want to raise in the group can be illustrated best with a custom-made exercise. To begin designing an exercise, think about the particular dynamic or issue you want to raise; then think about creating a similar or opposite dynamic through an exercise. Scenario 8 illustrates a custom-made exercise that mimics a group's dysfunctional behavior.

Scenario 8: Using a Familiar Experience

Robert was working with a group that had some very vocal members and some members who hardly spoke at all. He suspected that the quieter members of the group were being overshadowed by the more vocal members. He wanted the group to work on this dynamic so they could create an atmosphere where everyone's ideas could be heard.

Robert reviewed all the exercises that he knew, but he could not find one that fit the issue he wanted to raise. He thought about the dynamic in the group: it seemed that some people always went along with what the more vocal members of the group said, even when Robert expected them to disagree. He had the sense that the quieter members never got a chance to decide what they really thought before the other members had already taken a firm position. It reminded him of being pulled downstream by a powerful current.

He decided to have them act out this dynamic by singing the old song "Row, Row, Row Your Boat." He split the group up into three sections, and had them sing the song as a round. Since the more vocal members of the group always sat next to each other in the circle, it was easy to put them in the same section. As the group sang the song, one section was much louder than the others. In fact, they were almost yelling instead of singing. As the other sections tried to join in the round, they got drowned out by the loud section. Before long, the whole group was singing the song together, instead of as a round.

In processing the exercise, Robert asked the group why they had been unable to keep the song going as a round. Some people said they had gotten confused. Even though they had started singing separately, all they could hear was the loud section of the group, and before they knew it they had lost their ability to keep their own time. Robert asked the group if this sort of thing ever happened in their work together. After a bit of a silence, one of the more vocal members of the group said that she thought maybe others were quiet a lot during group discussions because she always had a lot to say. She said she thought everyone should speak their own mind. Robert closed the exercise by encouraging everyone to hold onto their own thoughts and opinions rather than just going "gently down the stream" with the loudest voice. He also suggested that the group make room in the boat (the group) for everyone, and give others a chance to think and talk too.

"Row, Row, Row Your Boat" had been a perfect fit for the issue the group was facing. It allowed the dynamics in the group to come to the surface in an unexpected, indirect way. If you have a good sense of the dynamics in the group, you can use experiences of all sorts to surface them.

Exercises can come from anywhere. What's important is that an exercise provide the group with a genuine experience and useful information about their work or the challenges they face. In designing an exercise, be sure that you know what you are trying to illustrate and that the risk level of the exercise is appropriate for the group. Consider carefully what is likely to happen, both positive and negative, during the exercise. Are the potential outcomes the ones you want? Develop clear directions about

how the exercise will be conducted and, if possible, try it out with co-workers before bringing it to the group.

Being innovative with interactive techniques takes time, practice, and openness to your own creativity. It also requires you to take some risks, and you should expect that some of your innovations will succeed and some will fail. If an exercise does not work as you had hoped and planned, give yourself points for trying, and recognize that our mistakes can often teach us more than our successes. Being able to pick yourself up after failed attempts at innovation and evaluate what went wrong is an important part of the learning process.

Take It Slow

This book describes many variations of exercises, each representing some adjustment that changes the dynamic or risk level. In general, it is best to begin with the basic form of an exercise and to save the more complex or challenging versions until the group has had experience with the basic exercise and with each other. However, there may be times when a variation suits the purpose better than the original version. As always, your decision should be driven by the group's needs.

Keep It Simple

Sometimes facilitators who are beginning to learn the *Moving Beyond Icebreakers* approach become caught up in complexity: choosing the more involved exercises over the simple ones, or creating elaborate exercises that take a lot of time. However, less is often more with interactive exercises; simplicity is more effective than intricacy. A sure way to increase resistance in a group and to undermine the value of interactive work is to use lengthy exercises that make people suspect the group is spinning its wheels. As you design agendas, keep the expenditure of time in proportion to the value of what you are trying to achieve. If you can reach your goal with either an exercise that takes five minutes or one that takes 15 minutes, using the five-minute approach is almost always preferable.

Be Inclusive

You should choose exercises in which all group members can participate. If some members have physical limitations that make participation difficult, make it a priority to design agendas that will include them. See Appendix B: Adapting Interactive Exercises for Physical Limitations. Similarly, you can adapt exercises to make them work for group members with mental or emotional limitations.

Facilitating the Meeting

The skill with which you are able to facilitate a meeting is even more important than the agenda design. A good facilitator can take a mediocre agenda and make it into a highly effective experience for the participants. On the other hand, a facilitator who is overcome by resistance, or one who either is unaware of the powerful potentials of the group experience or is not committed to maximizing them, can take the best agenda and achieve little or nothing with it.

This section describes the skills you need to facilitate an interactive agenda effectively.

Remain Aware of Your Purpose

If you have designed the agenda with care, forethought, and a clear purpose in mind, you will be much better able to retain faith in the importance of what you are asking the group to do. Knowing why you designed the agenda as you did and what you expect to accomplish will provide you with a firm foundation as you introduce each element on the agenda and lead the group through it. Solid awareness of your purpose will allow you to maintain the strength it takes to ride out the resistance coming from the group or from yourself. (See chapter 3.)

Give Good Instructions

Without good instructions, an exercise may not work at all, and if it does it is less likely to meet your goals. In a few cases (such as PAIR TAG, p. 270), an exercise can actually be dangerous if people are not well instructed. Before you lead an exercise for the first time, make sure you understand the instructions and can visualize how the exercise works. Practice giving the instructions in your own words. If possible, practice with someone else who can ask questions and point out difficulties and potential misunderstandings.

Observe the Group's Dynamics

While you are facilitating, try to be a keen observer of what is happening around you. Be receptive to any messages that the group's actions communicate. Be aware of how people are interacting or failing to interact. Try to determine where the leadership in the group is coming from. Is the leadership static, or does it flow through different people? Note the group or individual characteristics that are revealed as people go through the session's activities. Remember the ideas, perceptions, or understandings that are expressed by the group or come to mind for you. By paying attention to the details of what happens and what is said, you will gain important information that will empower you to bring the group to deeper levels of connection, understanding, and commitment to fulfilling its goals.

It is often helpful to take notes as you observe. For example, you might jot down a few key words from each response to the Warm-up Question, or note who volunteered to be first during the Springboard Exercise, who went last, or other actions that might be revealing of group dynamics or individuals' states of mind. This information is often very helpful in conducting an effective processing of the exercise. (Processing is discussed in detail below.)

Know When to Participate and When to Observe

Facilitators are also members of the group, and as such should always participate in Name Exercises, Warm-up Questions, and Evaluation Exercises. For most Springboard Exercises, however, it is more effective if you observe rather than participate. As a new facilitator you will need to observe in order to process effectively, and as you become more skilled, you will want to be an observer so that you can make adaptations to take advantage of dynamics as they emerge. Moreover, for exercises that require physical activity, such as the tag-style exercises in chapter 14, you need to enforce the rules from the sidelines to ensure that no one gets hurt.

Nevertheless, in some situations it may be important for you to participate, and there are some exercises in which you can easily participate and observe simultaneously. For example, the facilitator should always join in on THE WIND BLOWS (p. 377).

Enjoy Yourself

While your job as facilitator is to maintain order and keep the meeting moving along, remember that humor and jokes are not only OK, but are in fact desirable in creating a positive atmosphere for group work. Letting your own personality and style come out as you facilitate is one of the powerful and pleasurable aspects of the interactive process.

Don't Panic if What You Planned Doesn't Work

There may be times when you give clear instructions but the group, for whatever reason, does not follow them. Rather than interrupting with corrections, watch how the group deals with the exercise. Then use what you've observed, including the fact that the instructions were not followed, in the processing discussion. As you become more experienced, you will learn how to take advantage of this kind of situation, and you will come to see that sometimes both you and the group might learn more from an exercise that does not work as expected than from one that does.

Processing the Exercises

By "processing" we mean leading a discussion and/or making observations about a completed exercise in order to draw understanding from it. Processing can help people to think in a creative way about a decision they must make, appreciate the importance of their work, understand a dynamic that exists in the group, or learn some new piece of information.

Format for Processing

A general format for processing an exercise involves:

- Asking a few good questions that will spark discussion in the group about their experience of the exercise and how it relates to their experiences in the group. The best starting question is "What did people think of that exercise?" because it allows the group to create its own agenda and express its own understanding.

- Providing your own comments about why you selected that particular exercise and what you thought it illustrated about the group (based on your observations and/or the comments of other group members).

In certain circumstances, you may decide that the best approach is to do only one of these pieces—that is, to ask questions of the group but not to comment yourself, or to comment without asking questions. For example, in a one-time group where there are no formed dynamics to surface, it is often appropriate to limit your processing to a few comments making the point(s) you want to get across. In processing a Warm-up Question, you would generally only make some comments to sum up people's responses.

The discussion can look at areas such as:

- How people dealt with the challenges posed by the exercise.
- What the end result was (whether expected or unexpected).
- How the learning from the exercise relates to the work the group is doing or the issues they are facing.

Anything that happens during the exercise could be included in the processing, and the variability of human responses to experience virtually guarantees material for processing of any exercise.

Be Aware of Resistance

The few moments allotted for processing an exercise are when you are most likely to feel the impact of your own resistance. When you are experiencing a high level of resistance, much of your attention and focus will be directed inward on your own doubts, fears, and nervousness, rather than outward on the group dynamics and learning opportunities that are present. This inevitably leads to missing obvious process points. A garrulous facilitator in this situation may "overprocess" by talking more than necessary about the exercise, whereas a more reserved facilitator may "underprocess," saying very little and missing valuable and sometimes obvious opportunities to draw understanding from the exercise. In addition, when you are in the grip of resistance you are more likely to be thrown off when an exercise "doesn't work" as expected, and you may forget that the exercise often can be more powerfully processed than one that "does work."

It is important to be aware of your level of resistance so that you can work to focus your attention outward on what is happening around you. It will help you to do this if:

- before the exercise, you understand clearly what you want the group to learn from it, and
- during the exercise, you observe carefully what happens and what is said.

How Much Processing Is Enough?

You need to develop the ability to judge how much processing work the group needs around the issues raised by the exercise. Sometimes it will be appropriate to lead an in-depth discussion of the group dynamics that emerged during the exercise. At other times, a few comments may be all that is needed. Occasionally, you may decide not to process an exercise at all, but instead use the energy generated by the exercise to flow right into the next section of the agenda. See scenario 9, "Three Ways to Process Pair Tag," for different pictures of how an exercise can be processed.

Your sense of the appropriate amount of processing may change during the exercise itself. Be prepared to respond to critical dynamics that emerge during an exercise, even if you had planned not to process the exercise at all. On the other hand, be prepared to end the processing of an exercise after just a few comments if the lesson of the exercise is already clear to the group. Stay in the moment, remaining as aware as possible of what is happening in the group.

It is very easy to underprocess an exercise, spending so little time on processing that the group misses the learning opportunities inherent in the experience. Conversely, with so much that can be learned, you may be tempted to overprocess, to prolong the processing beyond the point where people can remain engaged. Pay attention to how many group members are participating; some people have a lower tolerance than others for reflecting on nuances of an experience. It is ideal to end the processing while most people are still thinking and attentive.

Processing should never take the form of the facilitator speaking at length. When you are speaking, you have about a two-minute window to make your point(s). Maintain an awareness of that window and how much time is left before it closes. You can reopen the window by making a good joke or asking a good question, and once it's reopened you can make additional comments, but be aware that the window is always on its way down again.

Each time you work with an exercise, you are building up your sense of how to do it and learning how to gauge the needs of the group so that your processing brings out the most valuable lessons and is neither too much nor too little.

Scenario 9: Three Ways to Process Pair Tag

A. Processing with a Few Comments

Keisha was preparing her group to run workshops at a conference. The young people would each be facilitating in teams of two. She wanted group members to practice working together and supporting their partners, even when they were not facilitating themselves. Keisha decided to use Pair Tag (p. 270) to illustrate her point.

She asked the group to form two lines facing each other, then explained that each person would be playing tag with the person directly across from them. Keisha watched and enforced the rules as everyone fast-walked around the room, laughing and hiding from their partners.

When it came time to process the exercise, Keisha said that PAIR TAG was like co-facilitating. The individuals on each team would be taking turns leading their workshop group, passing the agenda back and forth between them. But unlike playing PAIR TAG, when people are co-facilitating they need to work together throughout the meeting. When one person passes off the leadership to the other, the first person can't run away and hide; they need to stay present in every way, supporting and helping their co-facilitator.

Then Keisha had each pair go off and practice their workshops. She asked them to be especially aware of how they would share the agenda, how they would pass it off to each other, and how they would keep the energy flowing between them.

B. Processing with an In-Depth Discussion

Luis's youth group had just completed a community barbecue that had not been entirely successful. Although turnout for the event had been good, the group had spent much of the day bickering among themselves. The grills had been left unattended at several points, and some of the youth who gave speeches were flat and uninspired in their delivery.

As Luis prepared the agenda for a meeting to evaluate the barbecue, he tried to think of an exercise that would mirror the dynamic he had seen in the group during the event. He decided to try PAIR TAG. He thought that he would process the exercise by talking about the chaotic environment that PAIR TAG created and relating it to the way the group had worked together at the barbecue. He also planned to make points about people shirking their responsibilities (like not cooking the burgers) by passing them off on other people.

When the group played PAIR TAG, Luis observed a great many behaviors that seemed related to the current dynamic in the group. Ron and Steven insisted on running, though Luis kept asking them not to. Steven ran into Susan and stepped on her foot. Several pairs just stood in one place and tagged each other, rather than actually engaging in the exercise. Toya left the room to go to the bathroom, leaving her partner with nothing to do but sit on the sidelines.

After a few minutes, Luis settled the group down and began to work with what he had observed. He asked the group the following questions to stimulate discussion: "Did people enjoy this exercise? Why or why not?" "Why were some people standing still?" "Were the rules being followed?" "Did people feel safe?" "What was the energy in the group like during the exercise?" "Is this the same type of energy that the group had during the barbecue?"

As the group discussed their experience of PAIR TAG, it became clear that several people were taking the position that the exercise was stupid. Luis sensed a dynamic emerging that caring about the work of the group was also stupid. This was making it difficult for those who were truly invested in the work to act on their convictions, and it was letting those with a negative attitude take over.

Susan commented that when Steven stepped on her foot, she felt like quitting the exercise so she wouldn't get hurt again. Then Toya said that she had left her job of grilling at the barbecue because she'd almost burned her hand when someone jostled her and she didn't want to take any more chances of getting hurt.

Luis closed the processing of the exercise by making some comments. He pointed out that when people are not invested in the exercise or in the work of the group, it creates an unsafe environment where people can get hurt. When people don't feel safe, they are not able to take risks and try new things; Luis wondered if this explained the lackluster performance of those who had given speeches, as well as Toya's situation. He concluded by saying that he hoped they could create an environment where people felt safe and could work together.

Through his processing of PAIR TAG, Luis brought out some important issues. He knew that he would have to continue to work with group on these issues if he was going to change the dynamic that was developing. He learned from the exercise that he would need to design future meetings to push those who were not invested in the group's work to either get on board or leave the group.

C. Using PAIR TAG without Processing

Ellen and Dan were working with their group to organize a student/teacher workshop at their high school. In the Work Section of the agenda they planned to do BRAINSTORMING on the positive and negative aspects of student/teacher relationships. From past experience, they knew that this group had a hard time with Brainstorms; they tended to censor their ideas and feel shy about yelling them out in front of the group.

After the Introduction and Warm-up Question, Ellen and Dan had the group play a quick game of PAIR TAG. While the energy was high and the group was laughing and having a good time, the facilitators stopped the exercise and quickly started the Brainstorm. Still huffing and puffing from PAIR TAG, group members began shouting out their thoughts about student/teacher relationships at school.

Ellen and Dan had decided not to do a formal processing of PAIR TAG. Instead, they used the energy it created and the in-the-body experience of the back-and-forth nature of relationships to inform the BRAINSTORMING session.

Use Subtlety in Processing

On p. 59 we discuss the importance of being subtle when you select exercises; the points made in that discussion apply equally here. When the facilitator "names" the group's dynamics directly, this can eclipse the group's own process of learning and understanding.

As a facilitator, you have the power to determine an agenda and keep the group focused on it, enforce guidelines, and keep time limits. However, when it comes to changing group dynamics and creating new understanding, you have much less direct power to impact the group. Achieving this kind of deep change is accomplished most effectively when the group members come to a new understanding through their own collective and individual thought processes.

Your primary role is to create a field of experience where the group members can deduce, through their own perceptions, new understandings of themselves, the dynamics of the group, or the issues and societal dynamics that are the focus of the group. For an example of how this can work, see scenario 10.

Scenario 10: Subtle Processing of a Warm-up Question

Hanad's group was organizing a conflict resolution session between rival neighborhoods. In a planning meeting several days before the event, Hanad opened with the Warm-up Question, "Why did you want to be involved in this project?" Most members of the group cited various goals the group had set for the session, such as saving lives and creating peace in their community. But one young woman, Danielle, said that she was just coming to watch the fights.

Hanad had run into problems with Danielle's attitude in the past. In previous meetings he had tried to address her attitude on the spot by confronting her about the negative energy she was putting into the group, but he had found that this approach served only to further cement her in the role of the tough, uncommitted one. Occasionally his lectures seemed to make her even more removed and obstinate.

This time, he took a different approach. Instead of addressing the negative tone of Danielle's answer, he decided to try working with the information she had put out, and to be careful not to force her into her typical role. When processing the Warm-up Question, he said, "It sounds like people got involved in this project for a lot of different reasons. I heard people say that if we do this thing well we can make some important changes in this community. We can stop people from getting hurt; we can save lives; we can make it safer for young people to go where they want without looking over their shoulders. I also heard that there's the potential for fights and violence, so we really need to have our act together. We need to take the steps necessary to ensure everyone's safety, and to be sure we're putting out the right message to those who come. We also need to have our eyes open. So, if people in this group have information about possible conflicts, or concerns about how the session is set up, we should get those things out in the open so we can address them."

Hanad then made some adjustments in his agenda for the meeting. He made time for reviewing the safety measures the group had in place, the logistics of the session, and the way that the group intended to create a peaceful atmosphere. He asked for input from the group on each aspect of the event, which led to a discussion about those who might come who were notorious for stirring up trouble. Danielle said that she'd heard some guys talking trash about the session. The group strategized about how they would deal with these guys, and how they could help them feel invested in the success of the session.

By being less direct in his approach, Hanad had succeeded in keeping Danielle on board with the initiative. Even if Danielle's comment was motivated only by a poor attitude, by addressing her answer in an indirect way Hanad avoided freezing her in a negative role in the group. More importantly, he used the negative information she'd put out in a constructive way. The fact that Danielle expressed concern about the safety of the event, however negatively, was a signpost pointing toward important information for the group.

Being subtle and indirect in processing does not mean ignoring the information or dynamics in the group, but instead dealing with them in a non-confrontational, constructive, group-oriented way.

There is No One Correct Way to Process an Exercise
This book gives specific processing ideas for exercises based on our experiences in a variety of settings. However, many aspects of processing an exercise cannot be planned in advance. Effective processing involves being tuned in to what is happening in the group at a particular moment, taking responsibility for the safety of group members, and committing yourself to making these exercises meaningful experiences in the life of the group. These are skills that are developed over time.

As you gain confidence and experience, we encourage you to move away from the processing suggestions in this book, and instead to respond to what you see in the moment and to rely on your own understanding of your group's needs. The most effective processing comes when you are open to the lessons contained in the particular experience of the exercise at that moment, which may be different from the experience at any other time.

Making It Work for the Long Term

Even after you have experienced the advantages of working interactively, you may still find it tempting to revert to the old, familiar forms. It is difficult to think consistently about how to involve everyone through interactive techniques; it takes time and energy to plan for every new group and every new meeting in a way that will maximize productive interaction. Furthermore, resistance never goes away completely, and it is far easier in the short term to allow your natural resistance and the group's resistance to prevail.

But if you are convinced of the benefits of the Interactive Meeting Format, and if you are committed to reaping these benefits for your group and for yourself, here are two important practices to incorporate into your work:

Be Consistent
The tendency among people who use some interactive techniques is to use them occasionally, when there is extra time or a special purpose. And even in groups where interaction is the standard operating procedure, when the facilitator or the group is under stress or pressure there is a natural inclination to lower your expectations for the group and yourself and to lapse into a more commonplace, noninteractive format.

But occasional or inconsistent use of interaction sends the message that it is peripheral to the serious work of the group and does not serve an important function. Inconsistent use gives people a sense of justification for their resistance, and it allows resistance to build up. Therefore, each time you choose a static agenda over an interactive one, you make it more difficult to work interactively the next time you wish to.

Consistent use of interaction means that people are always given the opportunity to speak, to move, to interact, and to evaluate. In a group that has a culture of interaction, people recognize that their thoughts and insights are valued. Such an inclusive climate brings great personal rewards to both the group members and the facilitator, and it creates a productive and effective working environment.

Evaluate Your Work
Spend time after each meeting reflecting on what happened. If you are working with a partner, discuss and evaluate together. For example, ask questions such as these about the exercises you selected:

- Did they serve your purpose(s)?

- Were there any unintended results?
- Was there resistance? If so, how did you deal with it?
- Was the risk level appropriate?
- Were the instructions clear?
- Did the processing work to raise points or issues in the way you expected?
- How could the processing have been more effective? Did you overprocess, perhaps draining energy and momentum from the experience? Or did you underprocess, not spending enough time to bring home the points you wanted to raise?
- Do you consider the exercise a success? If so, why? If not, what can you learn from the experience?

Whether an exercise failed or succeeded, you need to understand why. In many cases, an exercise that felt like a complete failure may have been successful in surfacing the dynamics of the group. Evaluate whether or not you were able to stay with the unintended results and continue to work with the group's experience of the exercise.

Look in a similar critical way at the agenda design and the overall meeting facilitation.

Some Final Thoughts about Facilitation

The art of group facilitation has a steep learning curve. In the beginning, there is a lot to learn and there are many areas of questioning and anxiety: *What exercises should I use? How do I give the directions? What happens if the group won't do it? What if the exercises don't work?* But as you continue to work with groups in an interactive way, you will gain strength and confidence and come to better answers and deeper levels of understanding. The process of exploration and growth, however, is endless; learning to deal effectively with human interaction is a lifelong process.

When you set out to acquire the skills to be an effective group facilitator, you are beginning a journey toward overcoming your own fears so that you can experience the power, the joy, and the productivity of working in groups where all involved are engaged and feel valued. There is nothing quite as gratifying as being part of a group that likes to be together, where group members recognize each other's positive qualities, and where each person is encouraged to be creative in developing their ideas and skills.

In taking on the role of facilitator, you are choosing to experiment, to innovate, to open up your heart and mind, and to experience significant personal growth. To continue on this road, you will need the courage that it takes to risk failure in the pursuit of achieving meaningful success. With courage, commitment, and creative energy, you will be able to achieve the effective facilitative leadership that groups of all kinds need to succeed.

Interactive Agenda

Date: ______________________

Goals:

Materials and Timelines needed:

Introduction Info:

Name Exercise(s) / Warm-up Question:

Processing points:

Springboard Exercise(s):

Processing points:

Work Section (including agendas for small groups):

Summation Info:

Evaluation Exercise:

Chapter 6

Putting It Together

- The Super Exercises
- Exercises with Movement
- The Agendas

  Agenda 1. A Meeting to Begin Taking Action
  Scenario 11: First meeting of an action-oriented, ongoing group
  Agenda 2. A Drug and Alcohol Abuse Prevention Workshop
  Agenda 3. Evaluating an Event
  Agenda 4. A Workshop on Personal Goal-Setting
  Agenda 5. A Routine Staff Meeting
  Agenda 6. Freshman Orientation: Small Group Agenda
  Agenda 7. High School Senior Class Meeting

In some ways this chapter is the most important in the book. It contains agendas that show how the pieces of the Interactive Meeting Format come together and how the format can work in a variety of situations to create powerful group experiences. It also describes the benefits of using physical movement exercises, and it highlights the "Super Exercises," which are used more than once in the agendas and are some of the most consistently effective exercises in this book.

To gain a deeper understanding of how to use the meeting format and the exercises, it helps to see them working toward specific goals and within particular settings. For that reason, we've described the context for each agenda. While these contexts probably will not match your exact situation, the agendas do provide blueprints for formats that, with appropriate adjustments, will meet the needs of many kinds of groups coming together for a variety of reasons.

Notes on the Agendas

Remember that the Introduction section of every agenda should include a brief overview of the goals and a preview of the agenda, as well as the other elements outlined on p. 37.

In writing these agendas, sometimes we give directions to the facilitator (such as "Instruct the group to do the exercise at a faster speed than normal") and sometimes we use language that shows how the facilitator can talk with the group (such as "Today's meeting is designed to help us build our relationships…."). We've tried to use the wording that will be most helpful for you in learning to work with the agendas.

The Super Exercises

The "Super Exercises" are useful in a variety of settings and they are almost always successful in helping facilitators to achieve the goals they set for meetings. They are easy to implement, yet they can have profound effects on groups.

PAIRING (p. 237) and CONCENTRIC CIRCLES (p. 190)

PAIRING is simply putting people into pairs to discuss a specific topic for a limited period of time, and CONCENTRIC CIRCLES is a series of pairings. CONCENTRIC CIRCLES is the preferred exercise in agendas where building relationships is an important goal, and it is particularly valuable at an early meeting of an ongoing group. However, if an agenda calls for CONCENTRIC CIRCLES but you do not have the time for it, you can substitute one or two PAIRINGS.

The keys to success for these exercises are:

- a specified topic (for CONCENTRIC CIRCLES, a series of topics arranged logically),
- a specified and limited time, and
- most important of all, assigned partners.

It is essential to the effectiveness of PAIRING that the facilitator assign the pairs. When the facilitator simply says, "Find someone you don't know to talk with," most people will instantly feel anxious. Some people will connect right away, but in any group there will be some who are not so lucky. When pairings are eventually established for all, many people will be caught up in nagging thoughts about issues of acceptance and rejection (*why did that person turn away, why did I choose this person, why didn't anyone want to talk with me, I should have talked with so-and-so,* etc.), rather than about the pair question. Instead of a fairly relaxing experience, the exercise becomes filled with anxiety. By contrast, by assigning the pairs the facilitator creates a safe context for participants to explore issues and develop relationships.

In CONCENTRIC CIRCLES, the facilitator should set up the circles so that people talk with those they do not usually spend time with. In a meeting that includes people in different categories (for example, youth and adults, teachers and parents, staff members and board members, people on different sides of an issue), the facilitator may want to specify that people in one category sit on the inside of the circle and the others on the outside.

Speaking and listening one-on-one with another person are powerful experiences that humanize people to one another very quickly. As a listener, each participant in a pair is granted a window into the thinking and emotions of the other person about the discussion topic. When people are paired who would probably not talk directly under any other circumstances, this is a rare gift. Given time for follow-up, the connections made in these discussions can serve as the basis for the development of ongoing relationships of trust and respect.

Speaking in pairs allows people to organize their thoughts, explore issues, and develop new ideas or problem-solving strategies. For most people, speaking to one other person is generally not a stressful experience; it is far easier than speaking in front of a group. In pairs, people are able to think and talk about the issue at hand in a relaxed way, which opens up thoughts and emotions around the issue and makes them more accessible. People often will share an idea with one other person that they would not initially be willing to say to the whole group, and sometimes this makes it possible to share the idea with the group later.

At times you may want to follow up the exercise by hearing from people about what they discussed with their partners. Remember to stress that people can share what they said to their partners, but they cannot share what their partners said to them.

BRAINSTORMING (p. 385)

BRAINSTORMING is a tool for helping groups to set goals, solve problems, or create options for action. It is a mainstay of interactive group work because it allows a group to speak as individuals while encouraging all voices to be heard.

The key to effective BRAINSTORMING is for the facilitator to understand the importance of the rules for BRAINSTORMING and to follow them rigorously. The instruction to suspend judgment is particularly essential. This removes individual identity from the ideas and allows ideas to be judged on their merit,

thus opening up new sources of creative energy. By bringing out many ideas before any discussion takes place, group members can look at a wide range of ideas before deciding which ones to spend time discussing.

WORDSTORM (p. 413)
This exercise is deceptively simple. It can have extremely powerful effects for a group, but learning to work with it to achieve these effects can take time and practice.

The WORDSTORM operates with the same rules as for BRAINSTORMING, but asks the group to let their thoughts fly about a single word, rather than about a question or problem. In choosing the word, consider whether you want to be direct or indirect. When your goal is to explore a group's attitude or understanding of a particular concept, it is best to be direct. For example, if you are working with a group of students on the issue of morale at their school, a WORDSTORM on the name of the school would provide ample material for the group to begin exploring the issue. In most circumstances, a direct choice such as this works well. However, if you are working to surface a problematic dynamic within a group, it is more effective to choose a word that allows the group to find their own indirect route to the issue. See the discussion of subtlety on p. 60 for an example of a WORDSTORM choice in such a situation.

Processing a WORDSTORM effectively is a skill that takes practice to master. Frequently the jumble of words is surprising, reveals great depths of feeling, and contains fascinating connections and contradictions. It can be a struggle to deal with the wealth of material that the WORDSTORM brings up and to draw out the most significant areas for discussion. Unlike BRAINSTORMING, where processing often involves prioritizing issues, in a WORDSTORM it is not necessary to drive the discussion toward a conclusion. The discussion itself is enough to get people thinking in a way that feeds into the work that follows.

Exercises with Movement

There is a direct connection between generating energy and subsequent levels of group productivity. For this reason, most of the agendas in this chapter include an exercise (such as BAG TOSS, STOP TAG, or THE WIND BLOWS) that gets people up and moving. Scenario 11 includes a name exercise that involves movement, adapted for a participant in a wheelchair.

High-energy activities not only wake people up, but they also can help break down inhibitions, prompting group members to express their ideas more freely and creatively as the meeting progresses. In designing your agendas, always consider including a movement exercise.

The Agendas

This section presents a scenario and seven agendas that cover a variety of purposes.

A Note about Time

All of the agendas are set within specific time frames, but the times given are approximations. For many exercises, such as Warm-up Questions, the amount of time spent depends on the size of the group. For others, such as BRAINSTORMING and WORDSTORMS, the time spent will vary according to the openness of the group to participation and the depth and the direction of the processing.

As the facilitator, you should always be aware of time and honor your commitment to end at the appointed time, unless the group agrees to stay longer. If the meeting is taking longer than anticipated, think about how to shorten or eliminate various components. However, do not eliminate the Evaluation in order to finish on time; it is essential that everyone have the opportunity to provide input at the conclusion of the meeting. If the group's time is flexible, you can ask about 15 minutes before the meeting is scheduled to end if people are willing and able to extend the time by a specified amount.

Agenda 1. A Meeting to Begin Taking Action

Context

The general outline of this agenda can be used for the initial session of a new group that will be meeting on an ongoing basis to plan and take action. We are using the context of a group whose purpose is to create an improvement plan for a high school. To use this agenda with a group that has a different focus for its action, adjust the words for THE WIND BLOWS WITH WORDS, the questions for CONCENTRIC CIRCLES, and the topic for BRAINSTORMING.

Estimated Time: 2 hours or less

To make this session shorter than two hours, you can eliminate THE WIND BLOWS WITH WORDS and/or ROLE-PLAYS, and do PAIRING rather than CONCENTRIC CIRCLES.

Goals

- To build relationships by giving people an opportunity to share their experiences and their feelings about the work they will be doing together.
- To define the priority issues for the group to address.

Agenda Summary

Introduction

Names/Warm-up Section

NAME CHANT AND MOTION

Warm-up Question: Say your name and briefly finish the sentence, "My ideal school is a place where …."

Springboard Section

THE WIND BLOWS

THE WIND BLOWS WITH WORDS

PAIRING or CONCENTRIC CIRCLES

Work Section

BRAINSTORMING: What issues do students face in this school?

Discuss and prioritize the issues.

ROLE-PLAYS: Small groups create and present role-plays about the priority issues.

Summation

Evaluation

Agenda 1 in Detail

Introduction 2 minutes

Today's meeting is designed to help us learn each other's names, build our relationships, and discuss the importance of the work we'll be doing together to improve our school. We need to build relationships in order to work together effectively and gain an understanding of the reasons that each of us has chosen to do this work.

We'll begin with several exercises to learn names. Then we'll do two exercises to learn about each other and have some fun. Then we'll go on to brainstorm the issues that students in our school face. Toward the end of the meeting we'll review where we are and where we are going. Finally, we'll evaluate the work we've done today.

Names/Warm-up Section
1. NAME CHANT AND MOTION (p. 135) 8 minutes
Processing suggestions

- We did this exercise to begin the process of learning each other's names, which is the first step in building relationships.
- The exercise illustrates people imitating each other. In the school environment, students are looking around to see what their peers are doing, and often they start copying what they see happening around them. With the improvement plan that we create, we hope to change some patterns of behavior in our school.

2. Warm-up Question 10 minutes
Say your name and briefly finish the sentence, "My ideal school is a place where …."
Processing suggestions

- The responses to this question have given us a vision of what we are working toward in this group. The group has a lot of important work to do in figuring out how we can move our school toward the ideal that we have articulated.

Springboard Section
1. THE WIND BLOWS (p. 377) 5 minutes
optionally followed by THE WIND BLOWS WITH WORDS (p. 378) 5 minutes
Words for the second part could be "student," "teacher," "resources," "conflict," "unity."
Processing suggestions

- If you do both exercises, process them both together.
- This exercise shows what it feels like to be left out, which is often how students and teachers feel about the way things are decided in the school.
- In addition, it shows what it's like to be a leader and have to stand up in front of people and think on your feet; even though you only have to say something like "The wind blows for people who are wearing sneakers," it's not always easy. Developing leadership skills, including the ability to think on your feet in front of people, is an important element of this project.
- For The WIND BLOWS WITH WORDS: The addition of the words gave people a chance to express their opinions about important topics that we will be dealing with throughout this project.
- Refer to some of the things people said to highlight thoughts and opinions that are relevant to the work of the group.

2. PAIRING (p. 237) 5 minutes
or CONCENTRIC CIRCLES (p. 190) 20 minutes
For PAIRING, use the sixth question below ("What do you think is the biggest issue …").
Questions:

- Talk about where you grew up and your earliest memories of your neighborhood.
- Talk about a time you helped someone.
- Talk about a time someone helped you.
- Talk about your best elementary school teacher, and what you liked about that person as a teacher.
- Talk about your worst elementary school teacher, and what you disliked about that person as a teacher.
- What do you think is the biggest issue that students face in our school, and what do you think should be done about it?
- Talk about someone you know who has dropped out of school and what happened to that person.

- Talk about what you would do if you had a million dollars to spend on our school and why you would choose to do those things.
- What do you think this school will be like in five years, and where do you see yourself in five years?

Processing suggestions

- We did this exercise to begin building deeper relationships and understanding of each other within the group.
- Trusting relationships among members of the group is crucial to our ability to meet our goals.

Work Section

1. BRAINSTORMING (p. 385) 20 minutes

Do a Brainstorm on the question "What issues do students face in this school?"

Processing suggestions

- Begin a discussion of the issues by circling some of the more unusual responses and asking for comments about how each issue affects the school. Look for opportunities to make the discussion as broad as possible. The goal of this section is to engage group members in deep conversation and consideration of the issues that they face. Ask people, "Why do you feel that way?" and "What does everyone else think about [the opinions expressed]?"
- Then focus the question to the group: "If you had to choose one issue that has the biggest impact on the rest of the issues, which would you choose and why would you choose it?" You are looking for issues from which broad-based initiatives can flow, rather than narrow issues that are really symptoms of the larger issues. Your goal is to find the deepest issues, not the side effects of the issues.
- Work intensively with the list to pull out information, so that the whole group gains understanding about the layers of meaning behind the issues. For example, if the problem is "Respect," where does the problem lie—with students, teachers, parents, etc.? Do some of the other problems on the list actually stem from lack of respect? Can these issues be combined? How many dimensions does this problem have? How does it relate to other problems and issues?
- Work toward an agreement on the top four or five issues that students face. When you have reached that goal, summarize the discussion, then explain that we will be focusing on these issues and developing strategies to address them through our work in this group.

2. ROLE-PLAYS (p. 404) 40 minutes

Split the group into two or three small groups. Assign one or two issues to each group and ask them to create a Role-Play that shows how these issues affect the lives of the students in the school. Give the groups about ten minutes, then have them present their Role-Plays.

Processing suggestions

- Ask those in each Role-Play to talk about the issues they portrayed and why they made the choices they did in creating their Role-Play.
- Ask the group if they felt the Role-Play was realistic and what they thought about specific actions.
- Then ask what they think can be done to have a positive impact on these issues.

Summation 5 minutes

We are coming to the end of this session, and in a moment we will be ending with an evaluation. At the next meeting [note the date and time], we will begin creating strategies to address the issues discussed today, and then we will start to take the steps needed to implement these strategies. If we can work together, we will be able to create real, positive change in our school.

Evaluation
EVALUATION SCALES (p. 422) 5 minutes

Scenario 11: First Meeting of an Action-Oriented, Ongoing Group
Three friends, Helen, Eric, and Cassandra, decided to begin organizing to put an environmental issue on their town's ballot. They scheduled a meeting, then recruited for it by talking with friends, putting up flyers, and placing a notice in the local newspaper.

As they met to plan the meeting, the organizers set a number of goals, which included:

- Everyone who attends this meeting will plan to come to the next meeting.
- Everyone will be motivated to talk with their friends and neighbors about the issue.
- Everyone will resolve to bring at least one other person to the next meeting.

They reasoned that the more they could create a network of relationships at each meeting, the more people would be motivated to come back. Therefore, they agreed that the meetings should combine building relationships with tackling the business at hand in an organized and timely way. They decided to devote the first 15 minutes of the agenda to building relationships.

Recognizing that comfort with others' names is the cornerstone of relationships, they decided to begin the first meeting with a Name Exercise. They chose NAME CHANT AND MOTION (p. 135), and agreed that they would do the exercise if there were at least six people at the meeting (unless they were certain that everyone already knew everyone else).

They decided that Helen would facilitate, Eric would take minutes, and Cassandra would greet people, ask them to wear nametags, and deal with logistics.

Their outreach efforts were rewarded when 22 people showed up for the meeting, including a few people the organizers had never seen before. Helen opened the meeting by welcoming everyone and going over the goals and the agenda. She noted that the meeting, which started at 7:00 PM, would end by 9:00 PM.

Agenda Summary
Introduction
Names/Warm-up Section
NAME CHANT AND MOTION
Warm-up Question: Your name and (briefly) what you were thinking about as you came here tonight.
Springboard Section
PAIRING: What is the most compelling reason you can think of for working on this issue?
Work Section
BRAINSTORMING
1. Why should people care about this issue?
2. What are the tasks involved in getting this issue on the ballot and in winning?
Create a timeline and subcommittees.

Summation
Evaluation

She had planned to ask everyone to stand for the Name Exercise, but seeing that one participant was in a wheelchair, she modified the plan to do the exercise seated. One person expressed resistance: "Can we just talk about this ballot issue? We don't have all night." Helen felt an inner tug of desire to give in to her own resistance, but she was convinced that the planned agenda was the best approach to meeting their goals (which included ending on time). She said, "I promise we'll end by 9:00, but let's spend five minutes doing this. It will help us to have a better discussion."

NAME CHANT AND MOTION seemed to energize the group, most of whom had come out to this meeting after a day at work. Everyone learned to pronounce the two or three unfamiliar names, which was helpful in the discussions later on. Helen processed the exercise by saying a few words about how it is good to begin getting to know each other and creating a network to deal with an issue that everyone in the room cares about.

She then asked the group to go around and answer the Warm-up Question: "What is your name and (briefly) what were you thinking about as you came here tonight?" Some people responded with serious points about the issue, while others commented with humor about their dinner or the music on the car radio. By the end, people felt they knew each other a little. In her processing, Helen noted that the group had begun to grapple both with the issue at hand and with the world of distractions that keep people from working on the issue.

Helen then set up the PAIRING (p. 237) by quickly designating who should pair with whom. She told people to spend a few minutes discussing the question "What is the most compelling reason you can think of for working on this issue?" She had anticipated resistance at this point, but instead, with at least one person in each pair eager to discuss the question, the room began to buzz with conversation. After about two minutes she reminded everyone that the second person in each pair should give their opinion, if they had not done so already. After another two minutes, she asked the pairs to stop talking and requested that everyone return their chairs to the circle and turn toward the flip chart.

Quickly but clearly, she explained the rules for BRAINSTORMING (p. 385), and told the group to start calling out their ideas about the question "Why should people care about this issue?" When the sheet was filled, she called a halt to the Brainstorm, then spent a few minutes processing the ideas. She asked people to say which ideas they thought were the most important, and the group had a lively discussion. Helen suggested that these top-priority reasons could be the beginning of a publicity campaign for the issue.

Next, she said they would do a second Brainstorm, this time on the question "What are the tasks involved in getting this issue on the ballot and in winning?" People called out many tasks; Helen then led the group in prioritizing the tasks and setting deadlines. She asked for volunteers to handle the most pressing tasks and to head up subcommittees.

With the clock reading 8:50 PM, Helen briefly summarized the accomplishments of this meeting, told everyone the time and place of the next meeting, and suggested that everyone try to find one other person to bring along next time. Finally, she asked the group to do an Evaluation by going around the circle, with each person giving the meeting a numerical rating (1-10 scale) and/or commenting on the meeting. Several people said that the meeting had accomplished more than they thought possible, and everyone seemed to feel that the group was off to a great start.

Agenda 2. A Drug and Alcohol Abuse Prevention Workshop

Context

This agenda is a model for a drug-prevention workshop that can be used with both one-time groups and ongoing groups. The format gives participants the opportunity to think about the impact of drug use and abuse on their lives and their communities. It is designed to elicit discussion of experiences, and this could occur at any point; therefore, facilitators should not be rigid in terms of time. In particular, facilitators should not cut short a discussion in order to have time for the fact sheet, which is the least important aspect of the agenda.

Estimated Time: 1.5 hours

Goals

- To promote discussion of attitudes and behaviors related to drugs and alcohol.
- To provide information about resources available for dealing with drug and alcohol abuse.

Agenda Summary

Introduction

Names/Warm-up Section

Warm-up Question: Say your name and if you could have any power or ability, supernatural or natural, what would you choose to have and why would you want it?

Springboard Section

BAG TOSS

Work Section

1. BRAINSTORMING: What are the drugs most commonly used within [a geographic area, such as a school, neighborhood, state, or country, or a demographic group, such as an age group, a gender, a particular racial group, etc.]?
   Discuss and prioritize by prevalence and by damage caused.
2. Go over prepared fact sheet about drug use.

Summation

Evaluation

Agenda 2 in Detail

Introduction 5 minutes

Today we are going to spend time with each other discussing attitudes toward the use of drugs and alcohol. An important goal of today's work is to create a safe space for people to say what they think and to learn from each other about the best ways to deal with the issues associated with these substances.

Names/Warm-up Section 10 minutes

Warm-up Question: Say your name and if you could have any power or ability, supernatural or natural, what would you choose to have and why would you want it?

Processing suggestions

- It is important that we learn each other's names and begin building our relationships if we are

going to be able to talk with one another about such important issues.
- Review some of the powers and abilities that people said they wanted and why they wanted them.
- People are driven to have new experiences and gain new skills. However, some things are unattainable by any means; other things are attainable through working for them; nothing can be attained only by wishing.
- Some people seek new experiences through drugs and alcohol. Some can control the use of these substances, while others are controlled by them.
- We will be exploring these issues in today's session.

Springboard Section

BAG TOSS (p. 302) 10 minutes

Processing suggestions

- Think of the bags as the things you have to deal with in life. Even when you are in top form, it can be hard to "keep all your bags in the air." When your mind and/or body is impaired through drug or alcohol use, it's impossible.
- Some people use drugs to fill gaps in their lives, to seek something they feel is missing. Drug use can also be an attempt to cope with feeling overwhelmed. Just as in BAG TOSS, finding the right balance in your life is important; life needs to have enough going on, but not too much, and that varies with different people.
- You have to deal with what's coming at you.
- The kinds of things that get "thrown at you" vary from person to person, depending on your life situation and on what networks of relationships you are part of. It might be family obligations, academic work, perfectionist expectations, social pressures, drug use, or a variety of other things.

Work Section

1. BRAINSTORMING (p. 385) 30-40 minutes

Brainstorm a list of drugs most commonly used within a geographic area (a school, neighborhood, state, or country) or a demographic group (an age group, a gender, a particular racial group, etc.) that is relevant to the people in this workshop.

Processing suggestions

- First, discuss the list and prioritize the items listed in terms of prevalence.
- Then discuss and prioritize in terms of those drugs that cause the most damage (including physical and emotional damage) to people who use them. Encourage discussion among group members and explore concrete experiences and differences of opinion as much as possible. Some good questions to pose are: Why do people use drugs? What can be done to help someone who is doing drugs? What can you do if a person doesn't want help?
- In an ongoing group, you may want to state that the group will be able to explore some of these issues in depth at another meeting.

2. Prepared Information 15 minutes

Distribute prepared information sheets that outline the drugs most commonly abused by the target population, the impact of these drugs on individuals and communities, and the resources available for those who are seeking help dealing with these difficult problems. Go over this material and discuss with the group.

Summation 5 minutes

Summarize the big picture—the prevalence of various drugs and the damage they cause, and the small picture—how drugs affect individual lives and relationships.

Evaluation
EVALUATION SCALES (p. 422)   5 minutes
As part of the Evaluation, take care of any loose ends remaining from the discussion and emphasize the availability of resources for dealing with the problems discussed during the session.

Agenda 3. Evaluating an Event

Context
This agenda is for a group that has been working together over a period of time and has just completed a particular piece of work or a phase of its work. When the agenda refers to an "event," this can also mean some other piece of work or phase of work.

Estimated Time: Up to 1.5 hours

Goal

- To give the group the opportunity to reflect on its past work and to formulate recommendations for future work.

Agenda Summary
Introduction
Warm-up Section
Warm-up Question: Say a word that describes the event and why you chose that word.
Springboard Section
STOP TAG
PAIRING
Work Section
GROUP SHOUT EVALUATION of the event's goals
BRAINSTORMING: Positives, negatives, and recommendations
Discuss and prioritize the recommendations.
Summation
Evaluation

Agenda 3 in Detail
Introduction   2 minutes
If the event went well, acknowledge this, and if the event was not successful, acknowledge that there were problems. In either case, say that it is important to go through a process to determine to what degree the event did or did not meet its goals and to look at what worked well, what didn't work well, and what could be changed next time.

Warm-up Section   8-10 minutes
Warm-up Question: Say a word that describes the event and why you chose that word.
Processing suggestion

- Use the words and the reasons for choosing those words to review and summarize what happened at the event and to give permission for group members to think about and express both the positive and negative aspects of their work.

Springboard Section

1. STOP TAG (p. 272) 10 minutes

Processing suggestions

- The process of creating an order demonstrates group connection, which is important to success.
- The exercise demonstrates an interdependent system, and it can show both how systems work and how they malfunction. Frequently the chain will break down so that some people are never tagged while others are tagged repeatedly, which has consequences for everyone in the order. This dynamic can be used to show how systems work or fail and to make points about putting things in order.
- If the chain broke down, where did it happen and why? This can show that it's important to find the source of a problem in order to fix it and ensure that things will flow smoothly.
- People have different experiences of any event, and the evaluation process allows for sharing of those experiences.

2. PAIRING (p. 237) 5-10 minutes

Question: What was a highlight and "lowlight" of the event and why?

Processing suggestions

- The exercise helps people to reflect upon the positives and negatives of the event and to prepare for the activities of the Work Section. No processing is necessary.

Work Section

1. GROUP SHOUT EVALUATION (p. 423) of the event's goals 10 minutes

This exercise assumes that the group set goals for the event as part of its planning process. If this did not happen, the group could quickly set goals now. For each goal, evaluate the degree to which it was achieved on a scale of 1-10 and ask people to comment on their ratings if they wish.

2. BRAINSTORMING (p. 385) 30 minutes

Do three Brainstorms in succession. First brainstorm the positive aspects of the event, then the negative aspects, and finally the group's recommendations for a similar event in the future.

When the group does the third Brainstorm, they should be able to draw recommendations from both the list of positives and the list of negatives. In order to make this happen, tell the group to be mindful of not expressing negatives as recommendations. For example, if someone says, "We should have started later," the negative statement is "Started too early," and the recommendation to come out of that is "Start later." Help the group both to follow this approach and to be sure that they draw from both lists.

Processing suggestion

- Work with the group to prioritize the recommendations. Keep the list of recommendations and use them the next time the group prepares for a similar event.

Summation 5 minutes

Summarize what was learned from the evaluation and stress that the results of the evaluation will be used the next time the group plans a project.

Evaluation

EVALUATION SCALES (p. 422) 5 minutes

Agenda 4. A Workshop on Personal Goal-Setting

Context

This is an agenda for a group whose purpose is to work on setting individual goals. In an ongoing group, you would also want to create a mechanism to help participants track progress toward their goals.

Estimated Time: Between 2 and 2.5 hours. The time will vary depending on how many people wish to share their vision and goals with the whole group.

Goal

- To give participants a framework for creating long-term and short-term goals.

Agenda Summary

Introduction

Names/Warm-up Section

Warm-up Question: What three things would you want to have with you if you were stranded on a desert island?

Springboard Section

EVERYBODY'S IT

FINDING THE PATH

Work Section

WORDSTORM on "Future"

LIFE LINES TO THE FUTURE

Creating three short-term goals

Report-backs to the whole group

Summation

Evaluation

Agenda 4 in Detail

Introduction 2 minutes

Today you will have the opportunity to think about what your personal goals are and to define for yourself both a long-term vision of your future and some short-term goals that will lead you toward that vision.

Names/Warm-up Section

Warm-up Question 8 minutes

If you were stranded on a desert island (but all basic survival needs, such as food and water, were taken care of), what three things would you want to have with you? You cannot say people.

Processing suggestions

- There are many ways to envision a different life in a different place. Some of us think in very practical terms, while others are more fanciful. We are all striving to meet certain goals; to do this we need to combine a vision of where we are going with the tools we need to get there.
- This question helps us to begin thinking about what we value, what we need in order to feel fulfilled, and how we get the things we need and value.

Springboard Section

1. EVERYBODY'S IT (p. 265) 5 minutes

Processing suggestions

- The environment of this exercise can be chaotic and overwhelming, and often this is how we feel about our lives. It can seem as if there's no way to pull things together, to achieve our goals, or to avoid the things that are "out to get us."

- Even in the midst of a chaotic situation, there are strategies we can employ to take control of the situation. Did anyone in this group discover a successful strategy? (For example, a person can pretend for a while to be frozen.)

2. FINDING THE PATH (p.195) 25 minutes

Processing suggestions

- We each need to find the right path, but unlike in this exercise, each of us has our own path. How do we find the right path for ourselves?
- The exercise illustrates the importance of learning from others' experiences and from our own mistakes.
- It also illustrates the value of persistence. It may have taken several tries, but eventually everyone found the path.

Work Section

1. WORDSTORM (p. 413) on "Future" 10 minutes

Processing suggestions

- What aspects of "future" did the group focus on?
- Do the words represent a variety of emotional reactions to the idea of the future? (For example, does the future represent hope, despair, or change?)
- Processing for this exercise should be short so that the WORDSTORM serves as a jumping-off point into the LIFE LINES.

2. LIFE LINES TO THE FUTURE 30 minutes

- Follow the instructions for LIFE LINES (p. 401), except that in this exercise people represent their lives from the present into the future—to the end of life or to a specified point, such as 20, 30, or 40 years from now.
- Do not have the groups discuss their work in pairs until they have completed the next step, Creating Short-term Goals.

3. Creating Short-term Goals 10 minutes

Have each person create three goals for the year ahead that are consistent with achieving the vision represented in their LIFE LINE TO THE FUTURE. Goals should be specific and realistic.

4. Report-backs 20-30 minutes

Bring the whole group back together. Give people the opportunity to share their vision and their goals with the group.

Summation 5 minutes

Everyone now has created a roadmap to the future that they envision, as well as some concrete steps that they can start taking right away toward achieving that vision.

Evaluation

EVALUATION SCALES (p. 422) 5 minutes

Agenda 5. A Routine Staff Meeting

Context

This agenda is for a regular staff meeting taking place at a transitional point, such as the beginning of a program year or a business cycle.

Unlike the other agendas in this chapter, this one does not have an overriding theme; instead, the majority of the meeting is occupied with day-to-day staff business. The interactive exercises are designed to increase the level of staff productivity by bringing everyone into the group, helping people focus on their work, and building energy through movement.

Estimated Time: 1.5 hours to 3 hours, depending on the content of the Work Section

Goal

- To move through the day's business in an organized, timely, and inclusive way.

Agenda Summary

Introduction

Names/Warm-up Section

Warm-up Question: What is something you accomplished last week and something you plan to accomplish this week?

Springboard Section

FILL THE SPACE, SHAKE THE HAND

Work Section

Timeline

Agenda items

Summation

Evaluation

Agenda 5 in Detail

Introduction 2 minutes

Names/Warm-up Section 8 minutes

Warm-up Question: What is something you plan to accomplish this week?

Processing suggestion

- Comment briefly about the range of activities that staff members are involved in.

Springboard Section

FILL THE SPACE, SHAKE THE HAND (p. 282) 10 minutes

This agenda assumes that the group is familiar with this exercise. Instruct them to do it at a faster speed than normal.

Processing suggestions

- As our work speeds up at this time of transition, it is a challenge to stay in connection and to be aware of each other's needs. The tendency can be to rush by with barely a greeting. While we do need to keep up a fast pace, we also need to be aware of maintaining our connections.
- Our work flows best when everyone is conscious of the big picture and is willing to fill in where needed.

Work Section
1. Timeline 5 minutes
2. Agenda items as needed Between 1 hour and 2.5 hours
Use BRAINSTORMING and other Work Exercises as appropriate.

Summation 5 minutes

Evaluation
EVALUATION SCALES (p. 422) 5 minutes

Agenda 6. Freshman Orientation: Small Group Agenda

Context
This agenda is designed for an incoming class of high school freshmen, meeting in groups of up to 20. It can easily be adapted for older or younger students, primarily by adjusting the processing of THE WIND BLOWS and the nature of the CONCENTRIC CIRCLES questions.

Estimated Time: 90 minutes

Goals

- To build relationships within the class.
- To give students a sense of belonging in the school community.
- To have students define success in high school for themselves.

Agenda Summary
Introduction
Names/Warm-up Section
NAME CHANT AND MOTION
Warm-up Question: Say your name, and if you had $1 million, what's one thing you would spend it on?
Springboard Section
THE WIND BLOWS
CONCENTRIC CIRCLES
Work Section
WORDSTORM on "Success"
BRAINSTORMING: "Action Steps to Success in High School"
Summation
Evaluation

Agenda 6 in Detail
Introduction 2 minutes
In this group our task is to get to know each other and make some plans for a productive year, and we are going to do this through interactive exercises and discussion.

Names/Warm-up Section
1. NAME CHANT AND MOTION (p. 135) 5 minutes
Processing suggestions

- It's important to learn each other's names. This is the first step in building a community.

- We got to see a little bit about each person as we moved around the circle, so we are already learning things about one another.
- In this exercise, each person's attitude, tone, and style are picked up by everyone else. School is a lot like this. You put out a "motion," and you get a reaction from the people around you. You have to decide if you're going to put out motions that reflect who you truly are.
- Motions, vibes, and energy traveled around this circle, and they will travel around our school. We want you to be involved in creating and promoting positive energy.

2. Warm-up Question 10 minutes
Say your name and if you had $1 million, what's one thing you would spend it on?
Processing suggestions

- Those were some great *(imaginative, crazy, whatever)* answers to the question. It seems like people have some pretty good ideas already about what they want out of life.
- It takes hard work to get where you want to be in life, but it is not impossible. If anyone's ever told you that you can't be something, that's not true. What they should have said is that you need determination, skills, support, and a plan. You will need determination that you are going to succeed, skills to build your career and provide value to your community, support to get through those tough times that everyone faces, and a plan to help guide your decisions.
- Every success is made up of these elements. Now here's the important part: If you bring in that determination, we can help you get the rest. At this school, you'll get skills, find support from teachers and staff, and work with guidance counselors and mentors to develop your plan. But the determination is something that you have to bring to it.

Springboard Section
1. THE WIND BLOWS (p. 377) 10 minutes
Do several rounds, then announce that the next round will be the last. You want energy and fun to build up in the room.
Processing suggestions

- What did it feel like to be up in front of the group? Was it hard to think of something to say?
- How did it feel to lose out on a seat and know you would be on the spot?
- Did you look forward to being in front of the group, and not try too hard to get a seat?
- THE WIND BLOWS gives people the experience of being up in front of the group and taking on a leadership role, even if just for a moment.
- It's going to take leadership to be successful at school. You might feel nervous, or feel that you're not ready, but there will be moments in high school when success in a class, an activity, or some other area will depend on your stepping up.
- At this school, we will teach you how to be effective leaders because we think this is important for your growth and development.
- This activity is also about being left out. People were scrambling for a seat because they didn't want to be left out on their own.
- People who don't have high school diplomas are outside of a lot of circles in our society, and it makes life very difficult for them. We want you to think about this because many students do decide at some point to stop going to school. We know it's not always easy, but school will give you more options for your future.

2. CONCENTRIC CIRCLES (p. 190) 20 minutes
Questions:
1. What is your favorite TV show, and why?

2. Describe the neighborhood you grew up in and some of your earliest memories.
3. Talk about your favorite and least favorite teacher from elementary school.
4. Talk about one thing you are looking forward to this year and one thing you are concerned about.
5. Talk about someone who you feel is successful and what they did to become successful.
6. What do you think are your best methods of learning—through hearing, seeing, writing, reading, discussion, or a hands-on approach?
7. Talk about something you like to do outside of classes.

Work Section
1. WORDSTORM (p. 413) on "Success" 15 minutes
Processing suggestions
- Discuss the various ways that people measure success. Do not try to tie this discussion too directly into the high school experience; the Brainstorm will move the discussion to that level. Instead, use the WORDSTORM to stimulate thoughts and feelings, which will help to position the students for more productive work during the Brainstorm.
- What aspects of success are represented by the words? Did people include or omit elements such as health and emotional happiness? Explore these issues.

2. BRAINSTORMING (p. 385) 20 minutes
Do a Brainstorm on the topic "Action Steps to Success in High School."
Processing suggestions
- Discuss the action steps on the Brainstorm list and have the group prioritize the top five.

Summation 3 minutes

Evaluation
EVALUATION SCALES (p. 422) 5 minutes

Agenda 7. High School Senior Class Meeting

Context
This agenda is for a meeting at the beginning of the school year with a high school senior class. It is designed for 50-60 students. When the class is larger than 60, divide it into sections and use the agenda with each section.

This agenda, more than the others in this chapter, requires customization for particular circumstances. For example, the categories for GROUP-UPS should be tailored to the class and the processing suggestions should reflect the nature of the school and the class.

Estimated Time: 1.5 hours

Goals
- To build a sense of class identity.
- To build relationships within the class.
- To envision the transition to adulthood.
- To provide students with necessary information.

Agenda Summary

Introduction

Names/Warm-up Section

Warm-up Question: A word to describe senior year

Springboard Section

GROUP-UPS

CONCENTRIC CIRCLES

Work Section

Small Groups

Introduction

Warm-up Question: Say your name, then talk about one person you want to have present at your graduation and say why you chose that person.

HUMAN KNOT

WORDSTORM on "Adult"

Guidance Presentation

Evaluation

Agenda 7 in Detail

Introduction 3 minutes

We want to support this class in developing as leaders in the school, and most importantly we want you to take the steps you need to take to make it through this year successfully, prepared to handle the world beyond high school. This class meeting structure is going to be used throughout the year to communicate with seniors about your class and make decisions that will affect you. Later on in this meeting we are going to hear from the Guidance Department about what you need to be doing to prepare for next year.

Names/Warm-up Section

Warm-up Question 5 minutes

Say your name and a word to describe senior year. [Though this is a large group for a Warm-up Question, it can be done in just a few minutes since it asks for only one-word answers. If you decide the group is too large for a Warm-up Question, you could have people either shout or whisper their word on the count of three. See NAME SHOUT on p. 142 for how this works.]

Processing suggestions

- For some people, senior year seems to be just a continuation of all your previous years of schooling, while other people feel that it is a different time. You're a different person in many ways from the person who first came to this school, and now is the time to think about the positive changes you've experienced and how you can use those to move forward. These are the days to take care of business if you haven't, to reflect on your strengths and challenges, and make the most of your talents and wisdom gained from your last three years. If we can do it together, this will be a powerful senior class that leaves a positive legacy for those coming up after you—and you will have a lot of fun in the process.

Springboard Section

1. GROUP-UPS (p. 290) 12 minutes

Categories:

- Group up by the neighborhood you live in.
- Group up by cultural background.
- Group up by color of shirt.

- Group up by what you're planning to do next year.
- Group up by your favorite extracurricular activity.
- Group up by your favorite subject.

[Note that some of these categories would be high-risk in some schools but not in others.]

Processing suggestions

- This class is made up of lots of different groups, but you're all seniors. This year we want you to think of yourselves as seniors first, which means being leaders and role models for the other students in the school, and taking care of what you need to do to graduate with your class. Whatever your direction, whatever your background, whatever your choices in the past might have been, you're all poised at the end of this year to move on into adult lives.

2. CONCENTRIC CIRCLES (p. 190) 25 minutes

Questions:

1. What were your first impressions of high school and how are your impressions different now?
2. What was one of the challenges that you faced in getting to be a senior and how did you respond to it?
3. Talk about someone who helped you along the way, how they helped you, and what you would say to them if you could.
4. What's your favorite part of being a senior? What's your least favorite part?
5. What's a responsibility that you have outside of school and how does it impact you?
6. What's your plan for when you graduate from high school?
7. What do you want to be able to say in June about this year?
8. What is your own personal definition of adulthood?
9. Where do you want to be in five years? How are you going to get there?

Work Section: Break into Small Groups

Small Group Agenda

Introduction (small group) 2 minutes

We're going to continue the work that we started in the larger group, building connections and discussing the future.

Names/Warm-up Section (small group)

Warm-up Question 10 minutes

Say your name, then talk about one person you want to have present at your graduation and say why you chose that person.

(Note: Be aware that this question may surface concerns among some students about not making it to graduation.)

Processing suggestion

- High school graduation is a significant milestone for everyone who achieves it. As you go through this year, keep thinking about the achievement that you are working for and the pride that you will feel in yourself and that others will feel in you.

Springboard Section (small group)

HUMAN KNOT (p. 332) 10 minutes

Processing suggestions

- This exercise shows us working together. It is possible, even when things seem confused or tangled, to get through.

- We may have times when we are pulling in different directions, whether it's about a class trip, scheduling, where the prom is going to be, or some other issues, but if we keep working together, trying to figure out where others are coming from, we will get the best result.
- Everyone here has a stake in this class. Don't let go; don't break the circle.

Work Section (small group)
1. WORDSTORM (p. 413) on "Adult" 10 minutes

Processing suggestions

- Finishing high school is a major shift in your life. When you are out of high school, you've got to make things happen for yourself in a new way.
- Being cool means less and less as people expect you to be on time, do your job, treat people with respect, make your quota, pay your bills, etc.
- You need to be ready for adult life, and that means two things—changing your attitude if you've let things slide, and getting support from people to get to a place where you can fulfill your own dreams.

Summation 3 minutes

In this small group we've been thinking about getting to graduation, how we can work together to make this a great year, and what it means to step into the world after high school. Now we're going to go back to the large group where you'll get some concrete information from the Guidance Department about how to get where you want to go.

Return to the Large Group

Presentation from Guidance 10 minutes

Guidance counselors make a presentation covering the information they believe is most important for seniors to have right now.

Evaluation 5 minutes

If there is time, do a go-round evaluation. If there is not time, do a GROUP SHOUT EVALUATION (p. 423) with some comments. Collect written evaluations as well.

Chapter 7

The Engaged Learner: Interactive Methods in the Classroom

The Interactive Meeting Format is easily adaptable for the classroom. Most of what you read in this book can be understood in classroom terms if you think "lesson plan" whenever you read "agenda" and "class" whenever you read "meeting." The purpose of this chapter is to specifically translate the language of meetings into the classroom, and to provide you with some examples of lesson plans designed according to the format that Teen Empowerment staff have used successfully.

Achieving Important Goals through Interaction

Interactive methods in the classroom help teachers to create a healthy, lively, and respectful environment for learning and to achieve the following objectives, expressed as teachers have told them to us:

- I want all my students to become engaged in the learning process and passionate about the subject matter.
- I want my classes to be fun and meaningful at the same time.
- I want my students to learn to work together.
- I want to form positive and respectful relationships with my students that will allow them to learn more effectively from me and also allow me to learn from them.

Engagement. Teachers often feel that some of the students in their classrooms are "somewhere else." These are the students who sit in the back of the room and do not participate in class activities. Some of these students may be preoccupied with personal issues, while others may feel so disconnected from the subject matter that they find it difficult to concentrate. The *Moving Beyond Icebreakers* approach makes clear to all students that their participation and their authentic voices are valued. It helps to break down the barriers that may be holding students back from participation, and it helps teachers to gain insight into why students may be disengaged. When these barriers begin to break down, students are freer to engage with the class's academic content.

Also, use of interactive exercises allows teachers to tap into the range of "multiple intelligences" described by psychologist and educator Howard Gardner.[1] Most of the exercises work with bodily/kinesthetic and interpersonal intelligences, and many work with intrapersonal, musical, and spatial. Students whose strengths are in areas other than the types of intelligence most relied on for classroom work (linguistic and logical-mathematical) are more likely to become engaged as their own strengths are called upon.

---

[1]Howard Gardner, *Frames of Mind: The Theory of Multiple Intelligences* (New York, NY: Basic Books, 1983).

Fun. Experienced educators recognize that powerful learning experiences are often playful. The Interactive Lesson Plan includes both play (the Springboard Section) and work (the Work Section). These are not distractions from real learning, but instead allow students to explore their learning through play and apply their learning through work.

Study of mental life has made evident the fundamental worth of native tendencies to explore, to manipulate tools and materials, to construct, to give expression to joyous emotion, etc. When exercises which are prompted by these instincts are part of the regular school program, the whole pupil is engaged.

John Dewey, *Democracy and Education*, 1916

Working together. Cooperation fuels human development. The ability to communicate effectively and the ability to work in collaboration with others are essential skills for success in almost any sphere of life. The Interactive Lesson Plan allows the teacher to facilitate relationship-building and surface group dynamics so that collaboration becomes a classroom norm.

Positive student-teacher relationships. In the view of renowned educator Deborah Meier, "Greater, not less, intimacy between generations is at the heart of all the best school reform efforts around today and is the surest path to restoring public trust in public education."[2] Research reveals that the quality of student-teacher relationships is associated with students' academic motivation and attitudes toward school[3] and that youth who have positive relationships with teachers are more likely to achieve personal and professional success.[4] Carl Rogers' description of the teacher as "a real person… entering into a relationship with the learner without presenting a front or a façade"[5] reflects the teacher's role in the interactive setting. Through Warm-up Questions and Springboard Exercises, the Interactive Lesson Plan provides opportunities for teacher and students to build respect for each other's strengths and life challenges while learning together.

Preparing to Create an Interactive Lesson Plan

There are three areas to consider when thinking about the needs of the students and the purposes to be served by the lesson plan: content objectives, skill objectives, and group objectives. Note that the objectives below are broad ones that may encompass several lessons; objectives for individual lessons would involve taking steps toward achieving the broader objectives.

---

[2]Deborah Meier, *In Schools We Trust* (Boston, MA: Beacon Press, 2002), p. 13.

[3]Jacquelynne S. Eccles et al., "Development During Adolescence: The Impact of Stage-Environment Fit on Young Adolescents' Experiences in Schools and in Families," *American Psychologist*, Vol. 48, No. 2 (February 1993), p. 95.

[4]Emily Werner, "Protective Factors and Individual Resilience" in *Handbook of Early Childhood Intervention* (New York, NY: Cambridge University Press, 1990), p. 110.

[5]Carl Rogers, *Freedom to Learn for the 80's* (Columbus, OH: Charles E. Merril Publishing Company, 1983), p. 121.

Content Objectives: What do students need to know?
Setting content objectives is a familiar task for most teachers. Examples might be:

- for students to understand the concept of filial piety in Romeo and Juliet.
- for students to become familiar with the Pythagorean Theorem.
- for students to learn scientific method.
- for students to explore diverse perspectives related to a critical social issue.

Skill Objectives: What will students do?
After determining the content objectives, the next task is to think about what students will do to build their understanding. This step aims to ensure that students will apply their knowledge and it creates an observable result that aids in assessment. For example, working with the content objectives above, students might:

- script a play in which they compare a contemporary family's expectations to those in a play by Shakespeare.
- discover the Pythagorean Theorem from experimentation.
- use scientific method to research the health of a local pond.
- debate social issues in a public forum.

Group Objectives: How does the class need to develop more fully as a functional group?
Ideally, your classroom will be an environment where students' interactions both enhance learning and develop appropriate socialization skills. This step aims to move the class toward that ideal situation. For example:

- If it is the beginning of the school year or if new students have recently joined the class, all students need to learn each other's names.
- If classroom conflicts are brewing or if some students are frequently disruptive, you may want to surface group dynamics.
- If students are about to enter into their first long-term group project, you may need to prepare them to work in groups or to manage their time effectively.
- If there is something strongly affecting the overall environment in the school (for example, an incident of violence), you may want to give students the opportunity to share thoughts and feelings about the situation.
- If it is the day before vacation, you may want to use the relaxed atmosphere of the day to work on group-building.

Each day before you design an interactive lesson plan, reflect on these three key questions. It is not necessary to accomplish all types of objectives in every lesson, but you should strive to create a balance of learning, fun, and physical movement that is thematically organized. Once you have identified your objectives, use them to develop each component of the lesson plan.

If you work with a co-teacher, peer coach, or student teacher, reflect on the key questions together. Multiple perspectives create increased insight and students learn about professional growth as they see their teachers engaged in discussions about subject matter or best practices.

After you have created the lesson plan, review and revise it based on your original objectives. Write up a large final lesson plan on the blackboard in your classroom.

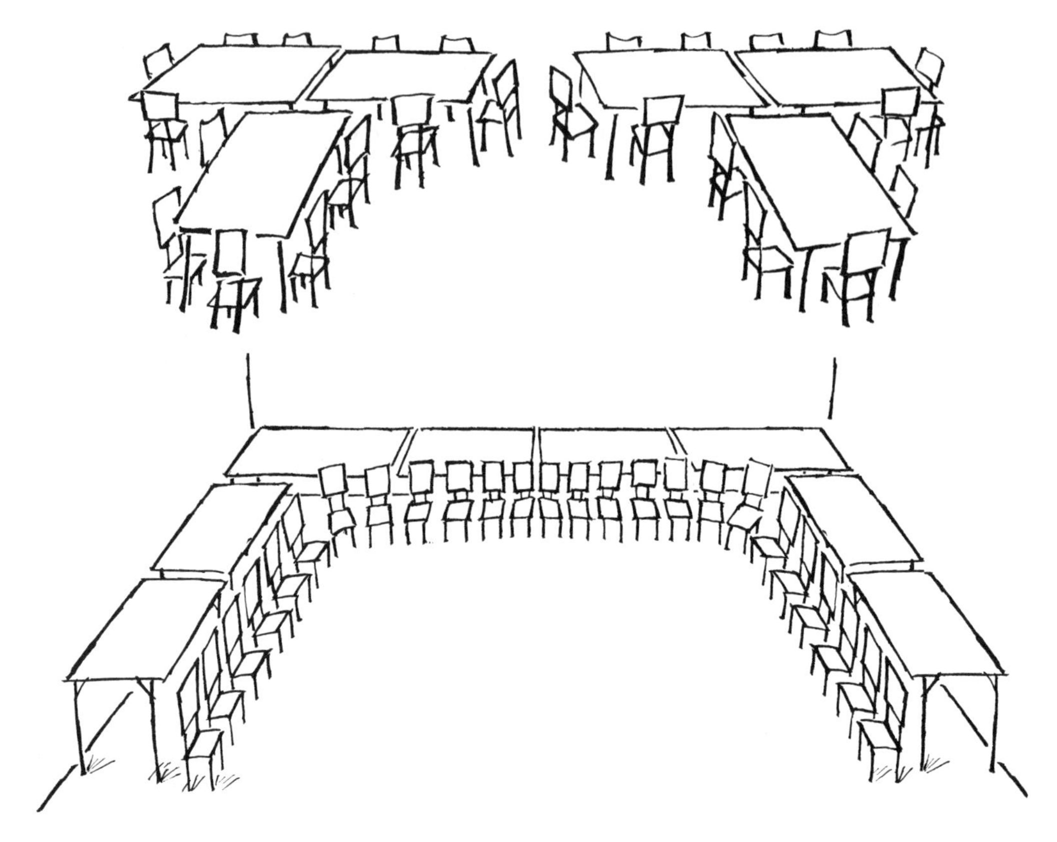

The Setting

Large classrooms and seating in rows were first promoted in the early 1800s when emerging public schools adopted the pedagogical methods of Joseph Lancaster. The Lancastarian system was praised for its low cost and its capacity to teach "subordination."[6] However, in an era when we encourage students to develop leadership and initiative, the legacies of the Lancastarian system are no longer practical.

Through our work with teachers, we have developed alternatives to row seating that meet multiple needs:

- "Double T" formation. This works particularly well when students are seated at tables rather than desks or desk-chairs. With six tables, arrange them in two parallel T's. The teacher can circulate easily to check on student work and reduce disruptive behavior. In a large classroom, you may be able to space the T's far enough apart to leave room for interactive exercises. In a smaller room, you can create space by moving one T or both to the side.

- "U" formation. Arrange tables or desk in a U shape around the perimeter of the room with students' chairs on the inside of the U. Students face their desks during individual or pair work, and during whole group activities they face the center of the room. This arrangement allows student to focus during individual/pair activities, makes it easier for teachers to circulate throughout the classroom during the Work Section, and provides a safe, open space for Springboard Exercises.

---

[6]Joel Spring, *The American School: 1642-1985* (New York: Longman, 1986), p. 55.

When planning for small group or pair activities, pre-arrange random or planned groups or pairs rather than asking students to choose their own groups or pairs. See "Pairing People Up" on p. 237 and "Structuring Small Groups" on p. 46 for reasons why this is important.

Components of the Interactive Lesson Plan

Chapter 4 explains the purpose of and procedure for each element of the Interactive Meeting Format. When using the format to create a lesson plan, consider the following:

Introduction

During the Introduction, the teacher shares information with the group for approximately five minutes:

- Welcome. Welcoming students to the classroom reaffirms that each individual is valued and needed for optimal learning to take place.
- Acknowledge who is present, who is missing, and where missing people are (if known). This communicates to students that their presence is so important that it is the first point of business. During this segment, also introduce any guest speakers or visitors to the classroom.
- Outline the goals of the class period (in terms of the objectives). Note, however, that if you plan to use the class period to work on group objectives, be subtle in your description of these goals. For example, it would be productive to say, "This class period will give you all a chance to think about the roles you take in class activities," whereas it would not be helpful to announce that "Today's class will be dedicated to learning why this class is so factionalized and how that hurts everybody." Read more about subtlety on p. 59.
- Establish the class situation in time (timeline). Include the objectives and the accomplishments of the previous day, important project dates, due dates, etc. This is also a good time to integrate reminders and announcements (permission slip due dates, grade report dates, etc.).
- Briefly preview the class period and explain how the time will be used.

The Introduction gives students an understanding of the purpose of the class and how the purpose will be achieved. When students understand the organization and relevance of their learning experiences, they are more likely to learn.

Name Exercises

Knowing names is the first step to building community in the classroom. Unless every person in the room knows every other person's name, include a Name Exercise or integrate names into the Warm-up Question. For an explanation of why this is important, see pages 41 through 43.

Warm-up Questions

With a class of 20 students or fewer, you can have everyone answer the Warm-up Question. If you have a larger class or limited time, you can pose the question but take only a few answers.

In addition to those purposes described on pp. 42-43 (such as assessing the general health of the group, energizing/focusing, and connecting students with upcoming work), Warm-up Questions in the classroom can be used for particular learning goals. See Table 3.

It is important to choose Warm-up Questions that allow students to share, but that do not require students to take risks that reveal sensitive and personal information in the group setting. For example, a

Function of the Warm-up Question	Example
Assess what students already know about a topic. Give students an opportunity to learn from each other.	What is one thing that you know or think may be true about the American Civil War?
Introduce a topic.	In a geometry class studying proofs: What is one thing about yourself that you can prove to be true?
Review concepts. Give students an opportunity to learn from each other.	If you were one of the elements in the periodic table, which element would you be and why?
Help students evaluate and reflect on learning.	If you were to go back in time and give yourself one piece of advice before starting this project, what would it be and why?

Table 3. Warm-up Questions for Specific Learning Goals

teacher introducing issues of filial piety in Romeo and Juliet might ask, "If you were a parent, what is one thing you would expect from your children?" While this question would not be threatening to most students, teen parents or students experiencing severe parental pressure might need to be in a well-formed group to answer this question comfortably.

Write the Warm-up Question on the blackboard with the lesson plan so students can prepare themselves for their first contribution of the day. Depending on the question, you might require students to offer original answers or allow them to use answers already offered.

Teachers should always participate in the Warm-up Question. This is a primary vehicle for helping you to build relationships with your students. Follow the guidelines on p. 40.

Springboard Exercises

The general purposes of the Springboard Exercises (see p. 44) are relevant to and important in the classroom setting in this slightly adapted form:

- Give students an experience (frequently a creative or a body-centered experience) of the tasks, objectives, or issues they will be addressing in the Work Section of the lesson plan, thus building a bridge to the work of the class.
- Provide the class with a chance to have fun, laugh together, and be energized to do the work of the day.
- Generate enthusiasm for being in the class and working together, or reflect the difficulties the class is experiencing and help people understand what needs to be changed to create an optimal learning environment for everyone.
- Provide students with insights into how they work together.

Many of the Springboard Exercises in chapters 11 through 16 can be used in the classroom either as given or with slight modifications to better meet your objectives. See below for examples of how some exercises can be used in the classroom, and see chapter 8 for in-depth information about choosing exercises to suit particular needs.

Numerous books and websites of teaching resources contain many other collaborative learning exercises. Two sources that we can recommend are materials from Teachers' Curriculum Institute (TCI) found at www.historyalive.com and *Get It Together: Math Problems for Groups Grades 4-12*[7] by Tim Erickson. Exercises from these sources may be appropriate as Springboard Exercises and/or Work Exercises.

As you design Interactive Lesson Plans, remember that students spend most of the day seated and they generally respond with enthusiasm to exercises that involve movement.

From chapter 10: Five-Minute Springboard Exercises
WAIT A MINUTE, p. 177
Objective: For students to engage in a discussion about managing time and meeting deadlines.
Modification for the Classroom: No modification needed.

From chapter 11: Fifteen-Minutes-Plus Springboard Exercises
CONCENTRIC CIRCLES, p. 190
Objective: For students to explore and discuss issues faced by characters or players in a work of fiction or a historical event.
Modification for the Classroom: Create one question related to the particular struggle of each character or individual. Reduce the total time for the exercise to 5-10 minutes, if necessary.

FINDING THE PATH, p. 195
Objective: For students to have an experience of learning (or not learning) from mistakes as a lead-in to a lesson in scientific or mathematical discovery, history, or literature that deals with people learning or not learning from the past.
Modification for the Classroom: In processing, emphasize learning from past successes and failures.

TWO-TEAM PATHFINDING (Variation), p. 196
Objective: To provide students with a body-centered experience of competing strategic interests as a lead-in to a lesson in history or current events.
Modification for the Classroom: In processing, discuss how groups of people have dealt with the fact that they required the use of the same space in order to meet their goals.

PICTURE WALL, p. 205
Objective: For students to self-evaluate group projects.
Modification for the Classroom: No modification needed.

From chapter 12: In-Your-Chair Springboard Exercises
FINDING THE FS, p. 218
Objective: For students to pay attention to details when doing schoolwork.
Modification for the Classroom: Relate processing to the attention to detail needed for specific projects or assignments.

SELF POEMS, p. 240
Objective: For students who are learning a language, to practice using the language and to express themselves creatively.
Modification for the Classroom: Add an introduction to the poem, such as: "My name is __, I am from __, and I live with __."

---

[7]Berkeley, CA: University of California Berkeley, 1989.

SNICKERSNACK, ANIKANIPANISAN, p. 242
Objective: For students to engage in a discussion about multi-tasking and managing stress (useful during finals).
Modification for the Classroom: Ask processing questions that allow students to identify their own stress responses. Then Brainstorm ways of managing stress and multiple tasks.

PAIRING, p. 237
Objectives: To prepare students for discussion and to build the group.
Modification for the Classroom: No modification needed. Choose discussion questions that lead in to the topic of the class. Be sure to assign pairs, rather than having students find their own partners.

SWITCH SWATCH, p. 246
Objective: To illustrate how controversial issues become polarized in the public debate.
Modification for the Classroom: No modification needed.

From chapter 14: Springboard Exercises for Groups Both Large and Small

STAND UP/SIT DOWN, p. 296, or DO WHAT YOU GOTTA DO (Variation), p. 297
Objective: To review material, to gauge students' level of knowledge about new material, or to prompt discussion about issues.
Modification for the Classroom: Prepare questions in multiple-choice format and ask students to stand (or to perform a specified action) for the answer they think is correct. Then ask students to explain why they chose their answers.

From chapter 15: The Rest of the Springboard Exercises

ALL ABOARD, ALL AHEAD , p. 300
Objective: For students to attend class regularly or to work with motivation.
Modification for the Classroom: Ask processing questions that allow students to realize the importance of their presence to the overall success of the group.

BAG TOSS, p. 302
Objective: To provide material for understanding probability.
Modification for the Classroom: Set up controlled situations such as: varying the number of bags entered into play, subtracting players, not saying names before throwing bags, and using THINK AHEAD BAG TOSS (p. 304). Have students graph the probability of bags being dropped under varied circumstances.

HIDE AND SEEK, p. 329
Objcctive: For students to attend class regularly or to work with motivation.
Modification for the Classroom: Ask processing questions that allow students to realize the importance of their presence to the overall success of the group.

PAY ATTENTION, p. 353
Objective: For students to engage in a discussion about multi-tasking and managing stress (useful during finals).
Modification for the Classroom: Ask processing questions that allow students to identify their own stress responses. Then Brainstorm ways of managing stress and multiple tasks.

POEM PUZZLE, p. 354
Objective: For students to work with sentence and paragraph structure.
Modification for the Classroom: Write a paragraph and give each small group of students a sentence, in POEM PUZZLE fashion, to put in the correct order. When all the sentences are correct, have the class work on ordering them to create the best possible paragraph.

RELAY RACE, p. 359
Objective: For students to review material (vocabulary, historical names, parts of speech, science terminology, etc.).
Modification for the Classroom: Prepare question sheets and post them on the walls. Each member of a relay team must fill in the correct word, term, etc., on the team's sheet.

THE WIND BLOWS WITH WORDS (Variation), p. 378
Objective: For students to review material (vocabulary, historical names, parts of speech, science terminology, math fundamentals, etc.).
Modification for the Classroom: Require each student who does not find a seat to provide the answer for one of the elements that you have posted (define a word, explain a term, solve a problem, etc.). If the definition (or the explanation/solution, etc.) is incorrect or incomplete, leave that element on the board for someone else to speak about.

Work Section

In a well-designed Interactive Lesson Plan, when students begin the Work Section they have been prepared by the preceding elements to be more comfortable in the classroom and ready to settle down to work. Depending on the effectiveness of the lesson plan thus far, they may also be better prepared to understand the work that is required and why they are doing it.

Generally the Work Section is the time for students to apply, or prepare to apply, their understanding of the objectives individually, in pairs, or in small groups. This is the part of the class that students might think of as the "real" classwork, and indeed, depending on your content objectives, this time might include traditional textbook or written work. While these forms of classwork are essential at times, be aware as you plan your lessons of other approaches that can help your students achieve the learning objectives you have set. For example, many teachers routinely include real-world tasks in their lesson planning (such as students in a Spanish class writing to pen pals in Puerto Rico, or students who are learning about bar graphs polling other students about school issues and graphing the results). In addition, most of the Work Exercises in chapter 17 can be used or adapted for the classroom, as follows:

BRAINSTORMING (p. 385)
This is a most valuable exercise that can be used in many types of classes for many purposes. BRAINSTORMING that is conducted according to the rules on p. 385 requires both students and teachers to suspend judgment of ideas as they are contributed. In a typical classroom, some students are reluctant to speak because they are afraid of how their contributions will be received and judged (both by teachers and by their peers). BRAINSTORMING reverses this negative classroom dynamic that keeps some students from sharing their thoughts. When students come to understand that the ideas they contribute to the Brainstorm will be received in a neutral manner, they are able to relax and to speak up.

In the discussion (processing) of the Brainstorm, both teacher and class do evaluate the ideas that were contributed, but the Brainstorm format allows each idea to stand on its own merit, without regard to whose idea it was.

In addition to creating an environment where all students can speak, BRAINSTORMING provides the teacher with a wealth of material and an approach to exploring a subject from a variety of angles. Here are two examples of how BRAINSTORMING can be used in the classroom:

- To understand the importance of a historical event, students can brainstorm the possible repercussions if the event had not occurred or had turned out differently.
- To explore the complexity of a scientific problem, students can brainstorm the questions to be answered or the obstacles to finding the answers.

WORDSTORM (p. 413)
Like BRAINSTORMING, WORDSTORMING helps students to relax and to speak up, and it is useful in many classroom settings. A WORDSTORM can open up discussion and examination of concepts in any academic discipline. Also, WORDSTORMING can help teachers explore social dynamics in the school (a WORDSTORM on the name of the school can give rise to excellent discussions) or in the classroom. As always, it is important to be subtle in your choice of words; see p. 60.

GROUP POEM (p. 397)
Can be used to sum up reactions to a project or a unit of work and to review material from it. You can specify that each student must write at least five lines and must include some piece of information learned in the project or unit.

INFO FLOW (p. 398)
Gives students the opportunity to present class material in a creative way. You can use this as one option for a project.

INFO PICTIONARY (p. 399), QUIZ-A-RAMA (p. 403), and WIND BLOWS FOR PRACTICE (p. 411)
Can be used to review any information.

INSIDE ME DRAWINGS (p. 400)
Can be used to think about fictional or historical characters.

LIFE LINES (p. 401)
Can chart the lives of fictional or historical characters.

ROLE-PLAYS (p. 404)
Can be used to understand how a novel or a historical event might have turned out differently.

THE SPEECH GAME (p. 405)
Can help students to learn and use new vocabulary or terminology in a meaningful context. You can introduce the words before the exercise. Instead of emotions, list authentic settings in which students can use the words.

STAND AND DELIVER (p. 406)
Can draw students into debate about issues in any discipline.

TAKE A SEAT (p. 407)
Helps students to understand the distribution of resources. It can be tailored to show the situation in a particular country or in the world.

VISUALIZATION (p. 409)
Can be used in many ways, such as: to help students to visualize a place and time in the past, present, or future; to see the world through the eyes of another person in the study of psychology, history, or literature; to generate ideas for creative writing.

WORLD PARTY (p. 416)
Helps students to understand stereotypes.

If students have been working individually or in small groups during the Work Section, be sure to include time for report-backs (see p. 47) so that students can present their accomplishments, seek support for their challenges, share what they have learned, and receive feedback when appropriate.

Summation

Before moving into the Evaluation, spend a moment summing up what the class has accomplished and assigning homework or clarifying questions about the assignment.

Evaluation

Providing time at the end of the class for students and teachers to evaluate the experience they have just shared helps students to create ownership of their own learning. This is just one of many reasons that Evaluations are a good idea; see p. 49 for others. For the teacher, research on effective teacher evaluation states that: "Teachers who want to improve their teaching are eager to know how other teachers and their students view them. These are the people who interact with the teacher every day; their perspective should not be ignored during the evaluation process."[8] The Evaluation allows you to gather this information directly from your students. In addition, students often use their evaluation to assess their own performance and engagement, and to assert a positive influence on other students.

Chapter 18 describes several approaches to doing the Evaluation.

Frequently Asked Questions

1. There is an element of silliness in some exercise, such as BOPPITY BOP BOP BOP and ZIP ZAP ZUP. Is this method serious enough to be meaningful?
Playful routes are often the best avenues to serious objectives. If you know what you plan to accomplish with an interactive exercise, the exercise is serious no matter how much laughter it may provoke. In addition, students and teachers need to see each other as real people, and being "silly" within the limits of an exercise is a helpful way of touching our common humanity without losing control of the classroom.

2. My class periods are only 50 minutes long. When is there time to do all this?
The Interactive Meeting Format described in this book fits most comfortably into a time period of 80-

[8] Ronald T.C. Boyd, *Improving Teacher Evaluations* (ERIC Digest No. 111 1989), http://www.ericfacility.net/ericdigests/ed315431.html

90 minutes or more. Adapting the format for a 50-minute period requires some compromises, particularly if there are more than 20 students in the class.

Warm-up Questions are too time-consuming for classes of more than 20, unless you take only a few answers. Even in smaller classes you may at times need to limit warm-up responses to a word or phrase, and Evaluations to a phrase or a number. For Evaluations in large classes, you can use a GROUP SHOUT (p. 423), GROUP WHISPER (p. 423), or GROUP THOUGHT (p. 424) EVALUATION.

For many of the Springboard Exercises and Work Exercises, you can spend less time than cited in their descriptions. The sample Interactive Lesson Plans in this chapter allot less time for most of the exercises than the descriptions call for.

Once your students become accustomed to the routine, you will find that you can move through the lesson plan in a timely way. In general, when all students are engaged, distractions will decrease and productivity will increase in your classroom.

It's best to form the habit of starting the class on time and moving quickly to either the Warm-up Question or the Springboard Exercise. Most students will not want to miss this element of the class and will try to arrive on time.

You can also create time for the Interactive Lesson Plan by giving extra attention to class preparation. Completing the following tasks before class will save time during the period:

- Prepare and lay out all materials for the Work Section.
- Set up pairs and groups.
- Prepare handouts or datebook-sized stickers (such as mailing labels) with the day's assignments, rather than have students copy assignments from the board.
- Prepare templates and examples for students to follow.
- Prepare follow-up or enrichment activities for students who complete the Work Section early.

3. When can new information or ideas be presented in this format?
In general, you would introduce new information in the Work Section. However, you can also use other parts of the lesson plan for this purpose, as in the following examples:

In the instructions for an exercise:

- A biology teacher could introduce the parts of a cell and then ask the Warm-up Question, "Which part of the cell are you most like and why?"
- A math teacher could introduce the concept of prime numbers, then facilitate GROUP COUNT (p. 221) using a set of prime numbers.

In processing an exercise:

- A math teacher can ask the Warm-up Question, "What are your three favorite foods, in order of preference?" or use the Springboard Exercise LINE-UPS (p. 340). During processing, the teacher can introduce the concept of the order of operations.

4. I've tried to use interactive methods in my classroom, but my students seem unwilling to try something new. What should I do?
It's not surprising that students are resistant to trying new things. Notice how, in classes that have no

seating plan, students generally sit in the same seats every day (just as adults attending meetings have their preferred seats). Most students have developed routines for getting by in school in ways that make them comfortable. By introducing interactive methods to your class, you are requiring students to step outside of their routines. Though you are offering an approach that focuses on student activity, brings fun to the classroom, and engages students in their learning, many students will prefer at first to stay within their comfort zones.

Read about resistance in chapter 3 and about being consistent on p. 70. Consistent use of Interactive Lesson Plans while recognizing and working through your own resistance are fundamental to the success of this approach for your students.

Interactive Lesson Plan: Themes in George Orwell's *Animal Farm*

Subject: English
Grade Level: 9-10

Content Objectives	To explore the following themes in the novel *Animal Farm* by George Orwell: the corruption of ideals by greed, the nature of leadership, and human weakness.
Skill Objectives	Students will take positions on issues related to these themes, then debate the issues and consider whether to change their positions.
Group Objectives	Students will engage in respectful discussion of issues related to the themes.

Notes:

- This lesson plan assumes that students have finished reading *Animal Farm*. However, a teacher could adapt the lesson to generate interest in reading the book and to serve as an introduction to the book's themes by gearing discussion in the Work Section to the themes themselves without particular reference to the book.
- The lesson plan is not a comprehensive study of *Animal Farm*. It touches on only one dimension of the novel and does not delve into other important aspects.

Introduction (2 minutes)

Warm-up Question (5 minutes)
If you could be any animal in the world, which would it be and why?
Processing suggestions

- People identify with different animals for a lot of reasons; various animals may represent power, grace, beauty, intelligence, speed, etc. In *Animal Farm*, the main characters are animals and they have different degrees of status in their society because of their traits. Through telling a story about animals, the author is making points about people, how they act, what they want, and what they will do to get what they want.

Springboard Exercise (8 minutes)
THE LEADER GAME (p. 227)
Processing suggestions

- Sometimes it is difficult to figure out who is exerting influence on others' behavior. At other times, it's clear where the influence is coming from, but it's not clear what the leader's motives are. If someone is waving a flag and wants you to do the same, it takes sophistication to stop and think about why the person is doing what they are doing and whether you agree with their reasons enough to follow them. You also need to think about the consequences of following or not following a leader. In *Animal Farm*, of course, those who don't follow are killed.
- Whenever we are in a new group, we observe what other people are doing. Each of us makes decisions about how this will help us to fit in (or not) and whether or not to change our usual behavior to conform to norms of the group. In this exercise, most people choose to go along with what everyone else is doing, just as most of the animals in *Animal Farm* chose to go along with Napoleon. In this school, what do most people choose to do in order to fit it? What happens to those who choose not to fit in? Is it difficult to identify the leaders here?

Work Section (25 minutes)
STAND AND DELIVER (p. 406)
Use the following statements:

- Leaders tend to be the smartest people in a group.
  Discussion points: What makes people ideal leaders? How are leaders selected in our community/school/society? How did the pigs become the leaders in *Animal Farm*? What motivates people to follow leaders? Was it a failure of intelligence that caused the other animals to let the pigs seize power? What is the meaning of "intelligence"? Are there different ways of being intelligent?

- Power corrupts.
  Discussion points: How did the pigs gain absolute power? Did they always intend to seize power? Which animals collaborated with them in that process? Could they have been stopped? How? What parallels do you see to institutions and governments that you know about?

- Money equals success.
  Discussion points: What are the various ways we can measure success? What equals success in *Animal Farm*, and how does that change between the beginning of the novel and its end?

General discussion points: How did you make your decisions? Consider how many people changed their minds after listening to the arguments of others. Did some people change their minds internally but not switch groups? How much of what you decide is based on your own beliefs? on what you hear from others? on the beliefs of people you identify with?

Summation (2 minutes)

Evaluation (3 minutes)

Interactive Lesson Plan: Introducing Percentages

Subject: Math
Grade Level: 4-6

Content Objectives	To introduce and practice percentages.
Skill Objectives	Students will understand the concept of percentages and will practice turning raw data into percentages.
Group Objectives	Students will work cooperatively in groups.

Preparation:

- Prepare about 20 questions for STAND UP/SIT DOWN (p. 296), using low-risk questions that will not make anyone in the class uncomfortable. Prepare questions that will give you a range of results from 100 percent (everyone will stand up) to zero percent (no one will stand up). Also, to make the math more challenging you could include some questions that will be for students only, others for everyone in the room (students and teacher), and others for subsets (for example, for all the girls or all the boys). You could also include questions that relate to other areas of study (for example, to tie in with genetics, "This is a question for people with blond hair only. Raise your hand if you have blond hair. Now stand up if you have blue eyes.")
- Prepare a chart to record the responses to the STAND UP/SIT DOWN questions. Include room for additional questions that you add at the last minute. Make copies of the chart to distribute to all members of the class.
- Make a large copy of the chart on flip chart paper or an overhead transparency.
- Depending on the length of the class, you could also prepare worksheets for practice with percents.
- If you wish, decide how you will divide students into small groups.

Introduction (2 minutes)

As you preview the agenda, include the following explanation: Today the class will be learning about ourselves as a group, what we like, don't like, and so forth, and then learning how to express that in percentages.

Warm-up Question (5 minutes)

What is one thing you think is true of most of the people in this room?

Processing suggestion

- Tell the class that if something is true for every single person in the room, we can say it is true for 100 percent of the group. If it is true for most of the people, we can say generally that it's true for 80 to 90 percent. Today you are going to learn about percents and how to calculate them.

Springboard Exercise (8 minutes)

STAND UP/SIT DOWN (p. 296)

- Appoint a student (or ask for a volunteer) to record the responses to the questions. The recorder should also participate in the exercise.
- Proceed as normally with the exercise, except that the recorder captures information about how people respond.
- If you wish, include additional questions that came up during the Warm-up Question, and remind the recorder to write these in.

Processing suggestion

- We got a lot of information about ourselves from this exercise. It would be interesting to know how to talk about this information in a clear way. We can always say, "14 out of 28 students like math," but it's also good to know that 50 percent of the class likes math.

Work Section (25 minutes)

1. Explanation of Percentages

- Using a question that everyone stood up for, ask what percentage of the class responded. For example, "What percent of our class likes ice cream?"
- Then use a question to which no one responded. For example, "What percent of our class likes to spend all day Sunday doing homework?"
- Then, beginning with these simple examples, explain the mathematical process for figuring percentages, using more examples from STAND UP/SIT DOWN.
- Pass out the charts. Have the class fill in all of the percentages that have been figured thus far and the information from the recorder about the numbers who stood up for each question.

2. Individual Work

Have students work individually on their charts to figure the percentages for several more of the STAND UP/SIT DOWN questions.

3. Small Groups

Create small groups of 3-4 students each. In their groups, have students compare the results of their individual work and settle discrepancies in their answers.

4. Report-backs

Have each group report back on two or three percentages, recording their answers on the large chart.

Summation (2 minutes)

Summarize briefly what the class has learned, and assign homework. For extra credit, students could write up the results of this class as a report on the class's likes and dislikes.

Evaluation (3 minutes)

Ask students to express their evaluation of the class as a percent. (For example, "I give this class a 90% because it was fun and I learned how to make percentages.")

Creating Springboard or Work Exercises

Many teachers are adept at creating ways to make learning interactive and fun in their classrooms. See p. 61 for information that may help you to think creatively about how to construct interactive exercises to meet your goals for your students. In the meantime, here are two exercises that Teen Empowerment staff devised for use in English classes. (Both can be adapted for any language arts or foreign language class.)

There, Their, They're Tag (Homonym Tag)

Goal	To reinforce the correct use of the homonyms "there," "their," and "they're." (Can also be used with other homonyms.)
Time	5-10 minutes
Physical contact	Tagging
Physical challenges	Ability to walk fast
Number of participants	8-25
Space requirements	Open floor space
Materials needed	Signs
Preparation	Prepare a sign for each of the homonyms. Post each sign in a different part of the classroom. Write 15-20 sentences, each including one form of the homonym, and write each sentence on an index card. Order the cards so that no form of the homonym is used twice in a row.

Instructions

1. Explain or review the homonym forms. Point out the signs around the room.
2. Ask for two volunteers, one to be the tagger and one to be the reader. Give the reader the stack of index cards.
3. Tell everyone else to scatter around the room. Emphasize that there is to be no running.
4. When the reader reads a sentence, everyone walks as fast as they can toward the sign with the homonym form that they think is included in the sentence. A person is safe when their hand is touching the sign.
5. The tagger's task is to tag two people before they are safe. The tagger must say "there, their, they're" as they tag someone. The first person tagged becomes the new tagger and the second person becomes the reader. If no one is tagged, the tagger and reader stay in their roles for the next round.
6. Continue until all the cards have been read.

Processing suggestions

- Sometimes it seems hard to be "safe" when dealing with these confusing words. But with practice, knowing which is which can become as automatic as walking.
- This exercise is a lot harder than trying to figure out the correct word when you're writing, because during the exercise you have to make snap judgments. When you're writing, you can be more careful and deliberate; you can stop and think it over. If you practice, think about what you know, and approach your writing carefully, you'll get it right.

Pop It into Place

Goal	To practice using words in proper context.
Time	5-10 minutes
Physical contact	None
Physical challenges	None
Number of participants	8-25
Space requirements	None
Materials needed	Slips of paper, balloons, tape
Preparation	For each team, write a paragraph on a subject of interest to the students. Then think about which words you will remove from the paragraph so that students can reinsert them in the correct places. Leaving space for the words you have removed, write each paragraph in a separate place on the board or on flip chart paper hung on the wall. Next, write each removed word on a slip of paper. Blow up a balloon for each word and insert the slip of paper into the balloon. Put the balloons for each team into a bag. (If popping balloons will be too noisy for the classroom setting, you can set up a different task, such as unwrapping words that you have wrapped in paper or tied up in rubber bands.)

Instructions

1. Divide the class into teams of up to six students. (Depending on the size of the class and the classroom, you may decide to have half of the teams watch while the other teams compete, then switch.)
2. Show each team the paragraph they will be working on.
3. Give each team the bag containing its balloons and the missing words.
4. Each team first has to pop the balloons using only their feet, then extract the words from the balloons.
5. Each team works together to tape their words to the correct places in their paragraph. When all the words are inserted, the team reads the paragraph to a teacher. If it is correct, the team reads it aloud to the whole class.
6. The first team to read its paragraph correctly is the winner.

Processing suggestion

- A word all by itself, out of any context, usually doesn't have that much meaning, and a bunch of separate words don't communicate very much, either. It's only when everything is in its place that we gain understanding.

Scenario 12: A Lesson Plan for Dealing with Test Anxiety

Sharon and Marcus, counselors at an urban high school, wanted to help students overcome the anxiety that was contributing to their poor performance on a high-stakes standardized test. They designed an Interactive Lesson Plan for this purpose, which they conducted in each of the school's test-preparation classes. (For a related scenario about this lesson plan, see p. 29.) The lesson plan's objectives were to address the students' frustration and stress and to increase motivation levels in the classroom.

They set up the classroom with chairs in a circle to facilitate discussion. Sharon introduced the agenda and gave the class the Warm-up Question "Say your name and a word that describes how you feel right now." Many of the words that came out had to do with being scared, frustrated, angry, upset, or tired. In her process, Sharon talked about the importance of feelings and how they can drive the decisions that people make. She stated that if you don't feel good about something, you may find it difficult to focus your attention on it and give it your best effort. She said that it was important to be aware of your feelings about the test, and not to let those feelings prevent you from trying your best.

Marcus then instructed the group in how to play BAG TOSS and told them that he would time the exercise so they played for one minute. The first time the group played, it was chaotic and frenzied. Marcus counted the number of bags that were dropped—a total of 15. Then he said they would play again for one minute, but he instructed the group to throw the bags more slowly, to focus and concentrate, and to set a goal of not dropping any bags. This time, with group members more focused on receiving and throwing, only six bags were dropped. In processing, Marcus brought out the awareness that the group had taken a task that seemed difficult and undoable and, with some structure, helpful strategies, and concentration, had come much closer to reaching their goal. He drew a parallel with the test, suggesting that just as in BAG TOSS, the task might seem undoable, but with structure, helpful strategies, and concentration, it could be done.

During this discussion, one student, Joe, said that he was sick of everyone making such a big deal about the test, that he was so worried about failing and not graduating that he couldn't even try to focus in class, and that he might as well drop out now. Sharon related people's answers from the Warm-up Question to Joe's concern, saying that when you feel afraid that you can't accomplish something, sometimes you don't even want to try. But if you work to overcome your fear, and realize that one test doesn't define who you are, your chances of succeeding are actually much greater.

The group then did CONCENTRIC CIRCLES, with discussion questions designed to help students reflect on their time in high school and on their own learning styles and to develop relationships in the class. Then they did a WORDSTORM on the word "Success," which brought out issues of hard work and sacrifice and the need to have confidence in yourself.

In the evaluations, the students rated the session very highly, and made comments such as, "No one ever asked me my feelings about the test before," "I think this session will change people's minds about giving up," and "I felt like I got to express myself and learned how I need to have confidence about this test." The sessions reduced anxiety about the test, and enabled the students to recognize the necessity of sustained effort in their test-preparation classes.

Agenda Summary

Introduction

Warm-up Question

Say your name and a word that describes how you feel right now.

Springboard Exercises

BAG TOSS, p. 302

THINK-AHEAD BAG TOSS, p. 304

CONCENTRIC CIRCLES, p. 190 (See questions below.)

Work Section

WORDSTORM on "Success," p. 413

Summation

Evaluation

Questions for CONCENTRIC CIRCLES

- What was your freshman year in high school like?
- How is it different now that you are an upperclassman?
- What is your strongest subject, and why?
- What is your weakest subject, and why?
- Talk about how you learn best, and why you think that is.
- How have you personally been feeling about this test?
- What do you want to do when you graduate from high school, and why?
- Where do you see yourself in five years, and how do you plan on getting there?

Interactive Lesson Plan

Date: ___________ Class Period: ____________ Subject:______________________________

Objectives:

Preparation and Materials:

Groupings or pairings:

Introduction Time:

- Welcome
- Who's here and who's not here
- Outline the goals of this class period
- Timeline and announcements
- Review the lesson plan

Other:

Name Exercise: ____ Time:

Warm-up Question: _______________________________________ Time:

Processing ideas:

Springboard Section: ______________________________ Time:

Processing ideas:

Work Section: ______________________________ Time:

Summation: ______________________________ Time:

- Review objectives
- Share observations
- Preview next class

Other:

Evaluation Technique: ______________________________ Time:

Learning Assessment:

Chapter 8

Choosing Exercises to Serve Your Goals

- Interconnection

- Focus
- Introspection
  Group
  Personal
  Group or Personal

- Communication
- Trust
- Surfacing Group Dynamics

- Group Problem Solving
- Personal Problem Solving

- Leadership
- Organizing
- Planning

- Different Perspectives
- Cultural Awareness

- Creativity
- Visual Arts
- Acting

- Reinforcing Information
- Learning Names
- Reinforcing Names

Choosing the right exercises for a meeting begins with defining your goals, and this chapter exists to help you find the exercises that will serve your goals. For example, if the goals for the first meeting of a new group include building relationships, you can look here under "Interconnection" to find exercises that will help meet that goal.

In addition to goals, there are other factors to consider in choosing the right exercise. Be sure to read the section on "Designing the Agenda" (p. 55) in chapter 5 for discussion of these factors.

With two exceptions, you will find all the Name, Springboard, and Work-Section Exercises listed here, with most listed under more than one goal. The exceptions are BRAINSTORMING and WORDSTORM; you will find the general goals of these exercises with the exercise descriptions in chapter 17.

Variations of exercises generally serve the same goals as the exercises they spring from. In this chapter variations are only listed when they have goals in addition to those of the original exercises.

Interconnection

These exercises demonstrate connection among participants, make new connections between people, or show the importance of working together.

Focus

These exercises require participants to pay careful attention. They are good lead-ins to Work Sections that will require focus, and they can be helpful for reining in scattered energy.

Introspection

It is often useful, and sometimes necessary, for the growth and development of a group to design agendas that require participants to reflect on a deeper level about group dynamics, their role in the group, personal qualities they may be struggling with, or their views on certain issues. Exercises with the goal of Introspection can set the tone for this type of work.

Some exercises in this category are especially useful for introspection related to the group, some deal more on the personal level, and some can be used in both ways. The exercise "World Party" is included in this category because it prompts participants to think about larger issues in the world.

Introspection: Group

Introspection: Personal

Introspection: Group or Personal

Communication

These exercises are useful for getting people talking with each other or for making points about the importance of good communication.

Trust

Most of these exercises require participants to trust the group or members of the group. Others demonstrate the importance of trust and can be used to make points about trust.

Some of the exercises require physical risk-taking that could result in injury to participants. Do not use an exercise such as Trust Falls or Pair Pyramids unless you feel confident that everyone in the group will take their participation seriously.

Surfacing Group Dynamics

While nearly every exercise in this book surfaces group dynamics to some extent, these exercises are particularly helpful in this area.

All Aboard, 299
Amoeba Tag, 258
Bridging the Barrier, 187
Chill, Chill, Run, 262
Conversation Web, 193
Dot Tag, 263
Elbow Tag, 264
Everybody's It, 265
Eye Connect, 156
Feeling About (variation), 324
Finding the Path, 195
Follow Me, Follow You, 161
Gab Fest (variation), 192
The Good Show, 394
Group Beat, 163
Group Count, 221
Group Mirror (variation), 317
Group Story, 224
Group the Group, 289
Head or Tails Tag, 267
Hide and Seek, 329
Human Knot, 332
Human Maze, 201
Leadership Circle, 338
Line Chase, 268
Machine-o-Rama, 203
Marco Polo, 269
Name Chant, 135
Name Chant, Motion, and Sound, 348
Name Dance Circle, 350
Name Face, 233
Name Jingle, 234
Name Octave, 170
Name Volley, 143
Napkin Race (variation), 360
Obstacle Course, 204
Pair Pyramids, 351
Pair Tag, 270
Poem Puzzle, 354
Private Eye, 355
Quiz-A-Rama, 403
Red Light, Green Light, 357
The River Wild, 206
Row, Row, Row Your Boat, 239
Slide by Slide, 364
Squat Ball, 368
Stop Tag, 272
Stuck in the Mud, 276
Surfing the Web, 211
Take a Seat, 407
Take a Shot, 370
Tentacle Tag, 277
Three-Chair Improv, 248
Too Much, 371
Word Association Contest, 254
Zip Zap Boing, 181

Group Problem Solving

These exercises call upon the group to come up with a solution to a challenge. They are useful for surfacing issues related to the way a group copes with problems and how the group makes decisions and takes actions. They can be especially dynamic—and higher risk—when they also call for physical contact or movement.

Personal Problem Solving

These exercises can provide insight into how individuals cope with challenges.

Leadership

In these exercises, some or all of the participants take on positions of leadership and people experience the dynamics involved in being leaders or followers.

Organizing

These exercises demonstrate some of the challenges or the dynamics involved in organizing people or events, or they can promote discussion about how systems work.

Planning

These exercises help the group to start thinking in terms of putting things in order (for example, Line Ups and Step by Step by Step), about time issues (Wait a Minute), or about how planning something changes its outcome (The Story Game). They are useful lead-ins to work sessions that will focus on timelines or other planning tasks.

Different Perspectives

These exercises give participants insight into how people can see the same experiences differently, interpret the same instructions in a variety of ways, or bring varied skills to the same task. Stand and Deliver asks people to stand up for their beliefs.

Cultural Awareness

These exercises have the potential to highlight the cultural diversity among participants or to raise awareness about diversity.

DIVERSITY IN MOTION, 391
MULTICULTURAL FILL THE SPACE, SHAKE THE HAND (variation), 282
MULTILINGUAL GROUP COUNT (variation), 222
NAME, FOOD, AND REMEMBER, 138
PEOPLE HUNT, 293
WORLD PARTY, 416

Creativity

Each of these exercises calls upon the participants to exercise their creativity in one way or another.

CONCENTRIC ACTING (variation), 317
FREEZE, 219
GROUP BEAT, 163
GROUP COLLAGE, 396
GROUP POEM, 397
GROUP SCULPTURE, 198
GROUP STORY, 224
INCH BY INCH, 226
INFO FLOW, 398
MACHINE-O-RAMA, 203
MAGIC BALL, 342
THE MAGIC BOX, 231
MOVE TOGETHER, 168
NAME DANCE (variation), 136
NAME DANCE CIRCLE, 350
NAME JINGLE, 234
NAME OCTAVE, 170
SELF POEMS, 240
THE STORY GAME, 245
THREE-CHAIR IMPROV, 248
TRIPLE DRAW, 251
WORD ASSOCIATION CONTEST, 254

Visual Arts

These exercises involve creation of visual art as their primary activity (though with GROUP SCULPTURE, the medium is human "clay").

GROUP COLLAGE, 396
GROUP SCULPTURE, 198
TIMED ART, 250

Acting

These exercises are excellent preparation for a group that will be working on theater.

BIGGER AND BIGGER, 308
CONCENTRIC ACTING (variation), 317
EXAGGERATION, 157
FREEZE, 219
THE GOOD SHOW, 394
THE MAGIC BOX, 231
NAME, EMOTION, MOTION (variation) , 349
SPEECH TAG OR CHARACTER TAG (variation), 273
THREE-CHAIR IMPROV, 248
THE WIND BLOWS WITH CHARADES (variation), 379
THE WIND BLOWS WITH SCENARIOS (variation), 379

Reinforcing Information

These exercises provide fun ways to review information that the group has been working on.

Learning Names

In a new group or one-time group that is not too large, these exercises and their variations will help people to learn each other's names. See the information about the Names/Warm-up Section in chapter 4 for guidelines about using Name Exercises.

Reinforcing Names

Use these exercises when a group has done some work to learn each other's names and you want to reinforce that learning, or when you want to emphasize the importance of knowing names and calling people by name.

Part II: Interactive Exercises

Chapter 9

Name Exercises

Name Exercises are part of the Name/Warm-up Section of the interactive meeting structure. Be sure to read the information in chapter 4 that tells you the purposes, the procedure, and how to structure and process this section.

Five Reasons

These exercises are important with one-time groups and in the early stages of ongoing groups. If you are *not* planning to use a Name Exercise in one of these settings, look for your reasons here:

- *The group is too big.* NAME RACE and its variations (p. 140) work well with groups as large as 50. NAME SHOUT and NAME WHISPER (p. 142) can be done with groups of any size.
- *The group will be meeting only once.* The meeting is more likely to achieve its goals when people have the opportunity to identify themselves, however briefly. This act of identification creates a degree of investment in the group. Also, a Name Exercise helps to dissolve the tension that inevitably exists in a group that has never met together before.
- *We don't have time.* Most Name Exercises take less than five minutes with a group of up to 25 people. NAME RACE can take as little as two minutes. NAME SHOUT and NAME WHISPER take less than a minute. The benefits easily justify the time spent.
- *I'm planning to do a Warm-up Question with names.* You're forgoing the energizing benefits of a Name Exercise, but your plan may be good enough depending on the circumstance.
- *People will be too embarrassed. They won't do the exercise.* You're the best judge of your group, and it's important not to alienate people. But please read about resistance (below and in chapter 3) and think about it before ruling out a Name Exercise. Also, be aware that some Name Exercises are low-risk and work well even with very resistant people.
- *We've been doing Name Exercises regularly for several sessions and I'm certain that everyone in the group knows everyone else's name.* It sounds as if your group is ready to discontinue Name Exercises. Remember to add names to your Warm-up Question whenever the group has a visitor or a new member.

Resistance

Because Name Exercises are most often used in new groups and one-time groups, the resistance among group members tends to be high. It is especially important to be aware of your own level of resistance and be prepared to demonstrate comfort and confidence in conducting the exercise. Read more about resistance in chapter 3.

It's likely that the group will maintain feelings of tension and discomfort while doing the Name Exercises, even as the exercises are functioning to remove a layer of tension and make people feel more comfortable being in the group. The effects will become apparent as the meeting progresses. By overcoming your own resistance and confronting the resistance of the group, you will be able to achieve this impact.

Purposes

The Name Exercises serve many purposes in addition to helping people learn each other's names. See chapter 4 for more, but the purposes briefly stated are:

- Giving everyone a chance to speak, identify themselves, and be heard.
- Creating fun and energy.
- Helping people feel more comfortable in the group.
- Assessing the mood of the group and of individuals.
- Establishing the degree to which people are ready to "buy in" to the group's work.
- In some cases, illustrating the purpose of the meeting or imparting information that can be helpful to achieving the groups' goal.

How to Use

Remember that each exercise in this section can be used independently, in combination with other Name Exercises, or paired with a Warm-up Question. For example, if you have a new group that will be working together consistently and needs to get to know each other, you could begin the first session with the

NAME RACE, followed by NAME CHANT and MOTION, and then a Warm-up Question.

Processing

How you process an exercise always depends on the circumstances in the group and on your purpose for doing a particular exercise. The first time or two that you use Name Exercises with a group, tell them either before the exercise or during the processing some of the reasons that it is important to learn names (see chapter 4). Depending on the group, you can stress the importance of names to personal relationships, group productivity, or whatever is most significant in this situation.

Specific exercises contain possibilities for other processing points, some of which are suggested in this chapter. In addition, what you observe as you watch the group go through the exercise can yield valuable information for you as the facilitator, and some of this can also be profitably reflected back to the group during processing.

Checking

The following are useful for checking whether the group has learned names and is ready to stop using Name Exercises:

NAME CONTEST p. 137
NAME CROSS-LINE RACE (variation) p. 141
NAME, FOOD, AND REMEMBER p. 138
NAME VOLLEY p. 143

Exercises for Reinforcing Names

There are other exercises in this book that can be used with ongoing groups to reinforce the importance of knowing everyone's name and calling each other by name. Some examples are:

BAG TOSS p. 302
WHO'S THAT THERE BEHIND THE CURTAIN? p. 376
WEB OF CONNECTION p. 374
YES GAME p. 381

Name Chant

Goals	Learning names, Surfacing group dynamics
Time	5-10 minutes (not including processing)
Physical contact	None
Physical challenges	None
Number of participants	8-80
Space requirements	None
Materials needed	None
Preparation	None

Note: NAME CHANT and its variations are useful for revealing how people are feeling and what the level of resistance is in the group. You can get a sense of both mood and personal style by the tone each person uses and (in the variations) by the motions called for. These exercises let people express themselves in a fairly low-risk way.

Instructions

1. Going around the circle, each person says their name in whatever tone of voice they choose.
2. The group repeats the name three times in the same tone.

Processing suggestions

- People have a range of different styles in how they choose to present themselves to others, as well as varying comfort levels in expressing themselves in the group.
- The exercise illustrates how a person's attitude, tone, and style are mirrored back to them by those around them.

Variation – Name Chant and Motion

Additional goal	Leadership

Note: The group can do this exercise seated or standing, but the standing version is more dynamic since people can move freely and use more of their bodies in their motions. Standing increases the risk level of the exercise.

Instructions

1. Follow the instructions for NAME CHANT, except that each person also makes a motion as they say their name.
2. The group repeats both the name and the motion three times.

Additional processing suggestions

- People repeating one another's motions can be an illustration of responding to peer pressure.
- Often in this exercise the group will repeat something that the person who originated the motion did not realize they were doing (such as scratching their head or making a facial expression). This is an illustration of "unconscious leadership"—people modeling behavior that they do not necessarily want others to follow.

Variation – Name, Talent, Motion

Additional goal	Interconnection

Instructions

1. Follow the instructions for NAME CHANT AND MOTION, except that each person says one of their talents and does a motion that represents that talent.
2. The rest of the group then repeats the name, talent, and motion three times.

Additional processing suggestions

- This exercise helps us to recognize the many talents that are in this group.
- The group can accomplish a lot when people are comfortable sharing our talents with each other.

Variation – Name Dance

Additional goals	Leadership, Creativity
Physical challenges	Must be able to do simple dance moves.

Note: This exercise is a good choice for a group that is about to work on some form of creative expression.

Instructions

1. Follow the instructions for NAME CHANT AND MOTION, except that each person's motion should be in the form of a dance move.
2. The group repeats both the name and the move three times.

Additional processing suggestion

- Often people become more expressive as the exercise progresses, illustrating how creativity can be released as people loosen up and become more comfortable.

Variation – Name Stretch

Physical challenges	Must be able to do stretches

Note: This exercise is a good choice when the group is about to engage in a physical activity.

Instructions

1. Follow the instructions for NAME CHANT AND MOTION, except that each person's motion should be in the form of a stretch (touching toes, rolling shoulders, etc.).
2. The group repeats the name and the stretch three or more times (the number of repetitions will depend on your goals for the group).
3. If the stretch exercises just one side of the body, the group should also do it an equal number of times on the other side.

Additional processing suggestion

- Emphasize the importance of warming up and stretching ourselves both mentally and physically.

Name Contest

Goals	Reinforcing names, Focus
Time	5-10 minutes (not including processing)
Physical contact	None
Physical challenges	None
Number of participants	8-20
Space requirements	None
Materials needed	None
Preparation	None

Note: This exercise is a good way to check if the group is ready to stop using Name Exercises.

Instructions

1. Ask for a volunteer to go around the circle and say everyone else's name.
2. When that person either completes the group or can't remember someone's name, ask for another volunteer to start over, but going in the opposite direction.
3. Continue in this way until someone is able to say all the names correctly.

Processing suggestion

- Unlike contests that deal with trivial matters, this exercise is about something essential to the health of this group.

Name, Food, and Remember

Goals	Reinforcing names, Focus, Cultural awareness
Time	5-10 minutes (not including processing)
Physical contact	None
Physical challenges	None
Number of participants	8-20
Space requirements	None
Materials needed	None
Preparation	None

Note: This exercise is a good way to check if the group is ready to stop using Name Exercises.

Instructions

1. With people sitting or standing in a circle, the first person says their name and their favorite food.
2. The next person in the circle repeats the first person's name and food before giving their own name and favorite food.
3. The third person repeats the names and foods from the first two before giving their own name and food.
4. This continues all the way around the circle. Whenever someone can't remember, they should ask for help.
5. Finally, the person who went first repeats everyone else's name and favorite food.

Processing suggestions

- If the group is culturally diverse, people's favorite foods may be quite different. Your process could focus on food as a bridge between cultural groups. If the group does not appear to be culturally diverse, this exercise might reveal a surprising diversity of background.
- If people have difficulty pronouncing the names of unfamiliar foods, comment on the challenge involved in bringing different cultures together.
- Stress the importance of being respectful of differences.
- The food we eat and enjoy can be very personal to each of us. Sharing this with the group is a step toward building trust and safety.
- Process any hurtful comments by saying that this group has a lot of personal resources to share, but that people must feel safe to do this. Insensitivity toward another member of the group violates the trust needed for the group to achieve its goals.

Note: If people mispronounce the name of someone's favorite food, rather than correcting the mispronunciation immediately the best approach is to wait until the end of the exercise and use this as a processing point. If someone deliberately makes a negative or hurtful comment, the usual reaction from a facilitator is to speak up immediately, stating that negative comments are not acceptable. However, this approach can set up a dynamic that is not helpful: the facilitator in the role of authority figure versus the person who made the negative comment, who often will feel defensive and be unwilling to accept responsibility ("It was just a joke!"). A more effective approach is to wait until the end of the exercise, then process the comment in a way that does not single anyone out, but gives information for everyone to think about. (See the processing note below.) In this way, the person who made the comment can reflect on what they said and its effect on the other person and on the group. This indirect approach avoids setting up a clash with the authority figure and is more likely to result in changed behavior and in group and individual learning.

Variation – Name, Something, and Remember

Instructions

1. You can substitute other questions for "favorite food." In general, you should try to substitute questions that need only short answers (such as your age, the high school you attended, or the month you were born) and that are fairly low risk within the context of your group.

Additional processing suggestions

- Processing will emerge depending on the topic.

Name Race

Goal	Focus
Time	1-5 minutes (not including processing)
Physical contact	None
Physical challenges	None
Number of participants	10 to 50
Space requirements	None
Materials needed	A watch or clock with a second hand
Preparation	None

Note: This is the best Name Exercise to use with a large group where there is no possibility of learning everyone else's name and where a more in-depth Name Exercise would be impractical. It raises the issue of learning names and provides the opportunity to state its importance, without creating an unrealistic expectation that people can learn so many names.

Note: In smaller groups, NAME RACE works well as a lead-in to NAME CHANT AND MOTION.

Instructions

1. Explain that the objective of this exercise is to go around the circle having everyone say their names in as short a time as possible.
2. Ask for a volunteer to begin, or indicate the starting point.
3. Note the time on the watch or clock, then give the signal to start.
4. When everyone has said their name, tell the group how many seconds it took. Then ask them to do it again, trying to beat their time. (For example, if they did it the first time in 12 seconds, tell them to try for 10 seconds.)
5. Do the second round as you did the first.
6. If you wish, have a third round. You can choose a different starting point or have the group go in the opposite direction.

Processing suggestions

- Though we can't learn each other's names through this exercise, each person had the chance to be heard, if only for a fraction of a second. In our work together, let's try to be efficient, while still hearing everyone's voice.
- For a group of any size, this exercise requires focused attention, which is important for completing any task. Practice generally results in making progress.

Variation – Name Race Times 2 or Times 3

Instructions

1. Follow the instructions for NAME RACE, except that for NAME RACE TIMES 2 everyone has to say the name of the person who went before them, as well as their own name. For NAME RACE TIMES 3, everyone has to say the names of the two people who went before them, as well as their own name.

Variation – Name Line Race

Note: This exercise can be used to set up PAIR TAG (p. 270).

Instructions

1. Have the group stand in two lines facing each other.
2. Point out the starting position (the end of one line).
3. Do a practice round: The person in the starting position says their name; then the person directly across from them says their name, followed by the person diagonally across from them, and so on, making a zigzagging path to the end of the lines and back.
4. Note the time on the watch or clock, then give the signal to start.
5. When everyone has said their name, tell the group how many seconds it took. Then ask them to do it again, trying to beat their time.
6. If you wish, have a third round. To increase the challenge, you can choose a different starting point or have the group go in the opposite direction.

Additional processing suggestion

- Someone who is not paying close attention can hurt the group's ability to meet its goals.

Variation – Name Cross-Line Race

Additional goal	Reinforcing names
Number of participants	10 to 30

Note: This exercise is a good way to check if the group is ready to stop using Name Exercises.

Instructions

1. Explain that this exercise is like NAME LINE RACE except that that each person says another person's name instead of their own, following this pattern: The first person says the name of the person directly across from them, then that person says the name of the person diagonally across from them, and so on, making a zigzagging path to the end of the lines and back.
2. Then proceed as for NAME LINE RACE, including doing a practice round.

Additional processing suggestion

- Knowing each other's names will increase our ability to function efficiently.

Name Shout

Goal	Interconnection
Time	1-2 minutes (not including processing)
Physical contact	None
Physical challenges	None
Number of participants	No maximum number
Space requirements	None. Will work with theater seating.
Materials needed	None
Preparation	None

Note: Name Shout can be used to raise the issue of names in a very large group, where there is no possibility of learning everyone else's name and an in-depth Name Exercise would be impractical. It provides the opportunity to state the importance of knowing names, without creating an unrealistic expectation that people can learn so many names.

Instructions

1. On the count of three, everyone shouts out their name as loudly as they can.
2. Do this several times, encouraging people to participate with more enthusiasm each time.
3. If you wish, you can provide a competitive element to enhance participation: have one half of the group shout, then the other half, to see who can be louder.
4. You can also add other variations, such as having people whose names begin with certain letters shout at once (for example, everyone whose name begins with a letter from A through H).
5. Always end with the whole group shouting their names together.

Processing suggestion

- Sometimes people feel that they are shouting and not being heard. Even though this is a large group, we want to establish an environment where everyone can speak out and have a chance to establish their identity.

Variation – Name Whisper

Instructions

1. Follow the instructions for Name Shout, except that everyone whispers their name instead of shouting it.

Name Volley

Goals	Focus, Communication, Surfacing group dynamics, Reinforcing names
Time	3-5 minutes (not including processing)
Physical contact	None
Physical challenges	None
Number of participants	8-20
Space requirements	None
Materials needed	None
Preparation	None

Note: This exercise is a variation of Zip Zap Zup (p. 182).

Note: This exercise is a good way to check if the group is ready to stop using Name Exercises.

Instructions

1. Have the group stand in a circle.
2. With your hands in front of you, palms together (prayer position), point to someone and say their name.
3. That person then points to someone else and says that person's name. This continues in no particular order. Tell people to proceed as quickly as possible, and to call on people who have not yet had a turn.
4. Continue until everyone has had a turn, or longer if you wish. If you think that some people have not been called on, stop and ask people whose names have not been called to raise their hands.

Processing suggestions

- If you are unsure of someone's name, you will probably avoid pointing to that person. The exercise illustrates how important names are to the group's ability to work together. Individuals are unlikely to connect with someone whose name they are unsure of or cannot pronounce.
- The better we know each other, the more easily energy will flow within the group.
- Watch to see who gets pointed to the most and who gets pointed to less often. People will tend to point to the people they feel most comfortable with. Does the exercise provide insight into the group's dynamics or to possible factionalism in the group?

Name Walk

Goals	Learning names, Leadership
Time	5-10 minutes (not including processing)
Physical contact	None
Physical challenges	Must be able to walk around the circle.
Number of participants	8-30
Space requirements	Open floor space
Materials needed	None
Preparation	None

Instructions

1. Have the group stand in a circle. Ask for a volunteer (Person 1) to start.
2. The group starts walking around the circle to the right.
3. Person 1 calls out their first name and does a gesture that can be repeated while people are walking.
4. Everyone says Person 1's name and does the gesture while they walk.
5. When the group has completed one circle (that is, everyone is back at their starting point), the person walking behind Person 1 says their name and does a gesture, which everyone repeats as they walk.
6. Continue in this way until everyone has had a turn.

Processing suggestions

- Everyone has a different style. We hope to create a group where everyone feels comfortable expressing their own style.
- How does one person's style affect others in the group?
- Where do different styles of leadership bring the group?

Name Wave

Goals	Learning names, Leadership
Time	3-5 minutes (not including processing)
Physical contact	None
Physical challenges	Must be able to participate in the "wave."
Number of participants	8-80
Space requirements	None
Materials needed	None
Preparation	None

Note: The group can do this exercise seated or standing, but the standing version is more dynamic since people can move freely and use more of their bodies in their motions. Standing increases the risk level of the exercise.

Instructions

1. Ask for a volunteer (Person 1) to begin, and tell the group whether to proceed right or left after Person 1.
2. Person 1 says their name and does a motion.
3. Moving in the specified direction, people send the name and motion around the circle in a "wave." Person 1 should be the last to end the wave that they started.
4. Continue in this way until everyone has had a turn.

Processing suggestions

- As ideas and emotions run through a group, each person reinterprets what comes to them.
- Rather than just being affected by the wave, each person has an opportunity to control the character of the wave.
- By putting our actions out into the world in an organized way, we can start a wave that will have an effect on others.

Chapter 10

Warm-up Questions

- All-Purpose Questions
- Time
- Personal and Work Goals
- Remembering Your Life
- Relationships
- Self-Analysis
- Food
- Entertainment
- Seasons/Holidays
- Community/School
- This Group/Program/Organization
- Ending the Group/Reflecting on Time Together
- Event Planning
- Event Outreach or Marketing
- Theme/Message
- Hypothetical
- Envisioning the Future
- Drugs
- Stereotypes/Prejudice/Racism
- Social Class
- Miscellaneous

The Warm-up Question is commonplace in meetings of new groups or one-time groups. A facilitator will often open a meeting with, "Let's go around and introduce ourselves," and suggest that people answer a question such as "What brought you here?" or "What do you want to get out of this meeting?" These Warm-up Questions are a good beginning and are sometimes the most appropriate questions for particular settings.

However, the range and purpose of useful Warm-up Questions goes well beyond this. This chapter will expand your view of the kinds of Warm-up Questions that can best serve your group.

Choosing the Question.

A thoughtfully chosen Warm-up Question can provide insight into the group and the individuals in the group and can set a tone of richness and creativity as the meeting gets underway. Using Warm-up Questions most effectively requires choosing a question that sparks people's interest and that simultaneously speaks to a need in the group and advances the goals of the meeting. A well-chosen question helps a facilitator to understand the mood of the group and of individuals in the group, begins to engage people in the process of achieving the group's goals, and sets the stage for the work that will come next.

The number of possible Warm-up Questions is virtually unlimited; your challenge is to find or think of the question best suited for your group on a particular day. This chapter has suggestions for more than 180 Warm-up Questions, but these questions are only a starting point. You might want to combine two questions, separate a question into parts, add or remove qualifiers, use variations, make up entirely new questions, or use an old standby like "what you want to get out of this meeting." What is important is that you think creatively about the needs and goals of your group and how this part of the agenda can get your meetings off to a great start.

Consider the following factors in choosing the question:

- Needs and goals. What does the group need in order to have a productive meeting? What are your goals for this meeting and how can the Warm-up Question contribute to achieving the goals?
- Risk level. How much risk does the question represent to individuals in the group? New groups should begin with low-risk questions, while formed groups may be ready for higher-risk questions. This chapter flags questions that are generally high-risk, but a high-risk question for one group may be low-risk for another, and vice versa. See p. 58 for more about risk level.
- Time. How much time do you want to give to the Warm-up Question? For a meeting with a long agenda or a large number of participants, choose a question with short and easy answers. In some

situations, asking for one-word answers might be appropriate. Conversely, when a major purpose of the meeting is for people to get to know each other, or when the group is going to delve into a serious topic, ask a question that invites lengthier and more reflective answers.

On some days, questions whose intent is obvious may be appropriate, but at other times the best question will be one that deals in a creative, non-linear way with the issue that you want to get at. See the discussion about subtlety on p 59.

Combining with Name Exercises.
There are many circumstances, such as when you first start working on building a group, when it is best to do one or more Name Exercises in addition to a Warm-up Question. Please review the information in chapter 4 on the Names/Warm-up Section as you plan your agenda.

In new groups and one-time groups, people should always say their names as they answer the Warm-up Question. In a continuing group, whenever there is a visitor or a new person (or if you think at any point that everyone may not be completely sure of others' names), tell people to say their names as they answer the question. Let people know that they do not have to answer the question, but they do have to say their names.

Processing.
Even a simple Warm-up Question can provide a great deal of information. Though your processing of the Names/Warm-up section should be brief, you should use the time to bring out those themes that are relevant to the work ahead. For example:

- The question "What is a food that you never want to eat?" can relate to cultural differences, tolerance, taking independent action, dealing with the unknown, and other broad themes.
- Questions related to entertainment provide information about the culture and values of members of the group.
- Questions related to goals can show the breadth of tasks and interests that people are involved in, as well as the areas where tasks and interests overlap and are interrelated.
- The question "What three things would you want to have with you if you were stranded on a desert island?" can relate to what people value and can show the importance of planning and the various ways people approach it.

When processing, you should always be aware of how people's answers can be viewed in a way that will shed light on the group's work and its mission. For more information about processing Warm-up Questions, see p. 40.

Categories.
This chapter divides Warm-up Questions into categories for your convenience. However, there is no need to stay rigidly within the categories when you are choosing a question. For example, if the Work Section of your agenda will be taken up with planning an event, it may or may not be appropriate to choose a question from the "Event Planning" category. Depending on the situation in your group on a particular day, it might make sense to ask a Warm-up Question that deals with personal or group issues.

All-Purpose Questions

- Say a word that describes ... [your community/the event we are planning/the world/ your work/how you are feeling today/this group/an upcoming holiday/etc.].
- Something that's going well and something you're concerned about [within a particular context, such as your work or an upcoming event].
- What were you thinking about this meeting on the way here today?

Time

- What would you be doing if you weren't here now?
- Name three things you have to do every day (without repeating something already said).
- A word that describes your week, and why.
- One thing that happened this weekend (or a comment about your weekend), and one thing you're looking forward to this week.
- A memorable moment from the past week.
- A highlight and a "lowlight" of your weekend/your day.
- What do you like to do on Saturdays?
- A change that you've noticed since [a significant event] and how you feel about it.
- What is your relationship with time?

Personal and Work Goals

- One priority for your work this week/the most important thing for you to get done this week.
- A phrase to describe what you want to accomplish today.
- A goal you have for yourself and the first thing you'll do after you accomplish it.
- A goal you have for yourself, an obstacle you may face in achieving it, and what you plan to do to overcome the obstacle.
- A personal goal and a work goal for the next month.
- One thing you plan to do this summer/winter/etc.
- Something you would like to have in the future.

Remembering Your Life

- What did you want to be when you were a child, and what do you want to be now?
- Your favorite fairy tale when you were a child.
- A birthday celebration you remember and why you remember it.
- Something you remember about the first day of school (any year).
- What do you remember about your high school graduation?
- At what point in your life did you first see yourself as an adult?
- Talk about a reunion that you attended.
- Talk about your first job.
- A rule that you broke and what happened as a result.
- A project that you did in school that was meaningful and/or exciting and why.
- A silly accomplishment you've had.
- A time when the weather changed your plans and what you did.
- A time you got lost and what you did about it.
- A time you tried something new and what happened.
- Something you got for free, how you got it, and how you used it.
- Something unexpected that happened to you and how you handled it.
- A time you had difficulty learning something that you eventually mastered.

- *High-risk:* A time you were injured or had an illness.
- *High-risk:* A promise that you kept and a promise that you broke.
- *High-risk:* A time you felt left out.
- *High-risk:* A time you believed a lie someone told you.

Relationships

- Someone in your life that you learned from and what you learned.
- Someone you taught something to and what you taught.
- Something you accomplished this week and someone who helped you do it.
- A time you helped someone; a time someone helped you [in the last year/someone in your family/other qualifier].
- The best teacher you ever had and why.
- The worst teacher you ever had and why.
- Someone you look up to and why.
- Someone who impressed you last week.
- A person who helped you when you needed it.
- Someone or something you had to take care of and how it went.
- What's the most important quality in a relationship and why did you choose that quality?
- Talk about a relationship you admire and why.
- A gift you'd like to give someone and why.
- Talk about a time someone made you feel comfortable.
- What's a quality you admire in people and why do you admire it?

Self-Analysis

- Something you've learned this week/this summer/this year.
- Something you did well today.
- What is a positive quality that you have?
- A talent you have, and a talent you'd like to have.
- What three gifts do you bring to our group?
- Name one of your strengths and one area of growth or improvement.
- One thing you would do differently based on learning from an experience.
- An impact that your work has had on someone [within a particular context].
- Something that made an impression on you this week/month/etc.
- Something you learned to value this past year.
- The most memorable moment of this year.
- Something you've done recently for the first time.
- Something you find frustrating.
- What do you like to do on a rainy day?
- Something you've never done but would like to try.
- Something you haven't done yet this year.
- Something you do that makes you feel free.
- Something you did recently that was relaxing.
- Something you're thankful for and why.
- *High-risk:* Something you do when you're upset that makes you feel better.
- *High-risk:* Something you think no one in the group knows about you.

Food

- Your favorite food.
- Your favorite dessert.
- A food that you cooked and what made it good.
- A food that you think you would never eat.

Entertainment

- Your favorite entertainer and why.
- Your favorite movie and why.
- Your favorite character in a book, movie, or TV show.
- Your favorite kind of music.

Seasons/Holidays

- Your favorite time of the year and why.
- An object that reminds you of a season.
- Your favorite thing about the summer/winter/etc.
- What's the first sign for you that summer is ending, and how does it make you feel?
- How do the shorter days of the early winter affect you?
- A holiday wish that you have.
- What would you like to be for Halloween?
- What do you have to say about Santa Claus? [Everyone in this culture has something to say about Santa Claus!]

Community/School

- A word to describe the state of this [community or school].
- A recommendation you have to improve this [community or school], and why.
- Your favorite place in this [community or school] and why.
- *High-risk:* A place you feel safe in this [community or school].

This Group/Program/Organization

Note: For "group" in these questions, you can substitute "program," "organization," or whatever term is appropriate.

- A word to describe this group and why you chose that word.
- What is something you value about this group?
- If there were a headline in the paper about this group (or this group's work), what would it say?
- Something the group did well this week.
- What was your best day so far with this group, and why?
- A team or group you have been a part of that was effective, and what made them work well.
- Give a weather report for our group and explain why.
- Something that drew you to this group.
- Something you like about this group.
- If this group [or a project of the group] were a food, what would it be and what ingredient or part of it would you be?
- One thing about how this group will look in five years.
- A motto for this group.
- Something you did for the first time with this group.
- A memorable moment from this week/month/year in the group.

- What three gifts would you give this group and why?
- What did you like best about [a recent event that this group was involved in]?
- One thing you remember about [a recent event].
- A highlight and a "lowlight" of [a recent event] and why.
- A word to describe your work, and why you chose that word.
- An essential quality in a [profession relevant to the group's work].
- *High-risk:* A role you see yourself playing in this group.
- *High-risk:* A word to describe our group on a good day and a word to describe it on a bad day.

Ending the Group/Reflecting on Time Together

- If this group stayed together for ten years, what would it be like?
- What was the best meeting of this group that you remember, and what was good about it?
- What will you miss about this group?

Event Planning

- What is the most important goal of the project we are working on?
- If you were stranded on a desert island (but all basic survival needs, such as food and water, were taken care of), what three things would you want to have with you? You cannot say people.
- An event or show you've been to that impressed you.
- Talk about [an event similar to the one we're planning] that you enjoyed.
- A time you had to prepare something and what happened.
- One thing you like doing and the steps you can take to do it.
- If this event were a car, what kind of car would it be and why?
- A task related to the event that you can finish by the end of today, and one you will finish next week.
- On scale of 1 to 10, where are we in readiness for the event, and what's most important for you to get done today?
- One thing you're looking forward to about the event.
- A word for how you're feeling about the event.

Event Outreach or Marketing

- What is your favorite commercial?
- Someone you think would want to come to the event [or buy the product] and why.
- One person you want to come to the event [or buy the product] and how you will get them to buy a ticket [or the product].
- How many people do you predict will come to the event [or buy the product], and how many will you bring?

Theme/Message

- Where do you get your best ideas?
- If this week of your life were a movie or book, what would the title be and why?
- If we had a radio or TV show to talk about this group, what would its title be and why?
- A theme or a song title for the next month/two months, etc. [or for an upcoming event].
- Think of a book, story, or movie that is important to you. What's the message in it?

Hypothetical

- If you were a plant, what kind would you be and why?
- If you were a food, what would you be and why?
- If you were an animal, what would you be and why?
- If you could be anyone in history, who would you be and why?
- If you could live in any period of history, which would it be and why?
- If you could be someone else for a day, who would you be and why?
- If you could be or play any character (book, TV, movie, or real person), who would it be and why?
- If you came back to life, what would you come back as?
- If you were in the circus, what would you be: ringmaster, lion tamer, high wire walker, ticket taker, or something else?
- If you could go to one place in the world, where would you go and why?
- If you could have dinner with anyone living or dead, who would it be, what would you say, and why?
- What is something you would tell or ask Nelson Mandela [or some other renowned person]?
- If you had a million dollars to spend, what would you spend it on?
- If you could put a sign on a blimp to communicate to a crowd for 24 hours, what would it say and why?
- If you had to have a picture or word drawn on your nose for a week, what would it be, and why?
- If you were recreating the world, what profession would you recreate first?
- If you could give constructive criticism to some celebrity, who would it be and what would you say?
- *High-risk:* If you had to give up your sight, your hearing, or your ability to walk, which would you choose and why?
- *High-risk:* If you had to volunteer for six months for any cause, what would it be and why?

Envisioning the Future

- What is your vision of what the future will be like in the next ten years/fifty years/hundred years?
- If you had magic glasses and could see this school/neighborhood/company/etc. ten years from now, what would you see?
- Close your eyes and imagine yourself ten years from now. Where are you? What are you doing? Notice one person or thing around you and describe it.
- A word that describes the future, and why you chose that word.

Drugs

- How does drug use affect this community?
- Talk about a time you wished that you were someplace else.
- *High-risk:* Talk about someone's experience with drugs.

Stereotypes/Prejudice/Racism

- Talk about a time you witnessed someone being treated according to a stereotype.
- Talk about a time you were stereotyped (or someone you know or have heard about was stereotyped) and what happened.
- A time that you (or someone you know or have heard about) acted according to a stereotype.
- Something you've seen in a movie or TV show that perpetuates a stereotype.
- Talk about a time you experienced or witnessed a racist act and how it made you feel.
- *High-risk:* Describe your cultural background.
- *High-risk:* What is a type of discrimination that really bothers you and why?
- *High-risk:* What's a common stereotype that people have about [a particular group] and how do you feel about it?

Social Class

- How does classism affect your everyday life?
- What is your definition of success and why?
- Who controls our society?
- *High-risk:* How would you describe the social class that you grew up in?

Miscellaneous

- What is your favorite cliché and why?
- How do you feel about flying?
- Something in the news that caught your attention this week.
- Where do you get your news?
- What is the most common cause of arguments?
- What is money?
- What's your problem?

Chapter 11

Five-Minute Springboard Exercises

With the minor investment of time required by these exercises, you can give the group a meaningful experience that helps to illuminate the work of the day and increase the group's ability to meets its goals. Some exercises, such as HANDS TOGETHER, WAIT A MINUTE, or MINI-MED, are about quiet, focus, and concentration, while others involve movement and physical contact and help to give the group energy. What they have in common is that each can be done in five minutes or less (with some additional time for processing) and in that time can provide a significant boost to the group's understanding of its work and a corresponding increase in productivity.

In addition to the exercises in this chapter, the following exercises can be done in five minutes or less:

CHILL, CHILL, RUN	p. 262
EVERYBODY'S IT	p. 265
FINDING THE FS	p. 218
GROUP COUNT and variations	p. 221
GROUP MOAN/GROUP SHOUT	p. 286
LINE CHASE	p. 268
HIDE AND SEEK: TIME LIMITED (variation)	p. 330
PAIR TAG	p. 270
RIVER WILD RACE (variation)	p. 208
ROW, ROW, ROW YOUR BOAT	p. 239
STAND UP/SIT DOWN and variations	p. 296
TIMED ART	p. 250
TRIANGLE TAG	p. 278

Also, most of the exercises in chapter 14 (Tag-Style Exercises) generally take 5-10 minutes, but can be done in five minutes or less.

Exaggeration

Goals	Communication, Different perspectives, Acting
Time	Roughly 30 seconds per participant (not including processing)
Physical contact	None
Physical challenges	Must be able to mimic and exaggerate a movement from another participant.
Number of participants	5 or fewer
Space requirements	Open floor space is ideal, but the exercise can also be done around a table.
Materials needed	None
Preparation	None

Instructions

1. Have the group stand in a circle.
2. Ask for a volunteer to begin.
3. The first person makes a tiny movement.
4. The person to their right makes the same movement, but does it in a large, exaggerated way.
5. This person then makes a different tiny movement.
6. Proceed around the circle in this way. End with the first person exaggerating the movement of the person to their left.

Processing suggestions

- In times of stress, small things can get exaggerated.
- The same thing can be perceived very differently depending on how it is communicated.
- Sometimes people may exaggerate movements that the person did not intend to make. How do patterns sometimes get repeated unintentionally in the group and elsewhere?
- This exercise can be used to discuss issues of gossip and "he said/she said."
- Watch the way people made their movements for aspects that might be valuable for processing. People have different styles that will be obvious.
- How does having a variety of styles both enhance the group and also present challenges?
- Some people will have difficulty with this exercise. Not everyone is comfortable with exaggeration or making "big" statements and those people will have a hard time doing this under pressure. How does this affect the group's work?

Eye Connect

Goals	Introspection, Surfacing group dynamics, Interconnection
Time	5-10 minutes (not including processing)
Physical contact	None
Physical challenges	Must be able to see across the circle.
Number of participants	10-30
Space requirements	Open floor space
Materials needed	None
Preparation	None

Instructions

1. Have everyone stand in a circle and keep their heads down, looking at the floor.
2. When you give the signal, each person will look up and across the circle and try to meet the eyes of another person. People should not speak throughout the exercise.
3. When eye contact is made, both people move toward each other and take each other's place in the circle. They should not lose eye contact until they have arrived in the other person's place. Caution people to move slowly and carefully across the circle, since a number of pairs will be crossing at the same time and people will be moving backwards.
4. As soon as they arrive in the new place, people should try to make eye contact with someone else.
5. Continue until time is called.

Processing suggestions

- This exercise explores what it is like to make a connection with someone else, and it provides an image of people actively looking for ways to make connections with others. There are many levels of connection in our lives, from casual contact on the street to deep relationships.
- What were the dynamics of the group? Did you tend to connect only with certain people, such as people you know best? Did people avoid eye contact altogether? Why?
- Sometimes people have the experience of trying to make contact and not being able to, when others are doing it easily. If that happened to you, how did it feel?
- Eye contact can mean different things depending on the culture and the context. It can be a sign of respect, a challenge to authority, or a desire for intimacy. What did it feel like to maintain eye contact with someone for such a long period of time? What positive and negative associations do people have with making eye contact?
- It takes courage to connect using your eyes and your perception, and to connect with and affect the world around you.
- Because prolonged eye contact can be intense and cause anxiety for some people, laughter may emerge in this exercise. You can discuss the use of humor as a way of diffusing anxiety.
- You can talk about what how difficult it can be to maintain a connection with someone. Could people keep connections and still move without bumping into each other? How did it feel to be in the middle of the circle? How do you maintain connections with people you've met?

- The exercise can illustrate how, even as you focus on maintaining one relationship, you also need to be aware of the social context surrounding that connection.

Variation – One-Eyed Eye Connect

Instructions

1. Follow the instructions for EYE CONNECT except that everyone keeps one eye closed throughout their connection (or covers one eye with a hand). Caution people to move even more slowly and carefully, since they will be lacking peripheral vision on one side.
2. When people arrive in their new places in the circle, they switch which eye is closed, then try to make eye contact with someone else.

Additional processing suggestions

- This exercise can illustrate what it is like to move through the world or through a project with limited vision or perspective. It is important to see the whole picture as much as possible when working on a project, because having a partially blocked view will affect the outcome of the work.
- When we lose our perspective, it can greatly affect how we react to situations. Problems can seem bigger or smaller than they actually are, and that can affect our strategies to address them. How did having one eye closed affect people's perception of depth? Did things seem closer or farther away than they actually were? How did this affect people's strategies and actions?
- You can also use this exercise to talk about responding and adapting to challenges.

Variation – Spinning Eye Connect

Instructions

1. Follow the instructions for EYE CONNECT except that as people move across the circle while maintaining eye contact, each person must spin around once.
2. People should reestablish eye contact as soon as possible after the spin.

Additional processing suggestions

- This exercise can be used to see what happens when connections are broken and how people find ways to reconnect with one another.
- Did people have strategies for trying to maintain eye contact?
- How difficult was it to reconnect?
- What kinds of situations allow members of this group to connect or disconnect?
- How about people in general? How hard is it to reconnect once you have lost connection? What prevents people from trying to reconnect?

Variation – Eye Connect with Everyone

Instructions

1. Proceed as usual with EYE CONNECT, except that each person's goal is to connect with every other person in the group. Note that it's OK for two people to connect more than once.

Additional processing suggestions

- What were people's feelings when they succeeded or did not succeed in connecting with everyone?
- What are the risks in this variation of the exercise?
- You can use this exercise to talk about the need to connect with everyone at an event that the group is planning. Did people have strategies they used to connect with everyone in the group? What strategies can be used to make sure we connect with everyone at the event? How do we pull in people who are harder to connect with?
- How did it feel to connect with someone more than once?

Variation – Long Distance Eye Connect

Note: This exercise can provide relevant images for a group that has been in close connection, that has done EYE CONNECT previously, and that is now about to disperse, spread out, or lose some members.

Instructions

1. Have the group stand in a circle, then step backwards to widen the circle as far as seems practical.
2. Have everyone turn around with their backs to the circle. Instruct people to position themselves so that they cannot see anyone else, or to close their eyes if they can see other people.
3. At the count of three, everyone turns around with eyes open and looks around the room. The exercise continues as for EYE CONNECT, except that the circle is much wider.
4. You can speed up the exercise if you wish by telling people to connect within a specified time, such as five seconds. Caution people to be careful.

Additional processing suggestions

- Processing can focus on the power of consciously staying in connection even at a distance.
- What are the difficulties and the opportunities when you have to find new ways of relating and of making connections with others in the wider world?

Follow Me, Follow You

Goals	Group introspection, Surfacing group dynamics
Time	5 minutes (not including processing)
Physical contact	None
Physical challenges	Minimal
Number of participants	12-20
Space requirements	Open floor space
Materials needed	None
Preparation	None

Instructions

1. Have everyone stand in a circle.
2. Ask each person to look around the circle and choose someone as their leader, but to keep their choice a secret.
3. Then ask everyone to think of a pose.
4. On the count of three, each person first strikes their pose, then looks at their leader and does whatever their leader is doing for the rest of the exercise.
5. End the exercise when the entire group is doing the same movement or is in the same pose. If this does not happen, end the exercise when group members stop switching poses.
6. The exercise will take only a few seconds to play out. You can have the group do it several times if you wish.

Processing suggestions

- Analyze leadership patterns in the group by looking at who chose whom to be their leader, and whom everyone was following in the end.
- How did people decide whom to choose as a leader? How did people's strategies relate to how they choose leaders in life, be they role models, mentors, or politicians?
- Did anyone change their mind at the last second and decide to follow someone else? Why?
- Other points for discussion include the idea that leadership lies within the group, and that individual actions on a daily basis serve as a model for everyone else in the group. What are our responsibilities if we are all leaders for each other?

Go Between, In Between

Goal	Group problem solving
Time	5 minutes (not including processing)
Physical contact	Minimal
Physical challenges	Minimal
Number of participants	15-30
Space requirements	Open floor space
Materials needed	None
Preparation	None

Note: It is difficult to make this exercise "succeed" in a traditional sense, especially with a large group, but processing the exercise provides people with interesting insights. Since each person is intent on their own goal, which is enmeshed in the conflicting goals of others, what develops is usually either perpetual motion or resignation. It rarely occurs to a group to stop and work together.

Instructions

1. Have the group stand in a circle.
2. Each person should select in their mind two other people in the room. They should not say the names of those people or indicate in any way who they are. The people selected do not have to be standing near each other.
3. When you say "Go," each person moves to try to stand between the two people selected. The exercise ends when everyone is satisfied with their position or when chaos ensues.

Processing suggestions

- The decisions we make affect others in ways we may not initially be aware of, and our ability to carry out our own decisions is often dependent on the decisions of other people. It is important to communicate what decisions are being made, and why they are being made.
- When our own goals are frustrated by others in a group setting, how do we react? Do we continue to pursue our own interests? Do we give up? Do we stand back, look at the larger picture, and try to make some order out of the chaos?
- What can we learn from this exercise about the complexity of consensus and about group versus individual decision-making?

Group Beat

Goals	Interconnection, Surfacing group dynamics, Creativity, Different perspectives
Time	5 minutes for a group of 8-20 (not including processing); see note
Physical contact	None
Physical challenges	Minimal
Number of participants	8-20 per group; see note
Space requirements	Open floor space. Can also be done seated at tables.
Materials needed	None
Preparation	None

Note: This exercise can be adapted for a large group or for a situation such as a banquet in which people are seated around tables. Divide the group into small groups of 8-20 if it is not naturally divided. Then give the instructions, telling each small group to come up with its own beat, following the instructions below. Give them a minute or so to create the beat, then call on one group at a time to do its beat.

Instructions

1. Have the group stand in a circle.
2. Ask for a volunteer to begin. That person starts by making a rhythmical sound, and they continue to make that sound until the end of the exercise.
3. Others join in whenever they wish with a sound of their own, such as a "beat-box" beat, a snap of the fingers, or a vocalization, until everyone in the group is contributing a sound to the "group rhythm." Each new sound should be something that fits with the sounds that others are making. The goal is to get the whole group making their sounds at once and (hopefully) for it to sound coherent. It is helpful if someone in the group provides a basic beat that others can build on.
4. Let the beat continue for a moment or two before calling time.

Processing suggestions

- Group Beat can be used to show the way that people's different talents, abilities, and points of view contribute to the work of the group. Each person has an individual sound (talent, etc.) to contribute.
- Does the group make room in its work together for different kinds of sounds (or skills, talents, points of view), or is there pressure for everyone to sound the same?
- Combining many people's sounds, the group has its own unique song or rhythm.
- Everyone has to work together and adjust to each other's rhythms. It is a challenge to coordinate your own rhythm, timing, and style with what others in the group are doing.
- The exercise might illustrate the importance of good timing in the group's work.
- Is there coordination among people's varied roles within the group?
- Was there one central sound that held the group's beat together? Is there a parallel with the group's work?
- Did people have difficulty coming up with a sound to contribute?
- Were the sounds very similar or very different?

Hands Together

Goals	Focus, Organizing
Time	5 minutes (not including processing)
Physical contact	None
Physical challenges	Minimal
Number of participants	Any number
Space requirements	Minimal
Materials needed	None
Preparation	None

Instructions

1. Ask everyone to stand up. Position yourself so that everyone can see you, and stand with your arms extended forward and hands about two feet apart.
2. The goal of the exercise is for everyone to clap their hands at the same time, following the lead of the facilitator. Tell the group to watch your hands and to concentrate on following your movements.
3. Try one clap, then comment on how the group did.
4. Try it two or three more times. There will most likely be progress with practice; however, the group may not be able to succeed, and that's OK.

Processing suggestions

- This exercise demonstrates the power of working together. When everyone is joined together, the sound is clear and powerful. In contrast, when people are not together, the sound can be disturbing and lacking in power.
- When people are able to focus and concentrate, they are better able to achieve their goals.
- Often dysfunctional dynamics will play out in this exercise, especially in large groups. Did anyone intentionally not clap together?
- In large groups, follow-up discussion may not be practical. In a smaller group, you can discuss whether the group generally acts together or separately.

Variation – Step Together

Physical challenges	Must be able to stand on one foot and to step forward.
Number of participants	10-20
Space requirements	Open floor space

Instructions

1. Follow the instructions for HANDS TOGETHER except that instead of clapping, the goal is for everyone to step forward at the same time, following the lead of the facilitator. Begin with the group standing in a circle, with everyone holding their right foot a few inches off the ground.
2. Depending on how much space you have, you can ask people to step back after each step forward, or the group could tighten the circle with each step.

Additional processing suggestions

- Making decisions together (that is, using consensus) allows us to move forward together.
- The moments before we step together can feel uncomfortable because we are all balancing on one foot and worried that we don't have a solid base. The process of decision-making feels a lot like this.

- If the group tightened the circle, you can look at how or if coming physically closer together affected the group's ability to step in unison.

Variation – Step and Clap

Physical challenges	Must be able to stand on one foot and to step forward.
Number of participants	10-20
Space requirements	Open floor space

Instructions

1. Have the group stand in a circle, with everyone holding their hands apart and their right foot a few inches off the ground.
2. The goal of the exercise is for everyone to step forward and clap at the same time, following the lead of the facilitator. Tell the group to watch you and to concentrate.
3. Try one step and clap, then comment on how the group did. Have everyone step back to their original places.
4. Tell the group that in the next rounds you are going to step and clap twice, then three times.
5. Step and clap twice, then step back.
6. Step and clap three times.

Additional processing suggestions

- This exercise is a good energizer. You can keep processing short and use the energy of the exercise to move into the work section of the meeting.
- The exercise illustrates how helpful it can be to get into a rhythm in your work. Note that most groups will find it easier to step and clap three times in unison than it was to do it once.
- When we are moving forward, there's always the possibility of crashing, so you need to be aware of the momentum and make adjustments as needed.
- Also, as the work of the group deepens, it gets more complex, and more attention and focus needs to be given to it.

Variation – Hands Together Circle

Physical contact	Hand clapping
Physical challenges	Clapping hands with people on either side, with arms crossed
Number of participants	10-20
Space requirements	Open floor space

Instructions

1. Have the group stand in a circle.
2. Cross your arms in front of you at shoulder height with your palms facing outward, and ask the group to do the same.
3. The goal is for everyone to clap hands with the people next to them in unison, following your lead.
4. Try it two or three times.

Additional processing suggestion

- This exercise can illustrate the difficulty of working together under challenging circumstances. It can be much more difficult to work with a group, rather than individually. However, a group that can "clap" together can be highly effective and productive.

Lap Sit

Goals	Interconnection, Group problem solving
Time	5 minutes (not including processing)
Physical contact	Extensive
Physical challenges	Must be able to go quickly from a standing position to a sitting one.
Number of participants	10-20
Space requirements	Open floor space
Materials needed	None
Preparation	None

Note: This exercise may be too high-risk for groups with members who are very heavy and for groups dealing with issues of sexuality or tensions between males and females.

Instructions

1. Have the group stand in a close circle, with shoulders touching.
2. Tell them that they are all going to sit on each other's laps at the same time.
3. Have everyone turn to their right and take a small step sideways toward the center of the circle.
4. On the count of three, have everyone slowly sit down on the lap of the person behind them, while the person in front of them sits on their lap.
5. Have the group hold the LAP SIT for the count of ten before they stand up again.

Processing suggestions

- LAP SIT is about creating a structure that can support all members of the group. For the exercise to work, each person has to be in position and has to sit down at the same time. If people do not put their full weight on the person behind them, they end up carrying a lot of the weight of the circle themselves.
- You can use this exercise to address the distribution of work in the group. Does everyone put their full weight behind the group? Are some people carrying a lot of the weight of the group? How can group members support each other while taking care of their own responsibilities at the same time?

Mini-Med

Goal	Introspection
Time	5 minutes or less (not including processing)
Physical contact	None
Physical challenges	None
Number of participants	Any number
Space requirements	None
Materials needed	None
Preparation	Write a brief statement related to the reason for doing this exercise; see note.

Note: A MINI-MED is a brief meditation on a subject that the group will soon be asked to think and speak about. For example, it can be used preceding a Warm-up Question (chapter 10), a WORDSTORM (p. 413), or BRAINSTORMING (p. 385).

Instructions

1. Ask everyone to find a comfortable position (in their own space—no heads on laps, etc.).
2. Once everyone is settled, ask them to close their eyes, relax, and breathe deeply.
3. When everyone is quiet, read the statement you have prepared.
4. Let the room be quiet for a short time—perhaps a minute or two. Then ask people to open their eyes.
5. Go directly into the next piece (Warm-up Question, BRAINSTORMING, or whatever).

Processing suggestions

- You can process the experiences that people had during the MINI-MED while processing the piece that it leads into. For example, when processing a Brainstorm ask people if they had thoughts during the MINI-MED that came out in the Brainstorm.
- Ask people if it helped to have some quiet time to think. Sometimes the best ideas emerge when there is quiet.

Move Together

Goals	Interconnection, Creativity, Focus
Time	5 minutes (not including processing)
Physical contact	None
Physical challenges	Must be able to move easily.
Number of participants	8-20
Space requirements	Open floor space
Materials needed	A source of music (optional)
Preparation	If using music, choose what to use and decide how many times people's movements will be repeated.

Note: This is a good exercise to use on a day when the group will be working to come to consensus about some decision. It shows how everyone needs to have input and how people can work with each other's ideas.

Instructions

1. Have the group stand in a circle.
2. Turn on the music, if you are using it.
3. Ask for a volunteer to go first. That person does some kind of dance movement (claps, kicks a foot, spins around, etc.). If you are using music, you may want to repeat the movement 2, 4, or 8 times to go with the music.
4. The next person does the first person's movement and adds a movement of their own.
5. The third person does the previous two movements and adds one. This continues around the circle until everyone has added a movement.
6. Finally, the group does the whole "dance" all together.

Processing suggestions

- This exercise illustrates the group working together creatively. Everyone adds something, and everyone does the final "dance" with their own style. You can use this to relate to the importance of having everyone's input when group decisions are made, and talk about how the group can work with and build off of each other's ideas.
- You can also discuss focus, since it can take a lot of focused awareness to remember all of the steps to the group's dance.
- How did people remember all the steps? Was it helpful to watch other people across from you in the circle? The group needs to be able to look to each other for support and help.
- Does the group "move together" well? Does everyone in the group take on leadership and make movements for the rest of the group to follow? Do we all follow each other's lead? How can the group "move together" better?

Name and Adjective

Goal	Personal introspection
Time	3-5 minutes (not including processing)
Physical contact	None
Physical challenges	None
Number of participants	8-20
Space requirements	None
Materials needed	None
Preparation	None

Note: If someone in the group makes a negative or hurtful comment about someone else's self-description, the usual reaction from a facilitator is to speak up immediately, stating that negative comments are not acceptable. However, this approach can set up a dynamic that is not helpful: the facilitator in the role of authority figure versus the person who made the negative comment, who often will feel defensive and be unwilling to accept responsibility ("It was just a joke!"). A more effective approach is to wait until the end of the exercise, then process the comment in a way that does not single anyone out, but gives information for everyone to think about. (See the processing note below.) In this way, the person who made the comment can reflect on what they said and its effect on the person who was ridiculed and on the group. This indirect approach avoids setting up a clash with the authority figure and is more likely to result in changed behavior and in group and individual learning.

Instructions

1. Going around the circle, each person says their first name together with an adjective that begins with the same sound and that reflects something about themselves (for example, "Sophisticated Susan" or "Electric Eric"). Ask the group to move quickly and to be respectful of each other.

Processing suggestions

- This exercise lets group members say something to the group about how they perceive themselves, and it shows how hard it can be to describe yourself.
- Like many areas of life, the exercise requires that you quickly think of a way to present yourself to people within a very restricted format.
- Did people find this exercise difficult? Did they try to find adjectives that applied to them, or did they just choose any word with the right sound?
- Process any negativity or put-downs that occur by saying that this group has a lot of personal resources to share, but that people must feel safe to do this. Criticism and negativity not only are hurtful, but also hinder, trust, creativity, and the work of the group. Insensitivity toward another member of the group violates the trust needed for the group to achieve its goals.

Variation – Name, Adjective, and Remember

Additional goal	Focus
Time	5-10 minutes (not including processing)

Note: This exercise combines NAME, FOOD, AND REMEMBER with NAME AND ADJECTIVE.

Instructions

1. Follow the instructions for NAME, FOOD, AND REMEMBER (p. 138), but instead of saying a favorite food, each person says an adjective that describes them and starts with the same letter as the first letter of their name.

Name Octave

Goals	Creativity, Surfacing group dynamics
Time	3-5 minutes (not including processing)
Physical contact	None
Physical challenges	None
Number of participants	8-20
Space requirements	None
Materials needed	None
Preparation	None

Note: This exercise can be used to loosen up people's voices before rehearsing speeches, songs, a play, or anything that requires voice projection.

Note: This exercise asks a lot of people and is appropriate only with groups that are at ease with each other and that are used to being creative. You can use it to gauge how comfortable people are with taking risks in the group.

Instructions

1. Going around the circle, each person says or sings their first name in a couple of different octaves (higher notes, lower notes, or anywhere in between).
2. The rest of the group, singing together, repeats the person's name in the same octave notes.

Processing suggestions

- This exercise can be used to look at the feelings in the notes that people use.
- It can provide insight into the varying energy levels of group members.

Operator

Goal	Communication
Time	5 minutes (not including processing)
Physical contact	None
Physical challenges	Requires the ability to hear.
Number of participants	8-20
Space requirements	Minimal
Materials needed	None
Preparation	Choose a message to be repeated that is a bit complex, but not overwhelmingly so.

Instructions

1. Have the group sit in a circle.
2. If you feel your group needs this warning, tell them that the message and all repetitions or distortions of the message can contain no put-downs, names, or profanity.
3. Whisper a message, rhyme, or sentence into the ear of the person to your right.
4. Each person who receives the message must whisper it to the next person in the circle.
5. If a person does not hear or understand the whole message, they can say "Operator," and the person whispering the message to them can repeat it. Each person can say "Operator" only once.
6. When the message has traveled all the way around the circle, have the last person say it out loud to the group.
7. Compare the final message to the original message.

Processing suggestions

- This exercise shows how a message can become distorted as it travels from one person to another. It is a helpful exercise to use with a group that has problems with rumors or gossip.
- Was the final message the same as the initial message? What was the message in the beginning? in the end? in the middle? Where did it break down and how? See if the group can figure out where and how the distortions to the message occurred.
- Were distortions in the message intentional or accidental?
- How does this experience compare to the way information gets passed around in real life? Are there ever distortions? Are they intentional or accidental? What is the result of these distortions?
- What can people do to make sure the information they are getting is accurate?

Variation – Operating Instructions

Preparation	Prepare a message that includes some instructions for action. The message can be fairly simple (for example, "Jump up and down on your left foot while holding out your right arm.") or more complex (for example, "Get the red book from the chair, give it to a girl in blue, pat your head and pull your hair, wipe your brow, and then say 'Phew.'").

Instructions

1. Follow the instructions for OPERATOR.
2. When the message has traveled all the way around the circle, point to three people, one from the beginning of the circle, one from the middle, and one from the end. These people must simultaneously carry out the instructions that they received. See if they all do the same thing.

3. Ask them to repeat to the group the instructions they received.

Additional processing suggestions

- What people hear affects what they do.
- Being precise in communication and in listening is important because actions often follow words.
- If the message is not clear, or if it is misunderstood, it will often be reflected in actions that reflect the lack of clarity.

Pass the Pulse

Goal	Interconnection
Time	2 minutes (not including processing)
Physical contact	Holding hands
Physical challenges	None
Number of participants	10-50
Space requirements	Open floor space, or can be done sitting around a table.
Materials needed	None
Preparation	None

Instructions

1. Have the group stand in a circle and join hands.
2. Tell the group that you are going to start a pulse—that is, a light squeeze on one of the hands you are holding. When each person receives the pulse, they should pass it on to the person next to them.
3. Pass the pulse with either your left or right hand. When you get it back in the other hand, the round is over.
4. You can do more than one round if you like.

Processing suggestions

- PASS THE PULSE raises the issue of how things move through groups.
- Were there any problems? Did the pulse stop?
- You can use this exercise to discuss flow in a group: Are there times when the energy or the work does not flow well, and times when it does?
- Did more than one pulse move through the group? Are there multiple "pulses" or messages in this group? How does this affect the group? Where in society do you see multiple pulses or messages being sent?
- This exercise demonstrates that we are all connected, whether we know it or not.
- We are always sending signals (pulses) of one kind or another to each other and to those around us. These might be direct or indirect; sometimes we have to be alert to pick up signals from others.

Variation – Pass the Pulses

Instructions

1. You can send a pulse in both directions simultaneously, with or without telling the group that you are doing this.

Additional processing suggestions

- What is it like to have things coming at you from both sides at the same time, and to have to react to both of these stimuli at once?
- Did either of the pulses get lost?
- If the group did not know that two pulses were coming around, how did they react? How does the group react when something happens that they are not prepared for?
- You can also use this variation to talk about the difficulties of working on two tasks at the same time, and the additional focus that this requires.

Variation – Pass the Pulse Speed Round

Materials	A clearly visible clock with a second hand

Instructions

1. Tell the group that they should pass the pulse as quickly as they can, and that you are going to time it.
2. Pass the pulse, note the time, and as soon as the pulse completes the circle announce the number of seconds.
3. Repeat two or three times, urging the group to try doing it faster and faster.

Additional processing suggestions

- Usually, groups get better at passing the pulse around each time they do it, unless their focus is off. You can comment that people usually get better at things with practice.
- If the group improved its time, why did this happen?
- Having a goal usually helps to focus the group on the task and to engage the group in reaching that goal.
- If the group didn't improve its time, what happened?
- What was the effect of being timed? Did it help to encourage people or did it cause them stress? You might relate this to the group's work if they are working under a deadline, or trying to improve upon work they have already done.

Psychic Shake

Goal	Communication
Time	5 minutes (not including processing)
Physical contact	Handshaking
Physical challenges	Minimal
Number of participants	15-50
Space requirements	Open floor space
Materials needed	A slip of paper for each group member
Preparation	Decide how many small groups you want and prepare slips of paper for the exercise. For example, if there are 32 people in your group and you want to create groups of four, prepare 32 slips of paper, four with the number "1," four with the number "2," etc., up to the number "8."

Note: This exercise offers an interactive method for breaking down a large group into small groups, and can be used to surface group dynamics.

Instructions

1. Give everyone a slip of paper, and tell them to keep the number secret.
2. Tell the group to mingle and shake hands with people according to the numbers on their slips: if your number is 1, you shake once; if your number is 2, you shake twice, etc.
3. When two people have the same number, they'll stop shaking at the same time and realize they are in the same group. Those with the same numbers should stay together and continue to search for others until all the groups are together.

Processing suggestions

- How do people identify others that they share things with and want to group up with? People sometimes do this by brands of clothing, material possessions, habits, social or civic concerns, geographic location, race, class, likes and dislikes, etc.
- Some ways of identifying people are superficial and easy, like the handshake, and some are deeper and harder to figure out.

Small Change

Goal	Focus
Time	5 minutes (not including processing)
Physical contact	None
Physical challenges	Minimal
Number of participants	8 to 30
Space requirements	Minimal
Materials needed	A watch or clock that counts seconds
Preparation	None

Instructions

1. Assign people to pairs and have the partners face each other.
2. Instruct the partners to observe each other carefully, trying to remember as much as they can about their partner's appearance.
3. After 30 seconds, have the partners turn their backs to each other. Instruct people to make two or three small changes in their appearance (such as pushing up a sleeve, removing a ring, or untying a shoelace).
4. Give the signal for partners to turn back toward each other. Tell people to take turns spotting the changes that have been made.

Processing suggestions

In the discussion of what people observed and what they failed to observe, you can make the following points:

- Small details, especially the most obvious ones, can be easy to overlook.
- Change happens incrementally.
- People should be given credit for the small changes they make, and it is important to focus on the positive changes people make.
- We need to pay attention to details, and to be able to focus outside of ourselves, so that we can notice small changes.

Wait a Minute

Goals	Planning, Different perspectives
Time	5 minutes or less (not including processing)
Physical contact	None
Physical challenges	None
Number of participants	Any number
Space requirements	None
Materials needed	A pen, a list of everyone in the group, and a stopwatch or a watch with a second hand
Preparation	Cover any clocks visible in the meeting room.

Note: This is a good exercise to do when you are trying to bring time awareness to the group—for example, when the work of the day includes preparing a timeline for the group's upcoming activities, or when people don't seem aware of how little time they have left to prepare for an event or meet a deadline.

Instructions

1. Ask everyone in the group to remove their watches, pagers, cell phones, or anything that could help them tell time.
2. The task is for each person to try to determine when they think a minute has passed, from the moment you say "Start." Everyone must be silent, and their eyes should be closed. When they think a minute has passed, they should raise their hand.
3. As each person raises their hand, write the number of seconds next to their name.
4. When everyone has raised their hand and been recorded, tell people to open their eyes, and read the list to the group.

Processing suggestions

- Ask if people had a strategy for determining the time, and if it worked.
- This exercise can be used to discuss how people have differing perceptions of time, and how this affects people's ability to work together.
- Sometimes a person can accomplish more in 20 minutes when they are ready than in an hour when they are not ready.
- The exercise can also be used to examine internal instincts and what people sense on their own, when they are not being influenced by what they see.

Variation – Eyes Open Wait a Minute

Instructions

1. In this variation, people keep their eyes open throughout the exercise.
2. When someone thinks a minute has passed, they say "Time."

Additional processing suggestions

- How was this different from doing the exercise with eyes closed?
- Did a minute seem longer or shorter with eyes open?
- How did hearing or not hearing other people say "Time" affect your own perception of time?

Variation – Walk a Minute

Physical challenges	Must be able to walk around the room.
Number of participants	8-20
Space requirements	Open floor space

Note: Depending on your goals, you can vary this exercise and its processing by giving people different instructions regarding how quickly or slowly to walk. You can even change the pace during the exercise.

Note: In a formed group where trust has been built, you can have people do this exercise with their eyes closed. Make sure to have everyone put up their hands as "bumpers," and ask them to be move carefully. Watch carefully to be sure that people do not run into any objects in the room.

Instructions

1. Have the group stand up.
2. When you give the signal, everyone begins moving slowly and in silence.
3. When each person thinks that a minute has passed, they stop walking. In a larger group, you might also want to ask people to raise their hands when they stop.
4. When each person stops, write down the time next to their name.
5. When everyone has stopped, have people sit down. Read the list to the group.

Additional processing suggestions

- This exercise can look at how time moves and how, as we move or become busy, our perception of time passing may feel different.
- How did this exercise differ from WAIT A MINUTE?
- Were you more easily influenced by others in this exercise?
- Did you have any interactions with others? How focused were you?
- If you did the exercise with closed eyes, did anyone bump into anyone else? How did this affect people's perception of time?
- How does time seem to pass when you are busy?
- How did your walking pace affect your ability to keep time?

Variation – Move a Minute

Physical challenges	Must be able to move around the room.
Number of participants	8-20
Space requirements	Open floor space

Instructions

1. This exercise is the same as Walk a Minute except that participants must move in other ways besides walking. There are numerous ways you can set up the exercise; for example, you can tell people to move in freeform, dance-like ways, you can give them specific movements to do, or you can have them stay in one place and move their arms.
2. When each person thinks that a minute has passed, they stop moving or freeze in place. You can also ask people to raise their hands and/or say "Time" when they stop.
3. When each person stops, write down the time next to their name.
4. When everyone has stopped, have people sit down. Read the list to the group.

Additional processing suggestions

- Additional tasks are often distracting, and it takes additional focus to stay on track. How did the movements affect people's ability to keep time?
- Was it difficult to stop moving?

Word in Motion

Goals	Different perspectives, Communication
Time	2-5 minutes (not including processing)
Physical contact	None
Physical challenges	Minimal
Number of participants	8-20
Space requirements	Open floor space
Materials needed	None
Preparation	Think about what word or words you will use in the exercise.

Instructions

1. Have the group stand in a circle.
2. Say a word that relates to the work of the group or an issue you want to surface, and make a motion to go with the word. Indicate which direction (to your left or right) the word should travel.
3. Going around the circle, each person says the word in whatever way they wish and also makes a motion to go with it.
4. Alternatively, each person can say a different word, with a motion, that relates to either the first word or the previous word, depending on instructions from the facilitator.
5. If you wish to have additional rounds, you can supply the opening word, as before, or you can ask for a volunteer to start.

Processing suggestions

- Processing can look at the word or words that went around the circle and the many different ways that people express or respond to the same word.
- How did the meaning of the word change as people varied the way it was said and the motion that went with it?
- This exercise can be used to talk about the consistency between words and actions. People can say and mean different things with the same word, depending on how it is said, and what nonverbal communication is associated with it.
- If participants supplied words, discuss the range of words and ideas that came out.

Variation – Emotion in Motion

Time	5 minutes (not including processing)

Note: This exercise often elicits deep feelings from participants.

Instructions

1. Brainstorm a list of emotions. You may want to limit the Brainstorm to 10 or 15 emotions.
2. Send the word for each emotion around the circle; each person says the word and makes a motion.

Additional processing suggestions

- What are the varied ways that people express these emotions? Was there a range of intensity?
- Discuss the emotions that came up in the Brainstorm. Do they fit into any categories? What types of emotions did not come up?
- Which were the easiest emotions to express? Which were more difficult? Which emotions looked the same?

Zen Clap

Goal	Focus
Time	5-10 minutes (not including processing)
Physical contact	None
Physical challenges	None
Number of participants	8-20
Space requirements	Open floor space
Materials needed	None
Preparation	None

Instructions

1. Have everyone sit in a circle.
2. Place one hand flat under your chin with the palm facing down and fingertips pointing to one side, and say "Yin."
3. Play passes to the person next to you toward whom your fingertips are pointing. That person places their hand under their chin in the same way and says, "Yang."
4. Play passes to the person toward whom the fingertips are pointing, and that person places the palms of their hands together, points with their fingertips to anyone in the circle, and says "Clap."
5. The person pointed to then starts the pattern over with "Yin." Play continues to volley around the circle in this way. A person is out when they make a mistake or take too long to respond to a hand signal.
6. People who are out step outside of the circle, but remain around the circle trying to distract the remaining players and cause them to get out, too. The last player to remain in the game is the winner.

Processing suggestions

Processing can reflect on some of the following areas:

- How players developed strategies to stay focused on the game and not be distracted, and how this relates to the group's ability to be focused and work together.
- The increasing difficulty of the game as more and more points of distraction developed.
- How difficult it is to maintain a smooth group flow when people are not working together.

Zip Zap Boing

Goals	Focus, Surfacing group dynamics
Time	5-10 minutes (not including processing)
Physical contact	None
Physical challenges	Minimal
Number of participants	8-20
Space requirements	Minimal
Materials needed	None
Preparation	None

Instructions

1. Have the group form a circle.
2. The person who starts says "Zip," and going around the circle to the right each person says "Zip."
3. However, at any time the person whose turn it is can say "Boing," and at that point the group changes both the direction and the word: "Zap" starts traveling around the circle to the left.
4. This continues until you stop the exercise: whenever someone says "Boing," the group changes the word ("Zip" or "Zap") and the direction the word travels.
5. After playing for a while, you can play so that people are out if they make a mistake.

Processing suggestions

- Processing can raise points about a group getting into a pattern, energy moving through the group, and paying attention.
- If people say "Boing" a lot and play goes back and forth among the same people, you can raise points about energy getting stuck and people being left out and uninvolved.

Zip Zap Zup

Goals	Focus, Communication, Interconnection
Time	5-10 minutes (not including processing)
Physical contact	None
Physical challenges	Minimal
Number of participants	8-20
Space requirements	Minimal
Materials needed	None
Preparation	None

Note: If it fits your goals, you can use different words in this exercise, especially words that relate to your work. For example, Teen Empowerment groups have used the words "Peace," "Power," and "Plan."

Instructions

1. Have the group stand in a circle.
2. Place the palms of your hands together and point with your fingertips to anyone in the circle.
3. The person pointed to must say "Zip," then place their palms together and point to someone.
4. The person pointed to says "Zap," and points to someone else, who says "Zup."
5. Play continues in this way, with people responding "Zip," "Zap," and "Zup" in order as they are pointed to. Emphasize that it is important to be clear whom you are pointing to.
6. You can play so that when someone makes a mistake in responding, they are out.

Processing suggestions

Points can be made about the following:

- Getting the flow of energy and information going in the group.
- People picking up the flow of energy as needed from others.
- The issue of competition—did people intentionally try to get others out? What strategies did people use to get people out?
- Communicating clearly with others when you are passing something on to them.

Chapter 12

Fifteen-Minutes-Plus Springboard Exercises

Many of these exercises provide the opportunity to delve into the group's dynamics or address a group issue more deeply than usual. They provide a rich experience that produces a lot of material to work with during processing.

Planning

Most longer exercises require preplanning of content and/or materials. In addition, processing for these exercises can be complicated; it's a good idea to spend extra planning time thinking about processing to help ensure that the group will achieve a level of understanding that will help them move forward in their work.

Concentric Circles

Take special note in this chapter of CONCENTRIC CIRCLES. This exercise helps people connect and build relationships within all kinds of groups: large and small, formed and unformed, containing people of all ages or demographics. People always report that taking part in CONCENTRIC CIRCLES was a powerful experience that allowed them to engage deeply with others in a way that was both safe and meaningful. See chapter 6 for further discussion about using CONCENTRIC CIRCLES.

Achieving Your Goals

Remember that the purpose of the Springboard Exercise is to position the group to enter into the work ahead with increased understanding and enthusiasm. An exercise that is too time-consuming or involved can have the opposite of the desired effect. Don't choose an exercise simply to take up time in the meeting; be sure that you're choosing it because it fits the needs of the group. If your goals can be accomplished with a five or ten minute exercise, choose that.

Some of these exercises can be done well in less than 15 minutes. CONVERSATION WEB, for example, will take less time with a small group or if you place a limit on speaking time.

Work Section

In some circumstances, such as a meeting that will focus on communication or surfacing group dynamics, you could use these exercises in the Work Section of the agenda.

More Exercises

The following exercises in other chapters are also "Fifteen-Minutes-Plus":

ALL ABOARD, ALL AHEAD (variation)	p. 300
ALL ABOARD, SOME AHEAD (variation)	p. 300
BACK-TO-BACK DRAW	p. 216
PEOPLE HUNT	p. 293
SELF POEMS	p. 240
TIMED ART	p. 250

Back-to-Back Feedback

Goal	Introspection
Time	15-25 minutes (not including processing)
Physical contact	Minimal
Physical challenges	Must be able to write on paper with a magic marker.
Number of participants	10-20
Space requirements	Open floor space
Materials needed	A magic marker and a piece of heavyweight paper for everyone (including facilitators), and tape
Preparation	None

Note: BACK-TO-BACK FEEDBACK is a high-risk exercise that can cause damage in a group that has a lot of tension or conflict among its members. It is a good exercise, however, for an experienced and highly functioning group that has just completed a project or piece of work together, since it allows people to acknowledge and praise each other's work. Facilitators who are an ongoing part of the group should participate.

Instructions

1. Give everyone a magic marker and tape a piece of paper to each person's back (including your own).
2. Have everyone go around and write some positive feedback about each person on that person's back. People do not have to write their names next to their comments. However, it is important to stress that people should write only positive comments. (Negative feedback should only be given face-to-face, never behind someone's back.) Be aware, as facilitator, of people who may be receiving very brief or very lengthy comments, and help to balance that out.
3. Once everyone has had a chance to write on everyone else's back, tell the group to return to their seats. When you say OK, people can take off their papers and read their feedback.

Processing suggestions

- If there are negative comments, process them with care, being mindful of protecting both individuals and the group.
- Positive feedback can be very powerful, and there are not many vehicles for genuine praise to come out in a group.
- People should be aware of our positive qualities, not just because it makes us feel good, but because these qualities are resources that we can call upon in life.

Bridging the Barrier

Goals	Group problem solving, Surfacing group dynamics
Time	15-30 minutes (not including processing)
Physical contact	Extensive
Physical challenges	Requires strength and agility. Carefully consider group members' physical issues, including weight issues, before choosing this exercise.
Number of participants	8-15
Space requirements	Open floor space
Materials needed	One or more objects to use as a physical barrier; possibly chairs or other objects to stand on
Preparation	Create some sort of physical barrier for the group to get over. To make the exercise very difficult, use a large object such as a table or desk. To make it easier, use smaller objects such as desk chairs or create a pile of random objects that are available. Also, decide on a metaphor to describe the barrier to the group. For example, it can be a fallen tree covered with scorpions and other poisonous insects.

Instructions

1. Instruct the group that they must all get from one side of the barrier to the other without anyone touching it.
2. Getting everyone over the barrier generally involves people lifting and carrying each other. Stay engaged in your role as an observer throughout the exercise and make sure that no one is injured. Depending on the size of the barrier, you may want to allow the group to use chairs or other items from around the room if the exercise seems too difficult.

Processing suggestions

- Discuss how the group approached the problem. Who took on leadership roles? Were some people afraid to cross over the barrier? How did the group respond to them? Did some people not want help? How did the group respond to that? Were there different expectations for the males and females in the group?
- What barriers do we face, individually or as a group? How do we deal with these barriers? Who is carrying whom?
- The beginning and ending of this exercise are usually the most difficult. This can illustrate the difficulty of transitions, getting started or completing a project, or the beginning and ending of a group's time together.

Call and Response

Goals	Communication, Trust
Time	15 minutes (not including processing)
Physical contact	None
Physical challenges	Must be able to call out a word, distinguish words in the crowd, and move through the crowd with eyes closed.
Number of participants	10 to 40
Space requirements	A large open space
Materials needed	None
Preparation	Decide on the pairs discussion format (see step 4) tailored to the purpose of the meeting. For example, the pairs could discuss where they are from and thoughts about issues that are pertinent to the goals of the meeting.

Note: With an unformed group, this exercise can be used to help people get to know each other. However, the exercise is somewhat high-risk.

Instructions

1. Ask the group to line up according to birthdays, from January through December. (For an additional challenge, do a silent line-up, as in the LINE-UPS exercise on p. 340.)
2. Once the line is formed, ask the January end to fold around so that it is across from the December end. Each person should have a face-to-face partner. If there is an uneven number of people, a facilitator should participate.
3. Tell the partners to shake hands and introduce themselves to each other.
4. Tell the group that when they reunite with their partners they are to have a brief discussion (2-5 minutes), and give them the format for the discussion.
5. Each pair then decides on a two-word phrase or compound word—examples are "peanut butter," "football," "ice cream"—and each partner takes one of the words as their own.
6. Go down the line and have each pair announce its word/phrase to be sure there are no duplications. (If there is a duplication, the second pair to announce the word/phrase must choose something else. This also applies to the duplication of half of the word or phrase, such as if one pair says "football" and a later pair says "baseball.")
7. The two lines then go to opposite sides of the room and mix themselves up so they are not lined up as they were before.
8. Everyone closes their eyes and puts their "bumpers" up—arms bent in front with palms forward.
9. Each person calls out their word and listens for their partner's word, and then moves slowly through the crowd with the goal of meeting up with the partner.
10. When the pairs meet, people open their eyes and talk (following the format that you gave earlier).
11. When all pairs have had a few moments to talk, call time.

Processing suggestions

- The exercise involved two different types of communication with partners (the "call and response" and the discussion). Did both styles serve their purposes effectively? Could they have been interchanged? What kinds of situations are the different styles best suited for?
- Did people have problems trying to find their partners? What caused problems?
- How did you choose your matching words?
- How do we identify our allies and those with similar interests? There are positive ways to do this (for example, joining an interest group) and negative ways (for example, gang colors).

- What was it like moving with your eyes closed? You can talk about the need to move slowly through things when you aren't fully aware of the situation.
- The exercise could also be used to discuss the importance of "meeting people halfway."

Concentric Circles

Goal	Communication, Interconnection
Time	20-40 minutes, depending on the number of questions you present for discussion
Physical contact	None
Physical challenges	Minimal
Number of participants	16-76 (ideally, about 30 people)
Space requirements	Open floor space
Materials needed	A chair for each participant
Preparation	Prepare topics (see "Preparing CONCENTRIC CIRCLES Topics").

Note: CONCENTRIC CIRCLES is a powerful bonding exercise because it gives individuals the opportunity to share their thoughts and experiences with others in one-on-one conversations. Because people are given an ordered situation in which to have these conversations, they are able to build relationships with others without the pressure or awkwardness that are often part of social interactions.

Note: If the group has an uneven number of people, a facilitator should participate in the circles. However, if there is not a second facilitator to keep time, you can either arrange one set of chairs as a triad or have one chair outside the circle in which a different person will sit out each round.

Preparing CONCENTRIC CIRCLES Topics

How you choose topics will be driven by your purpose for doing CONCENTRIC CIRCLES. For example, you might want to inspire the group to have an in-depth discussion about a topic, or the group might be on the verge of making an important decision and you want to be sure everyone has put some thought into various aspects of the decision.

It is best to structure the topics so that they build on each other and move forward chronologically. For example, you might begin by asking people to reflect on aspects of their own early lives, move toward the issues that will be addressed in the work section of the agenda, then move to more policy-oriented topics, and end with a chance for pairs to talk about the future.

The following set of topics would be appropriate for a training session for student teachers:

- Talk about the neighborhood you grew up in and some of your earliest memories.
- Talk about your favorite and least favorite teacher from elementary school.
- Talk about a time that you broke a rule, and what happened.
- Talk about what you want and need out of your education.
- Talk about what you like about teaching, and what are its greatest challenges for you.
- Talk about a lesson plan that worked and one that didn't.
- Talk about your approach to discipline – what works and what doesn't.
- Talk about something that scares you and how you deal with it.
- Talk about something that makes you angry and how you deal with it.
- Talk about standardized testing and how you think it impacts education.
- Talk about how you think racial dynamics affect education.
- Talk about what your hope is for the future of education, and how we can reach that goal.
- Talk about where you hope to be five years from now.

chapter 10 on Warm-up Questions contains many ideas that could be useful in CONCENTRIC CIRCLES.

Instructions

1. Have the group arrange their chairs so that they are facing each other in two circles, one inside the other. You can have the group count off by 2s (1, 2, 1, 2...). Then have all the 1s form their chairs into an inner circle, facing the 2s who were to their left. Or you can simply say that every other person should move their chair to face the person to their left. If the group includes people from different subgroups (for example, teachers and students), tell one subgroup to form the inner circle, so they will be talking with people from the other subgroup rather than to each other.
2. Once the circles have been created, tell the group that they will be having a series of short conversations with a series of partners. They should introduce themselves to each new partner, and they should share the time so that each person has a chance to speak.
3. Give the group a question that each pair is to discuss.
4. After one or two minutes, call time. Allow less time for younger people and more time for older. (Keep the time short enough so that people still have more to say when they need to move on.) Tell the ***inside circle*** to move one seat to the left so that everyone is facing someone new.
5. Remind people to be sure and introduce themselves to their new partners. Then give another question for the new pairs to discuss.
6. In smaller groups, this continues until the inside circle has moved completely around to where they began. In larger groups, have people move 10 to 20 times, depending on how long you can dedicate to the exercise. Adjust the time you give each pair and the number of times you have people move according to the needs of the group and the constraints of the meeting.

Processing suggestions

- In general, it is not necessary to do a formal process of CONCENTRIC CIRCLES, since the value of the experience is in the individual interactions.
- If you are planning a BRAINSTORM (p. 385) or another approach to a group discussion, it is often best to move directly from CONCENTRIC CIRCLES into that work.

Variation – Concentric Vision

Goals	Group introspection, Different perspectives
Preparation	Prepare a one-to-three minute visualization about a subject that you want to focus on. For example, the visualization could be about an ideal community or school, friendship, trusting relationships, or an effective work activity. (See VISUALIZATION in chapter 17.) Then prepare CONCENTRIC CIRCLES topics that relate to the visualization.

Instructions

1. Ask the group to sit quietly with eyes closed.
2. Read the visualization slowly.
3. Have the group move their chairs into concentric circles.
4. Follow the format for CONCENTRIC CIRCLES to discuss the questions.

Additional processing suggestion

- This exercise can be used to help group members to get a clear vision of a common goal, or to show how people can have varying perceptions of the same reality.

Variation – Gab Fest

Additional goal	Surfacing group dynamics
Physical challenges	Moving around the room
Number of participants	15-30
Space requirements	Open floor space enclosed by a circle of chairs
Preparation	Prepare questions (see "Preparing CONCENTRIC CIRCLES Topics"). Set up chairs in a circle.
Materials	A boom box with a tape or CD (optional)

Note: This exercise can be an effective segue into a Brainstorm or discussion. It should only be done with a formed group in which finding partners to talk with will not be awkward for people.

Note: See FILL THE SPACE, SHAKE THE HAND (p. 282) for a more structured way to begin this exercise.

Instructions

1. Tell the group to stand up and start walking around inside the circle of chairs, as if they were at a party. If you have music available, start playing it.
2. After a short time, stop the music or call time and tell the group members to turn around and find a person close to them to talk to.
3. Make sure that everyone is paired. If there is an odd number in the group, you can join the group, or you can point out three people to make a triad. (If you join the discussion, pay careful attention to keeping time.)
4. Read off the question and tell the group that they have about a minute to discuss it, being sure to share the time so each person has a chance to speak.
5. When the time is up, call time and/or turn up the music and tell people to mingle as they did before.
6. Repeat this process for the number of questions that are prepared.

Additional processing suggestions

- This exercise can be used to discuss group dynamics at an event (such as a party) or issues such as anxiety that people often feel at social events and ways to make people feel comfortable socializing. What did it feel like when people were choosing their partners?
- There may also be issues of dynamics within the group that come out of the exercise. What was it like choosing someone to talk with? How did you choose whom to talk with?
- You can also use this exercise to bring up issues of side conversations in a group. Was it difficult to have a conversation with people talking all around you? Did you find your attention wandering to other conversations?

Conversation Web

Goals	Communication, Group introspection, Surfacing group dynamics, Interconnection, Different perspectives
Time	Depends on how much time you allow for each person to speak
Physical contact	None
Physical challenges	None
Number of participants	Best with no more than 20
Space requirements	Open floor space is ideal, but could also be done around a table.
Materials needed	None
Preparation	Decide the subject for the conversation and how much time you want to allow for people to speak.

Note: If there are enough staff, one or more people should be along the route as monitors.

Instructions

1. People sit in a circle.
2. Introduce the subject that the exercise will be addressing, tell the group the limit on how long each person can speak, and ask for a volunteer to begin.
3. The first person addresses a comment about the subject to any other person in the circle.
4. That person answers the comment by addressing another comment to another person.
5. This continues until everyone in the circle has spoken. (Each person speaks only once.)
6. The last person speaks to the person who began.

Processing suggestions

- How did it feel to not be able to speak if you wanted to address another person's comments?
- What points or issues were brought up that did not get carried forward in the conversation? How can the group address those issues, either now or in the future?
- Was it difficult to decide to whom to address your comment?
- How did it feel to wait to have someone speak to you?
- This exercise was a public/private conversation, since you were told to speak directly to one person, yet your comments were heard by everyone. What are the advantages and disadvantages of this kind of discourse?
- Did the path of this conversation lead to a better understanding of the issue we were discussing?

Variation – Connection Web

Physical challenges	Must be able to throw a ball of yarn to someone else (but another participant could help with this).
Materials needed	A ball of yarn long enough to create a web connecting everyone in the circle

Instructions

1. Have the group stand in a circle.
2. This exercise is like CONVERSATION WEB except that people are standing and they also create a physical web with the yarn. To begin, the first person to speak holds the end of the ball of yarn and throws the ball to the person they speak to.
3. The next person holds the yarn and throws the ball to the person they speak to, etc. (See WEB OF CONNECTION, p. 374.)

Additional processing suggestions

- The web of commentary about the topic is symbolized by the web of yarn.
- What pattern did the yarn create? How do our conversations create real things in the world?

Finding the Path

Goals	Group problem solving, Surfacing group dynamics, Communication
Time	At least 15-20 minutes (not including processing)
Physical contact	None
Physical challenges	Must be able to move across a grid on the floor.
Number of participants	5-15
Space requirements	Open floor space
Materials needed	Masking tape
Preparation	See "Creating the Grid."

Creating the Grid

1. Use the tape to create a large rectangle on the floor, then add lines within the rectangle to create a grid of whatever size you think is appropriate for the group. A grid that is 10 blocks by 6 blocks works well for a group of 10-12 people. The more blocks in the grid, the more difficult the task will be for the group and the longer the exercise will take to complete.
2. Draw the same grid on a piece of paper.
3. Mark the grid on your paper to create a path from one side of the rectangle to the opposite side. The blocks in the path must be adjacent or diagonal to one another. The path cannot lead backwards—forwards or sideways only. See the example of a path below.
4. Keep the path out of sight of group members.

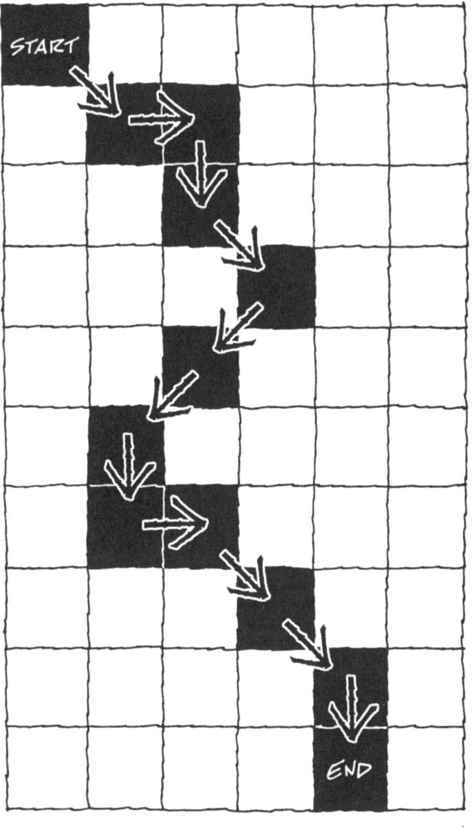

Note: You can increase the challenge by setting a time limit.

Instructions

1. Have the group line up at one end of the grid.
2. Instruct the group that that they cannot communicate with each other verbally or nonverbally during the exercise. They must be silent and they cannot write notes, make maps, or place any objects on the grid.
3. Tell them that the goal is for the group to figure out the path through the grid and for everyone, in consecutive order, to walk the path correctly.
4. The first participant steps into the grid. When they step into a block that is on the path, remain silent and let them continue. If they step into a block that is not on the path, say "no." They must then step out of the grid and go to the end of the line.
5. The person next in line then steps into a block and tries in the same way to determine the correct path.
6. When someone steps in a block that is not on the path, even if by accident, everyone who has made it through the grid must go back to the beginning.

Processing suggestions

- Relate the exercise to the mission, goals, or task of the group and how people must work together, deal with setbacks, etc. How did people feel when one person made a mistake? What did it feel like to have to go back to the beginning? Do things sometimes happen in the group that set the whole group back? How does this group deal with setbacks?
- Finding the path is an objective that the whole group has to achieve together. Did the group figure out a plan of action for how they could work together? How did people support each other?
- The exercise illustrates the importance of learning from others' experiences. Were people quick to do this or not? How can the group learn from others in their work together?
- Did people try to bend the rules?
- Were there clear leaders in this process? Was the leadership shared?
- You can also use this exercise to talk about obstacles, setbacks, and supports that people have to deal with on a societal level. How do we find the right path for ourselves? What institutions in society are set up to "send people back"? How do we as individuals react when someone sends us back as a group—for example, when someone doesn't confront a racial remark?

Variation: Two-Team Pathfinding

Additional goals	Interconnection, Different perspectives

Note: This exercise works best with two facilitators.

Note: This exercise can be helpful for groups that are experiencing factionalism.

Instructions

1. Divide the group into two teams.
2. Have the teams stand on opposite ends of the grid (on the sides with the start points/end points). A facilitator stands with each team to monitor the team's movement through the grid.
3. The teams begin traveling through the grid one person at a time, following the same rules as for FINDING THE PATH.
4. At some point, it is likely that someone will realize that the teams' paths are identical, but in reverse order. Notice if or when a team discovers that they can use this fact to learn from the other team, but do not comment on it during the exercise.
5. This exercise is not set up to be a race or a competition. However, if the teams do begin to compete, don't discourage this. Instead, use it as a processing point at the end of the exercise.
6. Depending on your purpose for choosing this exercise, you can end it either when one person from each team completes the path or when all team members complete it.

Additional processing suggestions

- We may be so focused on our own problem that we only look at it from one perspective, whereas sometimes we may find the answer by looking around and seeing what we can learn from others' experiences.
- If the teams race or compete, you can raise points about creating divisions or people competing against one another instead of working together.
- At what point did a team realize that their way out was the same as the other team's way in? Did they let the other team know this information, or did they keep it to themselves?
- The exercise illustrates people coming from different directions and heading for conflict. How did people manage to share the same space as they passed each other? Are there parallels to how people might deal with factionalism in the group or in society?

Variation – Path Ahead

Additional goal	Group introspection
Time	25-30 minutes (not including processing)
Physical contact	Requires the whole group to squeeze into a small space.
Physical challenges	Must be able to move across the grid on the floor. Could require the ability to balance, or to be surrounded by a lot of people.
Number of participants	Fewer than 20
Preparation	See "Setting It Up."

Note: This exercise is a combination of FINDING THE PATH and ALL ABOARD, ALL AHEAD (p. 300). It is best if the group has done one or both of these exercises previously.

Setting It Up

- Follow the preparation instructions for FINDING THE PATH.
- In addition, create a small, enclosed space (square or rectangle) at the end of the grid, following the preparation instructions for ALL ABOARD (p. 299). This space should be separated from the grid at a distance that is far enough away to be challenging but close enough to be possible.

Instructions

1. Follow the instructions for FINDING THE PATH.
2. When the first individual makes it through the grid successfully, that person must step or jump from the final square of the grid into the additional box and remain there. Each group member must complete the grid successfully and get into the box, as described in ALL ABOARD/ALL AHEAD.
3. If anyone steps on the floor in between the grid and the box or steps out of the box, the entire group must return to the beginning of the grid and start again.
4. Once everyone is in the box, they need to remain there until they have done something that you choose. This can be something quick, such as saying "We did it!" or counting to ten, or it can take more time, such as singing "Row, Row, Row Your Boat" three times.

Additional processing suggestions

- If the group is moving into another phase of their work or has a difficult project ahead, you can use this exercise to discuss what will be needed to reach their goals and to overcome setbacks.
- Most groups must go through a difficult process of learning to communicate, work together effectively, and build trust before coming to a common place. Each individual must do their part to make it work.
- What was difficult or easy for this group to complete this task and why?
- What strategies worked or didn't work?
- How did people feel if they were sent back? Were they discouraged, or ready to try again?
- You can use this exercise to talk about the importance of completing both individual and group goals. Once people were in the box, did they help each other out, or disengage?

Group Sculpture

Goals	Creativity, Group introspection
Time	15-20 minutes (not including processing)
Physical contact	Extensive for those who volunteer
Physical challenges	Must be able to move and hold a pose.
Number of participants	12-30
Space requirements	Open floor space
Materials needed	None
Preparation	Decide what you want the sculpture to represent. See "Choosing the Theme."

Note: This exercise is high-risk because it requires extensive physical contact. It should be done only in groups when there is a high level of trust.

Choosing the Theme

- You can use GROUP SCULPTURE to let the group recreate a scene from their work, examine it, and make adjustments to it. For this reason, it is a useful tool for evaluating their work and reflecting on what they could have done better.
- GROUP SCULPTURE could be used to create a common vision of a specific event that the group is planning.
- You can use the exercise to help the group examine a theme or an issue that is relevant to their work.

Instructions

1. Ask for a volunteer to be the "sculptor."
2. Ask for three or four volunteers to be the "clay" for the sculpture. Have them stand at the front of the group.
3. Tell the sculptor to create a scene about the theme you have chosen. The sculptor can move the clay people into positions, and the clay people must hold their positions. Make sure that the sculptor is respectful of the volunteers' bodies and physical space.
4. The sculptor then explains the finished sculpture to the group.
5. You can have other members of the group come up and adjust the scene, or you can ask how the scene could have been improved, and have the volunteers make their own adjustments.
6. Repeat with new clay volunteers and a new sculptor, if time allows.

Processing suggestions

- When creating a vision for a project or event, collaboration is very important. All members of the group offer different perspectives, and it is important to voice and incorporate those different perspectives into the work of the group. Did the sculptor's original representation reflect how you would have depicted the scene/theme?
- This exercise can be used to talk about the value of receiving feedback on one's work. What did the sculptor think about changes people made after the sculpture was "complete"? Was it difficult or easy to see your work being changed? Did you think the changes made the scene better?
- How did those who were the "clay" feel while they were being shaped? Did they have their own ideas of how they wanted to be positioned?

Human Machine

Goals	Group introspection, Personal introspection
Time	15 minutes (not including processing)
Physical contact	Minimal
Physical challenges	Must be able to contribute in some way to the machine.
Number of participants	8-20
Space requirements	Open floor space
Materials needed	A slip of paper for each group member
Preparation	Prepare slips of paper with actions on them. See "Actions."

Actions

The actions should be fairly simple, such as "Jump up and down on your left foot." You can also combine actions and noises, such as "Spin around and say 'beep, beep.'" Some possible HUMAN MACHINE actions are:

- Do deep knee bends.
- Spin around with your arms out, and sound like a helicopter.
- Pat your head and rub your stomach.
- Do jumping jacks while counting to ten.
- Jump up and down and say "boing, boing."
- Flap your arms.
- Lean over and touch your toes, then stand and reach for the sky.
- Imitate the hands of a clock and say "tick, tock, tick, tock."

Instructions

1. Give each person in the group a slip of paper.
2. Either ask for a volunteer or point to someone. That person must go into the center of the circle and do the action described on their paper. (If you choose someone to go first, try to pick someone who can do this without feeling unduly embarrassed.) Leave the first person alone in the center for a few moments.
3. Then point to another person, who must join the first, and continue pointing to people one at a time. As each person goes into the center of the circle, they add their action to the actions of the people already there, so that everyone together creates one "human machine."
4. When there's only one person left outside the center, wait a minute before pointing to that person to join.

Processing suggestions

- The HUMAN MACHINE deals with the way the group fits together and the functionality of the "machine" they create.
- Did the machine fit together?
- Was there one machine or were there several? What do you think the machine was? What did it do?
- People with different functions and different styles can come together to create a functional and

productive "machine."

- The exercise also deals with people's fears of looking foolish in front of the group. Throughout this exercise, people are typically very conscious of themselves and what they are doing while they are also looking at other members of the group.
- What was it like to be out in front of the group doing your motion—embarrassing, scary, fun?
- What did you think about the motions that other people were making?
- How did the last person left outside the center feel about that?
- The exercise illustrates how conformity is predicated on the context. Initially those who had to go in the circle were the nonconformists who felt embarrassed, but as the exercise progressed those who were left out (especially the last person) wanted to be part of what was happening.

Variation – Advanced Human Machine

Preparation	None

Instructions

1. Do not prepare actions ahead of time. Instead, let individuals come up with their own actions and sounds as the machine is being created.
2. Ask for a volunteer to come up and begin the exercise.
3. Instruct the group to come up one at a time when they are ready and add on to the machine.

Additional processing suggestions

- You can use this exercise to talk about identifying what needs to be done in the group or in people's work, and then taking the initiative to fill those needs.
- What motions did people choose to make? Did the motions fit into the machine? How did they choose these motions?
- Did people recognize a need for the machine? How does this group recognize and fill its own needs?

Human Maze

Goals	Surfacing group dynamics, Communication
Time	15-30 minutes (not including processing)
Physical contact	Participants can choose the amount.
Physical challenges	Must be able to move easily.
Number of participants	12-20
Space requirements	Open floor space
Materials needed	A chair and a blindfold
Preparation	None

Instructions

1. Ask for a volunteer to be the "maze-walker." Blindfold this person and have them sit in the chair until the maze has been set up.
2. The rest of the group sets up a maze or obstacle course with their bodies. They can work alone, in pairs, or in small groups to form the maze. For example, two people might stand facing each other making a bridge with their arms for the maze-walker to go under, while someone else gets down on all fours for the maze-walker to step over.
3. Once the entire group has become part of the maze, walk through it once yourself to make sure that the course is safe and that everyone understands which way the maze-walker is supposed to go.
4. Ask the maze-walker to stand up and try to walk through the maze, with the blindfold still on. The rest of the group should try to direct the person through the maze using sounds only. They are not allowed to speak or make noises that sound like words. Walk close to the maze-walker to prevent tripping or falling, but avoid touching or guiding the person unless it is necessary for safety.
5. Once the maze-walker has completed the course, ask for another volunteer and create a new maze.

Processing suggestions

- In this exercise, one member of the group is completely dependent on the rest for direction and safety. Did the group take their role seriously? Did they give good directions or mixed messages? Does the group take care of its vulnerable members or take advantage of their vulnerability?
- The maze-walker may be hearing a lot of different noises and sounds from the group. Their job is to determine what the sounds mean and how to translate them into actions.
- What noises helped the volunteer navigate the maze? Were the messages from the group clear or confusing?
- How did it feel to be blindfolded? Did it feel safe or unsafe?
- What process did the group go through to construct the maze? Did people work alone, only with their friends, or with others in the group that they do not usually connect with? How did people decide to work together?

Variation – Guided Maze

Instructions

1. Ask for someone to act as the maze-walker's guide.
2. In this version, only the guide makes noises to direct the maze-walker through the maze. The guide should walk along with the maze-walker to make sure no one gets hurt. (You should also be monitoring for safety.)

Additional processing suggestions

- In this version of the exercise, the dynamic of dependency is magnified in the relationship between the maze-walker and the guide. Did having a guide make the blindfolded person feel more or less secure?
- What was the attitude of the guide toward the job?
- Did others in the group feel more or less responsibility to help?

Machine-O-Rama

Goals	Group problem solving, Introspection, Surfacing group dynamics, Creativity
Time	15 minutes (not including processing)
Physical contact	Depends on how people configure their machine.
Physical challenges	Groups can work with individuals' needs.
Number of participants	8-20
Space requirements	Open floor space
Materials needed	Slips of paper
Preparation	For each small group that you anticipate, prepare a slip of paper with the name of a machine (for example: boom box, car, computer, pay phone).

Instructions

1. Divide the group into small groups of three to six people.
2. Give each group one of the slips of paper, and tell them they have five minutes to figure out how to "become" the machine, with each group member participating.
3. After the preparation time, have the groups take turns presenting their creations to the large group. You can either have the groups tell everyone what they represent or have the others guess.

Processing suggestions

- This exercise can be used to help people think about the tasks they are called on to do. Which ones build on their strengths and which help them grow?
- It also is useful for surfacing the dynamics in the group. How did groups decide who would be what part of the machine? What parts did you focus on? What parts did you leave out?
- If the group guessed what the machine was, did they guess correctly? What would have helped them understand the machine better?

Obstacle Course

Goals	Surfacing group dynamics, Group introspection
Time	15-30 minutes (not including processing)
Physical contact	None
Physical challenges	Must be able to do the tasks in the obstacle course.
Number of participants	8-15
Space requirements	Open floor space or a long hallway
Materials needed	A piece of paper and a marker for each group member, masking tape
Preparation	None

Note: With a group of ten or more, depending on how much time you have for this exercise you may want to pair people up to create stations.

Instructions

1. Give each person a piece of paper and a marker, and have the group spread out throughout the space.
2. Each person is to create a specific task that needs to be completed at their station, and to describe the task in words or drawings on their paper. Tasks must be brief, doable by everyone in the group, and in good taste. Examples of tasks are: "Hop on one foot five times," "Sing two lines from a song," "Put your index fingers on your nose and take a deep breath," or "Tap out a beat on your knees."
3. Go down the line and have each person demonstrate the task for their station. When each demonstration is completed, tape the paper on the wall or floor.
4. Once the group has learned what each step of the course is, have them line up at one end of the course and go through the course one by one.

Processing suggestions

- Discuss the kinds of obstacles that people came up with (creative, funny, hard, embarrassing), and how it felt to confront these obstacles.
- Do we place obstacles in each other's way in the course of our work together?
- Discuss the strategies that people used to get through the course and how people responded to frustration. What can we learn from the way people worked to overcome the obstacles?
- Obstacles can be an opportunity for growth for those who are willing to work to overcome them.

Picture Wall

Goals	Group introspection, Different perspectives
Time	20-30 minutes (not including processing)
Physical contact	None
Physical challenges	Minimal
Number of participants	8-15
Space requirements	A room with empty wall space
Materials needed	Markers and several pieces of flip chart paper or a length of butcher paper to extend over 6-10 feet of wall space
Preparation	Hang the paper on the wall horizontally. If using flip chart paper, hang the pieces end to end. Prepare 3-5 questions related to the work of the group. (See "Questions.") Write these on a separate piece of paper and hang it up.

Questions

The questions you choose will depend on your reasons for doing the exercise and the issues or topics that you want the group to think about. Examples of questions that could be used are:

How do drugs affect this school?
What is your favorite place in this building/this community?
What are the most important issues in this community?
What was a great experience for you this week?
What is one of your favorite leisure-time activities?

The 3-5 questions should be related. For example, if you are using the exercise to prepare the group to evaluate an event, questions might be:

What is something you remember from this event?
What was the highlight?
What was the lowlight?
What was your role in the event?

Instructions

1. Give each participant a marker.
2. Tell people they have ten minutes to draw a picture for each question. Everyone works at the same time, and people can draw their pictures anywhere on the paper.
3. When time is up, have people sit facing the picture wall.
4. Ask people to come up one at a time, point out their drawings and explain each one. With a larger group, ask people to keep their explanations brief.

Processing suggestions

- Comment on the similarities and differences in the ways people answered the questions through drawing. Did common themes emerge? Was there more or less difference in people's answers than expected?
- This exercise can highlight that it is important for people to find different ways to express themselves. Some people may be better at certain modes of communication than at others.
- This exercise will also illustrate the levels of trust in the group. Were the pictures and/or verbal descriptions specific and detailed, or vague and generalized? How deep were people willing to go?

The River Wild

Goals	Group problem solving, Surfacing group dynamics
Time	10-20 minutes (not including processing)
Physical contact	Contact is likely as people try to cross the "river."
Physical challenges	Must be able to cross from one side of the room to the other by stepping only on the "steppingstone" papers.
Number of participants	8-15
Space requirements	Open floor space
Materials needed	Masking tape and 2-4 pieces of paper (more or less depending on the ability of the group and the width of the "river")
Preparation	Mark two parallel lines 8-10 feet apart on the floor. The lines should be long enough to allow the whole group to stand shoulder-to-shoulder along one of them. Note: Depending on your purposes for doing this exercise, you may want to add a time limit (such as five minutes) for the whole group to cross and count down the minutes. This raises the stakes and brings out a lot of energy as the time limit nears. You can also divide the group into teams and have them compete to cross the river first.

Instructions

1. Explain to the group that they are on a journey and they need to cross this raging river (point to space between the two lines). To get across, they must use magical steppingstones, which are the pieces of paper.
2. Ask the group to stand behind one of the lines in the order that they want to cross the river. Give the first person in line the steppingstones.
3. Explain the rules:
   - If someone steps into the river without being on a steppingstone, they will be swept back to the shore where they started. They must go to the end of the line to await another turn to cross.
   - The stones must be in physical contact with a member of the group (hands or feet) at all times. If the group loses contact with a stone, even for a second, the stone is considered to be swept away by the river. (You will remove the paper.)
   - They can move the stones an unlimited number of times.
   - All members of the group must get across the river to complete the task.
4. Give the signal to begin.

Processing suggestions

- The group may struggle to come up with an effective strategy for getting across the river, and a lot of discussion can be generated out of what happened as they tried to solve the problem. Was everyone involved in problem-solving?
- Did the group take the time to develop a strategy, or did they start across without one? How does this relate to the way the group deals with other problems they face?
- If the group is having difficulty developing effective strategies in their work, does this experience illuminate that issue?
- Were any of the steppingstones swept away? How did the group feel when this resource was lost? Did they face the loss as a challenge or become discouraged? How does this group face setbacks?
- This exercise can bring out how a group supports members who aren't as skilled or motivated in a particular area. If someone is unable or unwilling to jump a distance, how did others react to

that? How did the group provide the level of support necessary to get that individual across?
- Conversely, there may be group members who cross the river easily but who are not very supportive of others—who get to the other side and just sit down. This can be just as much of a hindrance to the group as people who are more timid or uncoordinated.
- If there was a time limit, how did that affect the group's planning, decision-making, and effort?
- How did it feel when everyone had crossed the river?

Variation – Trivia River Wild

Additional goal	Reinforcing information
Preparation	Write some questions (enough for each person in the group) about a topic the group is working on.

Instructions

1. Give the group only two steppingstones to start.
2. After each person gets across the river, ask the group one of the questions. If the group is able to answer correctly, give them another steppingstone.

Additional processing suggestions

- How did it feel to answer incorrectly? How did the group react to incorrect answers and the failure to gain additional resources?
- What effect did additional steppingstones have on the group's effort? Were people still careful and focused when crossing, or were some of the stones lost due to carelessness? Sometimes we may let our own attention and responsibility slide when we have additional resources and support.
- You can relate this exercise to the importance of learning and education, and talk about how knowledge can move you forward in life and give you access to resources. The consequences of not educating yourself may mean that you have fewer resources with which to tackle obstacles in life.

Variation – Blindfold River Wild

Additional goal	Interconnection
Materials	One or more blindfolds

Note: This variation is higher risk, because members of the group are responsible for the physical safety of the blindfolded participant(s).

Instructions

1. Follow the instructions for THE RIVER WILD, except that before you begin ask for 1-3 group members to volunteer to be blindfolded for the exercise.

Additional processing suggestions

- How did it feel to be blindfolded? Did you trust those around you to keep you on the steppingstones? Do we trust each other to keep us safe in this group?
- How did people treat those with blindfolds on? Did everyone in the group take care of them, or were they left with little direction? Were they seen as a hindrance to the group's progress? You can use this exercise to talk about how the group treats each other's strengths and weaknesses. Are we always careful and helpful with people's different abilities?

Variation – River Wild Race

Instructions

1. Divide the group into teams (with at least four people in each team).
2. Give the teams preparation time of five minutes, ideally in separate spaces.
3. Have the teams race to see who can get their whole team across first.

Additional processing suggestions

- Did planning time help the teams be more efficient in crossing? In our work, does this group use time to plan, or does it rush into projects without planning?
- How were the teams' strategies similar and different? Which strategies worked best? Did any teams learn from watching the successes and mistakes of the others?
- This exercise can also be used to bring up issues of competition versus collaboration, and the difference between supporting your team and disparaging other teams. How did the fact that it was a race influence the teams' efforts? Is competition helpful or hurtful? You can also talk about how this group could support other groups with the same goals as theirs.

Sardines

Goals	Interconnection, Organizing, Planning
Time	15 minutes (not including processing)
Physical contact	Must squeeze into a small place with the rest of the group.
Physical challenges	Must be able to walk around the whole area used for the exercise, and to hide with the rest of the group.
Number of participants	10-15
Space requirements	This exercise is best played in an area of ample size that has lots of nooks and crannies. An open gymnasium is not a good choice; a large, multi-room floor space is ideal.
Materials needed	None
Preparation	None

Note: Because of the close physical proximity required, this exercise can be very high-risk.

Instructions

1. Ask for a volunteer to be "it."
2. While the rest of the group counts to 100, "it" finds a hiding place. This should be a place that will be difficult to find but can accommodate many people.
3. At the end of the count, everyone starts to search for "it." In a large group, send members out in pairs at ten-second intervals (so there will not be a pack walking around together). The goal is to

find "it" without alerting other people to where "it" is hiding.
4. When someone finds "it," they must join "it" in hiding by sharing the hiding place, and trying to remain unseen by the other searchers.
5. The exercise continues until everyone has joined "it" in the hiding place.

Processing suggestions

- This exercise can be used to talk about the group all "being in the same place" in terms of their goals or strategies.
- It can be used to talk about doing outreach for an event (everyone eventually getting the message/finding "it"). How do people's strategies for hiding and for looking relate to outreach?
- Who found "it" first? Who found "it" last? Did the number of people hiding with "it" correspond to how easy/hard it was to find "it"?
- Other possible areas of processing are peer pressure and faddism (people imitating others) and people looking outside themselves for "it" (something to make them feel fulfilled).
- Note that this is not an exercise to build trust, as players must be sneaky to join "it" without being seen.

Surfing the Web

Goals	Trust, Surfacing group dynamics, Communication, Group problem solving
Time	10-20 minutes (not including processing)
Physical contact	Might require people helping each other through the web.
Physical challenges	Must be able to get through the "web," which can be more or less challenging depending on how it is set up.
Number of participants	8-15
Space requirements	Open floor space and places to hang the web, such as hooks, high furniture, or sturdy lamps. Can also be done outside using trees.
Materials needed	Twine or thin rope
Preparation	See "Setting Up the Web."

Note: This exercise should be done only with a formed group, and a group that will be sensitive around weight/body issues.

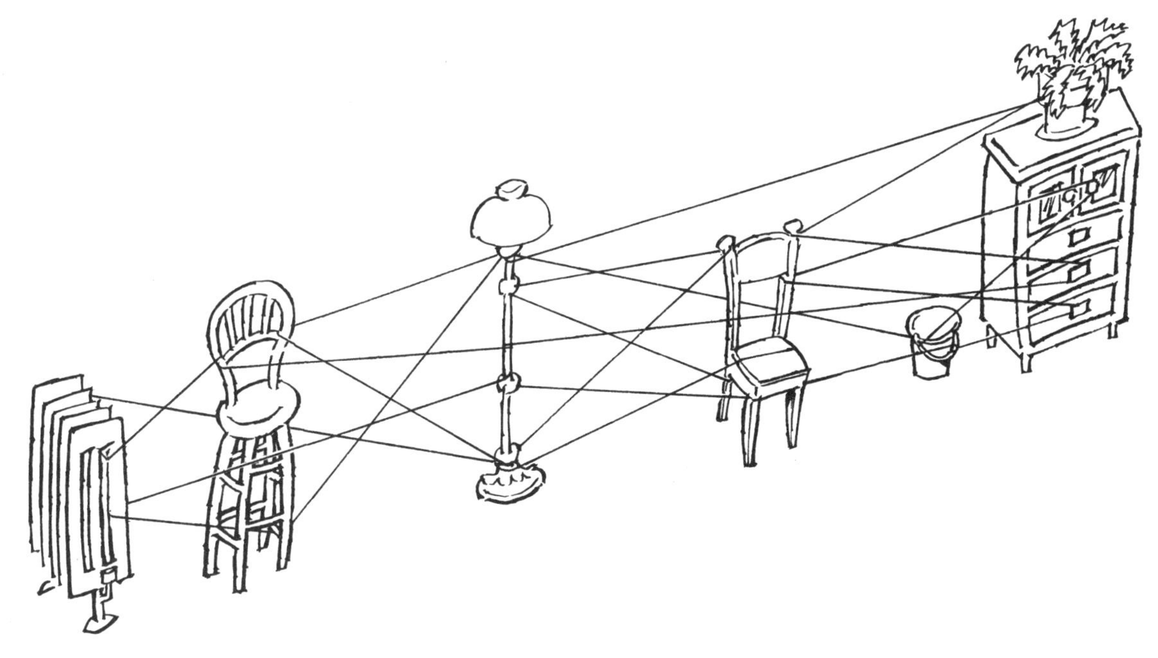

Setting Up the Web

Line up several objects, such as lamps, chairs, or bookcases. Use the twine or rope to connect the objects in such a way that you create a web. The web should have different sized spaces in it and holes low enough and big enough for people to get through.

Instructions

1. The goal of this exercise is for everyone in the group to get through the web without touching the twine or using props (such as chairs). Everyone can use the same hole in the web, or people can use different holes. As a variation, you can set rules about how people get through the web, such as that only two people are allowed to go through any particular hole. Stress that there is no competition involved.
2. People should "spot" each other on either side of the web, providing help so that those going through the web don't fall.

3. Depending on how difficult you want the exercise to be and on what dynamics you want to surface, you may want to send the whole group back to the starting side if one person touches the twine
4. If the group is having trouble, you can add a prop (such as a chair) to help them out.

Processing suggestions

- How did the group decide to get through? What techniques did they try? Did they make a plan, or just start moving through the web?
- Who took a leadership role?
- How did the group deal with the limitations of which holes people could fit through?
- If there were rules about how many people could go through the holes, what impact did this have on the group's progress? Sometimes having structure and rules forces people to use their creativity to solve problems.
- Were people focused on just getting themselves through, or on seeing that the whole group got through? How does this relate to how the group approaches difficult tasks or problems in general?
- What webs are there in our lives that we can get stuck in? How can we as a group help each other through those webs?

Who Am I?

Goals	Personal introspection, Trust, Communication
Time	15-30 minutes (not including processing)
Physical contact	None
Physical challenges	Moving from chair to chair
Number of participants	10-20
Space requirements	Open floor space
Materials needed	Pens or pencils and large sticky notes
Preparation	None

Instructions

1. Have the group sit in a circle. Facilitators should also be in the circle and participate.
2. Give each person a sticky note and a pencil.
3. Tell people to write five things about themselves on their sticky notes. Give some examples, such as: your favorite color, your favorite food, a career you are interested in pursuing, something you're afraid of, your favorite game as a child, what countries you have visited. Tell them to try to write some things that others in the group may not know.
4. When people have finished, have them fold the notes over to hide what is written, but leave the adhesive strip outside.
5. Collect the notes and stick them randomly on a flip chart or blackboard.
6. Take one note and read it to the group.
7. Ask that people raise their hands if they think they know who wrote the note (but the person who wrote the note should not raise their hand).
8. Call on the first person whose hand was up. If that person's guess is right, have them come up and read the next note. If the guess was wrong, call on the next person. The group has three tries to figure out who wrote the note. If no one guesses correctly by the third guess, ask the person who wrote the note to stand up. They then come and read the next note.
9. Continue until all the notes have been read.

Processing suggestions

- This exercise can be used to explore how well the members of a group know each other, and what assumptions they make about each other. Were some people's descriptions easier to guess than others? Was anyone surprised by something that was shared?
- The exercise also is a gauge of how much the group trusts each other. How did people choose what to write about? Did people try to hide themselves, or did they write things that others would be able to identify them by easily? How much do people hide or share in this group? How people choose to describe or show themselves can be related to the level of trust that they feel.
- It can also be an illustration of the fact that sometimes people are more comfortable writing about themselves than they are speaking about themselves. (Thus it is a good exercise when a group is working on any sort of written collection of information, such as a survey.)

Chapter 13

In-Your-Chair Springboard Exercises

Without requiring much physical movement, these exercises bring a feeling of movement to a meeting, as well as laughter, challenge, engagement, and insight into the work that the group will be doing.

The ideal configuration for most of the exercises is to have the group seated in a circle. However, they also work well in a classroom with desks, and many can be done in meetings where people are seated around a conference table (though it is almost always best to avoid having meetings around conference tables).

Audience-Style

Most of these exercises involve the active participation of everyone in the group. A few, however, are "audience style," with a small number of people coming up in front of the group as the most active participants for a time. Even in these exercises, though, the rest of the group has a role to play, as well as opportunities to take on more active roles if they wish. Note that you can use some of these exercises with very large groups, such as people sitting in an auditorium or at banquet tables. The "audience-style" exercises are:

More Exercises

The following exercises in other chapters can also be done "In-Your-Chair" style:

Back-to-Back Draw

Goals	Communication, Focus
Time	15-20 minutes (not including processing)
Physical contact	None
Physical challenges	Must be able to use a pencil and paper to draw.
Number of participants	12-30
Space requirements	Space for people to sit with their backs to each other, either in chairs or on the floor.
Materials needed	Two sheets of paper for everyone. Half of the group will need a pen or pencil and a hard surface (such as a clipboard, a book, or a piece of cardboard) to lean on as they draw.
Preparation	Prepare enough sheets of paper for everyone in the group to have two. Mark a dot in the middle of each sheet. Then on half of these, draw a shape or a simple picture (all should be at least slightly different). Arrange two rows of chairs back-to-back, with enough chairs for all participants.

Instructions

1. Assign people to pairs and have the pairs sit down so that their backs are to each other.
2. Give each person in one row a pen or pencil, a sheet with only a dot in the middle, and a clipboard or other hard surface. The people in this row will be the "drawers."
3. Then give each person in the other row a sheet with a shape or picture on it. These people will be the "guides."
4. The task is as follows: Each guide must describe the design on their paper in such a way that their partner can reproduce it on their own paper. The dot in the middle and the edges of the paper can be used as points of reference. The guides must not look at their partners' work. You can either tell the drawers to remain silent or allow them to ask questions; you can have them remain silent up to a certain point and then allow them to ask questions; or you can allow them to ask only a specified number of questions.
5. Each pair works until the drawer has completed the design to the best of their ability. Once everyone has finished, the drawers can compare their designs to the originals.
6. Drawers and guides then switch roles (not seats) and tackle a different design.

Processing suggestions

- Allow the pairs to compare the designs and the reproductions. You may want each pair to show their work to the entire group.
- The exercise illustrates the importance of giving clear and detailed directions. How close were the reproductions to the original designs? Was it easier to give instructions, or to receive them? Did the guides come up with any strategies to help transmit the information to the drawers? What worked and what didn't?
- Talk about assumptions and how powerful (and negative) they can be. The guides may assume that the drawers understand them, while the drawers may make assumptions about what the guides are saying.
- If the drawers had to remain silent, or could only ask a certain number of questions, what was that like? Were there any advantages to their limitations on speech? If they switched from silence to speech, how did that change the exercise?
- Groups can create something beautiful and innovative by accident, which is the power of non-judgmental communication in which the creative energies of the group are allowed to flow.

Essence

Goal	Personal introspection
Time	5-10 minutes per round (not including processing)
Physical contact	None
Physical challenges	None
Number of participants	10-20
Space requirements	None
Materials needed	None
Preparation	None

Note: This exercise can be high-risk and is best done with a group that knows each other well.

Instructions

1. Ask for a volunteer to be the "guesser," whose goal is to discover the identity of "it" by asking questions in a specified format. When someone volunteers as the guesser, ask that person to leave the room.
2. Then ask for a volunteer to be "it."
3. The guesser then returns and goes around the circle (or around the room) asking each person a question in this form: "If this person were a ... what would they be?" For example, the guesser could ask, "If this person were a flavor of ice cream, what flavor would they be?" The guesser may not ask questions like "What kind of ice cream does this person like?" Other examples: "If this person were a teacher, what subject would they teach?" "If this person were a car/a sport/a circus performer...."

4. After going around the circle once, the guesser has three tries to guess who "it" is.
5. If the first two tries are not correct, the guesser can ask one question of anyone in the circle before making the third guess.
6. Continue with additional rounds if there is time.

Processing suggestions

- This exercise provides indirect feedback to some group members about how others perceive them. What did people learn from the answers that others gave? Did they like what they heard? Was anything difficult to hear?
- This illustrates that we all have different impressions of and understandings about individual group members and their personalities. It also can demonstrate that group members will have different levels of understanding and knowing about one another. Did people agree or disagree with other people's assessments of "it"? How easy or difficult was it to guess who was "it"?
- Be alert to hurtful or inaccurate comments that may have been made. Acknowledge that this has occurred and try to offer some comfort and support as appropriate.
- The exercise illustrates how people in a group go through a process of learning about each other. Often it takes a while to discover important characteristics in others.

Finding the Fs

Goals	Introspection, Focus
Time	5 minutes (not including processing)
Physical contact	None
Physical challenges	Minimal
Number of participants	5-100
Space requirements	None
Materials needed	A square piece of paper for each group member
Preparation	Prepare squares of paper with one of the "Fs text" paragraphs printed on them. (Everyone in the group should have the same text.)

Fs Text

FEATURE FILMS ARE THE RE-
SULT OF YEARS OF SCIENTI-
FIC STUDY COMBINED WITH
THE EXPERIENCE OF YEARS.

THIS AUTHOR TURNS WORKS OF
SCIENCE FICTION INTO
ECONOMICS, FULFILLING THE
READER'S FANTASIES OF CON-
QUEST INTO ACTS OF HEROES.

Instructions

1. Place a square of paper face down in front of each person.
2. At your signal, people turn over their papers and read the statement on it. They have ten seconds to locate as many occurrences of the letter "F" as they can.
3. When ten seconds are up, ask them to place the squares face down.
4. Answers will probably range from three to seven (there are six Fs in the "Feature films" text and seven in the "This author" text).
5. Ask people to try again, with 15 seconds this time.

Processing suggestions

- What things or people in our lives do we not really see, even though they are right in front of us?
- It is important to pay attention to details, for they are what make up the bigger picture.
- How can we become more aware?

Freeze

Goals	Different perspectives, Acting, Creativity
Time	10-15 minutes (not including processing)
Physical contact	None
Physical challenges	Must be able to move freely.
Number of participants	8-30
Space requirements	None
Materials needed	None
Preparation	None

Note: This is a good exercise for a group that will be working on skits or role plays, but it can be used in other situations as well. It is a fairly high-risk exercise because it asks people to put themselves forward strongly in the group. Therefore, it is best when used with a group that is very comfortable with each other or that has had acting experience.

Guidelines

There are three guidelines for this exercise:

- Anyone who gets up to act must go along with whatever the other person initiates. For example, if one actor says, "Mom, I missed you!" the other actor must assume the role of the mother. They cannot say, "No, I don't want to be the mother; I'd rather be a friend."
- People in the audience should say "Freeze" before they have thought about what they will act out. Encourage the group to be spontaneous.
- Each scene should be distinct from the ones before it. When someone freezes the scene and steps into it, their task is to initiate a change in direction. They should let the frozen positions suggest a new scene to them, rather than just continuing where the previous pair left off.

Instructions

1. Explain the procedure and the ground rules (see "Guidelines").
2. Ask for two volunteers to come up in front of the group, and a third volunteer to be ready.
3. Ask the rest of the group to call out a couple of actions, such as "brushing your teeth" or "swinging a baseball bat." Quickly assign each volunteer one of the suggested actions. Let them do their motions for a few seconds, and then say "Freeze." The volunteers freeze in position.
4. Then say "Go." The volunteers begin to improvise a scene between them based on the positions they are in. They should do whatever comes to mind and just go with it.
5. Let the scene play out for at least 30 seconds, until the third volunteer calls out, "Freeze."
6. The actors freeze in position, and the third volunteer takes the place of one actor, assuming the position of the actor who is replaced. The other actor remains frozen.
7. When you say "Go," the actors begin to improvise a scene based on the positions they are frozen in. The scene should be a new one, not picking up where the last one left off. In general, the new actor should be the one to initiate the scene, but the "experienced" actor can do so if the new person falters.
8. The audience should let this scene play out for at least 30 seconds, and then anyone who wants to

can call out "Freeze" and take the place of the first actor. Go on in this way for as many rounds as you like.

Processing suggestions

- You can talk about the content of the scene. What new actions came out of the frozen positions? Did scenes sometimes go in surprising directions after the freezes?
- Processing could focus on how the ability to be spontaneous and creative can be a powerful instrument for changing an environment.
- You can also discuss how people interpret situations differently.
- Sometimes it helps to "freeze" and take a break so that you are able to come at situations with a fresh perspective. Stopping, reflecting, and evaluating is an important part of improving a group's work and the way they work together.

Group Count

Goals	Group problem solving, Surfacing group dynamics
Time	5-10 minutes (not including processing)
Physical contact	None
Physical challenges	Minimal
Number of participants	10-20
Space requirements	None
Materials needed	None
Preparation	None

Instructions

1. The object of the exercise is to have the group count to 10, as a group, by means of random individuals successively saying each number out loud. For example, one person says 1, someone else says 2, and so on. If two people speak at once, or if someone says a number out of order, the group goes back to 1. The group is not allowed to plan how they will accomplish the task, to use body language such as pointing, or to speak in any particular order. People must try to anticipate when they should say a number and when they should remain silent.
2. If the group is unable to accomplish the task, you can have subgroups try it, such as all the males and then all the females. If you try the exercise with subgroups, it might be best to end by trying to do it as a whole group again, to avoid leaving the group feeling factionalized.

Processing suggestions

- GROUP COUNT illustrates the difficulties a group can have in accomplishing a task.
- It can raise awareness about the need to be considerate of each other's voices.
- It may bring up the different ways that people take on or avoid responsibility in a group. Did every one say a number? Did anyone say more than one number? Did two people keep saying numbers at the same time? Why? Are these dynamics present in the group's work together?
- What allowed the group to accomplish the task (or what prevented them from doing it)?
- This exercise can also be used to talk about planning, and about getting things in the right order.

Variation – Group Spell

Preparation	Decide on a word or phrase related to the work of the group that you want the group to spell. Post the word where the group can see it.

Note: This variation works well to bring some fun and variety to an established group that has had experience with GROUP COUNT.

Instructions

1. Following the instructions for GROUP COUNT, the group spells out the word or phrase.

Additional processing suggestions

- How did doing this exercise compare with doing GROUP COUNT? Was it more difficult to spell a word out than count to ten? Familiarity often makes tasks easier, and it may take more effort and focus when you are working on a task that is new to you.
- What thoughts did you have about this word/phrase while spelling it out?

Variation – Multilingual Group Count

Additional goal	Cultural awareness

Instructions

1. Following the instructions for GROUP COUNT, but encourage people to say the numbers in languages other than English.

Additional processing suggestions

- This exercise illustrates how being inclusive of many cultures adds a layer of difficulty to working together, while it also makes the work more fun and more interesting.
- Was this easier or more difficult than regular GROUP COUNT? Why?
- Was it more interesting? What were the challenges?
- Being able to speak in more than one language can be a real asset in our world. In this exercise, did some people have an advantage over others? How did it feel if you did not understand what was being said?

Variation – Name Count

Instructions

1. Following the rules for GROUP COUNT, group members say the names of everyone in the group in any order.

Additional processing suggestions

- This exercise is a good tool to help explore group membership and/or the role of the facilitator as a member of the group. For example, participants might name people who are no longer members of the group, they might forget someone who is absent, or they might or might not name the facilitator.
- This exercise can be used to highlight the importance of including and valuing each member of the group. It can also help to make people more aware of each of the other individuals in the group. You can also look at whose voices were and were not heard.

Variation – Blind Count

Instructions

1. Follow the instructions for GROUP COUNT or any of its variations, except that everyone must have their eyes closed throughout the exercise.

Additional processing suggestions

- This exercise can be used to see how well the group can listen to others and focus only on listening. Sometimes when people are not able to take physical or visual cues from others, they are forced to truly listen to one another.
- Was this exercise easier with eyes closed? What did people notice with their eyes closed? Was it easier or harder to focus and concentrate?

Group Modeling

Goals	Communication, Group introspection
Time	5-15 minutes (not including processing), depending on the number of rounds
Physical contact	None
Physical challenges	Minimal
Number of participants	10-30
Space requirements	None
Materials needed	None
Preparation	None

Instructions

1. Have the group stand in a circle.
2. Ask for a volunteer to be the "poser." The poser leaves the room.
3. While the poser is gone, have the rest of the group choose a simple pose, such as standing on one foot with arms out, for the volunteer to try to guess. The group does not assume the pose; they just decide on it.
4. Once the group has selected the pose, call the poser back into the room. The poser has about two minutes to try to assume the right pose without receiving any verbal information from the group. The poser should just start trying different positions. The group responds with applause and other nonverbal responses to let the poser know if they are close or if they have guessed correctly.
5. You can repeat the exercise with a number of different posers.

Processing suggestions

- This exercise demonstrates people trying to figure out how to act based on nonverbal cues from their peers—a dynamic that occurs frequently in groups. In particular it can be helpful for a group that is about to integrate a new person. You can use the exercise to process issues around peer pressure.
- Was it easy to tell if the volunteer was on the right track or not?
- How did the poser feel when they were getting negative feedback from the group? positive feedback?
- Were the messages ever mixed?
- What kind of messages do we give each other about behavior in real life?
- Does the group encourage its members to act in positive or negative ways?
- How can we encourage positive behavior inside or outside of this group?

Group Story

Goals	Surfacing group dynamics, Creativity
Time	5-10 minutes (not including processing)
Physical contact	None
Physical challenges	Minimal
Number of participants	8-20
Space requirements	None
Materials needed	None
Preparation	None

Instructions

1. Begin the story by saying, "Once upon a time there was a ..." and complete the sentence.
2. Go around the circle and have each person contribute one meaningful sentence to the story. Each person's sentence should build on the sentence that came before it.
3. The story should travel around the circle once (twice for smaller groups), with the last person in the circle contributing the final sentence and then saying, "The end."

Processing suggestions

- In Group Story, each person contributes ideas to the group. When all of the contributions are put together, the group has created its own unique story or product.
- You can use this exercise to address issues around the need to make room for diverse ideas and styles.
- It can also be used to surface issues around productivity—whether or not everyone is putting themselves into the work of the group.
- Watch to see if people are able to work with the ideas that came before them in the circle or if individuals took the story in a different direction.
- Was the story coherent? Did it make sense? If not, why not?
- Did everyone have an idea to contribute?

Mix and Match Variations

The variations of this exercise can be integrated to create additional variations: SIX WORD LEADER STORY, SIX WORD THEME STORY, and LEADER THEME STORY.

Variation – Six Word Story

Instructions

1. Follow the instructions for GROUP STORY except that each contribution to the story is limited to six words. The six words do not have to form a sentence, but each person's contribution must allow the next person to go forward in such a way that it will form a sentence.

Additional processing suggestion

- This exercise placed a limitation on our ability to communicate and to be creative. What were the positive and negative effects of this limitation?

Variation – Leader Story

Instructions

1. Follow the instructions for GROUP STORY, but instead of going around the circle in order, you point to people to indicate that it is their turn to speak. Depending on what your specific goals are for the exercise, you can give some people multiple chances to speak while leaving others out, or you can conduct the exercise evenhandedly.

Additional processing suggestions

- This exercise can look at issues of authority, power, and control in groups and in society.
- It can look at what it feels like to be chosen and what it feels like to be left out. Who was chosen to speak? Who was left out, and how did that feel?
- What did those who were chosen do with the opportunity to contribute? Who feels that they have the opportunity to contribute in this group, and who feels left out?
- Who is selected to contribute in our society, and who is left out? Which people are given opportunities?
- Was the person in control inclusive or exclusive? What role did that play in the exercise?
- How do those who are left out react?

Variation – Group Theme Story

Preparation	Decide on a theme that you want the story to be about. Ideally it will relate in some way to an issue facing the group. See the discussion of subtlety on p. 59.

Instructions

1. Tell the group the topic or theme for the story, then follow the instructions for GROUP STORY.

Additional processing suggestions

- Did people interpret the topic differently? Where did different people go with it?
- What surprised you about the way the topic was covered?
- Were there elements that you wish had emerged, but they didn't?

Inch by Inch

Goals	Communication, Creativity, Different perspectives
Time	10-15 minutes (not including processing)
Physical contact	None
Physical challenges	Must be able to draw and write.
Number of participants	8-20
Space requirements	None
Materials needed	Paper (preferably lined), pens or pencils, and hard writing surfaces if the group is not around a table
Preparation	None

Instructions

1. Have the group sit in a circle, if possible.
2. Give each person a piece of paper, a pen or pencil, and a hard writing surface.
3. Each participant uses the top inch of the paper to write something—a sentence, a quote, a phrase, a song lyric, etc.
4. Everyone then passes their paper on to the person at their right.
5. On their new piece of paper, everyone uses the next inch down to draw (without using any words) a picture or depiction of the words above. (You can impose time limits of perhaps 30-60 seconds for each round.)
6. Everyone then folds over the first inch of writing so that only the picture is showing, and passes the paper to the right.
7. The next person then writes something in the next inch that describes the picture, folds over the picture so that only the second line of writing is showing, and passes the paper to the right.
8. This continues until the papers are filled, perhaps a total of nine or ten rounds.
9. After the last round, people unfold the papers they are holding and pass them around to be shared.

Processing suggestions

- This exercise can be used to explore the issue of change and how things evolve from an original concept or idea.
- It can also be used to discuss how to build off of each other's creativity and how to work together in a collaborative process.
- It is interesting to see how others interpret your words and drawing differently from what you intended. Processing can explore the difference between what is said or meant and what is heard or understood.
- Was it difficult to see your ideas take a different shape?
- How do we share creativity when we work together?
- What do we do when things change from our original idea of how they should be?
- Is change positive or negative?

The Leader Game

Goals	Introspection, Leadership
Time	10-15 minutes (not including processing)
Physical contact	None
Physical challenges	Minimal
Number of participants	10-30
Space requirements	Open floor space. With 10-15 people, this can also be done seated at a table.
Materials needed	None
Preparation	None

Instructions

1. Have everyone sit or stand in a circle.
2. Choose one person, or ask for a volunteer, to leave the room and be the "outsider."
3. While the outsider is gone, ask for a volunteer to be the leader for that round.
4. Instruct the leader to do a simple, repetitive motion, such as clapping or pulling on an earlobe, and to switch actions frequently but unobtrusively. Tell everyone else to follow, but without making it obvious who the leader is.
5. The outsider is then called in, asked to stand in the middle of the circle, and given three tries to guess who the leader is.
6. For the next round, the leader becomes the outsider. Play for a few rounds.

Processing suggestions

- This exercise illustrates feelings associated with being an insider or an outsider in a group and how groups can function to keep new people out.
- It can raise issues for discussion about how groups establish their norms.
- Processing can look at what it's like to take on different roles in the group: being a leader, being a follower, or being an outsider and not knowing something everyone else knows.
- The exercise can look at styles of leadership. Were there different styles? What happens when the leader is too fast, too slow, too complicated, etc.? There may also be points to bring out about individual leadership styles that you observed during the exercise.
- How did the "outsider" guess who the leader was? Was there anything about the leader's motions that gave away who it was? Did group members give it away?

Variation – Double Leader Game

Instructions

1. Follow the instructions for THE LEADER GAME, but select two people as leaders. Make sure the outsider knows that there are two leaders to be discovered.
2. The leaders must try to share the leadership without communicating verbally. If one leader changes the motion, the other should follow along.
3. The outsider has five guesses to discover both leaders. After the first leader is discovered, the group keeps playing until either the second leader is discovered or the outsider runs out of guesses.

Additional processing suggestions

- This exercise can be used to discuss shared leadership. For the leaders, what was it like to switch suddenly from leading to following, and vice versa? Did the leaders share leadership, or was one more dominant? Did having another leader make the leaders more or less likely to change the motion?

- When there is more than one leader, there can often be miscommunication and mixed messages if the leadership is not consistent. What was it like for the group to follow two leaders? Were there times when there were two different motions to follow? How did people decide which motion to follow? How do we make choices when we are being pulled in two directions?

Variation – Not the Leader Game

Instructions

1. Follow the instructions for THE LEADER GAME, except that in this version the outsider's goal is to eliminate everyone from the exercise except the leader.
2. When the outsider is called back in, they start to pick people who they think are not the leader. Whenever a person is picked who is not the leader, that person sits down and stops participating in the exercise.
3. This continues either until everyone but the leader has been eliminated or until the outsider accidentally picks the leader.

Additional processing suggestions

- In this variation, you may find people trying to pretend they are the leader, when they are actually following others. You can discuss this illustration of "false leaders" in relation to peer pressure.
- You can also discuss what real leadership is and how the group wants leadership to be shown.
- Sometimes it is easier to know what is wrong than what is right. It can be easier to make decisions when you eliminate some of the wrong answers that confuse the situation. This strategy can be effective in groups if everyone agrees on what to eliminate.

Variation – Dueling Leaders Game

Instructions

1. Split the group in two.
2. Each group huddles briefly to decide who its leader will be.
3. The groups then stand in a semicircle facing each other.
4. Tell one group (Group A) to begin. The leader in Group A starts the motion for everyone in the group to follow. As in THE LEADER GAME, the leader must change motions frequently and unobtrusively.
5. Group B has three chances to guess who the leader is.
6. The groups switch roles, with Group A trying to guess the leader of Group B.
7. If you have time, you can award each team a point for guessing correctly, and play several rounds to determine a winning team.

Additional processing suggestions

- How did the groups handle their three guesses? Did they coordinate or did people call out guesses randomly?
- Were there successful strategies used by leaders, followers, and guessers?

Variation – Noisy Leader Game

Materials	A blindfold

Instructions

1. Follow the instructions for THE LEADER GAME, with the following exceptions:
   - The outsider wears a blindfold.
   - A volunteer leads the outsider into the room and into the circle.
   - The leader makes sounds instead of motions, and the outsider tries to guess the leader based on

where the changes in sounds originate.

Additional processing suggestions

- This exercise illustrates some of the subtleties involved with interacting in groups and determining leaders.
- It shows the importance of developing the skill of listening.
- You can discuss how to develop awareness of leadership styles or qualities that are not visually apparent.

Listen Up

Goals	Trust, Communication, Personal introspection
Time	10 minutes (not including processing)
Physical contact	None
Physical challenges	Minimal
Number of participants	8-100
Space requirements	None
Materials needed	A watch or clock with a second hand
Preparation	Decide on two topics, such as what you plan to do this summer, or the best teacher you ever had. Topics can be related to the purpose of the meeting or not, depending on your goals.

Instructions

1. Pair people up and have the pairs sit together.
2. Ask the pairs to decide which of the two people will go first.
3. Give the first topic. The person who is going first from each pair must close their eyes, then talk about the topic for 90 seconds. The other partner should listen, but is not allowed to answer, touch, or communicate with the talking partner in any way.
4. After 90 seconds, tell the group to stop. Give them another topic and have people switch roles in their pairs.

Processing suggestions

- This exercise lets group members explore how it feels to be really listened to, and the trust necessary for true communication.
- Having your eyes closed while talking requires a lot of trust on the part of the speaker. How does it feel to speak without knowing for sure if someone is listening? Could you feel whether the person was listening or not? How could you tell?
- The listeners are also challenged in having to try to communicate their presence and attention without being able to speak or touch their partners.
- When you were the listener, was there anything you did to try to connect with the other person? Were you actually listening?

Magic Box

Goals	Creativity, Acting
Time	5-15 minutes (not including processing)
Physical contact	None
Physical challenges	Minimal
Number of participants	8-100
Space requirements	None
Materials needed	None
Preparation	None

Note: THE MAGIC BOX is a good exercise to use with a group that will be doing role-plays, skits, or other creative work. It requires participants to follow their imaginations and not worry about appearances. It is most appropriate for groups that know each other well or have some acting experience.

Instructions

1. Ask for a volunteer to come to the front of the room.
2. Tell the group that there is a "Magic Box" on the floor in front of the volunteer. You might want to pretend to show the group the dimensions of the box by patting the sides, mime-style.
3. When you are ready to begin, tell the volunteer to open the box, take something out, and hold it up. Then anybody in the group can call out questions for the volunteer to answer about the imaginary object, such as "What color is it?" "How big is it?" "What's that thing on the top of it?" "What is it used for?" etc. The group and the volunteer should let their imaginations take over.
4. If the volunteer gets tired of one object, they can throw it away and pick something else out of the box.
5. Repeat the exercise one or more times with new volunteers.

Processing suggestions

- You may choose not to process this exercise heavily but instead move directly to the work of the group.
- If you want, you can ask the group what helped them to "see" the object. Were there any movements made by the volunteer or any questions that particularly helped to clarify the object?
- What did people choose to pull out of the box? Why did they choose these things?

Memory

Goals	Focus, Personal problem solving, Different perspectives
Time	10-15 minutes (not including processing)
Physical contact	None
Physical challenges	Minimal
Number of participants	8-12
Space requirements	Open floor space or around a table
Materials needed	40-50 index cards
Preparation	Prepare the index cards so that you have 20 to 25 matched pairs, each with a word or symbol. For example, you could write "Hat" on two cards, draw the same stick figure on two cards, draw a house on two cards, write "X" on two cards, and so forth.

Instructions

1. Mix up the cards and lay them out in a grid, face down, on the floor or table.
2. Have the group sit at the table or in a circle on the floor around the cards.
3. The person who begins turns over two cards in an attempt to find a matched pair.
4. When a person uncovers a pair, they pick it up and set it aside, then take another turn. A player continues choosing cards until they fail to pick a match. In this case, the cards are returned to their positions face down and play moves to right, going around the circle.
5. At the end of the exercise, the person with the most pairs wins.

Processing suggestions

- Discuss what kinds of strategies people use to help them focus on and remember details, in the work they do as well as in this exercise.
- How can we help each other to remember the work of the group?

Variation – Memory with Movement

Instructions

1. Follow the instructions for Memory, except that after each person's turn, everyone in the group rotates one position to the left.

Additional processing suggestions

- What new challenges are presented when the group is constantly shifting position? What additional strategies are effective in dealing with these challenges?
- When you are forced to change your perspective, how does this affect your ability to function?
- Did it get easier or harder to adjust to the shifting perspectives as the exercise went along?

Name Face

Goals	Communication, Trust, Surfacing group dynamics
Time	5-10 minutes (not including processing)
Physical contact	None
Physical challenges	None
Number of participants	8-20
Space requirements	None
Materials needed	None
Preparation	Decide based on your goals for the exercise whether the facial expression should relate to how people are feeling at the moment or to something the group may be dealing with or working on.

Instructions

1. Going around the circle, each person says their name and makes a facial expression.
2. The group repeats the name and the facial expression three times.
3. Group members can then offer up to three guesses about what the face meant.
4. If no one has guessed correctly, the person who made the face tells the group what it represented.
5. Continue until everyone has had a turn.

Processing suggestions

- This exercise can be used to look at non-verbal clues that people give through their facial expressions and body language.
- Do we carry ourselves the way that we want to be seen? How can you tell if you are communicating to others what you want to communicate?
- We don't always know what our faces are saying. Others, seeing us, may know more than we do about what we are feeling.
- Which facial expressions were the most difficult to interpret? Which were easiest?

Name Jingle

Goals	Creativity, Surfacing group dynamics, Personal introspection, Communication
Time	5-10 minutes (not including processing)
Physical contact	None
Physical challenges	None
Number of participants	8-20
Space requirements	None
Materials needed	None
Preparation	None

Note: This exercise asks a lot of people and is appropriate only with groups that are at ease with each other and that are used to being creative. You can use it to gauge how comfortable people are with taking risks in the group. It is also a useful exercise in a meeting that will call on people's creativity.

Instructions

1. Going around the circle, each person says their name and sings a jingle (a simple tune with words) that expresses who they are or how they are feeling. It can be original, but it does not have to be.

Processing suggestions

- You may choose to forego processing and just use the energy generated by the exercise to move ahead with the meeting.
- This exercise can be used to look at creative ways to express who someone is or how they feel.
- It can be used to talk about the challenges of being creative and being true to yourself
- What elements contribute to the power of a message (rhyme, melody, artfulness, surprise)?

The Numbers Game

Goal	Focus
Time	5-10 minutes (not including processing)
Physical contact	None
Physical challenges	Minimal
Number of participants	10-20
Space requirements	Open floor space with chairs in a circle
Materials needed	Chairs
Preparation	None

Instructions

1. Have the group sit in chairs in a circle.
2. Starting with yourself as number 1, go around the circle and verbally assign numbers in consecutive order to each seat, leaving out a few numbers (more or fewer depending on the size of the group). For example, you could assign numbers 1, 2, 3, 5, 6, 7, 8, and 10 (leaving out 4 and 9), and so on.
3. Stress to the group that the numbers are assigned to the chairs, not to the people sitting in them.
4. Call out one of the numbers in the circle. The person sitting in the chair with that number must call out the number of another chair; the person in that chair then calls out another number; and so on. People cannot call out the number of the chair they are in or any of the excluded numbers.
5. When a person calls out their own number or an excluded number or they pause before calling out a number, that person has to move to the last seat (that is, the highest numbered chair), and other people move up one seat as needed. Then restart the exercise by calling out a number.
6. Do a warm-up round so people can practice responding quickly. Then play as follows.
7. The goal is to get to seat #1. If the person in seat #1 makes a mistake and has to move, the person who is now in seat #1 becomes the leader.
8. End the exercise at a high point, while people are still enjoying it.

Processing suggestions

- This exercise illustrates the importance of focus in a group. If one person is not focused, it slows things down and affects the whole group. As in this exercise, one person's being unfocused or distracted has consequences for others.
- Lack of focus can drag you backwards instead of moving you forward.
- Details and memory are important. If everyone remembers the details, we are less likely to forget them as a group.
- This exercise also illustrates issues of collaboration versus competition. People are competing to get to seat #1, but people may also work with each other to unseat someone in a lower numbered chair by calling their number more frequently, and trying to throw them off focus.
- In formed groups, you will see dynamics played out, such as who makes a mistake on purpose, who is not committed to the goal, etc.

Variations

You can vary the exercise in different ways—for example, by timing it, or by telling the group to see if they can keep the numbers going without mistakes for a specified period, such as 30 seconds or 45 seconds.

One Word, Two Words, Three Words

Goals	Focus, Organizing
Time	10-15 minutes (not including processing)
Physical contact	None
Physical challenges	Minimal
Number of participants	8-20
Space requirements	Minimal
Materials needed	A watch with a second hand (optional)
Preparation	None

Note: This is a good exercise to use when the group is dealing with change.

Instructions

1. Ideally, have the group sit in a circle.
2. Person #1 begins by saying one word.
3. Person #2 (sitting next to #1) says two words: a word that relates in some way to person #1's word and a word that relates to their own first word.
4. Person #3 then says three words: the first relating to the last word said by person #2, the second word relating to the previous word, and the third relating to the second.
5. Person #4 says only one word, which must relate to the third word said by person #3. The exercise continues in this way around the circle. Here is an example:

Person #1:	Peach
Person #2:	Orange (relates to "Peach"), Sunset (relates to "Orange")
Person #3:	Dusk (relates to "Sunset"), Night (relates to "Dusk"), Sleep (relates to "Night")
Person #4:	Snore
Person #5:	Nose, Eyes
Person #6:	Mouth, Smile, Happy
Person #7:	Sad

6. Have the group do one round.
7. After the group has learned how to do the exercise, you can opt to have people be "out" if they make a mistake. Alternatively, or in combination with outs, you can set a time limit: see if the group can finish within the limit, or have them do several rounds striving for their fastest time.

Processing suggestions

- This exercise illustrates the difficulty of thinking on one's feet and responding appropriately to a given situation without planning ahead. To do this exercise well, you must be flexible and adjust to change fluidly; you never know what's coming next. In the exercise, as in life, change is constant.
- Discuss the challenges of the exercise. Explore whether participants were able to develop a strategy for responding appropriately.
- If you played with outs, discuss how people got out and how they felt about it.
- If you played with time limits, how did it feel to be under pressure?

Pairing

Goal	Communication, Interconnection
Time	10-15 minutes (not including processing)
Physical contact	None
Physical challenges	Minimal
Number of participants	8-100
Space requirements	Minimal
Materials needed	A watch or clock
Preparation	Plan one or two questions for people to discuss in pairs (see "Questions"). With a large group, decide on the pairing technique you will use and plan for it (see "Pairing People Up").

Note: Pairs can be helpful in setting the stage for BRAINSTORMING (p. 385). Discussing a topic one-on-one helps people formulate and articulate their ideas, making it easier to participate in the Brainstorm.

Questions

Well-selected pair questions bring the work of the group and the experience of being in the group down to an individual level where everyone can feel comfortable. Depending on the amount of time you have for this exercise, you need one or two substantive questions for the pairs to discuss. Ideally, the questions will relate to and feed into the topic or the work of the meeting. In this way, people have a chance to think about the topic or the work in a more personal way before they are asked to bring their ideas to the larger group. Additionally, pairings provide the most powerful opportunity to build relationships and trust.

Pairing People Up

Do not tell people to find their own partners for a pairing. When people are responsible for finding a partner, many will feel anxious and some may experience moments of confusion or rejection—all feelings that are counterproductive to the goals of the exercise. It is always worth taking the time for facilitators to pair people up.

With a small group, you should tell people with whom to pair up. If most group members do not know each other, you can pair people with those they are sitting next to (but be sure to indicate where the pairings should start and be sure that everyone has a partner). Before the pairings, you can do an exercise such as THE WIND BLOWS (p. 377) that will move everyone around so they are less likely to be sitting next to people they know.

In formed groups, you may want to make a list of pairings beforehand, especially if there are people you specifically want to pair up. Try to pair people who are unlikely to have other opportunities to talk one-on-one; try not to pair people with their friends. To do the pairings, call out names and ask people to raise their hands so partners can identify each other.

With a large group, use a pairing technique. For example, as people arrive for the meeting you can give out name tags with numbers; those with the same number form a pair.

You can also have people form two facing lines, have the lines move in fairly close to each other, and tell the people standing opposite to shake hands and consider themselves a pair.

Instructions

1. First, put people into pairs or instruct them to locate their partners. (See "Pairing People Up.")
2. Tell people to introduce themselves to their partners.
3. Tell the group the question(s) for discussion and how long they have to talk. (About 3-5 minutes is a good amount of time for a pair. People should leave their pairs feeling that they have more to say. Note that adults tend to need more time in pairs than younger people do.) Remind people to share the time so that each member of the pair has time to speak.
4. Let the group know when they are about halfway through the allotted time, and note that the second person should begin speaking if they have not already done so.
5. If you do not process the work of the pairs, the group should go directly into work that is related to the pairs questions.

Processing suggestions

- Most pairs do not need processing.
- In some cases you may want to allow a short time for processing by bringing the large group back together and asking some questions about the experience of being in pairs. However, it is important to stress that people should not divulge information that their partners told them; they should share with the group only their own personal opinions or stories.
- Processing can look at how discussion in pairs helps people get to know each other and feel bonded with the group, and how building relationships is an important part of being able to work well together.

Row, Row, Row Your Boat

Goals	Surfacing group dynamics, Introspection
Time	5 minutes (not including processing)
Physical contact	None
Physical challenges	Minimal
Number of participants	No maximum number
Space requirements	None
Materials needed	None
Preparation	None

Note: See scenario 8 on p. 61 for an example of how one group used this exercise.

Instructions

1. Divide the group into three or more equal sections. They can remain seated in their places.
2. Tell the group that they are going to sing the song "Row, row, row your boat" as a round, and indicate the order that the teams will enter the singing.
3. Have the whole group sing the song together once.
4. Have team 1 begin the song.
5. As soon as team 1 finishes the first line ("Row, row, row your boat"), have team 2 start singing from the beginning of the song.
6. As soon as team 2 finishes the first line, have team 3 start singing.
7. Each team should continue singing until you tell them to stop.
8. To illustrate the processing points you wish to bring out, change the pattern as the teams continue to sing. For example, you can have certain teams sing louder or softer, have teams sing faster or slower, point out people to sing solos, have a team skip a turn, have the teams compete to see which can sing the loudest, and other variations that suit your needs.

Processing suggestions

Specific processing will depend on the instructions that you gave throughout the exercise. For example, points for discussion could be about:

- Finding your voice in the group.
- Being able to hold an opinion that goes against the flow.
- Different voices being heard in the group.
- Finding the appropriate pace for certain activities.
- Working together and coordinating everyone's contributions to meet a common goal.

Self Poems

Goals	Personal introspection, Creativity, Different perspectives
Time	15-20 minutes (not including processing)
Physical contact	None
Physical challenges	Minimal
Number of participants	8-30
Space requirements	None
Materials needed	A pencil and a copy of the template for each group member. If necessary, supply hard surfaces (such as books or clipboards) to make it easier for people to write.
Preparation	Prepare a self poem template (see "Making the Template") and make enough copies for each group member.

Note: You can do this exercise more than once over the course of the time that the group meets, and keep the poems so that group members can compare their new and older poems.

Making the Template

Here is a template for a Self Poem, which can be altered to fit the needs of your group.

Self Poem by ______________________________
Title:____________________________________

I am
I hear
I see
I am

I am
I think
I feel
I am

I am
I care
I wish
I am

I am
I hope
I know
I am

Instructions

1. Ask people to find a comfortable place to sit where they will be able to write.
2. Pass out the templates and pencils.
3. Tell people that they will have a certain amount of time (for example, five minutes) to write their "self poems," everyone should be quiet during the writing time, and the poems do not have to

rhyme. Also, say that there will be time for people to share their poems with the group if they wish, but that people can choose to keep their poems private.

4. Tell people to begin writing. Be sure the room is quiet for the specified amount of time.
5. When the time is up, ask that everyone put down their pencils.
6. Ask who would like to read what they have written. Remind the group to listen respectfully as others share their poems and to be aware that negative comments about other people's work would be hurtful and inappropriate. Give everyone a chance to read their poems if they wish.

Processing suggestions

- The poems are a form of self-exploration, and the exercise allows for shared reflection.
- Process the content of the poems. What themes do you see?
- This exercise can bring up issues of trust levels in the group. How deep or shallow were the poems, and how willing were people to share their poems with the group?
- If the group has done this exercise more than once, you can ask them what they see that was different or the same in their new and old poems.

Snickersnack, Anikanipanisan

Goals	Communication, Focus, Planning
Time	10-15 minutes (not including processing)
Physical contact	None
Physical challenges	Minimal
Number of participants	8-15
Space requirements	None
Materials needed	Two small objects (for example, a marker and a paper cup)
Preparation	None

Instructions

1. Have the group sit in a circle.
2. Explain that, in the dialogues that take place in this exercise, everyone must confirm the name of object with you, the facilitator, before passing it on.
3. Hold out the first object (for example, the marker) to the person on your right (Person #1), and have the following dialogue:

Facilitator:	This is a snickersnack.
Person #1:	A what?
Facilitator:	A snickersnack. *Hand the marker to Person #1.*
Person #1:	Oh, a snickersnack!

4. Person #1 then begins a dialogue with the person on their right (Person #2). However, Person #1 must turn to you to confirm the name of the object before passing it on. The dialogue goes like this:

Person #1:	This is a snickersnack.
Person #2:	A what?
Person #1 *[to the facilitator]*:	A what?
Facilitator:	A snickersnack.
Person #1 *[to Person #2)*:	A snickersnack. *Hands the marker to Person #2.*
Person #2:	Oh, a snickersnack!

5. Person #2 then turns to the person on their right and begins the dialogue. This continues around the circle. Each person who gets the object must confirm its name with you before passing it on.
6. As soon as the "snickersnack" is moving around to the right, hold out the second object (for example, the paper cup) to the person on your left and say, "This is an anikanipanisan." A dialogue takes place in the same form as above for the "anikanipanisan" as it moves around the circle to the left.
7. If the group is able to control the confusion enough so that one or both objects get back to you, you can either end the exercise or continue for another round.

Processing suggestions:

- Discuss the way in which communication was hindered by the structure that was set up. The group could not progress in its task without the explicit and repeated approval of one person.
- Did it become easier to go through the expected dialogues? This could be an illustration of how

people can get used to dysfunctional ways of communicating, and even find them comfortable and normal.

- The group was dealing with two messages traveling in opposite directions. How is this like the mixed messages that we encounter in a variety of situations?
- Ask who was the person who had to deal with both objects at once. What was that like?
- When many things are happening at once, it can be difficult to focus. How did people cope with the confusion?

Step by Step by Step

Goals	Communication, Planning
Time	10-15 minutes (not including processing)
Physical contact	None
Physical challenges	Minimal
Number of participants	Any number
Space requirements	None
Materials needed	A jar of peanut butter, a jar of jelly, a loaf of bread, a knife, and a paper plate or cutting board
Preparation	None

Note: This exercise uses the procedure of making a peanut butter and jelly sandwich, but you can substitute any simple procedure that can described step by step.

Note: This exercise is good preparation for a group that is about to do specific planning of the tasks involved in an event.

Instructions

1. Ask for two volunteers: one to be the "instructor" and the other to be the "follower."
2. Tell the instructor that their task is to tell the follower how to make a peanut butter and jelly sandwich, going step by step and being as clear as possible.
3. Tell the follower that they must do exactly what they are told—no more and no less. (So, for example, if the first instruction is, "Put the peanut butter on the bread," the follower might put the jar on top of the loaf.)
4. Give the follower the materials and have the pair proceed with their tasks until the follower is able to complete the task of making a peanut butter and jelly sandwich.

Processing suggestions

- This exercise emphasizes the importance of not taking anything for granted and not making assumptions about what other people do and do not know. In any project, there can be tasks that might be overlooked because they seem so apparent.
- What assumptions did the instructor make? How about the follower? Why did they make these assumptions? What were the consequences?

The Story Game

Goals	Planning, Different perspectives, Creativity, Interconnection
Time	5-10 minutes (not including processing)
Physical contact	None
Physical challenges	Minimal
Number of participants	No maximum number
Space requirements	None
Materials needed	None
Preparation	None

Instructions

1. Ask for three volunteers to be the "Storytellers" and one volunteer to be the "Pointer." (In a group with 12 members or fewer, you can have all but one person be Storytellers if you wish.) All Storytellers come up in front of the group.
2. Ask the whole group to supply three elements to get the story started: a name (not the name of a particular person), an occupation, and a location. For example, you might get "Tom," "plumber," and "Main Street." Announce to the group, "This is a story about Tom, the plumber from Main Street." You can vary the number and nature of the elements depending on the purpose of the exercise.
3. The Pointer then points to one of the Storytellers, who begins to make up a story about this character. Whenever the Pointer points to one of the Storytellers, that person must pick up the story where the previous Storyteller left off.
4. After the story has gone on for a while, say something like, "Three more pieces before the story ends," to let the Storytellers know they should bring the story to a conclusion. How long you let the story continue depends on how it is going, the needs of the group, and the time available for the exercise.

Processing suggestions

- Use the exercise to discuss goal-setting: How could this story have developed if one person had a plan in mind, or if the Storytellers had agreed on a goal beforehand? Stress the importance of being clear about the content and messages of what you are planning to do.
- When you start out in a certain direction, you can't be sure where you will end up.
- We can't predict how our actions will be modified by the actions of others.
- People working together build on each other's work. However, it is important to coordinate our efforts to build a coherent message.
- Who was pointed to? Who was not pointed to? How did it feel to be or not be pointed to?
- How was the content of the story affected by the elements supplied at the beginning? Were the elements transformed in surprising ways? You can explore how people work within the limitations of what they are given, and how they sometimes push beyond the limitations.
- Processing the content of the story will depend on how the story developed.

Switch Swatch

Goal	Communication
Time	5-15 minutes (not including processing)
Physical contact	None
Physical challenges	Minimal
Number of participants	No maximum number
Space requirements	None
Materials needed	Two chairs
Preparation	Place two chairs facing each other in front of the group. Choose topics, and prepare some people if necessary (see "Getting Ready").

Note: This exercise is useful when the meeting is focusing on communications skills or conflict resolution.

Getting Ready

- Decide on one or more general topics for participants to discuss. The purpose of the exercise is to look at communication styles rather than to seriously debate the topics, so the topics do not have to be relevant to the meeting. Choose topics that people can argue about easily but that are not too serious or divisive; you want to avoid hurt feelings or serious disagreements. For example, topics might be: television (good or bad), teens (annoying or terrific), money (love it or hate it), rain (love it or hate it).
- If you will be doing the exercise in front of a large group, you may want to prepare two people in advance to be the first volunteers.

Instructions

1. Ask for two volunteers to come up and sit in the chairs at the front of the room.
2. Tell them that their goal is to defeat each other in an argument by arguing as vehemently as they possibly can for their position. They are not to listen to each other, but to talk over each other. They must stay seated, and swearing and physical contact are not allowed. Also tell them that when you say "Switch!" they must immediately start arguing for the position they were just arguing against.
3. Give them the topic of the argument and the position (for or against) that each will take. For example, if the topic is school, tell one person that they are for school (it's fun, important, etc.) and the other person that they are against school (it's boring, useless, etc.).
4. When you say "Go," the pair begins the exercise by arguing their position for or against the topic.
5. After about 30 seconds, say "Switch!"
6. Say "Switch" several times before stopping the argument. If you wish, you can decrease the amount of time between switches as you go along. The switch usually creates laughter from those watching.
7. After several switches, tell the pair to stop.
8. Ask the group to declare the winner by their applause. (Note that since each person has taken both positions in the argument, the group will be voting for the person's ability to argue, not for a particular position.)
9. Let the winner stay up for a round with another volunteer. You can do a number of rounds.

Processing suggestions

- This exercise illustrates the kind of communication that is not productive in solving problems. When people are having an angry discussion, they are playing Switch Swatch. Trying to defeat

each other is conflict, not communication.
- Could you hear what anyone was saying?
- Were the people who were arguing listening to each other?
- What did it take to "win"? What was "winning"? Was it the loudest, most animated, or most convincing argument?
- Have you ever seen situations where people are playing Switch Swatch in everyday life? How do people "win" in these kinds of arguments?

Variation – Multiple Switch Swatch

Materials	Additional chairs at the front of the room (optional)

Note: This variation shows how small issues can turn into major conflicts.

Instructions

1. Play SWITCH SWATCH in the regular way for one round.
2. Before starting the second round, point to someone from the audience and tell them to join one side of the argument or the other.
3. Depending on what you are trying to illustrate, you can either add people evenly to each side or put more people on one side so that they gang up against one person or a small group on the other side.

Additional processing suggestions

- When more people get involved in arguments, factions become more important than facts. As the numbers grow, so too does contention and conflict. The side you are on becomes more important than the truth.
- The more solidified the factions, the less listening takes place.
- This happens on local levels, such as in gangs, as well as on international levels.

Three-Chair Improv

Goals	Creativity, Acting, Surfacing group dynamics
Time	5-10 minutes (not including processing)
Physical contact	None
Physical challenges	Minimal
Number of participants	No maximum number
Space requirements	None
Materials needed	Three chairs
Preparation	See "Setting It Up."

Setting It Up

How you set up this exercise will depend on the issues you are working with in the group.

Set up three chairs in front of the room, and label each with a sheet of paper taped to the back of the chair that will tell the person sitting in the chair something about how to act. The labels can be roles or they can be emotions. For example:

- teacher, student, administrator
- police, youth, resident
- having fun at a party, about to have a fight, a peacemaker
- afraid, happy, hostile
- bored, angry, joyful

In addition, you can create a situation for the three people to act out, if you wish. For example: "In this chair is a student who was ten minutes late for school. In this chair is an administrator who is about to enforce the school's lateness policy and send the student home. In this chair is a teacher who knows the student well and does not like the lateness policy."

Instructions

1. Ask for two volunteers to come to the front of the room and sit next to each other.
2. If you have created a sketch of a scene, tell this to the group and the actors. Otherwise, tell the actors to improvise the scene themselves.
3. Tell the actors to play the role or the emotion stated on the label, and let them improvise for at least 30 seconds.
4. Give a signal to the group that someone should volunteer to sit in the third chair and join the scene. The new actor must take the role labeled on the third chair and join the scene that is in progress.
5. Tell the group that every 30 seconds or so, someone from the group should come up to take the "new person" chair (where the third actor is sitting). The actors must shift over one place, and the original actor who was sitting on the end must leave the scene. The scene continues, but the actors take the new roles that are assigned to the chair they are now sitting in.
6. Let this process continue for several rounds. Each new person who enters the scene always enters from the same side and takes the "new person" chair, while the other actors move down chairs in the same direction.

Processing suggestions

In addition to looking at the content of the scenes that developed, you can consider these issues in processing:

- Changing roles within the group.
- Making room for new ideas.
- Being able to adapt to new situations and changing situations.
- Making things up as you go along.
- How different people interpreted the roles or the emotions.

Timed Art

Goals	Communication, Different perspectives, Visual arts
Time	5-20 minutes (not including processing)
Physical contact	None
Physical challenges	Minimal
Number of participants	8-30
Space requirements	Space to work in small groups
Materials needed	Paper and art supplies such as markers, pencils, scissors, and glue
Preparation	Decide what theme, if any, you want to suggest or mandate for the groups' drawings. Decide how long you want to give the groups to work (from 1-15 minutes, or as long as seems appropriate to the situation).

Instructions

1. Divide people into small groups of 3-6, and provide each group with paper and other supplies.
2. Tell people that they will have the specified amount of time to create a picture using the materials provided. Tell them the theme, if there is one, or tell them the picture can be on any theme.
3. Give the groups the specified amount of time to work on their pictures.
4. This exercise can be done with or without talking, depending on what you want to get out of it and the dynamics of the group.
5. When the time is up, have the groups come back and present and discuss their work and the process they went through to make it.

Processing suggestions

- Processing can look at what it's like to work together on a vision—the pros and cons of developing a product as a group or creating a group vision.
- What was it like to create a message that reflects the group rather than just one individual?
- If people were not allowed to talk, discuss the importance of communication (both verbal and nonverbal) when developing a product.
- Discuss what people drew and what they have to say about it.
- How is the theme expressed differently by different people? In what ways are people's individual pictures connected to the whole? Do the drawings come together as a coherent whole? If not, what is needed to bring them together in a larger picture?

Triple Draw

Goals	Group problem solving, Creativity
Time	10 minutes (not including processing)
Physical contact	None
Physical challenges	Must be able to draw using a pen or marker.
Number of participants	5-15
Space requirements	Minimal
Materials needed	For each group member a piece of paper, a pen or marker, and a hard surface for writing (such as a book or a clipboard) if needed
Preparation	None

Instructions

1. Ideally, have the group sit in a circle or around a table. If they are at desks, establish the order for drawings to be passed on.
2. Give each person a set of materials (listed above).
3. Each person should quickly draw a shape or scribble on their paper. Give people about ten seconds and call time.
4. Each person then passes the paper to the person on their right.
5. Everyone adds something to the shape or scribble on the paper they received. After about ten seconds, call time.
6. Pass the papers to the right once more and allow the third person to elaborate on the drawing or turn it into something new. Give people 10-20 seconds for this.
7. Collect the drawings and post them for discussion and processing.

Processing suggestions

- This exercise illustrates the benefits and challenges of working together in a group.
- It provides a direct experience of integrating other people's skills and ideas with your own and of making your contributions to others.
- What changes did the original scribble go through?
- Was it difficult to watch your drawing change?
- Did it become "better" as it became more defined?
- At what stage did you feel you contributed more to the drawings? Are you better at initiating or finishing a project?

Two Truths and a Lie

Goals	Trust, Personal introspection, Interconnection
Time	10-15 minutes (not including processing)
Physical contact	None
Physical challenges	Minimal
Number of participants	8-12
Space requirements	Minimal
Materials needed	None
Preparation	Think about what "truths and lies" you will share with the group. Depending on your purposes, you may want to set a light tone or a tone of deep sharing; however, you would only want to move away from a light tone with a group that knows each other very well and is prepared to work on a deeper level.

Note: People in the group must have some degree of familiarity with each other in order to do this exercise, but it's a good exercise to help people get to know each other better. It can become very high-risk, depending on what people choose to say about themselves.

Note: With a group that has already done Two Truths and a Lie, you can vary the format by asking the group to come up with two lies and a truth about themselves.

Instructions

1. Ideally, have the group sit in a circle.
2. Ask for a volunteer to begin, or begin yourself if you feel it is necessary to set the appropriate tone.
3. Each person in turn shares three pieces of information about themselves—two pieces that are true and one that is not true. Tell people to lie as skillfully as they can by using the following tips: Say true things that people in the group may not know; make the lie something that is believable; and say the lie in the same way as the truths.
4. After each person shares their information, the rest of the group tries to decide which is the lie.

Processing suggestions

- What surprising things did people learn about each other?
- Was it harder to think of lies or of truths that you wanted to tell?
- Was lying difficult?
- Which lies seemed the most believable? Why were some not believable?
- Were there any truths that seemed unbelievable?
- How does this exercise change the way you think about the members of the group?

Who's That?

Goal	Communication
Time	10 minutes (not including processing)
Physical contact	None
Physical challenges	None
Number of participants	12-20
Space requirements	None
Materials needed	None
Preparation	None

Instructions

1. Give the ground rules for the speakers: No profanity, no put-downs, people should limit themselves to a word or a phrase, and they should try to disguise their voices.
2. Ask for three volunteers to be the guessers.
3. Have the guessers stand in front of the group with their backs turned.
4. Point to a member of the group (or the group can decide silently who will speak). The person who is chosen walks to within a few feet of the guessers and says a word or phrase in a disguised voice.
5. The guessers take turns (left to right) making guesses about who spoke.
6. If no one guesses correctly, the speaker speaks again.
7. If the guessers cannot identify the speaker after a second round, point to someone else to be speaker.
8. When a guess is correct, the speaker and the guesser change places.
9. Play for several rounds.

Processing suggestions

- People often disguise their true selves with different "voices." What is it like to try and get behind the façade that someone presents to you?
- You can use this exercise to discuss the importance of authenticity and "being real" in the group and in life. What are the advantages of being authentic or "real?" What does it take in order to show your true self?
- How can you try to tease out what's real and what's not, or what's sincere and what's insincere?
- When you work with limited information and input, you may make assumptions about who people are. To truly know someone, you must know them deeply, and they must want to share their true self with you.
- There are many ways to use your voice, and you can use your voice for different purposes, both positive and negative. You have the choice of how to use your voice, and whether or not you articulate the truth.

Word Association Contest

Goals	Organizing, Introspection, Surfacing group dynamics, Creativity
Time	5-10 minutes (not including processing)
Physical contact	None
Physical challenges	None
Number of participants	8-20, or work in teams with groups up to 40
Space requirements	None
Materials needed	None
Preparation	Prepare a list of words. See Appendix A for sample lists of low-, medium-, and high-risk words. Decide on any rules that you want to have. For example, you can disallow proper names or words that have already been used.

Instructions

1. Tell people the rules.
2. Begin with one or two warm-up rounds, in which you go around the circle and say a word from the list to each person. That person should reply with the first word that comes to their mind.
3. For the rest of the exercise, people will be out if they do not reply within one second or if they break one of the rules (such as using a word that's already been said).
4. Continue until only two people are left. Those two face off, and the last person left is the winner. During this final round, the contestants respond to each other's words rather than to words from your list, and they cannot use names, numbers, or repeat words. (If you wish, you can begin to use this method before the final round.)

Processing suggestions

- This exercise does not need to be processed heavily. It is a good warm-up for a WORDSTORM (p. 413) or BRAINSTORM (p. 385), or another task that requires people's thoughts to flow freely.
- You can comment or ask for comments about some of the associations that people made during the exercise.
- You may want to ask people how easy it was to let their minds free-associate and let the words just come out. Did people censor any ideas that came to them? What is the value of censoring your ideas, rather than just speaking anything that comes to your mind?

Variation – Unfair Word Association Contest

Note: With a large group, do the exercise with two teams and two facilitators. When each team is down to one person, the two compete against each other.

Instructions

1. Do one or two rounds of WORD ASSOCIATION CONTEST enforcing the rules fairly.
2. Then begin to be unfair: call some people out when they should not be and let others stay in the game when they should be out. You can say that a word does not relate when it does, or that a word relates when it does not, or give some people less time to reply and others more time. Try to be subtle enough so the group does not catch on that your purpose is to raise issues of fairness.
3. Continue until there is a "winner."

Processing suggestions

This exercise is useful for initiating a discussion about fair rule enforcement:

- How did those who were treated unfairly feel?
- How did they deal with their anger?
- What did they do and what might they have done? Were there ways to organize a response to the unfairness?
- Did those who benefited from the unfairness do anything to help the others?
- How did it feel to win when you found out the exercise was unfair?
- How do the feelings raised by this exercise relate to other situations in life?

Chapter 14

Tag-Style Springboard Exercises

The activity level of the tag exercises makes them especially popular with teens and young adults. Because they wake people up and relieve tension, tag exercises are useful for people who are tired and for groups that are feeling tense. They contribute to the group's productivity because they generate energy that can be directed toward the work of the day. In addition, they are effective at illustrating group and societal dynamics and can be adapted for many educational purposes.

Space Requirements

Tag exercises can be done in all kinds of spaces, including classrooms and offices, as long as there is some room for people to move around. In terms of safety, in fact, it is preferable for the group to be in a confined space when doing a tag exercise, since a smaller space is a natural check on people's tendency to run.

Because all the tag exercises require the same type of space—some open space with adequate room to move around and with well-defined boundaries—the category of "Space requirements" has been removed from the heading information.

Safety

Safety is a key factor in these exercises. Before beginning a tag exercise, be sure to do the following:

- Point out the boundaries for the exercise and emphasize that no one can step outside them. If the group is seated in chairs in a circle, have people push back their chairs a few feet; the chairs form the boundary.
- **Emphasize that everyone must walk, not run.** Running may be fine if the group is outside on a grassy surface, but in many other situations, particularly in an indoor setting, the no running rule is important to avoid injury.
- Give clear and complete instructions, and insist that everyone listen carefully.
- Make clear that anyone who is unable to participate can sit out for the exercise.
- Do not begin the exercise until you are sure that everyone understands the rules.

As a facilitator, you should not participate in the exercise, so that you are able to monitor compliance with the rules (as well as to observe the group dynamics). It is helpful to issue frequent reminders; often this means saying "Don't run!" over and over until the exercise is completed. It is likely that there will still be some running, but emphasis on this rule will remind people to move more slowly and carefully. When you process the exercise, you may want to make points related to people's compliance with the "no running" rule.

Time

Most of the tag-style exercises take between 5 and 10 minutes (not including processing), while a few take less than 5 minutes. In general, these exercises are fast and efficient. In addition, most require no props or preparation. They are "no fuss, no muss" exercises that present ample opportunities for raising issues and making processing points.

Number of Participants

Many of these exercises work well with groups of up to 50 or 60 people, while also being effective with smaller groups. Monitoring for safety is particularly important with a large number of participants.

Processing

The processing suggestions given for each exercise may or may not be appropriate for your group at the time you do the exercise. Watch the group dynamics carefully and process the exercise based on what you see.

Variations

This chapter gives variations for some of the exercises, but remember that any exercise has an infinite number of variations that you can create to meet the needs of your group. Remember, too, that any change, large or small, that you make in the exercise contains potential for processing.

Amoeba Tag

Goal	Surfacing group dynamics
Time	5-10 minutes (not including processing)
Physical contact	Linking arms
Physical challenges	Must be able to move fast enough to tag or avoid being tagged.
Number of participants	12 to 60
Materials needed	None
Preparation	None

Instructions

1. Ask for a volunteer to be "it."
2. Everyone else in the group spreads out around the room, trying to avoid being tagged.
3. When someone is tagged, they link arms with "it," become part of the "it" chain, and move together trying to tag everyone else. Only those on the ends of the "it" chain can tag people, and those who are trying to avoid being tagged must go around the ends of the chain, not under the linked arms.
4. When an "it" chain grows to four people, it splits in half, becoming two groups of two that are both trying to tag people. When these groups grow to four people, they split again. This continues until everyone has been caught. Note that in very large groups, you may want to have the chains divide at six or eight people rather than at four.

Processing suggestions

- AMOEBA TAG is useful in surfacing issues of fragmentation in a group. Rather than bringing everyone onto one chain, as in CHAIN TAG (p. 261), each small group competes to get the last people onto their own chain.
- Does the exercise mirror the dynamics of the group—that is, does the group usually operate as one large group, or as smaller "amoebas"?
- Conversely, the exercise can also illustrate a functional way to organize, in which people take on tasks in smaller groups or committees.
- Who got caught first? What was that like?
- Who got caught last? How did they hold out so long?
- Did people want to get caught by one group rather than by another?

Variation – Competitive Amoebas

Preparation	Decide what movements or sounds to assign to the competitive "its." See "Distinguishing the Its."

Distinguishing the Its

Decide on a distinguishing movement or sound for each of the two "its" in this exercise—for example, yelling "beep, beep," shaking their heads, saying "come here, come here," or waving one arm in the air. Try not to assign something that would seriously interfere with the ability to catch people, such as running backwards or hopping. However, in some situations you may want to assign a movement to one side that will put them at a disadvantage, so that you can discuss unequal/unfair circumstances. Waving an arm in the air, for instance, gives "it" only half the capacity for reaching out to tag people.

Instructions

- Ask for two volunteers to be "it," and assign each "it" a movement or sound.
- Proceed as in AMOEBA TAG, except that when someone is added to an "it" chain they must also make the movement or sound that the original "it" was making. Each time the chain splits, both ends continue making the movement or sound of the original chain.
- Once everyone has been caught, figure out which of the original "its" got the most people by seeing how many people ended up doing each of the movements or sounds.

Additional processing suggestions

- Points can be made and discussion sparked about competitiveness and about factionalism. Did people respond during the exercise in ways that are typical of the group's dynamics?
- The exercise can be used to illustrate multi-tasking and/or having too many things to do at once.
- If one of the original "its" was assigned a sound or movement that put them at a competitive disadvantage, discuss the issues that this brings up.

Cartoon Tag

Goal	Organizing
Time	5-10 minutes (not including processing)
Physical contact	Tagging
Physical challenges	Must be able to move fast enough to tag or avoid being tagged.
Number of participants	12-30
Materials needed	None
Preparation	None

Instructions

1. Ask for a volunteer to be "it." In a group of 20 or more, you might want to start out with two "its."
2. When you say "Go," the person who is "it" will try to tag other people in the group.
3. Those being chased must stay within the boundaries. They are "safe" if before they are tagged they squat down, touch the ground, and say the name of a cartoon character. They remain "safe" for 20 seconds; then they must stand up and continue playing.
4. Everyone who is tagged before they can think of a cartoon character becomes an additional "it." The exercise continues until everyone is "it."
5. Each person can use a particular cartoon character only once. For example, John can say "Fred Flintstone" and Pam can say "Fred Flintstone," but no one can say "Fred Flintstone" more than once.

Processing suggestions

- CARTOON TAG can be very frustrating for the person who starts out as "it," because it is often difficult to capture people. You can use this exercise to process how it feels to be doing something all by yourself—such as when some individuals in the group are doing most of the work, or when the group as a whole is having a hard time reaching people with their message.
- Was it difficult for the person who was "it" to catch people? How did they deal with that frustration?
- As the exercise progresses, people run out of cartoon characters, more people are "it," and it becomes increasingly easier to catch people. This can illustrate persistence and being able to stay on task.

Variation – "Something" Tag

Additional goal	Reinforcing information

Instructions

1. In a smaller group, instead of cartoon characters you can use elements specific to your group, such as the goals of an upcoming event, or people to be invited to a workshop, etc. You might want to set a rule that each item can be used only once. You will have to listen carefully to enforce the rule.

Additional processing suggestion

- You need to understand information (rules, goals, etc.) and be able to use it under pressure.

Chain Tag

Goal	Organizing
Time	5-10 minutes (not including processing)
Physical contact	Tagging
Physical challenges	Must be able to move fast enough to tag or avoid being tagged.
Number of participants	12 to 50
Materials needed	None
Preparation	None

Note: Frequently when groups do this exercise, the chain will break and the people in it have to regroup and get organized so the chain won't break again. It is best if the facilitator does not get involved in this process.

Instructions

1. Ask for a volunteer to be "it."
2. When "it" tags someone, the two link arms and both are "it." Everyone who is tagged links arms and becomes part of the "it" chain. Only the people on the ends of the chain can tag the people being chased.
3. Those trying not to be tagged must go around the ends of the chain; they cannot go under people's linked arms. If someone does this, or goes out of bounds, they are automatically caught.
4. Ultimately, almost the whole group is "it," trying to tag the last person. At this point the chain becomes very powerful and the last person will be unable to avoid capture.

Processing suggestions

- CHAIN TAG can be used to illustrate that a group can gain power as it grows if it is well organized. In the beginning it can be difficult to get the first few people together, but as the group becomes larger, it is easier to get more people involved. The group may split, or people may want to go off in different directions. When this happens, the group loses its power. But if there is enough leadership to keep everyone together, the movement will start to function in a rational way and it will gain adherents.
- Ask the person who began as "it" what it felt like to be alone, and how it felt as more people joined the chain.
- How did it feel to be captured, or not to be captured until the end?
- If the chain broke apart, did someone organize getting it back together? Did people take leadership to help the chain operate more effectively?
- For a formed group, did what happened in the exercise reflect the group's day-to-day dynamic?

Variation – Safe Tag

Instructions

1. Create a zone where participants are safe from being tagged. Depending on your purpose, you can vary the size of the safety zone and the amount of time that people are allowed to stay there.

Additional processing suggestion

- Depending on the purpose of your group, you can discuss how people find or are able to create "safety zones" or places of respite that are more or less temporary.

Chill, Chill, Run

Goal	Surfacing group dynamics
Time	5 minutes (not including processing)
Physical contact	Tagging
Physical challenges	Must be able to move fast enough to tag or avoid being tagged.
Number of participants	12-20
Materials needed	None
Preparation	None

Instructions

1. Ask for a volunteer to be "it."
2. Have the rest of the group stand in a circle or sit in a circle on the floor. Make sure there is enough room for people to move around the circle without tripping or bumping into things.
3. "It" walks around the circle, touching each person's head and saying "chill." At some point, "it" touches someone's head and says "run." That player then chases "it" around the circle (but both must walk), trying to tag "it."
4. "It" tries to get to the player's space in the circle without being tagged. If this happens, the player becomes the new "it." But if "it" gets tagged, the player returns to the circle and the person who is "it" begins again.
5. The exercise has no set ending point. End it after five minutes or less.

Processing suggestions

- CHILL, CHILL, RUN can be used to process the different ways people act when they are calmly sitting with the group versus when they are running around outside of the group. Did people act differently while they were in the circle than when they were outside the circle? Do these same differences exist when people are with the group and when they are out in the community?
- It can also surface issues related to the anxiety around being chosen or not being chosen to participate in the exercise. Did everyone get chosen? Were some people chosen more or less frequently than others? How did that feel? Did people perceive being chosen as positive or negative? Are there parallels with the work of the group, or with larger social dynamics the group is working with?

Dot Tag

Goals	Organizing, Surfacing group dynamics
Time	5-10 minutes (not including processing)
Physical contact	Tagging
Physical challenges	Must be able to move fast enough to tag or avoid being tagged.
Number of participants	10 to 30
Materials needed	Enough stick-on dots (available in stores with office or household supplies) for everyone in the group to have about ten. The dots should be evenly divided between two colors.
Preparation	None

Instructions

1. Divide the group into two teams.
2. Designate a "safe zone" in the meeting room for each team.
3. Give each team dots of one color, to be divided up among the members of the team.
4. When you give the signal, players begin trying to stick their dots on the arms of players on the other team, with the goal of getting rid of all their dots.
5. When a player has no more dots, they enter their team's safe zone. Players in the safe zone cannot be tagged with any more dots.
6. The first team to have all of its members in the safe zone wins.

Processing suggestions

- This exercise can be a lively lead-in to a work session that involves doing outreach. What are the most effective ways to reach others? How does the "outreach" in this exercise differ from trying to reach others with information and ideas?
- There may be group dynamics issues that surface during the exercise and would be useful to process—for example, leadership in the teams, how the teams divided up the dots, or whether people followed the exercise guidelines (no running, staying in bounds) in getting rid of their dots.
- You could discuss how the exercise might reflect ways that people relate to those they think of as "other" (for example, of a different race or class). Think of the dots as labels or stereotypes that people stick on each other before running into their own safety zones.

Elbow Tag

Goals	Group introspection, Communication, Surfacing group dynamics
Time	5-10 minutes (not including processing)
Physical contact	Linking elbows
Physical challenges	Must be able to move fast enough to tag or avoid being tagged.
Number of participants	12-30
Materials needed	None
Preparation	None

Instructions

1. Ask for two volunteers—one to be the "chaser" and the other to be the "linker."
2. Have the rest of the group stand in two lines facing each other. If there is an uneven number of people, ask for a volunteer to sit out (perhaps to help enforce the "no running" rule), then play a second round with another volunteer sitting out.
3. Have people partner up with the person across from them. Partners should link arms, and each person should place the hand of their unlinked arm on their hip.
4. Pairs should spread out through the available space, staying within the boundaries. Once they are spread out, they remain in place. Hands must remain on hips.
5. The chaser's goal is to tag the linker before the linker links arms with someone in a pair. If the chaser tags the linker, they switch roles, so the linker becomes the chaser, and vice versa. But if the linker succeeds in linking arms with someone, the other person in that pair must break off and become the new linker.
6. Everyone must stay in bounds. If the linker goes out of bounds, the linker and the chaser must switch roles.
7. Let the exercise run for a few minutes, then call time.

Processing suggestions

- This exercise shows a chain reaction—how an action by one person affects another person, which affects another, and so on.
- It can be used to illustrate a variety of points about how things relate to one another— for example, one person or group gaining what another loses, or groups struggling over limited resources.
- How did the group respond to the situation? Did they come together to isolate the chaser? How did it feel to be the outsider trying to get in?
- How did the exercise illustrate the group's dynamics? Who paired up with whom and why? Was it intentional? Did people try to not let certain others link up with them?

Everybody's It

Goal	Surfacing group dynamics
Time	One or two minutes (not including processing)
Physical contact	Tagging
Physical challenges	Must be able to move fast enough to tag or avoid being tagged.
Number of participants	12 to 25
Materials needed	None
Preparation	None

Note: EVERYBODY'S IT is a good way to enliven a group quickly. It is fast and a great energy booster.

Note: The exercise creates a chaotic environment, with many things going on simultaneously. It is difficult to tell if people are following the rules or not. Watch to see how they deal with the chaos.

Instructions

1. Have the group stand up.
2. When you give the signal, the group will begin to play tag—but in this exercise, everybody is "it." Each person should try to tag as many people as possible, while avoiding being tagged by others.
3. When a person is tagged, they must freeze until the exercise is over.
4. The exercise ends when there is only one person left unfrozen.

Processing suggestions

- The exercise shows a situation where everyone is out for themselves, with no responsibility to the group or to anyone else. Frequently one or more people will start to break the rules (for example, by running), and soon others will also break the rules. Dysfunction is contagious, and it is very difficult for individuals to choose to function within the established order. How do people react to this? Some may withdraw; others may be determined to "win."
- Conflict and chaos are the products of an environment such as this one, which is set up so that responsibility to the group is neither expected nor enforceable. How did people feel about everything being so chaotic? What happens in a situation where it's difficult to enforce rules?
- If you do the exercise again at a later time, discuss what strategies people may have learned, and how experience counts. (For example, people sometimes realize they can pretend for a while that they've been tagged.)
- The exercise can open a discussion about how people react under new and stressful circumstances.
- Did anyone avoid being tagged the entire time? If so, how?

Variations – Meditative, Time Limited, and One Handed

Number of participants	12 to 30
Materials needed	A clock or watch with a second hand (optional)

Instructions

You can vary the exercise in one of the following ways, or you can combine variations:

- Before you give the signal to begin tagging, instruct everyone to close their eyes and to walk around slowly with eyes closed. Count ten seconds, then give the signal to open eyes and begin tagging.
- Follow this procedure, but do not count the seconds. Instead, instruct the group that each person should count ten seconds silently on their own before opening their eyes. People will most likely

open their eyes at different times, and this creates an area for processing.
- You can vary the amount of time that people walk before opening their eyes. How does this change the dynamic?
- Allow people to use only the right hand (or the left hand) to tag others.

Additional processing suggestions

- The exercise requires people to adapt quickly to a new situation when they open their eyes.
- Ask how people felt at various points: while walking in the dark, while trying to tag others, while being tagged, while being frozen.
- How did the last person still moving manage to avoid being tagged?
- While people had their eyes closed, were they strategizing how to avoid being tagged or how to tag others?
- Did everyone keep their eyes closed? Are there issues of trust that emerge through this dynamic?
- If people used their left hands, how did this affect the experience of those who are right-handed and those who are left-handed?

Heads or Tails Tag

Goals	Organizing, Surfacing group dynamics
Time	5 to 10 minutes (not including processing)
Physical contact	Tagging
Physical challenges	Must be able to move fast enough to tag or avoid being tagged.
Number of participants	12 to 60
Materials needed	None
Preparation	None

Instructions

1. Have the group stand in a circle.
2. When you give the signal, everyone puts one hand on either their head or their "tail." Then, with their free hands, the "heads" try to tag the "tails," and vice versa.
3. When a person gets tagged, they switch sides.
4. The exercise ends either when everyone is on the same side or when chaos ensues.

Processing suggestions

- Frequently the "tails" side wins because those with hands on their heads are at a disadvantage (the raised arm hinders vision on one side and makes it a bit more difficult to move quickly). This can be used as an illustration of societal disadvantages.
- The exercise can lead to a discussion about what it takes to bring someone, or a group of people, over to your point of view.
- It can also bring up issues about people switching allegiances or making decisions based on fast-moving factors beyond their control, such as fashion or style.
- Switching sides can be compared to seeing other people's points of view. Some people may find that they switch sides several times; have they faced similar situations in their lives?

Line Chase

Goal	Surfacing group dynamics
Time	5 minutes (not including processing)
Physical contact	Everyone holds the waist of the person in front of them.
Physical challenges	Must be able to move fast enough to tag or avoid being tagged.
Number of participants	10 to 20
Materials needed	None
Preparation	None

Instructions

1. Have the group stand in a single line with each person holding the waist of the person in front of them.
2. The object of the exercise is for the first person in the line to tag the last person, without breaking the chain.

Processing suggestions

- LINE CHASE can be about the various pressures that people face. The people in the front of the line tend to become invested in catching the end of the line, while those toward the end of the line tend to become invested in avoiding capture. What happens to the people in the middle? Do they identify with one end or the other, or are they just pulled this way and that?
- The exercise can be an illustration of a group that is ambivalent about its work or its direction, or of a group in which people are working at cross-purposes.
- Points about the group running in circles or chasing its own tail can be made if appropriate.
- You can make points about the nature of leadership: what happens when leaders are aggressive or passive, unsure of how to proceed or focused and directed?

Marco Polo

Goals	Surfacing group dynamics, Introspection
Time	5-10 minutes (not including processing)
Physical contact	Tagging
Physical challenges	Must be able to move fast enough to tag or avoid being tagged.
Number of participants	8 to 20
Materials needed	A blindfold
Preparation	Set up boundaries, if necessary, so that the space is confined and not too large for the group. Clear the space so that there are no obstacles that someone could trip over.

Instructions

1. Ask for a volunteer to be "Marco."
2. Blindfold the volunteer.
3. Marco's task is to tag someone else in the group, who will then become Marco. The person who is Marco tries to figure out where people are by calling out "Marco," to which everyone must respond "Polo."
4. The exercise has no set end point. Let it run for a few minutes, then call time.

Processing suggestions

- This exercise can be used to discuss what it is like to try to find your way, especially when limitations have been placed on your ability to do so.
- It shows that people need accurate information in order reach their goals.
- Was it difficult for the person who was Marco to tag someone? How did it feel to be blindfolded?
- Was it easy for the rest of the group to avoid being tagged?
- Does the group ever seem to be walking around blindly?
- Watch to see how people relate to the blindfolded person. Do they take advantage of this person's vulnerability?
- The exercise can be related to people or groups who are marginalized, and how those in the majority may band together to keep the marginalized ones at a disadvantage.

Pair Tag

Goals	Group introspection, Surfacing group dynamics
Time	5 minutes (not including processing)
Physical contact	Tagging
Physical challenges	Must be able to move fast enough to tag or avoid being tagged.
Number of participants	8 to 30 (10-12 is ideal)
Materials needed	None
Preparation	None

Instructions

1. Have the group stand in two lines facing each other. If there is an uneven number of people, ask for a volunteer to sit out (perhaps to help enforce the "no running" rule), then play a second round with another volunteer sitting out.
2. Have people shake hands with the person across from them, so that it is clear who is paired with whom. Each person will be playing tag with the person directly across from them.
3. Designate one side as "it."
4. When you give the signal to begin, each "it" has to try to tag their partner.
5. The person tagged tries to tag their partner back, and the exercise continues in this way.
6. After a few minutes, call time.

Processing suggestions

- This exercise can be used to illustrate a dysfunctional group, in which everyone is trying to give the responsibility to someone else, then hiding behind the ensuing chaos.
- Contrast this with the way you hope this group will function, with people working together and taking responsibility.
- What did the room look like during this exercise? When we work together, do we ever look like this?

Variation – Hospital Tag

Physical contact	Tagging on different body parts

Instructions

1. Follow the instructions for Pair Tag, except that when a person is tagged, whatever part of the body they are tagged on becomes "paralyzed." For example, if a person is tagged on the right arm, they can no longer use that arm for the rest of the exercise.
2. The tagging and "paralyzing" between partners goes on for the duration of the exercise.

Additional processing suggestions

- You can use this exercise to talk about the group's ability, or individuals' abilities, to keep going despite setbacks.
- Was anybody tagged so many times they could not move anymore? When people had a lot of parts they could not move, did they give up or keep trying? How does this relate to the work of the group?
- Hospital Tag illustrates that the competitive behavior of Pair Tag and its variations is disempowering and can cause injury.

Variation – Hospital Tag with a Healer

Physical contact — Tagging on different body parts

Instructions

1. Ask for a volunteer to be the "healer." The healer sits at one end of the room and must remain seated throughout the exercise.
2. Follow the instructions for HOSPITAL TAG, except that as people get tagged and are unable to move certain body parts, they can make their way to the healer. If the healer touches them, they have full use of their body parts once again and return to the exercise. Note that the healer may decide not to heal certain people.

Additional processing suggestions

- This exercise can be used to discuss the role of helping or "healing" others and what it is like to ask for help.
- It can also bring up the ways in which people use power or react to those in positions of power.
- What was it like for the healer? What did the healer do, and how effectively did the healer use the power given to them?
- Did people use the healer? What was it like to ask for help?
- How well do individuals in this group ask for help when they need it? Are others willing and able to help them? How is power used in this group? in society?
- Do we choose to heal each other when we can?

Stop Tag

Goals	Surfacing group dynamics, Organizing
Time	5 to 10 minutes (not including processing)
Physical contact	Tagging
Physical challenges	Must be able to move fast enough to tag or avoid being tagged.
Number of participants	10 to 20
Materials needed	None
Preparation	Decide what people must do when they are tagged, such as say the name of the person who tagged them three times, count to 5, count to 10, etc. With shorter stops, the exercise will be more chaotic, but with stops that are too long it can lose momentum.

Establishing an Order

Establish an order in one of the following ways:

- One person walks or reaches across the circle and shakes someone else's hand and says that person's name. (They are free to pick whomever they want.) Then that person reaches across and shakes someone else's hand and says their name. This continues until everyone has been picked once (and only once). The person who started the process should be the last one picked.
- Use the same process as above but, instead of shaking hands, have each person throw a ball or beanbag to some one else in the circle and say their name.
- You can also use other ways to establish the order that might help you to meet additional goals for your group. For example, you can have each person walk over, shake someone's hand, and tell that person something about themselves.

Instructions

1. Have the group stand in a circle.
2. See "Establishing an Order" and use one of the methods described.
3. Explain that the group will be playing tag. Each individual will be trying simultaneously to tag the person they picked when the order was established and to stay away from the person who picked them. Although everyone will be involved in the exercise, each individual is concerned with only two other people: the person they are chasing, and the person they are being chased by.
4. When someone is tagged, they must freeze. Before they can continue playing, they must say whatever it is that you have specified (counting to 5, saying the tagger's name, etc.).

Processing suggestions

- This exercise shows how systems work or malfunction. Frequently the chain will break down so that some people never get tagged, which has consequences for the person they are chasing and for everyone else in the order. This dynamic can be used to make points about putting things in order and to show how systems work or fail.
- Who got tagged a lot? Who got tagged very little? Why?
- If the chain broke down, where did it happen and why? This can show that it's important to find the source of a problem in order to fix it and ensure that things will flow smoothly.

Variation – Backward Stop Tag

Instructions

There are three ways to do STOP TAG backward. Depending on the needs of the group and the processing points you wish to make, you can choose one way, combine two, or do all three together.

- Each person chases the person who picked them and runs from the person whom they picked.
- Everyone walks backward.
- When tagged, people must say the person's name backward the specified number of times (e.g., "Keisha" becomes "Ahsiek").

Additional processing suggestions

- When the rules are changed, everyone has to adapt.
- There may be some advantages to the backward approach. What are they?
- It's important to be move forward with your eyes open as you approach difficult situations. Backing into things can create chaos, because if you do not see potential problems you may not be able to deal with them.

Variation – Stop Tag with Reverse

Additional goal	Introspection

Instructions

1. Follow the instructions for STOP TAG except that when you say "Switch," everyone tries to tag the person who was just trying to tag them.
2. Switch three or four times before ending the exercise.

Additional processing suggestions

- This exercise can be used to discuss how difficult change can be for individuals or for a group. When you shout "Switch," each individual must change their way of thinking about whom they must tag and who is trying to tag them. This change can be confusing and disorienting when it first occurs. This can also be true in the lives of individuals or when a group must change or alter a decision or a plan of action. You can discuss how people cope with change and explore strategies to deal with internal or external changes that happen.
- How did people react when you said "Switch" the first time?
- Did it get easier or more difficult to deal with the changes as the exercise went on?
- Did anyone have a strategy that worked or that didn't work so well?
- These questions can lead to more direct questions about the group or a particular situation, such as: How do we deal with changes in this group? What strategies can we use to deal with difficult changes in healthier, more productive ways?

Variation – Speech Tag or Character Tag

Additional goals	Reinforcing information, Acting

Note: This exercise can be used to generate physical and emotional energy when the members of the group are preparing to deliver a speech or to perform in a skit or play.

Instructions

1. Follow the instructions for STOP TAG except that when a person is tagged, before moving forward they must deliver a line from their speech or recite one of their character's lines with exaggerated emotion.

Additional processing suggestions

- Was it easy or difficult to generate emotional energy for the speech or the character in this spontaneous setting?
- Were people surprised at the lines that came out under pressure? Did they have difficulty remembering any lines at all?
- You can explore the issue of anxiety when speaking or performing in front of audiences. Did anyone experience stage fright during the exercise? Does it help to treat the material in a playful manner?

Variation – Praise Tag

Additional goal	Introspection

Note: This exercise is appropriate only with a group that has been together long enough so that the group members know a good deal about one another and can identify each other's strengths. Also, before choosing this exercise, consider whether or not it is too high risk for your group or for individuals in the group.

Instructions

1. Follow the instructions for STOP TAG except that when a person is tagged, they must stop and verbally praise the individual who tagged them before they can move on. The words of praise must be said three times—for example, "You have a great laugh, you have a great laugh, you have a great laugh."
2. Each time someone is tagged, they must come up with a new piece of praise and cannot repeat one that has already been given.
3. Stress to the group that the praise they give must be genuine, and that jokes and negative statements are not allowed.

Additional processing suggestions

- Sometimes it may be difficult to think of and give an authentic piece of praise to someone. We have to be actively searching for and observant of each other's strengths.
- Often we don't take the time to give real praise to others. We may be more critical in our approach and assume that individuals only learn from their weaknesses.
- We can also learn from the things we do well and as a group we can build on our strengths.
- How does it feel to receive praise?
- Were you surprised by any of the praise you received? Did it seem true?
- How difficult was it to come up with praise for someone?
- How often do we take the time to give real praise?
- What does empty praise feel like?

Variation – Spinning Stop Tag

Instructions

1. Follow the instructions for STOP TAG except that when a person is tagged, they must stop and spin around three times before moving on.

Additional processing suggestions

- This exercise can be used to discuss being clear and directed versus "spinning in place" or "going around in circles." How difficult was it to move forward toward your goal after you'd been spinning?

- Are there times when it feels like the group is spinning? What does it take to get clear with one another or to make decisions as a group?

Variation – Blind Stop Tag

Additional goal	Group introspection

Instructions

1. Follow the instructions for Stop Tag except that when someone is tagged, they must stop and close their eyes for five seconds before moving on.

Additional processing suggestions

- This exercise can be used to discuss situations when it is important to be aware at all times. When you opened your eyes after five seconds, did you notice how much had changed? Had other people moved on while you were unaware? Was it difficult to continue with what you had to do?
- Some people might find that the moments with their eyes closed provided time for centering. The exercise can be an illustration of finding the balance between reflection and action.

Stuck in the Mud

Goals	Organizing, Surfacing group dynamics
Time	5-10 minutes (not including processing)
Physical contact	Tagging
Physical challenges	Must be able to move fast enough to tag or avoid being tagged.
Number of participants	12 to 50
Materials needed	None
Preparation	None

Instructions

1. Ask for one or two volunteers (depending on the size of the group) to be "it." The task of "it" is to tag everyone else in the group.
2. A person who is tagged is "stuck in the mud" and cannot move. However, everyone who is not stuck can free those who are stuck by tagging them.
3. The exercise could continue until the "its" have accomplished their goal of tagging everyone, or until it becomes clear they will not accomplish it anytime soon. You could stop the exercise for a moment to ask for one or more additional volunteers to be "it."

Processing suggestions

- With a group that is focused on a work outcome, you can talk about the difficulty of completing the job. For all the energy that the group puts in one direction, there are forces pulling in the other direction at the same time. Sometimes the work they do gets undone. It's important not to be discouraged when that happens, but to keep up our energy for our work.
- Teamwork is critical; how well did the "its" work together?
- Sometimes people will pretend they are "stuck in the mud" to avoid being tagged or to free more people. Discuss what people think of these tactics, if they happened. How does it apply to the work the group is doing?
- If you added additional "its," this is an illustration of how important it is to have sufficient resources to accomplish a task.

Tentacle Tag

Goal	Organizing
Time	5-10 minutes (not including processing)
Physical contact	Tagging
Physical challenges	Must be able to move fast enough to tag or avoid being tagged.
Number of participants	12 to 60
Materials needed	None
Preparation	None

Instructions

1. The area in which the exercise will take place is the "lagoon."
2. Ask for a volunteer to be the shark; in very large groups you may want more than one shark. The shark stands in the middle of the space.
3. Tell the rest of the group that they are fish. They must go to one end of the lagoon. As long as they are touching the wall (or whatever the boundary marker is), they are safe and cannot be tagged.
4. When you give the signal, the fish must run to the opposite end of the lagoon without going out of bounds. When they reach that wall, they are safe. After resting by the wall for a short time, they must run across the lagoon again. No one can stay in either safety zone for more than 30 seconds at a time.
5. As the fish run across the room, the shark tries to tag as many people as possible.
6. Anyone who is tagged has to freeze where they are. They are now considered to be sea anemones—sea plants with tentacles.
7. Using only their arms and without moving their legs, the anemones try to tag anyone who goes by them. If an anemone tags someone, that person also becomes an anemone.
8. As more and more people are tagged, it becomes harder for the fish to get across the lagoon safely. The exercise ends when the last person is caught.

Processing suggestions

- TENTACLE TAG can show how an idea or movement gains momentum. At first there is only one person alone in the middle of the lagoon trying to catch the fish; it can be difficult to catch the first few. But once enough people are caught and start acting as anemones, it becomes easier and easier to catch the rest of the people. This exercise can be useful with a group that is trying to reach people with their message, or recruit participants for an event.
- Was it difficult for the shark to catch the fish?
- How did the fish feel about becoming anemones?
- Was there a point in the exercise when it became easy to catch the fish?
- Who was the last fish caught and how did they avoid being captured for so long?

Variation – Tentacle Tag with Traits

Instructions

1. Follow the instructions for TENTACLE TAG, except that the shark calls out characteristics and only those fish to whom each characteristic applies run across the lagoon. If the characteristic does not apply, they can stay in the safety zone. For example, if the shark says "all the red fish," anyone wearing red must cross. The shark can call out any characteristics they want, such as "all the fish that are a part of this group" or "all the female fish," etc.

Additional processing suggestion

- Sometimes people are required to take risks because of characteristics that are beyond their control.

Triangle Tag

Goal	Organizing
Time	One to two minutes (not including processing)
Physical contact	Tagging
Physical challenges	Must be able to move fast enough to tag or avoid being tagged.
Number of participants	9 to 60
Materials needed	None
Preparation	None

Note: This exercise is similar to STOP TAG except that the people who are trying to tag each other are a self-contained unit. In that way it is similar to PAIR TAG.

Instructions

1. Break the group into groups of three.
2. Each group of three must decide who will be tagging whom. For example, person 1 will try to tag person 2, person 2 will tag person 3, and person 3 will tag person 1.
3. Just as in STOP TAG, when you give the signal everyone tries to tag their designated person.
4. When a person gets tagged, they must stop and say the name of the person who tagged them three times before moving on.
5. End the exercise after about a minute.

Processing suggestions

- This exercise can be used to talk about focusing when a lot of other things are going on.
- Were the activities of the other triads distracting for some people? You can look at how distractions can be used to avoid focusing on the task at hand.
- Some people may find it easy to have only those in their triad to worry about. You can explore the pros and cons of single-minded focus and narrowing your field of awareness.
- The exercise can illustrate the dynamics of working in smaller groups.
- The exercise can illustrate people getting caught up in a triangle and not being open to new possibilities.

Chapter 15

Springboard Exercises for Groups Both Large and Small

These exercises are effective with a "group" that fills an auditorium as well as with a group of 10 or 20. To give some examples:

- We've used PEOPLE HUNT at events with more than 400 participants of all ages and at a birthday party with 20 young teens.
- STAND UP/SIT DOWN has the power to create points of connection in a group of 10 and in a room full of hundreds.
- GROUP MOAN/GROUP SHOUT provides a sense of release and shared purpose for two people or 1000 people.

Engaging a Large Group

While integrating interactive methods in large settings can be challenging, the effort is always worthwhile. No matter how large the group, a meeting is more productive and more likely to meet its goals when people are given a directed outlet for their thoughts and feelings rather than being in a passive role throughout. For example, in a program of speeches, you can intersperse interactive exercises that engage people directly and give them the opportunity to move, speak, or in some way establish their identity. Within this format, people are able to be more receptive to the presentations. After you try some of these exercises with a large group, you will quickly see the difference in people's level of engagement.

Lots More Exercises

This chapter describes only a few of the more than three dozen exercises in the book that you can use with large groups. All the exercises in this chapter involve active participation by up to 75-100 people. However, there are exercises elsewhere in the book that also fit this criterion (see especially some of the Five-Minute Exercises). In addition, there are numerous exercises that actively engage 40 or more people, and there are others that that involve people "audience-style" (see the list on p. 215). If you are working with a large group, check out these exercises:

Call and Response	up to 40	p. 188
Concentric Circles	up to 50	p. 190
Group Beat	up to 100	p. 163
Group Modeling	audience	p. 223
Hands Together	unlimited	p. 164
Human Machine	audience	p. 199
Listen Up	up to 50	p. 230
Magic Box	up to 100	p. 231
Name Chant, Motion, and Sound	up to 80	p. 348
Mini-Med	unlimited	p. 167
Pairing	unlimited	p. 237
Pass the Pulse	up to 50	p. 173
Psychic Shake	up to 50	p. 175
Relay Race	up to 50	p. 359
Row, Row, Row Your Boat	unlimited	p. 239
Dueling Simon Says (variation)	audience	p. 362
Step by Step by Step	audience	p. 244
Story Game	audience	p. 245
Switch Swatch	audience	p. 246
Three-Chair Improv	audience	p. 248
Wait a Minute	up to 50	p. 177
Wind Blows	up to 50	p. 377

Tag-Style Exercises

If you have a group of 30 to 60 active people and space to move around, many of the tag-style exercises in chapter 14 will work with your group. Here's a chart to help you locate an exercise that might meet your group's needs:

Up to 30	Up to 50	Up to 60
Cartoon Tag	Chain Tag	Amoeba Tag
Dot Tag	Freeze Tag	Heads or Tails Tag
Elbow Tag	Stuck in the Mud	Tentacle Tag
Pair Tag		Triangle Tag

Names and Evaluations

When you're designing a meeting for a large group, remember these Name Exercises and Evaluation Exercises:

Name Shout / Name Whisper	p. 142
Name Race	p. 140
Name Chant and Motion	p. 135
Group Shout / Group Whisper Evaluation	p. 423
Group Thought Evaluation	p. 424
Stand-Up Evaluation	p. 424

Fill the Space, Shake the Hand

Goal	Interconnection
Time	10 minutes (not including processing)
Physical contact	Handshaking
Physical challenges	Must be able to move around the room.
Number of participants	20-100
Space requirements	Open floor space
Materials needed	None
Preparation	None

Instructions

1. Ask everyone to stand up, and point out the boundaries within which the exercise will operate.
2. The object of the first part of the exercise is to fill spaces that are empty in the room or in a defined space. When you give the signal to begin, everyone should look around the room, identify an open space, and walk into it. After pausing for a moment, they move on to fill another open space.
3. Let this go on for 30 seconds or so. Watch to see if people distribute themselves equally around the room, or if they are all clumped up.
4. Ask everyone to freeze, then add the next element.
5. In the second part of the exercise, everyone must shake hands (using one hand and then the other) with someone else as they move around the room. Before they can let go of one person's hand, they must be starting to shake hands with someone else. People should keep moving in a chain-like movement around the room, shaking one hand, reaching with the other hand, and so on. As they shake hands with each new person, they should introduce themselves.

Processing suggestions

- This exercise shows how a group can work well, with everyone moving in to fill the empty spaces (to do what needs to be done).
- The second part of the exercise shows how important it is to nurture interpersonal relationships in the group or in the community. Being personally connected to others is what will make the environment fluid and productive. You can use this exercise to stress the importance of reaching out to people, especially those you don't know well.
- Were people spread out equally in the first part of the exercise? Did people fill all the empty spaces? What empty spaces are there in the group's work that still need to be filled?
- In the second part of the exercise, did anyone have no one to shake hands with? How did that feel?

Variation – Multicultural Fill the Space, Shake the Hand

Additional goals	Communication, Cultural awareness
Preparation	Prepare a list of greetings in other languages.

Instructions

1. Do the first part of the exercise as described for FILL THE SPACE, SHAKE THE HAND.
2. Before introducing the second part (in which people shake hands and introduce themselves), show the group the list of greetings in other languages and have them practice saying each greeting together.

3. Instruct people to use as many greetings as they can as they move around the room shaking hands.

Additional processing suggestions

- Adding the multicultural element allows you to make points about reaching out to people of different backgrounds and cultures, and about taking the risk of addressing people in their own language.
- What did it feel like to speak in different languages? If you know those languages, what did it feel like to hear those languages spoken?

Group Argue

Goal	Communication
Time	10 minutes (not including processing)
Physical contact	None
Physical challenges	Movement around the room
Number of participants	10 to 100
Space requirements	Open floor space
Materials needed	None
Preparation	None

Instructions

1. Have the group stand in a circle.
2. At your signal, everyone starts to move into the circle with the goal of pairing up with someone. (If there is an uneven number of people in the group, a facilitator should participate. Alternatively, you can instruct the group that it's all right to form a group of three.)
3. When two people pair up, they start to argue about any topic that comes to mind.
4. After a short argument (30-40 seconds), the pairs split up and each person looks for someone else to pair up and argue with. If the group needs the structure, you can give a signal for the pairs to split up.
5. Let the exercise continue until people have had a chance to argue with four or five others. Then call time.

Processing suggestions

- What did people argue about? How did the arguments start? Did the pair agree upon the topic, or did one person just start arguing?
- Did everyone listen as well as talk? What is the difference between having an argument and a discussion?
- Did any pairs start arguing and then realize that they were on the same side of the issue? Was anyone convinced by someone else's argument?
- This exercise can be used to discuss how to make connections with people or groups with opposing viewpoints.
- What was it like to try to make connections with other people? People may feel anxiety around having to find someone to argue with, and may experience feelings of confusion or rejection.

Variation – Directed Group Argue

Preparation	Prepare a list of topics for argument (or there could be just one topic).

Note: This exercise can be used as an introduction to a BRAINSTORM (p. 385) or WORDSTORM (p. 413).

Instructions

1. Give the group a topic for their first argument.
2. With multiple topics, call time to end each pair and give the topic for the next argument.

Additional processing suggestions

- How did people decide which side of the argument to take?
- How do we learn our opinions and which sides of arguments to take (from media, parents, etc.)?
- What opinions or arguments were stated?

- What is the difference between communication and conflict?

Variation – Group Argue in Whispers

Instructions

1. Do GROUP ARGUE or DIRECTED GROUP ARGUE, except that everyone must whisper while arguing.

Additional processing suggestions

- Was it difficult to hear others' voices? Was it hard to keep whispering?
- Was communication improved when voices were lowered?
- This exercise can be used to discuss whose voices get lost in discussion, either on a societal level or within the group. It can be particularly helpful if the group is having difficulties with people not listening or not speaking up.

Group Moan/Group Shout

Goal	Interconnection
Time	5 minutes
Physical contact	None
Physical challenges	Minimal
Number of participants	Any number
Space requirements	None (see note).
Materials needed	None
Preparation	Decide on the word or phrase for people to say during the GROUP SHOUT. It should be something related to the group's work or to a project they are involved with.

Note: If the group does not have open floor space in which they can stretch, you can adapt this exercise by having people stand by their seats and minimizing the movements you ask them to do.

Instructions

1. Have everyone stand up. If the group is small enough, have them stand in a circle.
2. For GROUP MOAN, the first part of the exercise, tell everyone to reach up to the sky, and then stretch however they want.
3. Then tell them to think about all the things they have to do that they don't feel like doing or don't have time for, about how difficult it is to do the work the group is engaged in, and/or other challenging aspects of their lives. On the count of 3, everyone will slump over at the waist and let their negative feelings run out their fingertips, while they let out a big moan. Count to 3 and have everyone do the GROUP MOAN.
4. You may want to do this part of the exercise more than once to let everyone get all their moaning out.
5. Then do the GROUP SHOUT. Tell the group to think about all the things they have accomplished and all the things they feel good about. With a small enough group, you can have everybody put their hands into the center of the circle. On the count of 3, have everyone shout the word or phrase that you give them.
6. You can do the GROUP SHOUT a couple of times to get the group energized.

Processing suggestions

- GROUP MOAN/GROUP SHOUT acknowledges the pressures that people are facing, while also being an energizer for the group and reminding them of the positive aspects of their work together. In general, it does not need formal processing, and you can move directly into the next part of the meeting.

Group Slide

Goal	Interconnection
Time	10 minutes (not including processing)
Physical contact	None
Physical challenges	Involves movement forward, back, and to the side.
Number of participants	10-100
Space requirements	Open floor space. Could also work in more constricted settings, such as people standing at their tables, as long as everyone has a little room to move around.
Materials needed	A CD or tape player with appropriate music
Preparation	Choose music. Write out the instructions (see "Creating the Instructions").

Creating the Instructions

You need four instructions: one that fits with a forward movement, one that fits with stepping back, and two that are more generic. All should be things that are simple and that everyone in the group can respond to positively. Here are some examples:

1. "Step forward if …"
   This step should relate to ways in which you make progress during the day or in life. Examples: you got out of bed this morning, you made it to this meeting, you've ever achieved a goal you set for yourself.
2. "Take a step back to reflect on …"
   This step should relate to how this year has been, or how you feel about a particular subject relevant to the group. Example: the connections we've built in this group, the progress we've made toward putting on an event, how you've changed since you've been a part of this group.
3. "Slide to the right if …"
   The right and left steps should involve things that everyone can respond positively to. In a school in May you might say "you're looking forward to summer vacation." In the middle of a cold snap you could say "you're ready for temperatures over 15 degrees." The directions will be more or less generic, depending on factors such as how well the group knows each other and how many experiences they have in common.
4. "Slide to the left if …"
   Ideally this will invoke a common positive goal, such as "if you want this meeting to be productive" or "if you want every student in this school to have a successful year."

Instructions

1. Ask everyone to stand up and to clear a space around them if necessary (move bags, chairs, etc.).
2. Ask people to follow your directions. Lead people slowly through the four steps two or three times. Then tell them you're going to put it to music.
3. Turn on the music and call out the steps, if you wish, the first few times as people move (for example: "Got up this morning! — Think about it! — Summer's coming — A great meeting").
4. Let it go for three or four rounds, or longer if the group seems to be enjoying themselves.

Processing suggestions

- Processing can go in many different directions depending on the instructions that you gave. One element is the fact that people were moving together, and that with some simple choreography they created something bigger than themselves. You can talk about the power of a large number of people moving in the same direction.

- If many people did not participate, you can comment about motivation and being part of a team or movement, and what happens when everyone is not making the same movement.
- Were people really able to reflect during the step backward? Often we are so caught up with the dance movements of our everyday lives that we do not have time to stop and reflect on what we have achieved. However, this is an important step in order to move forward.

Group the Group

Goal	Surfacing group dynamics
Time	5-10 minutes (not including processing)
Physical contact	Contact with others in small groups
Physical challenges	Must be able to move from one group to another.
Number of participants	20-100
Space requirements	Open floor space
Materials needed	None
Preparation	Plan the numbers you will call out. Choose numbers that are appropriate for the size of your group (larger numbers for large groups and smaller numbers for small groups). Use numbers that will leave some people out as well as numbers that will work out evenly.

Note: This exercise is a good lead-in to small group work. Have the last number you call be the number that you want in the small groups. You can also use the exercise solely as a way to form small groups, in which case you will not do any processing.

Instructions

1. The object of this exercise is for people to get into groups of different sizes based on the number you call out. (People are in a group if they are touching each other.) For example, if you call out "Five," everyone tries to get into a group of five. Then call out "Three," and have everyone get into a group of three. Those who are left out of a group should sit down until the next call.
2. Continue calling out numbers in random order for five or six rounds.

Processing suggestions

- Processing can look at people's ability to move through many different groups and work in all of them productively.
- The exercise can lead to discussion of not getting stuck in a particular clique.
- Watch to see how groups realign themselves. How does a group of five become a group of four? What are the dynamics of these realignments?
- How did people get into groups?
- What happened when a group had too many members? How did the group decide who would leave? What happened when a group did not have enough members?
- What feelings came up around being left out of a group? Do these feelings ever occur in the group at other times?

Group-Ups

Goal	Interconnection
Time	10-20 minutes (not including processing)
Physical contact	None
Physical challenges	Must be able to move from one group to another.
Number of participants	15-75
Space requirements	Open floor space
Materials needed	None
Preparation	Decide on the categories to use for grouping up. (See "Creating Categories.")

Note: See LINE-UPS on p. 340 and STAND AND DELIVER on p. 406 for exercises that are similar to GROUP-UPS.

Creating Categories

In creating the instructions for GROUP-UPS, think about the group's needs, your goals for doing this exercise, and the risk level that each instruction entails for members of the group.

Use instructions that fit the size and nature of your group. With small groups, use instructions that will create only a few groups, such as "Find everyone with the same color shirt as you." In large groups, you can use instructions that create more groups, like the first two in the list below. Be careful not to use instructions that will leave some people without a group.

Some sample instructions are:

- Find everyone with a birthday in the same month as yours.
- Find everyone whose first name starts with the same letter as yours.
- Find everyone with the same shoe size as yours.
- Think of your own favorite way to express creativity, and find everyone who shares it.
- Find everyone who lives in the same neighborhood as you.

Instructions

1. Have the group stand up.
2. Read the first instruction, and tell the group that they have about 30 seconds to get into small groups according to the instruction.
3. When everyone is in groups, ask the groups to say what category they are grouped in (for example, "Where are the January birthdays? ... February? ..."). If there are a lot of people doing the exercise, you may want to stand on a chair or elevated platform in order to see all the groups.
4. Give people a moment to look around and see who is in each group.
5. Read the next instruction, and repeat the process through all of the instructions.
6. As an extra challenge, you can conduct this exercise without allowing any verbal communication, except for people to respond when the facilitator asks what category the group is.

Processing suggestions

- This exercise allows group members to see some of the commonalities and differences in the group. While there may be things that separate members of the group, there are also many similarities around which we can come together. Did people find points of commonality with others in the group that they were unaware of?
- Is it more important to emphasize that which makes us similar, or that which makes us different?
- Some of the things that separate us or that we have in common are very meaningful, and others

are not. Some are the result of choices we make, while others are not.

- When we are arbitrarily separated into groups, competition can erupt between those groups. Did any competition between the groups emerge? How does this play out in the larger society? What groups are pitted against each other?
- If you did the exercise without verbal communication, you can use the exercise to talk about the role of non-verbal communication. What did people do to find their groups? Did anyone find themselves in the wrong group when the groups were called out?

Variation – Self Group-Ups

Number of participants	15-20
Preparation	None

Note: Use this exercise with groups that have already done GROUP-UPS. The exercise can be high-risk, and you should remind everyone to be respectful of what they ask people to group themselves by.

Instructions

1. Divide the group into two to four small groups.
2. Ask each group to come up with three GROUP-UP instructions. Remind them to keep the risk level low.
3. Do the exercise with the whole group, using these new instructions as read by members of the small groups that wrote them.

Additional processing suggestions

- How did people decide how to group themselves? What did people want to know about each other? Did people want to find out particular information about the group? Did people want to intentionally point out similarities or differences in the group?

Musical Cups

Goals	Communication, Personal introspection
Time	10-15 minutes (not including processing), depending on the number of questions
Physical contact	None
Physical challenges	None
Number of participants	Minimum of 7 or 8. Maximum number is unlimited, as long as people can be broken into small groups of 10-12.
Space requirements	Can be done seated around one or more tables or in an open circle.
Materials needed	A CD or tape player with appropriate music, and a cup or mug. (If there will be more than one subgroup, have a cup or mug for each.)
Preparation	Prepare questions or topics on small slips of paper that can be folded up and placed in the cup(s). Questions/topics should relate to the group's pur pose for the day or should be designed to open up discussion about a topic that the group will work on later in the agenda.

Note: MUSICAL CUPS is an exercise that allows a small group to share information in a dynamic way. It can be used before a BRAINSTORM (p. 385) or discussion to get people thinking about the topic or the purpose of the meeting. In some cases you may want to forego processing and move directly into the BRAINSTORM or discussion.

Instructions

1. Give the cup with the questions in it to one of the group members, start playing the music, and indicate the direction for the cup to travel.
2. While the music plays, people pass the cup around the circle.
3. After a short while, stop the music. Whoever is holding the cup when the music stops pulls out a slip of paper, reads the question or topic to the group, and then answers the question or responds to the topic. The slip of paper does not go back in the cup.
4. Allow one or two minutes for the person to speak. No one should interrupt while the person is speaking.
5. Start the music again. The group continues passing the cup around the circle. If someone who has already spoken is holding the cup when the music stops, that person can pass the cup on until it reaches someone who has not yet spoken.
6. The exercise continues until all the questions are answered.

Processing suggestions

- Processing will depend in part on the topics that were addressed.
- You can also talk about the anxiety of being chosen or not, about speaking on the spot in front of a group, and about the randomness of being chosen to do something.
- Did anyone want to respond to the question after they heard someone else speaking about it? How did it feel to not have a chance to be heard? You can discuss how people often do not get their voices heard, even if they want to speak out.
- Did people try to pass the cup even after the music stopped? Sometimes we try to get out of our responsibilities by passing them on to others, especially if the task is something that seems diffi-cult or anxiety-producing.

People Hunt

Goals	Communication, Interconnection, Cultural awareness
Time	15 minutes up to several hours. Depending on your goals, this can be done while people are arriving at an event, getting settled, getting food, etc., or it can be done during the entirety of an event.
Physical contact	None
Physical challenges	Generally must be able to get around and make connections with others in a group of people.
Number of participants	More than 15. No maximum number
Space requirements	None specific; open space is best.
Materials needed	PEOPLE HUNT sheets for each participant, pens or pencils, a place to return the completed PEOPLE HUNT sheets, and a raffle prize (if needed to give people an incentive to participate)
Preparation	Prepare the PEOPLE HUNT question sheet, being sure it contains a "Name" line. Make enough copies for everybody to have one. See "Preparing the PEOPLE HUNT."

Preparing the PEOPLE HUNT

The PEOPLE HUNT question sheet is a page that instructs the participants to "Find someone who…." Generally the page is designed in a grid format with between 16 and 24 boxes, and each box contains an ending to a phrase such as "Find someone who…" or "Sign here if …." Here are some examples.

Find someone who:

- has lived in this city all their life
- is a student
- has performed in front of an audience
- is wearing red

Sign here if

- you speak a language other than English. What language? __________
- you like to eat curry
- you have recently learned a new skill
- you remember [a historical event that only an older person would remember]

The endings that you use on your PEOPLE HUNT sheet will depend on the group you're working with and your goals for the exercise. It's important when designing the sheet to cover as many elements as possible of the population that will be doing the exercise. For a small group, be careful to design the sheet so that everyone will be asked to sign.

Be sure to include at the top of the sheet a line for the participant's name and the instructions for completing the sheet.

Instructions

1. Give each participant a question sheet and a pen or pencil. At a large event, people can pick up the question sheets whenever they arrive.
2. Instruct participants to find people who fit the criteria in each box and ask those people to sign

or initial the box. If there is information requested in the box, the person should supply it. (For example: "Sign here if you play at least two sports. Which ones?")

3. When a participant gets all the boxes filled in, they bring their sheet to the designated place.
4. Announce the deadline for all sheets to be turned in.
5. When everyone has turned in their sheets, thank people for participating, then draw out one sheet and award a prize to the winning player.
6. Alternatively, instead of ending with a raffle you can use the PEOPLE HUNT to engage the group in discussing what they learned about each other.

Processing suggestions

- Note that in some circumstances you will not do any processing. The exercise can stand on its own as a way of getting people to connect with each other.
- In a large group, processing can take the form of the exercise DO WHAT YOU GOTTA DO (p. 297).
- In a small group, you can ask people to comment on what they have learned about the group as a whole, what stereotypes they might have had about who could fill in which boxes, and what it felt like to approach people and ask about certain items.

PEOPLE HUNT

NAME: ______________________________

FIND A PERSON WHO FITS THE DESCRIPTION IN ONE OF THE BOXES AND HAVE THEM SIGN THEIR NAME. YOU MUST FIND A DIFFERENT PERSON FOR EACH BOX. WHEN ALL BOXES ARE FILLED, PUT IN BOX FOR RAFFLE. HAVE FUN AND GOOD LUCK!

FIND SOMEONE WHO...

...GOT AN A IN CLASS	...CAN FREE-STYLE OR RAP	...PLANS TO GO TO COLLEGE	...HAS WON AN AWARD
...HAS A YOUNGER BROTHER OR SISTER	...SPEAKS MORE THAN 2 LANGUAGES	...HAS PERFORMED IN FRONT OF AN AUDIENCE	...WRITES POETRY
...IS A POSITIVE LEADER	...IS LEFT-HANDED	...LIKES TO TRY NEW THINGS	...IS ARTISTIC
...CARES ABOUT OTHERS	...LIKES BEING RESPECTED	...DOESN'T LIKE SEAFOOD	...HAS BEEN OUTSIDE THE U.S. MORE THAN FIVE TIMES

Rainstorm

Goals	Organizing, Focus
Time	10-15 minutes (not including processing)
Physical contact	Minimal
Physical challenges	Must be able to make the movements.
Number of participants	No maximum number
Space requirements	None
Materials needed	None
Preparation	None

Instructions

1. With a smaller group, have everyone sit comfortably on the floor or in chairs. People can be in a circle or facing forward. A large group can remain in their seats.
2. Tell people to follow your lead, joining in as you point or nod in their direction, and to continue with one motion until you indicate they should begin the next. With each new motion, start with the people on the left and move gradually to the right. You may want to have more than one facilitator in a large group, with each facilitator picking up the motion from the one before and leading their segment of the group in that motion.
3. Rub your hands together lightly, then with increasing speed and intensity.
4. Snap your fingers (first one, then the other) lightly, then harder and faster.
5. Lightly pat your hands against your legs, then increase the speed and intensity.
6. Then reverse the order: snap your fingers hard, then less intensely; rub your hands together hard and fast, becoming lighter and slower until the sound fades away.

Processing suggestions

- By joining together in an organized way, people created something beautiful and powerful—the sound of a rainstorm.
- The arc of this rainstorm resembles a movement to create change in the way it starts slowly, gathers intensity and momentum, and then subsides.

Stand Up/Sit Down

Goal	Interconnection
Time	5 minutes (not including processing)
Physical contact	None
Physical challenges	See note.
Number of participants	No maximum number
Space requirements	Can be adapted to nearly any space.
Materials needed	None
Preparation	See "Preparing the Questions."

Note: The exercise can be easily adapted for various physical disabilities. If repeated standing up/sitting down is difficult for members of the group, have people wave their arms instead of standing up. Also, see the variation of this exercise, DO WHAT YOU GOTTA DO.

Preparing the Questions

- Prepare a series of 5-20 questions, depending on the needs of the meeting and the time available. The questions will depend entirely on the group you are working with and your goals in doing this exercise.
- A good approach is to begin with general questions, then integrate a few questions that touch on the purpose of the meeting. It is also helpful to mix questions that nearly everyone can stand up for with those that only a few will stand for. Try to end the exercise with a positive question that almost everyone can stand up for, such as "How many people want this day to be successful?"
- In general, this should be a fun, low-risk exercise, but with certain groups in certain situations you might want to include a few higher-risk questions that relate to your purpose.
- Remember that questions that are low-risk in one group can be high-risk in another. For example, in a group where some members come from difficult family situations, a question like "How many people have a brother or sister?" could pose problems.

This is a sample series of questions for a community meeting:

- How many people like ice cream?
- How many people play a musical instrument?
- How many people put on their shoes today?
- How many people speak another language besides English?
- How many people have ever worked at a fast-food restaurant?
- How many people have been out of the country?
- How many people have ever helped to resolve a conflict?
- How many people have ever performed in front of an audience?
- How many people like rap music?
- How many people like classical music?
- How many people are willing to work for a better community?

Instructions

1. Tell the group that you are going to read them a series of questions. If their answer to the question is "yes" or the question pertains to them, they should stand up. If their answer is "no" or the question does not pertain to them, they should remain seated. If they do not want to answer the question, they should remain seated. When someone does stand up for a question, they should remain standing until the next question is read.

2. Go through the questions you have prepared. At the end, ask everyone to be seated.

Processing suggestions

- In-depth processing is not needed for this exercise. However, you may want to note that STAND UP/SIT DOWN lets people see that they have similarities they may not have been aware of with other people in the group. It also points out the differences in experience and preferences in a group.
- You can comment about the numbers of people who did and did not stand for certain questions.
- This exercise can be used to surface particular experiences that may relate to the work of the group. For example, the question "How many people have known someone who was a victim of violence?" could lead into a discussion about that issue.
- You can also use the exercise to express commitment to the purpose of the day with a question such as "How many people are ready to work for social change?"

Variation – Do What You Gotta Do

Physical challenges	Depend on the actions that you ask people to do.
Preparation	Instead of questions, prepare statements and corresponding actions. See "Preparing the Statements."

Preparing the Statements

Follow the guidelines for STAND UP/SIT DOWN questions, except that you are preparing statements and actions to accompany the answers to the statements. For example:

- Stand up and stretch if you went to bed before 11:00 pm last night.
- Rest your head on your hands if you went to bed after 1:00 am last night.
- Jump up and down if you are happy to be here today.
- Sneeze if you remember at least one other person's name in this room.
- Wave your hands in the air if you were here for last week's meeting.
- If you speak a language other than English, say "Hello, how are you?" in that language.
- Play an imaginary instrument if you play a musical instrument.
- Stand up and make a fist if you have ever spoken out for something you believed in.

Instructions

1. Follow the instructions for STAND UP/SIT DOWN, except that you ask people to follow specific directions in response to statements. You should make the motions that you are asking the group to make.

Chapter 16

The Rest of the Springboard Exercises

These are the exercises that don't fit the criteria for chapters 11 through 15, so they share certain characteristics:

- They take more than five but less than fifteen minutes.
- They are suitable for groups of moderate size (generally between 8 and 30 people).
- They require either open floor space or room for the group to sit or stand in a circle, but they are not for an audience or for people seated at desks or tables.
- While some are quite active, they don't involve tagging.

They are useful for many different purposes and can help your group meet a variety of goals.

All Aboard

Goals	Group problem solving, Group introspection, Surfacing group dynamics
Time	5-10 minutes (not including processing)
Physical contact	Requires the whole group to squeeze into a small space.
Physical challenges	Could require the ability to balance oneself or to be surrounded by a lot of people.
Number of participants	Fewer than 20
Space requirements	Open floor space
Materials needed	Masking tape
Preparation	Use the tape to create a small, enclosed space (square or rectangle) on the floor. It is important that the space be small enough to make the exercise difficult, but not so small as to make it impossible. This requires some practice, and by adjusting the level of difficulty you can make different points or bring new dynamics to the surface. These changes will have a significant impact on how you process what occurs in the group.

Instructions

1. Tell the group that the instructions are simply for the whole group to fit into the space on the floor at one time.
2. Once everyone is in the space, walk around it and ensure that no one's feet are outside.
3. Have the group count to three before they get out of the space. You can make the task more difficult by having them sing "Row, Row, Row Your Boat" completely through three times before they leave the space.

Processing suggestions

- This exercise can be used to surface issues of motivation by raising the question of whether everyone is "on board" with the work of the group.
- Discuss the points in the exercise at which people chose to get involved. Who went in first? second? last? Are these the same people who are always first and last to take initiative in this group? How do we as a group make sure that everyone is "on board"?
- It also illustrates the way the group deals with a challenge and how they solve problems. Did some people or the whole group give up?
- How was leadership manifested? Were there clear leaders, or did everyone have a role?
- How well does the group adjust to different stresses?
- Can everyone fit within the space that this group represents?

Variation – All Aboard, All Ahead

Time	10-15 minutes (not including processing)
Additional physical challenge	Must be able to leap from one space to another.
Number of participants	Fewer than 20
Preparation	Create two enclosed spaces with tape on the floor, a good long step away from each other. Vary the size and shape of the spaces. The spaces must be big enough to make the task possible, but not so large as to make it too easy.

Instructions

1. Have the group start out by getting into the bigger space, just as you would in ALL ABOARD.
2. Then have them move into the smaller space without anyone stepping outside of the taped lines.

Additional processing suggestions

- When a group can work together under difficult circumstances and experience success, many opportunities open up. People can grow and feel free to take risks and try new things.
- Sometimes the difficult work of building trust, respect, and communication must be tackled first. As the group moves through these stages successfully, members may then feel more comfortable physically and emotionally, and be ready to take on bigger challenges together.
- Some people fall into patterns of always or never taking the lead. If this dynamic is present in the group, it will emerge in the exercise and can be discussed.
- The exercise can also be used to help a group reflect on acting strategically (for example, do they just keep trying the same thing even when it is not working?), and on how they make decisions (for example, who is listened to when deciding order, etc.).

Variation – All Aboard, Some Ahead

Preparation	Tape out three enclosed spaces of decreasing size on the floor, a good long step away from each other. The spaces can be different shapes (for example, square, circle, triangle). Decide how many people you want to fit into each space, and make the spaces big enough so that the task is possible, but small enough so that it is a challenge.

Instructions

1. Have the group start out by getting into the biggest space, as in ALL ABOARD.
2. Tell the group to have a certain number of people, fewer than the whole group, move into the second space. The group decides who will move ahead.
3. Tell the group how many people must move to the third space.

Additional processing suggestions

- Work becomes more focused in small groups as we move from the big picture to a more detailed level.
- As the group moves forward in its work, they will confront more and more difficult choices.
- You can also use this exercise to talk about dynamics of race and class preference in society, or more generally about group selection processes. Who got moved ahead and by what criteria? Who took the leadership during the exercise, at what point, and what were the decisions based on about who gets to go forward?

Further Variations

You can vary ALL ABOARD in a number of other ways. For example:

- To illustrate getting out of a stressful situation, have the group move from a small space to a larger space.
- To raise the issues associated with a group that has experienced changes in its form or membership, have the group move through a series of spaces of different shapes.

Additional processing suggestions

- Even subtle changes to an exercise can have a significant impact on the dynamics that emerge. Try to maintain a heightened awareness to how the changes play out and what messages they might convey to the group.

Bag Toss

Goals	Interconnection, Focus, Communication
Time	10 minutes (not including processing)
Physical contact	Minimal
Physical challenges	Must be able to throw and catch a beanbag.
Number of participants	12-30
Space requirements	Open floor space
Materials needed	Between 5 and 15 beanbags, depending on the size of the group
Preparation	None

Instructions

1. Have people stand in a circle.
2. To begin, establish an order for throwing the beanbags (see "Establishing a Pattern").
3. Once the pattern has been established, begin the exercise by calling someone's name and throwing a beanbag underhand to that person. Tell the group to throw underhand throughout the exercise.
4. While the first bag is making its way around the circle, tell the group that you are going to start adding more bags. Remind them that it is important to continue calling names.
5. Start throwing out more beanbags. By varying the number of bags and the speed at which you are throwing them, you can make the exercise more manageable or more overwhelming, depending on the needs of the group and the issue(s) to be illustrated. Note that when someone drops or fails to catch a bag, they simply pick up the bag and continue.
6. When you are ready to end the exercise, hold the beanbags as they come back to you, rather than sending them around the circle again.

Establishing a Pattern

You can establish the pattern with handshakes or with beanbags:

1. With handshakes, the facilitator (person A) calls the name of someone (person B) across the circle, makes eye contact with the person called, then walks across to shake their hand. Person B calls the name of someone else (person C) and shakes that person's hand. Person C calls someone else who has not yet been called. This continues until everyone has been chosen once (and only once). Everyone is free to choose whomever they want among those who have not yet been chosen. The last person to be called closes the loop by calling the name and shaking the hand of person A. Ask everyone to remember whose hand they shook, as that is the person to whom they are going to throw the bag. Before moving on with the exercise, practice the pattern with another quick round of handshakes to make sure that everyone remembers to whom they are throwing.
2. With beanbags, the procedure is to call the name and then throw a beanbag.

Processing suggestions

- You can use this exercise to demonstrate the various ways in which everyone is connected, both giving to and receiving from each other.
- We choose to whom we throw, just as we choose with whom we connect in the group or in our lives. (Often people will throw to someone with whom they have a higher comfort level, or someone they want to get to know better.)
- You can also talk about the importance of names and eye contact. Did anyone stop calling out a name? What happened?

- People or pairs often find ways to adapt to the circumstances, giving cues to each other or helping each other out. What strategies did people use to focus on catching and throwing the bags? How do these relate to the strategies people use in their lives?
- In this exercise, and in the work of the group, everyone needs to maintain focus if the group is going to "keep all its bags in the air." When many bags are used, the exercise can be used as a metaphor for how people react when conditions feel overwhelming. How did people cope? Did they drop bags, start whipping the bags, throw more than one at a time, or hold on to some bags and wait until their catcher was ready?
- BAG TOSS also shows the importance of establishing a clear structure, and how much fun and how productive working within a structure can be.
- Was the group functional or dysfunctional, and were you as an individual contributing to the order or contributing to the chaos? We each have power over the function of the group.

Variation – Bag Toss with a Reverse

Instructions

1. Follow the instructions for BAG TOSS, but tell the group that at some point in the exercise you will say "reverse."
2. At that point, everyone should switch the direction they are throwing the bag—that is, they will start throwing it to the person who had been throwing it to them, and they need to switch to saying that person's name as well. They will now be receiving the bag from the person they had been throwing it to.

Additional processing suggestions

- Adding a "reverse" to the exercise is helpful in talking about having to adjust to new circumstances or to change direction in your work together.
- It also shows how the group can fall apart and then with practice (experience) come back together again.
- Depending on the speed with which you call out reverses, the exercise can show how quick changes, or many changes in a row, can lead to chaos.

Variation – Bag Toss with Movement

Additional goal	Different perspectives

Note: This exercise works well with a group that is very familiar with BAG TOSS and some of the other variations, but it is too complicated for a group that is new to the exercise. This variation is very challenging and chaotic. Expect it to fall apart a bit.

Instructions

1. Play BAG TOSS using only one bag.
2. After the bag has gone around a few times, stop the exercise and tell the group the new procedure: Once they have thrown the bag to the next person and that person has caught it, they are to move to that person's place in the circle. Meanwhile, the person to whom they threw the bag will be calling the name of the next person in the order, throwing the bag to them, waiting for them to catch it, and then moving to *their* place in the circle.
3. Have the group practice once to help them remember the order of the tasks they must complete.
4. Start the bag and the movement
5. Add bags, as in BAG TOSS, up to or beyond the group's tolerance level.

Additional processing suggestions

- If your group is dealing with changes, or looking at making changes, this variation can get everyone thinking about how changes affect them and how the group can make adjustments that help it succeed through the change.

- It can be challenging to see things from another person's point of view.
- There is a fine line between chaos and dynamic movement within a group, and each individual plays a part in determining whether the group crosses the line.
- You can use this exercise to talk about the importance of speaking directly to someone and getting their attention. Communication is essential to the success of this exercise and to the work of the group.

Variation – Think Ahead Bag Toss

Additional goal Planning

Note: This variation should be used with a group that has played Bag Toss before.

Instructions

1. Before you begin throwing the bags, ask the group to think ahead about the exercise. For example:
   - What are some useful strategies?
   - What are some things to watch out for?
   - How many bags can the group handle?
   - How many bags do you predict might be dropped?
2. Then ask the group to set a goal regarding the number of times that bags will be dropped.
3. Play Bag Toss, keeping count of the dropped bags.

Additional processing suggestion

- Consider how planning and thinking ahead changed the experience of the exercise. For instance, were there fewer dropped bags when the group set a goal regarding keeping the bags in the air?

Variation – Bag Toss with Left Outs

Additional goal Group introspection

Note: This variation can be high-risk depending on the group. It brings out issues of exclusion, which can be difficult for people to deal with.

Instructions

1. Begin by playing regular Bag Toss.
2. Stop the exercise and arbitrarily pick someone from the group (person X). Tell the group not to throw the bag to X anymore. You will have to readjust the order so that the person who was throwing the bag to X now throws to the person that X was throwing to.
3. Continue with the exercise.
4. Stop several more times, taking more and more people out of the exercise. Do not give those who are taken out any particular instructions, but instead watch what people do as the exercise goes on without them.

Additional processing suggestions

- The exercise illustrates the experience of being left out and being an outsider. It can be used to illustrate a dynamic in the group, or to represent how someone on the margins of society (for example, a homeless person) might feel.

- How did those who were left out react to being excluded? If there were dysfunctional responses, talk about where the behavior came from.
- The exercise can show age, class, and race dynamics, what it feels like to be excluded, and how people who are excluded sometimes resort to dysfunction to try to get power.

Variation – Bag Toss with Outs

Instructions

1. This is the same as regular BAG TOSS except that people are "out" whenever they drop a bag or fail to catch a bag.
2. People who are out must drop back from the circle, and everyone else must adjust for their absence.

Additional processing suggestions

- This exercise could be used to talk about how the group might respond to losing a member.
- It can also be used to discuss the feelings that come out when things are high-stakes (when failure has immediate and significant consequences). How did it feel to be out? Did people pay more attention because they knew they would be out if they dropped the bag? How does our work and effort change when we are accountable to someone versus when we are working of our own accord?
- If group members expressed anxiety at seeing people pushed out, you can comment on the level of interdependence in the group.
- Did people try to intentionally get each other out by throwing the bags in a manner that made it difficult to catch them? What does competition do to a group? Does it help or hurt?

Variation – Hot Bag

Preparation	Choose an object to be thrown from person to person that is easily distinguishable from the ordinary beanbags. It could be a beanbag with a special marking or wrapping on it, or it could be a different object such as a small rubber toy.

Instructions

1. Play BAG TOSS using the "hot bag" along with the regular beanbags.
2. When you say "Freeze," whoever is holding the hot bag is out.
3. If play continues from that point, people must adjust so that the person throwing to the person who is out will now throw to the next person in the order.
4. You can continue playing until several more people are out.

Additional processing suggestions

- This exercise exposes how people respond to a person who is marked as the "outsider." Often the response will be to shun them or make comments about them, which will force the group to reckon with its own assumptions and attitudes.
- The exercise can show what happens when people begin to pass responsibility off to others. (For example, the person who's holding the hot bag may throw it to another person or onto the floor when you say "Freeze.")
- It can also be used to demonstrate the arbitrary nature of who gets passed by for opportunities (since people are stuck with the bag and its consequences through no fault of their own). Through this exercise you can set up discussions about power in society, as well as dynamics such as racism and classism.

Variation – Object Toss

Additional goal	Group introspection
Preparation	Collect a number of objects that are small enough and safe enough to be thrown from person to person.

Instructions

1. Follow the instructions for BAG TOSS using the objects instead of beanbags.

Additional processing suggestions

- In this exercise, groups and individuals must throw and catch objects of different shapes and sizes. Problems or issues also come in all different shapes and sizes, and that can throw us off unless we learn to adapt.
- What was the most difficult item to catch? What are the more difficult things we encounter as a group or as individuals? How do we deal with the more difficult objects/issues? What are the strategies we use?
- Did anyone feel overwhelmed or unable to handle an object? If so, how did they feel or react? How did others react?

Variation – Bag Toss with Words

Additional goal	Group introspection
Preparation	Write words on slips of paper or stickers and affix a word to each bag. The words should be related to the group's work; for example, they could be about the group's goals or about issues that will be discussed at the meeting.

Note: This exercise is similar in many ways to WIND BLOWS WITH WORDS (p. 378), except that it does not put anyone in a position where they must speak.

Instructions

1. Begin by playing regular BAG TOSS.
2. After a while, yell "Freeze" and ask if anyone would like to speak about the word on the bag they are holding.
3. Continue playing and freezing periodically.

Additional processing suggestions

- Focus on the type of words that people chose to speak about and some of the points that were made. Were some words skipped because of their complexity?
- Who chose to speak about their words, and why did they choose to do so?
- Having to speak extemporaneously can be difficult. You can use this exercise to make this point, to give people practice with impromptu speaking, and to discuss the benefits of being prepared.
- The exercise can also look at the fact that the external work of the group must give way at times to the need for discussing important issues inside the group.

Variation – Long Distance Toss

Additional goal	Group introspection

Instructions

1. Have the group stand in a circle and establish a pattern, as in BAG TOSS.
2. Have everyone take 5-10 (or more) steps back.
3. Follow the instructions for BAG TOSS with the circle spread out.

Additional processing suggestions

- LONG DISTANCE TOSS can be used to illustrate a range of barriers that separate people (such as race, class, or different parts of a large organization). What kind of "bags" need to be thrown in order to make connections across these barriers?
- It can also show how much more difficult, yet exciting and empowering, it can be to make connections when people are separated by social distance, conflict, or lack of trust.

Bigger and Bigger

Goals	Communication, Acting
Time	Roughly one minute per participant (not including processing)
Physical contact	None necessary, but there may be some if participants choose to initiate it.
Physical challenges	None
Number of participants	15 or fewer
Space requirements	Open floor space is ideal, but the exercise can also be done around a table.
Materials needed	None
Preparation	None

Note: This exercise can be hard work emotionally, and it is likely that some people will not be able to do it. If someone is having difficulty, allow them to pass if they wish.

Instructions

1. Have the group stand in a circle.
2. Explain that each person will take a brief turn (less than a minute) telling a story to the person to their left, who faces the speaker and listens to what they have to say.
3. There are three rules for the storytelling:
   (a) Your story cannot make sense.
   (b) You must start softly and quietly and get more and more emotional and physically animated (bigger and bigger) through your tone, gestures, and volume as you tell your story. You may want to give an example for the group to demonstrate the range you are looking for.
   (c) You must begin your story where the last person left off, but then may take the story in any direction.
4. Ask for a volunteer to start and then go around the group. The facilitators should participate. The person who listens is always the next to speak.

Processing suggestions

- While there are many issues that this exercise can be used to examine, be careful not to lose the energy that the exercise can create by "overprocessing." This is a powerful exercise that opens up the subconscious without much processing.
- This exercise can be used to talk about the importance of bringing emotions into speeches or acting, and the importance of having a large range of emotional and physical expression when trying to engage an audience. What kinds of emotions did people see in this exercise?
- What did it feel like to let things get bigger? Was there a point when you pulled back? How did the listener have an impact on what you did?
- What was it like to listen to the story? What was the body language of listening?
- Body language and other non-verbal forms of communication can be very powerful, even in everyday conversation.

Variation – Smaller and Smaller

Instructions

1. As each person tells their story, they start out very animated, but then make their tone, gestures, and emotions "smaller and smaller" as they go along.

Additional processing suggestion

- SMALLER AND SMALLER can be used to look at the nuances of emotions and emotional expression.

Blind Walk

Goals	Interconnection, Trust
Time	5-10 minutes (not including processing)
Physical contact	Holding hands
Physical challenges	Must be able to walk without using sight.
Number of participants	10-20
Space requirements	Open floor space
Materials needed	None
Preparation	Decide on the route for the walk and check it for safety (for example, look for places where people might trip). The walk need not be long; a short walk, even circling around in one room, will be enough to allow you to process the exercise effectively.

Note: If possible, one or more facilitators should stand along the route as monitors.

Instructions

1. Have everyone line up behind you, holding hands.
2. Explain that you are going to lead the group on a walk, but that everyone (except for you) will have their eyes closed. Stress the need to walk carefully and quietly, with no pulling or fooling around.
3. Ask people to close their eyes, and begin the walk.

Processing suggestions

- BLIND WALK can surface issues of connection and trust in the group as people struggle with giving up control and trusting themselves to someone else's leadership.
- Were people able to keep their eyes closed the entire time? If not, why not? Did people feel safe? Did people trust the leader?
- In a group that is preparing for leadership, you can discuss the role of the leader in this exercise. A leader needs to have vision and perspective that will help others to move forward.

Boppity Bop Bop Bop

Goal	Focus
Time	10 minutes (not including processing)
Physical contact	None
Physical challenges	Must be able to respond quickly.
Number of participants	12-30
Space requirements	Open floor space
Materials needed	None
Preparation	None

Instructions

1. With the group standing in a circle, ask for a volunteer who will be "it" and step into the middle of the circle. The task is to get out of the middle. This can be done in one of two ways:
   (a) The person who is "it" can point to anyone in the circle and say "Boppity Bop Bop Bop." If the person pointed to does not say "Bop" before "it" finishes saying "Boppity Bop Bop Bop," that person becomes "it" and goes into the middle of the circle, while the former "it" joins the circle.
   (b) The person who is "it" can also get out by trying to fool those forming the circle into saying "Bop" unnecessarily. "It" does this by pointing to someone in the circle and saying "Bop" instead of "Boppity Bop Bop Bop." If the person responds with "Bop," they must take the place of "it" in the middle of the circle. If they do not say anything, "it" stays in the middle.
2. "It" can point to anyone in the circle, in any order, and as many times as they want, until they succeed in getting out of the middle.

Processing suggestions

- This exercise can generate a lot of frustration for someone who gets trapped in the middle and cannot get out. Feeling trapped can be connected to a range of difficult situations, especially ones where someone is visibly vulnerable (for example, teen parents, someone living with a disability).
- What was it like to be in the middle? Did people use any strategies to stay out of the middle? How did you feel about the person in the middle while you were on the outside?

Variation – Boppity Name Bop

Note: This exercise can be used with a group that has been learning each other's names as a lively way to reinforce the importance of knowing names.

Instructions

1. In this variation, when "it" points to someone and says "Boppity Bop Bop Bop," before "it" finishes the person must respond with the name of the person to their right. If the person is too slow or gives the wrong name, they become "it."
2. "It" has the option of saying "Boppity Bop Bop Left." In this case, the person pointed to must say the name of the person to their left.

Additional processing suggestion

- If we don't have a grasp of each other's names, it can make our time in the group together lack a powerful level of connection. Names help you to reach out more easily, which is important when your work together calls for regular communication or split-second decisions.

Variation – Palm Tree, House, Viking

Additional goal Interconnection

Note: It is best to use this variation with a group that is already familiar with Boppity Bop Bop Bop. Introduce only one new element at a time; for example, let the group get used to doing the "Palm Tree" for a couple of rounds before adding the "House." It is also helpful if you demonstrate the motions required for each element as you add them to the exercise.

Instructions

1. Instead of saying "Boppity Bop Bop Bop" when pointing to someone, "it" says "Palm Tree," "House," or "Viking."
2. Both the person pointed to and the people on either side of that person must react as follows:
   (a) If "it" points to person A and says "Palm Tree," A has to stand like a palm tree—both arms up with hands draping down. The two people to the immediate left and right of A have to do a hula dance and sing "Aloha-waii, Aloha-waii."
   (b) If "it" points to person A and says "House," the people to the immediate left and right of A form a roof over A by turning toward A and putting their arms up to meet each other's outstretched fingers. Person A makes welcoming gestures and says "Come in, come in, come in."
   (c) If "it" points to person A and says "Viking," A must form a Viking's helmet by putting their hands on their head with index fingers curled out. The people to the immediate left and right of A become the oarsmen, pretending to row a boat and saying "Stroke, stroke, stroke."
3. If any of the three people fails to react or makes the wrong motion, that person becomes "it." If more than one of them makes a mistake, person A becomes "it." If none of them makes a mistake, "it" remains in the middle of the circle and must continue trying to get out.

Additional processing suggestions

- How did the exercise change when the new elements were added? What additional skills are required in this adaptation?
- This exercise requires that people learn and react very quickly, and some will have difficulty with this. What did the exercise show about different learning styles? Did some people have more difficulty with certain parts of the exercise than with others?
- This exercise can also be used to talk about the group's interdependence, since each person was dependent on those near them to create the "Palm Tree," "House" or "Viking." The group is dependent on everyone to help create and carry out the vision and mission of the group.

Circle of Support

Goals	Group problem solving, Interconnection
Time	10-15 minutes (not including processing)
Physical contact	Holding hands, being in a close circle with others, pulling or being pulled
Physical challenges	Must be able to go from a seated position on the floor to a standing position.
Number of participants	6-30
Space requirements	Open floor space
Materials needed	None
Preparation	None

Note: This exercise may be too high-risk if any members of the group would have difficulty coming to a standing position.

Instructions

1. Divide the group into smaller groups of three to six people.
2. Have each group sit in a circle with their legs extended and feet touching.
3. Have everyone cross their arms and hold hands with two other people in the circle. If there are five or six people in the circle, people should take the hands of those who are not right next to them.
4. Then instruct the group(s) to pull themselves up to a standing position. Some people will be able to stand right up, while others will need to be pulled up by the rest of their group. Group members may need to realign themselves so that their weight or strength is equally distributed around the circle before they are able to achieve the task.

Processing suggestions

- CIRCLE OF SUPPORT requires everyone to adjust to others' strengths and weaknesses in order to achieve the group's goals. This is also often the case when groups are working together.
- Did the groups need to make adjustments in order to achieve the task? Were those adjustments made easily? How is the support or mindset necessary to succeed in this exercise reflected in group's day-to-day work? How did people deal with the frustration associated with the task?
- The exercise can also be used to look at the dynamics of who is pulling and who is being pulled. At times, the load of the work may shift onto different people. How does this group make sure that everyone is able to pull their share of the work, and that people feel that the workload is fair and balanced?

Circle the Circle

Goal	Group problem solving
Time	5-10 minutes (not including processing)
Physical contact	Holding hands
Physical challenges	Must be able to get through a large hoop while holding hands. (This is easier than it sounds.)
Number of participants	10-15
Space requirements	Open floor space
Materials needed	Large plastic hoop
Preparation	None

Instructions

1. Have the group stand in a circle and hold hands.
2. Put the hoop on one person's arm, and explain that each member of the group must pass their body through the hoop without letting go of hands. In this way, the hoop will move around the circle until it reaches the starting point.

Processing suggestions

- CIRCLE THE CIRCLE illustrates teamwork and using everyone's creativity to complete a task. In the work of a group, the end product is stronger when ideas are put out into the group and everyone's input is included. Did anyone learn strategies from watching others in the group?
- Flexibility determines success with this exercise, and in the work of a group as well.
- A group works best when the people in it support each other whenever a particular task or action is difficult for an individual.
- How did group members feel when they finished with the hoop? Did people pay attention to others as the hoop went around?

Variation – Circle the Circle Squared

Materials	Two large plastic hoops

Instructions

1. Use two hoops moving around the circle in opposite directions.

Additional processing suggestions

- This illustrates the challenges associated with working on multiple tasks at the same time.
- You can use this exercise to talk about how to support group members when they are going through a particularly challenging time, or about how to help each other when group members are overwhelmed with tasks. What happened when the two hoops met? How did that person who faced that situation deal with the additional challenge?

Concentric Mirrors

Goals	Leadership, Communication, Introspection
Time	5-10 minutes (not including processing)
Physical contact	None
Physical challenges	Must be able to mirror the partner's actions.
Number of participants	12-30
Space requirements	Open floor space
Materials needed	None
Preparation	None

Instructions

1. Have the group stand up and create two concentric circles, so that half the group forms an outer circle facing in and the other half forms an inner circle facing out. Everyone should be facing someone from the other circle. If there is an uneven number of people, either you can participate or you can designate one place in the circle where people will form a triad.
2. Tell the group that the outside circle will start off as the leaders, while the inside circle will be the followers.
3. When you say go, the leaders start making motions. The followers pretend to be mirror images of their partners, each person doing everything that their leader does. Ask the group not to talk or make other noises during the exercise.
4. Whenever you say "Switch," the followers become the leaders and the former leaders become the "mirrors." This lets people experience both aspects of the exercise. You can switch frequently.
5. After 20-30 seconds, tell the outer circle to rotate one position to the right, so that everyone is facing a new partner.
6. Continue until the outer circle has rotated all the way around the inner circle.

Processing suggestions

- Concentric Mirrors lets individuals see their actions and expressions reflected back at them by their peers. What did it feel like to be imitated? Did the image in the "mirror" look funny?
- We are always mirroring and reflecting back what we see. People follow each other's motions, whether we are conscious of it or not. Often the best way to learn is to see ourselves through other's eyes, although this can sometimes be a painful experience.
- This exercise also deals with differences in style and personality, as people try to imitate various other group members. Was it easier to do the exercise with some people than with others? Were people always able to mirror their partners?
- Did people prefer leading or following? Which was easier for you? Did the leaders try to lose their partners or did they try to help them?

Variation – Concentric Mirrors with Words

Preparation	Prepare a list of words designed to surface issues or points for discussion in the group. The words you choose depend on your group's needs, but some examples might be: trust, community, work, help, leisure, together. You might choose to have the words name emotions (sad, joyful, worried, depressed, excited, hopeful, etc.).

Instructions

1. Proceed as for Concentric Mirrors except that before each new set of pairs begins, give them a word from the list you have prepared. The leaders' motions must represent the word.

Additional processing suggestions

- Some topics and emotions are easier than others for people to represent, express, and talk about. Which words were easiest or hardest for the leaders to represent, and why? How does this group handle discussing difficult subjects? How do we handle difficult emotions in this group or in society?
- This exercise can also be used to talk about communicating clearly so that others understand your message. How were the different words represented? Did the followers understand the leaders' interpretations? Did the followers have other ideas about how to represent the words?

Variation – Long Distance Mirrors with Words

Number of participants	10-20
Preparation	Prepare a list of words for people to act out—for example: easy, fun, important, joy, profound, life, truth, sadness, youth, justice. In choosing words, think about the purpose of the meeting and your reasons for doing this exercise.

Instructions

1. Have people stand in two facing lines at opposite ends of the room. The lines should be at least ten feet apart.
2. Tell people that each person is paired with the person opposite them in the other line. With an uneven number of participants, pair two people on one end of one line with the one person who is facing them in the other line.
3. Designate one side as the leaders and the other as the followers.
4. Give the group a word. The leaders act out the word however they wish, while each follower mirrors the actions of their leader.
5. Call time after 10-15 seconds.
6. The person at one end of the follower line moves directly forward to the end of the leader line, bumping everyone over one place. Likewise, the person at the other end of the leader line moves forward to the end of the follower line, bumping everyone until the original follower's place is filled.
7. You can decide if everyone then takes a step toward the center, or if only one side should move toward the center, while the other side stays where it is.
8. Give the next word. Continue in this way for several rounds. It is not necessary for everyone to have turns as both leader and follower.

Additional processing suggestions

- The exercise can illustrate what it's like trying to have an effect on people who are far away.
- When our perspective changes, it gives us the opportunity to see things that we hadn't noticed before, and often can help us to improve the work we are doing. How did your perspective change as the pairs got closer? Were the followers able to see different movements depending on their distance from the leaders?
- What distance was most comfortable for you to do this exercise? People have different levels of comfort around closeness of personal space, which can come from both personal preferences and cultural norms.
- How did people keep up energy while dealing with profound, important, or sad things? (Processing will vary depending on the words chosen for mirroring.)
- How did it feel to not have the chance to lead or follow?

- If there were an uneven number of participants, what were the experiences of those who were in two-on-one situations?

Variation – Group Mirror

Additional goals	Surfacing group dynamics, Focus

Instructions

1. Divide the group in half, and have people stand in two lines facing each other. The lines should be far enough apart so that everyone in one line can see everyone in the other line. People do not need to be lined up opposite each other.
2. Designate one side as the leaders.
3. When you say "Go," each person on the leader side starts making motions. People on the follower side mirror what people on the leader side are doing, without discussing who will mirror whom.

Additional processing suggestions

- Was there any order to whom people were following? Did followers stay focused on one leader, or did they switch? Does this mirror how the group functions in terms of our organization or our focus?
- Was there more than one person following the same person in the other group? Was everyone in the leadership group being mirrored?
- This exercise can be used to talk about positive and negative aspects of leadership, and of the simplicity and complexity of messages put forth by leaders. What kinds of actions were more likely to be mirrored by the follower group? In society, do people tend to follow positive or negative actions? simpler or more complex actions?
- You can use this exercise to talk about how we choose whom to follow. What strategies did people in the follower group use to decide whom to mirror and how to focus? What strategies do people use in life to choose who their role models, mentors, politicians and leaders will be? Are these effective strategies?

Variation – Concentric Acting

Additional goals	Creativity, Acting
Preparation	Prepare several scenarios or interactions that can take place between two people. See "Creating Scenarios" for suggestions.

Note: You can use this exercise primarily to work on acting skills or primarily to focus on issues, or you can use it for both simultaneously.

Creating Scenarios

Some or all of the scenarios could deal with issues or situations that are present or under discussion in the group. Other scenarios may be designed just for fun or to help people loosen up and release their creativity. The following are included to give you a general idea of the types of scenarios that a group could use; however, the scenarios you create should grow out of the needs of your group.

- A parent and teenager arguing over what time the teen is expected home at night
- A person talking with a friend, claiming to have won the lottery (but this isn't true)
- Two people arguing over whether it makes sense to vote or not
- Two people discussing what to do that night; one wants to go to the movies and the other wants to go to a party
- A student and a teacher having an argument over a bad grade
- A person who has just lost their job breaking the news to their spouse
- A person telling another person that someone they care about has been hurt in an accident

- A person telling another person that there is going to be a fight after school
- Two people arguing over a member of the opposite sex
- Two people are camping; one sees a bear in the distance but the other doesn't believe it.

Instructions

1. Have the group stand up and create two concentric circles, so that half the group forms an outer circle facing in and the other half forms an inner circle facing out. Everyone should be facing someone from the other circle. If there is an uneven number of people, either you can participate or you can designate one place in the circle where people will form a triad.
2. Describe one of the scenes and designate which circle (inner or outer) will take which part.
3. Give the pairs about 30 seconds to act out the scene.
4. When the allotted time is up, say "Switch." The people in the inner circle move one person to their left.
5. Describe another scene, and repeat the process several times, depending on how many scenes you want the group to act out. You can repeat scenes if you wish, so that people are experiencing the same scene with different partners.

Additional processing suggestions

- If you are using this exercise primarily to practice acting skills and to bring out the group's creative energy, it's important not to "overprocess." The exercise can generate energy that can be used effectively in the work section of the meeting.
- How did people feel in particular roles? Which ones were hardest to play? Which ones were easier, and why?
- Did the scenarios play out realistically? Did anything happen that was unexpected?
- Discuss the issues that the scenarios dealt with.

D-Chain

Goals	Group problem solving, Interconnection
Time	10-15 minutes (not including processing)
Physical contact	None
Physical challenges	Minimal
Number of participants	8-12
Space requirements	Open floor space or a large table that everyone can stand around
Materials needed	Dominoes
Preparation	None

Instructions

1. Give each member of the group five dominoes.
2. Tell the group that they must each place their dominoes so that, together with everyone else's dominoes, they create one chain that will tip over when the domino at the end is pushed over.
3. Give the group several minutes to place their dominoes.
4. When they have finished, push over the first domino in the chain and see if the entire chain falls over.

Processing suggestions

- This exercise is helpful in raising issues around the way that things or events are connected. If there are breaks in the chain and the entire structure does not fall together, this can be equated with the way that some issues/ideas/areas of society become disconnected. Did the D-Chain work? Did it all fall down? If not, why not?
- Is the work or communication of this group smooth and connected, or are there gaps? If there are gaps, what needs to be done to bring the pieces together?
- You should also watch the process by which the group lays down its dominoes. How did the group decide what shape the chain would take? Did one person take the lead or was it a group effort? Did anyone work to undermine the group in doing its task? If any conflicts arose, how did the group deal with them?

Eye Lines

Goals	Interconnection, Organizing, Leadership
Time	5-10 minutes (not including processing)
Physical contact	None
Physical challenges	Must be able to see across the circle.
Number of participants	10-30
Space requirements	Open floor space
Materials needed	None
Preparation	None

Instructions

1. Ask for a volunteer to start off as "it." "It" is the only one with the power to make a connection.
2. Have the group stand in a circle and look at the ground.
3. At the count of three, everyone looks up. The person who is "it" makes eye contact with someone else, and those two change places in the circle. The new person in the "it" position now has the power.
4. Continue in this way through several rounds. This is the first phase of the exercise.
5. Process the first phase (see below).
6. In the second phase, the power does not stay in the "it" position but spreads throughout the group. As before, the first person with the power makes eye connection with someone else and changes places with that person. But now the first person retains the power to make connections as well as to pass the power on, and each person who receives the connection has the power to make a new connection and to pass the power on.
7. Continue until everyone in the group has received the power.

Processing suggestions

- For the first phase, raise questions about what it is like to have power and to lose power, to get attention but then to lose it and not regain it. What did it feel like for those not "it" to not have the power to connect with others? Did anyone try to connect with "it" that "it" did not choose to connect with?
- The second phase, in contrast, illustrates power shared: how it feels to empower others and to be empowered.
- The exercise illustrates the difference between one person having power (the exercise proceeded in a simple and orderly fashion) versus shared power (which was chaotic, dynamic, and exciting). Which model did people prefer? What are the advantages and disadvantages of each?

Eye to Eye

Goal	Interconnection
Time	5-10 minutes (not including processing)
Physical contact	None
Physical challenges	Minimal
Number of participants	12-30
Space requirements	Open floor space
Materials needed	None
Preparation	None

Note: This exercise is best done with groups that already know each other and that have previously done EYE CONNECT (p. 158). Even with a formed group, it's likely that people will be anxious and have a lot of difficulty. Expect laughter as people try to diffuse their anxiety, and be prepared for the likelihood that some people will not be able to do the exercise.

Instructions

1. Have the group stand up and form two concentric circles, with half the group in the outer circle facing in and the other half in the inner circle facing out. Everyone should be facing someone else. If there is an odd number in the group, either a facilitator should participate or someone should be an observer in each round.
2. When you give the start signal to begin, the people facing each other simply look directly into each other's eyes for seven seconds.
3. When you call time, the inner circle moves one place to the right.
4. Repeat until the inner circle has moved all the way around. Be sure to keep time, calling out "Start" and "Stop" for each pair.
5. Once the group has had experience with the basic exercise, you can experiment with holding each eye contact for a longer period of time and/or with varying the amounts of time for the contacts.

Processing suggestions

- This exercise addresses both the power of direct contact with others and the fear that such contact can arouse. It can illustrate the importance of developing the confidence to look people and the world directly in the eye.
- Having someone look directly into your eyes can be an intensely personal experience. This exercise allows the group to practice engaging with others and remaining engaged, which is a skill that will improve with practice.
- How did it feel to look at someone directly? Was it more difficult with some people than with others? What did people do when they felt uncomfortable with the exercise?
- If you have used varying lengths of time for the eye contacts, ask how these experiences were different.

Variation – Eye to Eye with Words

Additional goal	Group introspection
Preparation	Prepare a list of words for the group to think about. Any words could be used that have relevance to the work or issues of the group; words such as "anger," "hope," "friendship," "trust," "honesty," or "unity" might be appropriate at different times.

Note: This exercise can be useful preparation for sessions that deal with group issues. However, it makes a high-risk exercise even more risky, so it should be used only with a group that has done EYE TO EYE several times and feels comfortable with it.

Instructions

1. Follow the instructions for EYE TO EYE, but for each eye contact give the group a word for each person to think about. Ask that they think about the word in relation to the whole group, rather than in relation to their current partner.

Additional processing suggestions

- What words were most related to what this group is experiencing now?
- Was it difficult to concentrate on the words while you were looking into someone's eyes?
- Would you be able to think about the words more without the eye contact? Did the eye contact bring you more or less in touch with the meaning of the words?
- Be open to a discussion evolving about the words and related emotions.

Variation – Eye to Eye with Visualization

Additional goal	Group introspection
Preparation	Prepare a brief visualization about the group's life and experiences together. For information about visualizations, see p. 409 and Appendix D.

Note: This exercise helps to get people thinking about themselves in relation to the group, and to motivate them to work together.

Instructions

1. Follow the instructions for EYE TO EYE except that you read or speak the visualization while the group is doing the exercise.

Additional processing suggestions

- Were you able to listen to the visualization while looking into people's eyes?
- Was this easier with some people than with others?
- Are there things in the visualization that you particularly remember, or that struck you forcefully when you heard them?

Feeling Labels

Goal	Introspection
Time	10-15 minutes (not including processing)
Physical contact	None
Physical challenges	Minimal
Number of participants	10-30
Space requirements	Minimal
Materials needed	Tape, a board or flip chart, and construction paper in seven or eight different colors
Preparation	See "Preparing the Labels."

Note: This exercise is high-risk and should be used only with groups that know each other well and have a high degree of trust.

Preparing the Labels

1. Cut the construction paper into name-label size strips, with enough labels for everyone in the group to have one of each color.
2. Designate an emotion for each color, choosing the emotions according to issues that you want to get at in the group (see the examples in "Emotions and Colors").
3. Write the color/emotion correspondences on the board/flip chart.
4. Set out the labels and tape where they are accessible to the group.

Emotions and Colors

Here are some examples of emotions you might want to use in this exercise, and colors that could correspond to the emotions:

blue = depressed
red = angry
white = hyper
yellow = happy
green = fearful
brown = peaceful
orange = self-destructive
purple = not sure what I feel

If you use colors associated with skin colors, be careful not to play into racial stereotypes when you designate the related emotions.

Instructions

1. Invite people to tape on the label that best fits the way they feel now or have been feeling lately.
2. When everyone is finished, ask them to get into groups according to their labels. Place singles in a "mixed emotions" group.
3. Ask people to discuss in their groups one incident that seems to contribute to the feeling they've been experiencing. Make it clear that no one has to speak if they don't want to.

Processing suggestions

- Ask people to share with the whole group, if they wish, the incidents they discussed with their small group.
- How do people's individual emotions and experiences affect

the group as a whole?
- What have we learned about the group by doing this exercise?

Variation – Feeling About

Additional goals	Surfacing group dynamics, Different perspectives
Preparation	In addition to preparing labels, decide what issue or experience you want people to express their feelings about.

Notes:

- This is less high-risk than FEELING LABELS, since you are not asking people to discuss their personal lives.
- This is a good exercise for a group that has recently shared or is about to share an important experience, such as going on a trip together or the group coming to an end.
- This exercise could be a good lead-in to BRAINSTORMING (p. 385) about the issue that the exercise focuses on.

Instructions

1. Ask people to tape on the label that best expresses their feelings about a specific issue, event, or incident.
2. Follow the procedure for FEELING LABELS.

Processing suggestions

- Is the group largely in agreement on the subject, or is there broad disagreement?
- What have we learned about the main reasons for disagreement on this issue?
- What have we learned about how we could go about resolving the differences?

Follow the Leader

Goal	Leadership
Time	10-20 minutes (not including processing)
Physical contact	None
Physical challenges	Must be able to walk and move.
Number of participants	12-20
Space requirements	A large space, such as an entire school building, a large office space, a neighborhood block, or a community center
Materials needed	None
Preparation	None

Instructions

1. The group lines up and the person at the front of the line leads. Everyone else follows the leader's actions. The leader can do any kind of movement or walk, as long as it is appropriate and safe and everyone is capable of doing it.
2. After a short while, yell "Switch." The leader then moves to the back of the line, and the person now at the front is the new leader.
3. Continue through several leaders.

Processing suggestions

- The processing of this exercise can bring out points regarding leadership styles and about bringing leadership out into the community.
- What kinds of movements did people choose when they were leading? What does this say about their leadership styles?
- When was it difficult to keep up with the leader? Why? When was it easy, and why?
- Watch to see if people were affected by how those in front of them interpreted the leader's actions, and if these interpretations carried on down the line. Were some people following the leader, while others were following one of the followers? Are there parallels to this in the group and in society?
- If people from outside the group were watching, did this affect your actions? If so, how?

Freeze Frames

Goals	Communication, Reinforcing information
Time	10-15 minutes (not including processing)
Physical contact	None necessary
Physical challenges	Minimal
Number of participants	10-30
Space requirements	Open floor space
Materials needed	A sheet of paper for each small group
Preparation	See "Words or Concepts."

Words or Concepts

Decide on the words or concepts you want to highlight, and write one on each piece of paper. Choose words or concepts that relate to the purpose of the meeting and that can be represented visually. For example, you might use emotions, like "pride" or "hate," or whole scenes like "graduation day" or "a conference about ____." You could also use information that you want to reinforce (for example, Rules for Brainstorming on p. 385).

Instructions

1. Divide the group into small groups.
2. Give each small group one of the sheets of paper with a word or concept.
3. All the members of the small group should look at the paper to learn what their word or concept is, but they cannot discuss it with each other or let the other groups know what the paper says.
4. The task of each group is to create a tableau that illustrates the word or concept they have been given. The groups will proceed one by one as follows: One member of the group comes to the front of the room and freezes in a pose that they think illustrates the concept. Then other members come to the front in turn and strike poses that add to the scene. Everyone should be facing in the same direction, so that all aspects of the scene are visible to the audience. Once people are frozen, they cannot move, and no talking or sounds are allowed.
5. When everyone in the small group has become a part of the Freeze Frame, the rest of the group tries to guess what the Freeze Frame represents. After a few guesses, the small group announces the theme of their Freeze Frame.

Processing suggestions

- Work with the content of each Freeze Frame to make points about what is being illustrated.
- People had different ways of communicating the same message. Are there additional ways that others in the group can think of?
- Everyone adds their perspective to create a more complete picture.
- How were those in the audience able to guess what each Freeze Frame represented? Was it a particular addition to the Freeze Frame that clarified the meaning, or did it sometimes take the whole picture?
- This exercise can illustrate the importance of body language in communication.

Group Pulse

Goals	Focus, Interconnection
Time	5-10 minutes (not including processing)
Physical contact	Physical closeness is required as people place their hands on the floor.
Physical challenges	Must be able to kneel and tap hands on the floor, unless done around a table.
Number of participants	10-20
Space requirements	Open floor space. Can also be done seated around a table.
Materials needed	None
Preparation	None

Instructions

1. Unless the group is seated at a table, ask them to kneel on the floor in a circle.
2. Have people place their hands on the floor (or table) in such a way that each person has one hand between the hands of someone next to them.
3. To begin the pulse, you lift one hand and tap the floor once.
4. The pulse travels around the circle to the right—that is, the person whose hand is to the right of the hand that just tapped uses that hand to tap the floor.
5. At any time, the person whose turn it is can tap their hand twice; this reverses the direction of the pulse.
6. When someone taps the wrong hand, misses the opportunity to tap, takes too long to respond, or taps on someone else's turn, the hand that made the mistake is out and must be placed behind the person's back.
7. After one round, take a count of the number of hands that have been taken out of play. Then have everyone return both hands to play and go around again, to see if practice improves people's ability to focus.
8. After these warm-up rounds, begin to play with "outs," so that people who have both hands

behind their backs must sit out, and the rest of the players continue until there is a winner left (with either one or two hands left in the game).

Processing suggestions

- Discuss the focused attention and the cooperation that are necessary to keep the group's energy always moving in the right direction. If one person makes a mistake, everyone else is thrown off.
- Anyone in the group can change the direction of the group at any time, and the ramifications can be positive or negative. Is this reflected in the day-to-day life of the group?
- What are the motives for the change of direction?
- If people change direction too often, the group's movement can get stuck in one area, leaving others out of the process. The work of the group needs to include everyone, but the actions of a few can make this impossible.
- The group needs to be flexible and able to respond to changes in direction, but it also requires people to act for the good of the whole, and not out of self-interest or in a way that is randomly oppositional.
- If you played with outs, you can use this exercise to talk about elements of competition. Why did people get out? Was it lack of focus, or were people trying to get people out by switching direction frequently? You can also ask the group to think about if this group ever tries to get people "out."

Hide and Seek

Goals	Surfacing group dynamics, Introspection
Time	10-15 minutes (not including processing)
Physical contact	None
Physical challenges	Must be able to move and hide.
Number of participants	10-15
Space requirements	A well-defined area that has places to hide
Materials needed	None
Preparation	Decide whether or not to use a "safe" area. (See step 5.)

Instructions

1. Choose one to three people to be "it."
2. Tell the group the limits of the area available for the exercise and point out the "safe" area, if there will be one.
3. Have those who are "it" close their eyes or go to another room while the rest of the group has one minute to hide.
4. When time is up, those who are "it" look for those who are hiding.
5. When someone is found, they are either sent to the "safe" area or they join those who are "it" in searching for the rest of the group.

Processing suggestions

- You can use the experience of hiding to discuss motivation among group members. Are people hiding from the responsibilities or work of the group? Do people hide or do they go right to work? Are people hiding from the entire group, or just some parts of it (such as the leadership)?
- In some groups, you can look at "hiding" from the point of view of emotional engagement and letting yourself be truly seen by the group. Are people hiding emotionally? Do you want people to know where you are, or don't you? When you were hiding, did you want to be caught? Why? Were you so well hidden that you were uncomfortable? Are you comfortable in the little space that you're in, or would you just as soon come out of that space and engage?
- The dynamics among the members of the group who are hiding are different depending on whether or not they will join the seekers when they are discovered; if they will, it becomes important to keep your hiding place secret from everyone, not just those who are initially designated as "it."
- While searching, it's important to keep your emotional balance and to stay focused on your goal.
- Processing can also focus on how the group can reach out to people who would benefit from what the group has to offer but are not currently taking advantage of it. What are the dynamics that keep people "hiding" from the group?

Variation – Time Limited Hide and Seek

Additional goal	Focus

Instructions

1. Follow the instructions for Hide and Seek, but place a limit (such as five minutes) on the amount of time allowed for searching.

Additional processing suggestions

- Did the time limit make the searchers approach their task more efficiently, or did they miss a lot because of time pressure?
- Especially when time is limited, it is very important to stay focused and use all your senses and awareness to accomplish your task.

Holes in the Ice

Goals	Trust, Communication, Focus
Time	10-15 minutes (not including processing)
Physical contact	None
Physical challenges	Must be able to move across the room with eyes closed.
Number of participants	12-20
Space requirements	Open floor space
Materials needed	Ordinary objects that are durable and safe, and a blindfold
Preparation	None

Instructions

1. Have the group stand in a circle. The inside of the circle is the "ice."
2. Ask for a volunteer to be the first "skater" across the ice. Blindfold the skater.
3. Place some objects in the circle, such as books, pencils, paper, or anything you have around the room that is not sharp or breakable. You can also ask people to contribute objects they might have, such as keys or jackets or purses. Spread the objects evenly around in the space.
4. The skater's task is to walk to the opposite side of the circle without touching any of the objects. Each object is a "hole in the ice." If the skater touches an object, you say "Splash" to indicate they have fallen into a hole and their turn is over.
5. Everyone else in the circle tries to help the skater navigate around the holes by calling out directions. They cannot allow one person to be the navigator; everyone has to be part of the process.
6. Continue the exercise for three or four more rounds with other volunteers. In between rounds, you can have everyone close their eyes while you rearrange the objects.

Processing suggestions

- How did the skaters feel as they listened for information about how to navigate the ice? Was it difficult to hear? Was there conflicting information? Did some voices stand out?
- The exercise illustrates what it's like to be vulnerable and dependent, and the various ways that people help others out.
- For those skaters who fell in a hole, what do they think contributed to their falling? Did they feel they weren't able to stay focused?
- What was it like to be in the circle trying to help the skater?
- Did the group work together to help the skaters? Was everyone part of the process? Did anyone intentionally try to get the skater to fall in the ice?
- You can look at issues of authoritarian structure versus everyone being involved. Different perspectives are available, but too many voices can cause confusion.
- Was it helpful to have the whole group involved in the navigation process? What was gained in this exercise by having everyone take part? What was lost?

Human Knot

Goals	Group problem solving, Surfacing group dynamics
Time	10-15 minutes (not including processing)
Physical contact	Extensive
Physical challenges	Must be able to move, twist, and turn.
Number of participants	8-20
Space requirements	Open floor space
Materials needed	None
Preparation	None

Note: This exercise and all of its variations are high-risk due to the level of physical contact involved. Observe carefully to ensure that people are respectful of each other's bodies.

Instructions

1. This exercise works well with "knots" of between five and eight people. If the group is larger than eight, break into smaller groups.
2. Have each group stand in a circle.
3. Have people cross their arms in front of their bodies and join hands with two other people. People who join hands should not be standing next to each other, and everyone should be connected to two different people (that is, not holding both of one person's hands).
4. The group has now formed a "human knot," and their job is to get out of it without letting go of each other's hands. In most cases, with a lot of twisting and turning and stepping over and under each other's arms, this can be done in a few minutes. It is all right if people end up facing outside the circle.
5. If the group seems hopelessly entangled, have them pass a pulse (see PASS THE PULSE on p. 173). If everyone in the knot receives the pulse, they are in just one knot and are likely to be able to get untangled. If not, they are in more than one knot and should probably break up and try it again.

Processing suggestions

- The HUMAN KNOT can be used to illustrate the importance of group cooperation, trust, being considerate of each other, and working together.
- You can make points about teamwork and the flow of leadership in a group.
- What was it like trying to get out of the knot? Did people think they would be able to do it when they first began?
- Did anybody take the lead? If members of the group were not helping to get out of the knot, how did that affect the outcome of the exercise or people's feelings about it?
- If the group gave up trying to get out of the knot: Who gave up? What were the dynamics of it?
- If you had two knots going at once: Did the groups become competitive? Did one group give up because the other group had finished?
- What kind of "knots" is this group in? What do we need to unravel those knots?

Variation – The Human Knot Director

Additional goal	Leadership
Number of participants	8-10

Instructions

1. Select someone or ask for a volunteer to be the Director. Ask the Director to leave the room.
2. Have the rest of the group get themselves into a human knot. They can do this by the method described above, or they can stand holding hands in a circle and create the knot by stepping over and ducking under each other's arms.
3. Once the knot is formed, the group calls for the Director, who comes back into the room and tries to undo the knot. The rest of the group should just follow the Director's instructions and not try to untangle themselves.

Additional processing suggestions

- This exercise can illustrate different things depending upon the success of the Director. Exploring the role of the Director can lead to insights into the nature of effective leadership.
- If the Director gets the group out of the knot smoothly, this can illustrate how sometimes a person who is not involved in a problem can see the situation more clearly than those who are involved in it.
- Conversely, if the group felt that the Director did not direct them well, it can show how sometimes an "outsider" cannot solve a problem as well as those who are directly involved in it.

Variation – Stuck Knot

Preparation	Make a slip of paper for each participant. Leave most of the slips blank, but write an X on one or two of them.

Note: If it suits your purposes, you could leave all the slips blank, so that no one has an X (although the group thinks that someone does).

Instructions

1. Pass out the slips and ask people to look at their slips, put them away, and not let anyone else know what is on the slip. Explain that anyone who has an X on their slip should *not* try to help the group get out of the knot.
2. Follow the instructions for HUMAN KNOT.

Additional processing suggestions

- Ask the group to identify the person or people who had the X. This exercise can be used to raise issues of how the group deals with the lack of input or subtle resistance of some of its members.
- It can also be used to open up a discussion about what forces outside the group are impeding the group's process toward its goals, and how to address those forces.

Variation – Backward Human Knot

Instructions

1. Have the group stand in a circle facing outward.
2. Have them back in closer and join hands behind their backs with others in the circle (two different people, and not people they are standing next to). They do not cross their arms before joining hands.
3. Proceed as for HUMAN KNOT.

Additional processing suggestions

- This exercise can illustrate how the group approaches difficult problems.
- It can also show how difficult it can be to find solutions when people "back into" a situation and have limited ability to see what's going on. How did people deal with not being able to see the knot? Were people frustrated, or did they take it on as a challenge?
- It can also illustrate the need to have faith that you can succeed at least partially, even when things seem hopeless.

Note on "blind" adaptations: Be aware that asking people to have their eyes closed during the physical contact involved in the HUMAN KNOT raises the risk level considerably.

Variation – Half-Blind Knot

Additional goal	Communication

Instructions

1. Follow the instructions for setting up the HUMAN KNOT.
2. Select some members of the group, or ask for volunteers, to keep their eyes closed during the exercise. The dynamics of this exercise can vary greatly, depending on the number of people you choose to have their eyes closed.
3. Those with their eyes open are then responsible for communicating with the others about the movements they should make to help untie the knot.

Additional processing suggestions

- The "blind" versions of the HUMAN KNOT create a dynamic where some members of the group are dependent on others' verbal instructions to complete the exercise. How did that feel for those who had their eyes closed? Did they trust the voices they heard?
- How did it feel for those who had to tell the others what to do?

Variation – Half-Blind Knot with Stops

Additional goal	Different perspectives

Instructions

1. Follow the instructions for HALF-BLIND KNOT, but several times during the exercise ask the group to freeze and select different people to close their eyes.

Additional processing suggestion

- This variation can be useful in raising issues around different viewpoints or understandings of how an event occurred.

Variation – Blind Knot, Sighted Leader

Additional goals — Leadership, Different perspectives

Instructions

1. Follow the instructions for setting up Human Knot and then ask everyone to close their eyes.
2. Select one person in the knot either by saying their name or by tapping them on the shoulder. This person opens their eyes and begins attempting to untangle the group by giving instructions.
3. After a minute (more or less depending on your objectives for the exercise), select another person to take over as the leader.
4. The first leader closes their eyes; at any given time, only one person in the knot should have their eyes open.
5. Continue to select different leaders until the group is untangled.

Additional processing suggestions

- This exercise is useful for exploring people's relationship with authority—both the authority of the person designated as leader and the authority of the facilitator who is running the exercise.
- Did people communicate with each other or did they just follow the instructions of whoever was leading at the moment?
- Did anyone move independently and take steps to untangle the group when not instructed to do so?
- Did anyone open their eyes when they weren't supposed to? Why or why not?
- The exercise can also be used to illustrate how a group of people in the same situation may have many different perspectives on it.

Instant Impulse

Goals	Communication, Interconnection
Time	10-15 minutes (not including processing)
Physical contact	Holding hands
Physical challenges	Sitting on the floor. Some players must try to grab a ball.
Number of participants	10-20
Space requirements	Open floor space
Materials needed	A medium-size ball, a coin to flip, and blindfolds (optional) for each player
Preparation	None

Instructions

1. Divide the group into two teams of equal size.
2. Have the teams sit cross-legged on the floor in two lines facing each other, with about a foot between them.
3. Have each team hold hands down the line. The players at the far end of each line are the "grabbers"; tell them to place their free hands on their knees.
4. Place the ball on the floor equidistant between the grabbers.
5. The players at the head of each line are the "see-ers." Everyone except the see-ers must close their eyes (or you could have people put on blindfolds). No one may talk.
6. Stand at the head of the line (near the see-ers) and flip the coin. If it comes up tails, the players do nothing and wait for another coin flip. If it comes up heads, the see-ers send an impulse (hand squeeze) down the line.
7. When the grabbers receive the impulse, they try to grab the ball with their free hands.
8. The team that grabs the ball first wins the round. The see-er on that team takes the grabber's position, and everyone moves up one space.
9. The first team to have its see-er move back to their original position wins the game.
10. If a see-er mistakenly sends an impulse when the coin came up tails, the team is assessed a penalty by having to rotate one spot in reverse order.

Processing suggestions

- How did communication (impulses) work within the teams? Did teams lose ground because of faulty or false communication? Does this group ever lose ground because of miscommunication?
- If a team had to move backwards, how did that feel?
- What was it like to be in the different roles? How did it feel to have to switch roles?
- Which positions did people like or dislike the most? You can talk about the importance of all roles in a group. Some will like the more passive role of passing the impulse, while others will like the active responsibility of the see-ers and the grabbers. How are responsibilities shared in this group? Do people take on the tasks that they don't enjoy as much?
- What sorts of competition arose from the groups (for example, people making comments about the opposing team)? This can be used to discuss arbitrary groupings and how competitiveness can set people up against each other.

Keep Your Balance

Goal	Focus
Time	10 minutes (not including processing)
Physical contact	None
Physical challenges	Must be able to balance on one leg.
Number of participants	Any number
Space requirements	Any area in which everyone has room to stand with at least a foot of clear space around them. Open floor space is best.
Materials needed	None
Preparation	Decide on the balancing pose you will ask people to take, being sure that it is not too difficult. (It could be as simple as standing with one foot off the ground.) A good position for this exercise is the yoga pose referred to as the "tree."

The Tree

Place the sole of one foot on the inside of the other leg at whatever point (ankle, calf, knee, or thigh) is comfortable. Place the hands in front of the chest in the prayer position. For extra challenge, stretch the arms overhead.

Instructions

1. Ask that each person stand quietly in an uncluttered space a couple of feet away from everyone else.
2. Give the instructions for the pose. Demonstrate if you can.
3. Ask people to assume the pose, to be quiet, and to remain balanced in the position for as long as they are able without undue strain.
4. Everyone should come out of the position whenever they feel they need to. When they do come out of it, they are to remain quiet and continue standing.
5. When only 3-4 people are left in the pose, direct them to close their eyes. (Most people cannot remain balanced for long with eyes closed.)

Processing suggestions

- Ask people what strategies they used to stay balanced. Some people may say they found a stable point to focus on; this is a good analogy for staying focused on a goal.
- What happens if your point of reference shifts position or becomes unstable?
- Struggling to keep your balance can be exhausting. Conversely, attaining a state of balance can feel peaceful. How do you try to achieve balance in your life? Do you ever feel perfectly balanced, or is it always a process of trying to achieve balance?
- What happened when you noticed other people losing their balance? Did it affect your balance?

Leadership Circle

Goals	Leadership, Interconnection, Surfacing group dynamics
Time	10-15 minutes, depending on the number of participants (not including processing)
Physical contact	None necessary, though the exercise can be done with people sitting in close proximity (nearly knee-to-knee).
Physical challenges	Must be able to make motions.
Number of participants	10-20
Space requirements	Open floor space, although it can be done around a table.
Materials needed	None
Preparation	None

Instructions

1. Have the group sit in a circle. For a more intense experience, you can have people sit very close to each other (knee-to-knee).
2. Ask for a volunteer to be the first leader and tell them in which direction the leadership will travel.
3. The leader starts making motions and everyone mimics what the leader does.
4. After 15-20 seconds, the leader indicates by a motion that they are passing the leadership on to the person to their right or left.
5. The next person leads for a short time and passes the leadership on (going around the circle in the same direction), until everyone has been the leader.

Processing suggestions

- There are many different styles of leadership. What styles do people feel most comfortable with?
- People who are following can gain something from each style.
- People feel varying degrees of comfort in the leadership role. Some people will be very comfortable in that role and may keep the leadership longer; others will pass it on quickly.
- Who was easiest to follow and who was hardest, and why?
- What do your movements say about you as a leader?
- What were you thinking about while you were leading?
- Was it easier to follow or to lead?
- In a group (or society), everyone is making motions that others are following, either consciously or unconsciously. Each of us can choose to put positive or negative motions out into the world, as well as to follow either the positive or negative that we see others doing.

Leadership Spin

Goal	Leadership
Time	10-15 minutes (not including processing)
Physical contact	Minimal
Physical challenges	Must be able to move to move across the room and circle around a chair.
Number of participants	10-40
Space requirements	Open floor space
Materials needed	A chair for each team
Preparation	None

Note: Watch carefully to be sure that everyone is safe as they do the spin and walk back to their team.

Instructions

1. Divide the group into teams with 5-10 people per team.
2. Have people line up in their teams.
3. Put a chair about 30 feet in front of each team. Have volunteers or other facilitators sit in each chair.
4. The LEADERSHIP SPIN operates like a relay race. The first person from each team walks (not runs) to the team's chair, circles around the chair three times, then walks back to the team and touches the hand of the next person in line. As each person circles around the chair, the volunteer seated in the chair will count the rotations. The first team to have each of its members complete the course is the winner.

Processing suggestions

- This exercise functions to break down stereotypes of physical dominance in the group because people who are in better shape physically tend to have a harder time maintaining their balance as they circle the chairs. Discuss why the winning team came in first and how their ability to win may (or may not) contradict stereotypes.
- You can also relate this exercise to any unproductive "spinning" that the group may be experiencing, such as belaboring details, getting stuck in their work, or not coming to consensus on an issue. When the group gets stuck spinning its wheels, it can't move forward. How can the group get itself unstuck?

Variation – Leadership Spin with Assigned Leaders

Instructions

1. Follow the instructions for LEADERSHIP SPIN, but before beginning the race, arbitrarily assign one person from each team to be the leader.
2. Tell the leaders that they have one minute to put the members of their teams in the order that they will race in.
3. Once the teams have been organized, start the race.

Additional processing suggestions

- This variation can open a discussion on leadership styles as well as the process by which leaders are selected.
- How did the leaders feel about being chosen?
- How did the rest of the group feel about the process by which the leaders were assigned?
- Did the people assigned to be leaders actually take on leadership roles?
- Which leadership qualities were effective and which were not?

Line-Ups

Goals	Group problem solving, Communication, Planning
Time	10-15 minutes (not including processing)
Physical contact	None
Physical challenges	Minimal
Number of participants	10-20
Space requirements	Open floor space
Materials needed	None
Preparation	Determine what four or five criteria to use for lining up. See "Line-Up Criteria."

Line-Up Criteria

The criteria you choose can be almost anything that will result in a definite order. You may want to choose one or two that relate to the purpose of the meeting. Here are some examples:

- Birthday order: January to December
- Alphabetically by first or last name
- Shoe size: smallest to largest
- Height: smallest to tallest
- Opinion about how much money we will make at our fundraiser: not enough to plenty and more
- Opinion about how many people will come to our event: a modest number to more than we can count
- How long it takes you to leave the house after you get up in the morning: not long to hours and hours
- How much you love chocolate: not at all to more than anything else
- How vegetarian you are: not at all to completely
- How late you stay up at night: not late to very late

Instructions

1. Tell the group that they have 30 seconds to line up in the right order *without talking*, based on the criteria you give them.
2. Read off the first criterion.
3. Once everyone is in line, find out whether people are in the right place (for example, by asking people to state their birthdays, or by looking at people's shoe sizes) and have them adjust their positions if necessary.
4. Read the next criterion, and follow this procedure through all the criteria.

Processing suggestions

- Line-Ups is about putting things in the correct order. It is a useful exercise for a meeting that will focus on setting timelines or otherwise deciding in an orderly way how to approach a problem.
- The "no talking" rule makes the group find ways to communicate nonverbally. What methods of communication did they come up with? How effective were they?

Variation – Blind Line-Ups

Physical challenges Must be able to move to the correct positions without using sight.

Instructions

1. Follow the instructions for LINE-UPS, except that participants can talk but must keep their eyes closed. For safety, ask group members to put their hands out in front of them to use as "safety bumpers."

Additional processing suggestions

- This exercise can be used to talk about the importance of having a vision when planning or putting things in order. Without a vision of the big picture, it is difficult to put the details in place.
- How did the ability to speak compensate for the inability to see? Was communication more or less difficult than in LINE-UPS? What communication strategies did people use?

Magic Ball

Goals	Focus, Creativity
Time	5-10 minutes (not including processing)
Physical contact	None
Physical challenges	Minimal
Number of participants	10-20
Space requirements	Open floor space is ideal, but can also be done around a table.
Materials needed	None
Preparation	None

Instructions

1. Have the group stand in a circle.
2. Explain that you are holding an imaginary ball that you will pass around the circle. Everyone should do something with it, then pass it on.
3. Do something with the "ball" (for example, act out bouncing it or throwing it in the air, or changing its size by squashing it down or blowing it up), then pass it to the person to your right or left.
4. Each person does something with the "ball" before passing it on.

Processing suggestions

- The power of the exercise is derived from the tacit agreement of the group to pay attention to an invisible object. The point is the importance and the power of focused attention. You can draw an analogy with other invisible forces that draw the group's focus, such as a belief in the goals that motivate their work.
- This exercise can be used to talk about the group's mission or vision for a project. Everyone needs to be able to "see" it, even if it isn't visible to the eye.
- You can use this exercise to talk about clarifying a vision or goal. Were you able to "see" the ball more clearly through certain people's actions than through others?
- Usually, the more care and attention and details put into the action of doing something with the ball leads to the ball seeming more "real." You can relate this to the need to put care, attention, and detail into the work of the group to make it become real.
- How did people's creativity come out through holding the imaginary ball?
- Were you surprised by anything people did to the ball?

Variation – Invisible Clay

Instructions

1. Have the group stand in a circle.
2. Ask for a volunteer to begin.
3. Give that person an imaginary lump of clay.
4. The first person has about 30 seconds to do whatever they want with the "clay" (play with it, create something, etc.). When they are through, they pass it on in its new form to the person on their right.
5. The next person receives it in this form and then has about 30 seconds to do what they want with it.
6. The "clay" continues around the circle in this fashion until everyone has had time to work with it.

Additional processing suggestions

- This exercise can illustrate beginning a project or a movement and the various stages of development it will go through.
- It can also show the power to transform what you interact with, whether relationships, ideas, policies, procedures, etc.
- Did you have an idea of what you wanted to create, or did you just create in the moment? It can be helpful to have a creative vision of how to build or shape something, but sometimes the most creative ideas can happen when you are thinking in the moment.
- What was it like to see you ideas or creation altered by others?
- What do people do with what they are given? Are there opportunities that people do or do not take?

Make It Up

Goals	What your group needs at this time
Time	You decide.
Physical contact	None, a lot, or anything in between
Physical challenges	Adapted for your group
Number of participants	8-25 people
Space requirements	What you have to work with
Materials needed	Whatever you need to accomplish the goals
Preparation	It depends.

Note: MAKE IT UP is for groups that are very familiar with interactive exercises and understand their importance in the group's development.

Instructions

1. Ask the group to do a quick Brainstorm (p. 385) about what they need emotionally as a group right now. Write down whatever people say on the flip chart.
2. Tell the group that you want to design an exercise to meet some of those needs, and ask for suggestions about what the exercise could include. Write down the responses on the flip chart.
3. Ask people to suggest how the elements that have been proposed could fit together into an exercise. In other words, ask the group to make up an exercise that will meet the needs they have stated.
4. Depending on the group's size, you may want to split them up into two or three groups to come up with different exercises. Each small group should choose someone to facilitate.

5. Discuss the suggestions and refine the elements until the group has created an exercise.
6. Do a quick Brainstorm about what this exercise could be called.
7. Do the exercise. Whether or not the facilitators participate will depend upon the situation. If there is more than one small group, each should lead the whole group in doing their exercise.

Processing suggestions

- How did the group interpret their needs?
- Did the exercise adequately meet those needs?
- What did the process of "making it up" show about how the group works together? Is it similar to other ways the group has worked to meet their own needs?
- How did the group communicate in this exercise, and how is that related to the group's communication in general?
- Everyone in the group has to take responsibility for how the group functions.
- Being creative and "thinking outside the box" can help to enliven the work of the group and give people new perspectives.
- This exercise also demonstrates that you can make something out of nothing when you have the resources of people's ideas and willingness to engage.

Mirror Squared

Goals	Leadership, Introspection
Time	10 minutes (not including processing)
Physical contact	None
Physical challenges	Minimal
Number of participants	8-30
Space requirements	Open floor space
Materials needed	None
Preparation	None

Instructions

1. Divide people into groups of four. (If necessary, one or two of the groups can have three members.)
2. Within each small group, members will rotate through the following roles: leader, observer, and two followers (one follower in a group of three). Tell the groups to decide who will take which role for the first round.
3. Each round lasts about a minute and consists of the leader making motions, the followers imitating the leader, and the observer watching.
4. Do the exercise three times.

Processing suggestions

- How did it feel to be in each of the roles?
- Which roles did people prefer, and why?
- What are some characteristics of good leadership that emerged from this exercise?
- Did some people have trouble being followers? Discuss the reasons: Were they distracted, unwilling to follow, or unable to understand?
- Discuss the role of the observer: Could they see what those involved could not see?
- The role of observer is an important one in the group, and we are all each other's observers. When you stand back from what is happening, you often get a unique perspective that those involved do not have. Sharing this perspective helps the group to grow.

Mixed Messages

Goals	Communication, Group problem solving
Time	10-15 minutes (not including processing)
Physical contact	Minimal
Physical challenges	Activities can be tailored to the abilities of the group.
Number of participants	10-30
Space requirements	Minimal
Materials needed	Index cards, paper, and pencils
Preparation	See "Scrambling the Instructions."

Scrambling the Instructions

Decide how many small groups you want to have and prepare an index card for each group. Each card should contain a simple instruction for an action to take, with the letters of each word scrambled. Some examples are:

od a atp acden	(do a tap dance)
dnast yb onwdswi	(stand by windows)
olok yalerl trseseds	(look really stressed)
yalp ophtocshc	(play hopscotch)
pksi nodura het omor	(skip around the room)

Also, place some paper and pencils around for people to use if they want.

Instructions

1. Divide people into small groups.
2. Give each group a card.
3. Each group must try to decipher the instruction on their card.
4. When a group unscrambles its instruction, they do what it says.
5. You can play so that the first group wins, or simply play until every group has followed their instructions.

Processing suggestions

- How did people work together to unscramble their messages?
- Did people use the tools available to them (paper and pencils)?
- Sometimes it's hard to know exactly what is expected of us. People send mixed messages and don't always say what they mean. It is important to clarify messages before you take action on them.
- How can we help each other to decipher mixed messages?

Musical Conversations

Goals	Communication, Movement
Time	10 minutes
Physical contact	None, unless people try to sit on the same seat
Physical challenges	Must be able to move quickly.
Number of participants	12-30
Space requirements	Open floor space
Materials needed	Chairs and a source of music
Preparation	Prepare four or five discussion questions related to the work of the meeting.

Note: This exercise gets people moving around the room, thinking and sharing ideas about the work of the day. It works well as part of an agenda where the questions from the exercise will be discussed more in depth later in the meeting. An added benefit of the exercise is that it gives some people the chance to practice speaking in front of others.

Instructions

1. Arrange the chairs in a large circle, with three fewer chairs than there are people in the group.
2. Have everyone stand inside the circle of chairs.
3. Tell the group the first question, and start the music. Everyone should find someone to discuss this question with during the time that the music is on.
4. Turn the music off after 30-60 seconds. When the music stops, everyone should try to find a chair.
5. The three people left standing speak briefly about the question to the whole group.
6. When they are finished, give the next question and start the music for the next round.

Processing suggestions

- Generally no formal processing is necessary. You can move directly from MUSICAL CONVERSATIONS directly into BRAINSTORMING (p. 385), a WORDSTORM (p. 413), or discussion about the topics that people spoke about.

Name Chant, Motion, and Sound

Goals	Surfacing group dynamics, Leadership
Time	5-10 minutes (not including processing)
Physical contact	None
Physical challenges	None
Number of participants	8-80
Space requirements	None
Materials needed	None
Preparation	None

Note: This exercise and its variations are useful for revealing how people are feeling and what the level of resistance is in the group. You can get a sense of both mood and personal style by the tone each person uses and by the motions called for.

Note: The group can do this exercise seated or standing, but the standing version is more dynamic since people can move freely and use more of their bodies in their motions. Standing increases the risk level of the exercise.

Instructions

1. Going around the circle, each person says their name in whatever tone of voice they choose, makes a motion, and makes a sound to go with the motion.
2. The rest of the group repeats the name, motion, and sound three times.

Processing suggestions

- People have a range of different styles in how they choose to present themselves to others, as well as varying comfort levels in expressing themselves in the group.
- The exercise illustrates how a person's attitude, tone, and style are mirrored back to them by those around them.
- People repeating one another's motions can be an illustration of responding to peer pressure.
- Often in this exercise the group will repeat something that the person who originated the motion did not realize they were doing (such as scratching their head or making a facial expression). This is an illustration of "unconscious leadership"—people modeling behavior that they do not necessarily want others to follow.

Variation – Name, Characteristic, Motion, and Sound

Additional goal	Interconnection

Instructions

1. Follow the instructions for NAME CHANT, MOTION, AND SOUND, except that each person says a characteristic that they possess and makes a sound and a motion that reflect the characteristic.
2. The rest of the group repeats the name, characteristic, motion, and sound three times. Ask the

group to move quickly and to be respectful of each other.

Additional processing suggestion

- As groups work together, they learn more about each other. People need to feel safe enough to express themselves and share more of their personal characteristics.

Variation – Name, Emotion, and Motion

Additional goals	Group introspection, Personal introspection, Acting
Preparation	Decide based on your goals for the exercise what to instruct the group about the emotions to bring up. It could be emotions they are feeling at the moment or emotions about something in particular related to the work of the group.

Note: There are two circumstances in which this exercise can be particularly helpful:

- When the group needs to deal with emotional issues. This exercise can be used to surface emotions that you know are present in the group.
- When people will be doing skits or role-plays or working on speeches.

Instructions

1. Follow the instructions for NAME CHANT, MOTION, AND SOUND, except that instead of making a sound each person states an emotion and does a motion that signifies or acts out that emotion.
2. The rest of the group then repeats the name, emotion, and motion three times.

Additional processing suggestions

- Emotions can empower or disempower us individually and as a group, depending on how we choose to deal with them.
- When people are motivated by emotions that they are not fully aware of, this can be disempowering for the individuals and destabilizing for the group.
- It's important for people to feel safe enough in this group to let others know what emotions they are dealing with. We are trying to create a group where people feel safe to express their emotions, and to seek help around emotional issues when they need it.

Name Dance Circle

Goals	Creativity, Trust
Time	5-10 minutes (not including processing)
Physical contact	None
Physical challenges	Must be able to do simple dance moves.
Number of participants	8-20
Space requirements	Open floor space
Materials needed	None
Preparation	Decide (based on time and the size of the group) if each person's dance move will be repeated for a full rotation of the circle or a half rotation. Decide if the group should say each person's name once or continue repeating the name as they walk around the circle.

Instructions

1. Have the group stand in a circle, then have everyone turn to their right (so that each person is facing the back of the person in front of them).
2. Ask for a volunteer (Person 1) to begin the NAME DANCE CIRCLE.
3. When you give the signal, everyone starts walking forward in the circle.
4. Person 1 says their name and does a dance move.
5. While the group remains walking in a circle, everyone say Person 1's name and imitates their dance move until Person 1 has moved either halfway or completely around the circle.
6. After Person 1 reaches the designated spot, the person behind them says their name and does their dance move, and the whole group repeats the name and move while walking.
7. Continue until everyone has had a turn.

Processing suggestions

- Do people in the group feel safe to take risks in expressing themselves? Is the group supportive or not?
- Do people feel free to be creative?
- How did people deal with the limitations imposed by their own self-consciousness?
- Safety in the group can lead to creativity and fun, while not feeling safe can lead to fear, self-limitation, and alienation.

Pair Pyramids

Goals	Surfacing group dynamics, Group introspection, Trust
Time	10-15 minutes (not including processing)
Physical contact	Extensive
Physical challenges	Must go from a standing position to squatting, and then to standing under constrained circumstances. Not appropriate for people with back or knee problems.
Number of participants	8-20 (even number)
Space requirements	Open floor space
Materials needed	None
Preparation	None

Instructions

1. With the entire group standing, make two circles, one inside the other. Everyone must have a partner. If there is an odd number, have one person stand outside the circle as an observer.
2. Have people turn so that everyone is standing back-to-back with someone from the other circle. Make sure that each pair has enough room to do the exercise.
3. The pairs attempt to lower themselves to a squatting position and then stand up again while keeping their backs flat against each other.
4. The outer circle moves one place to the right. If there is an observer, make sure the observer is integrated into the circle, and that a different person stands outside the circle.
5. Have the inside circle rotate one person over to form new pairs.
6. Repeat several times.

Processing suggestions

- PAIR PYRAMIDS can show the ways that different elements of the group balance each other and work together. People fit together differently. Sometimes people work well together even though they are very different (different sizes in the exercise). Conversely, people who seem well matched may have a hard time working together.
- Everyone has their own style and comfort level. Some people lean more; some people never take the lead; some pairs barely touch; others link arms and lean hard against each other.
- Would it be possible for a pair to move up or down if one partner did none of the work? How is the work of the group affected when people don't contribute?
- When we are trying to accomplish a goal as a group, there are times when we need to lean on each other.
- Was it easier with some people than with others? What made it easier or harder? Were you more comfortable with some people than with others? Did you lean on people more or did they lean on you? Did people communicate with their partners about how they would do the exercise?

Variation – Pair Stand

Instructions

1. Have people paired in concentric circles as in PAIR PYRAMIDS.
2. Ask the group to sit on the ground back-to-back in pairs, with their arms locked together.
3. The goal for each pair is to stand up together without touching the ground with their hands or breaking from the pair.
4. Have the inside circle rotate one person over to form new pairs.
5. Repeat this several times.

Additional processing suggestions

- Working together is important in groups. Sometimes this means supporting one another, meeting pressure with pressure. It's about pushing upward together, not pushing one another.
- In order to stand up as a pair, both people must work with one another and push against one another. Sometimes this pressure is uncomfortable or unequal if the two people are significantly different in strength, size, or height. The key is to vary pressure (give and take), work together, and take a gradual approach.

Variation

You can try this exercise with groups of four, or even with larger groups.

Pay Attention

Goals	Focus, Introspection
Time	10-15 minutes (not including processing)
Physical contact	None
Physical challenges	Minimal
Number of participants	8-30
Space requirements	Minimal
Materials needed	One or more decks of cards, depending on the size of the group
Preparation	None

Note: This is a card game in which each player's goal is to be the first to have a hand consisting of four of a kind—four queens, four 6s, etc. The value of the cards is not important; a hand with four kings is no more valuable than a hand with four 2s. The goal is to get four of any kind.

Instructions

1. Divide the group into small groups of four to eight people and give each small group a deck of cards. If you have a larger group (up to 12) that you would prefer to keep together, simply give them two decks of cards to work with.
2. Have each group decide on a dealer.
3. The dealer gives everyone four cards; everyone looks at their own cards but keeps them hidden. Throughout the game no one can have more than four cards.
4. The dealer picks up the remaining cards one at a time, looks at each card, and either passes it on or keeps it (passing on another card from their hand, to keep a total of four cards in hand).
5. Each person looks at the card that comes around and either passes it on or keeps it and passes on another card. The discarded cards are piled face down near the dealer.
6. The first person to get four of a kind sticks out their tongue but continues to play the game. As soon as the other players see that someone has their tongue stuck out, they too stick out their tongues, but also go along with the game as if nothing has changed. The loser is the last person to stick out their tongue.
7. If there is no winner by the time all the cards have run out, the dealer reuses the discard pile.
8. The game moves quickly, so you will probably want to play two or three rounds. If you have three or more groups playing, you can reconfigure the groups by having the losers of each round form their own small group.

Processing suggestions

- The exercise illustrates the importance of paying attention to more than one thing at a time. Sometimes we get so focused on one aspect of what we're doing, such as collecting four of the same kind of card, that we forget the bigger picture.
- It also illustrates the importance of paying attention to what's going on around us as well as what we are going through ourselves. We can get so focused on our own needs and emotions that we fail to see what everyone else is going through.
- It can show what it's like to feel left behind, realizing that everyone else has moved on but you are still dealing with old issues.
- The exercise touches on what it's like to take the risk of feeling foolish (sticking your tongue out).
- How does the group relate to the person who is left out?
- What strategies did people use to win or to avoid losing?

Poem Puzzle

Goals	Group problem solving, Surfacing group dynamics, Interconnection
Time	10 minutes (not including processing)
Physical contact	None
Physical challenges	Minimal
Number of participants	8-15
Space requirements	Open floor space
Materials needed	Paper
Preparation	Prepare a short poem or rhyme that relates to the work of the group and that contains as many words as there are members of the group. Then write each word on a separate sheet of paper.

Instructions

1. Distribute the sheets of paper randomly to the group members.
2. Tell people to hold their papers in front of them and to arrange themselves so that the words they are holding form a poem that makes sense. If people are absent and you have extra words, facilitators can participate but should not provide any input regarding the order of the words.
3. When the group has finalized their order, have each person say their word or hold up their paper so the group can hear the resulting poem. If it is different from the poem that you planned, read the original poem to the group.

Processing suggestions

- This exercise requires each member of the group to contribute their piece of the puzzle; the group has to work with each person's input to find the solution. Discuss people's willingness to contribute their viewpoints and skills to the group, as well as the group's ability to use everyone's skills and input in their work.
- As with all group problem-solving exercises, the POEM PUZZLE allows you to observe how the group works together and who takes on leadership roles.
- You can also discuss the content of the poem—is it true, false, or somewhere in between? Are there differing perceptions about what the poem says in the group?

Private Eye

Goals	Surfacing group dynamics, Trust
Time	5-15 minutes (not including processing)
Physical contact	None
Physical challenges	Ability to wink
Number of participants	8-20
Space requirements	Open floor space
Materials needed	One playing card for each group member. Cards must include the Queen of Spades.
Preparation	None

Instructions

1. Have the group sit in a circle and be sure that everyone has a clear view of everyone else's face.
2. Count out as many playing cards as there are group members, being sure to include the Queen of Spades.
3. Give each person one card. Whoever gets the Queen of Spades is the "private eye." The private eye's weapon is a wink; the goal is to "knock out" everyone in the circle by winking at them without being identified by any of the "conscious" group members.
4. When you say to begin, everyone should look around the room at each other. If someone is winked at, they should count to three in their head, and then say out loud, "I'm knocked out." That person is now out of the game, but they continue sitting in the circle.
5. Be prepared for people to cheat. You may have someone other than the private eye winking at people, or some people may ignore winks and refuse to be out.
6. If someone thinks they know who the private eye is, they should raise their hand and say, "I solved the mystery."
7. Ask the person who they think the private eye is, and check the card of that person. If the guesser is right, the exercise is over. If they are wrong, they are now knocked out too.
8. Continue until everyone but the private eye is knocked out, or until someone solves the mystery. You can redeal the cards and play several rounds.

Processing suggestions

- This exercise can be used to reflect back certain dysfunctional situations in a group—such as some people trying to immobilize others, or people hiding their intentions or identities from the group.
- You can use this exercise to surface the anxiety associated with keeping things secret from the group—the anxiety of being discovered and the anxiety of being taken out of the game. You can also discuss the relief of having secrets surfaced and revealed.
- Since there is a real temptation to cheat in this exercise, it can be used to raise issues around following directions and the chaos that ensues when rules are not followed.
- How did people feel as they looked around the circle?
- How did the group deal with the rules? Were the rules followed?
- Was the private eye easy to discover or able to go undetected? Why?

Puzzle Hunt

Goals	Group introspection, Group problem solving
Time	10-15 minutes (not including processing)
Physical contact	None
Physical challenges	Minimal
Number of participants	8-12
Space requirements	Open floor space, preferably several rooms
Materials needed	Two large pieces of poster board, pencil, markers, scissors, transparent tape
Preparation	See "Preparing the Puzzle."

Preparing the Puzzle

1. On a piece of poster board, prepare a two-sided puzzle. On one side, draw a picture (or write some words) that depicts the whole group. This can be as simple or as elaborate as you wish to make it.
2. On the other side, use a pencil to draw lines dividing the poster board into puzzle pieces, with one piece for each member of the group. You can include the facilitator(s) if this seems appropriate.
3. Within the puzzle pieces, draw pictures (or write some words) that depict the various skills, talents, or personal qualities that people bring to the group. While the pieces do not have to correspond one-to-one to members of the group, be sure that each individual can identify in the drawings something that they bring to the group.
4. Cut the pieces out.
5. Hide the pieces, preferably throughout several rooms near the meeting space so that people have to disperse to find them.

Instructions

1. Tell the group about the hidden puzzle pieces. If necessary, give them some clues about how to find the pieces, and send them off to look.
2. As people return with pieces, they should begin to put the puzzle together on another large piece of poster board, with the whole-group drawing facing up.
3. When the puzzle is complete, tape the pieces together.
4. Have the group look at and comment on the drawing.
5. Flip the poster board over and have the group look at and comment on the smaller drawings.

Processing suggestions

- Discuss the dual nature of the group experience—how each member of the group has talents and skills that contribute to the whole group, and how the group itself holds all these people and skills together to make a complete picture.
- Process the message of the pictures or words.
- Could everyone in the group recognize themselves in the depictions? Are there any skills or talents missing?
- Talk about how we need to search to find these skills within ourselves that may yet be unknown to us, and how we need to value everyone's contribution to the group.
- Sometimes people see within us talents and abilities that we are not aware of, and other times there are skills and talents that we have yet to share with people. It is as important to share ourselves as it is to listen to the positive feedback of others.

Red Light, Green Light

Goals	Group introspection, Surfacing group dynamics
Time	10-15 minutes (not including processing)
Physical contact	Minimal
Physical challenges	Requires the ability to move across the room and stop suddenly.
Number of participants	8-20
Space requirements	Open floor space. This exercise is more exciting in a larger space, but it can be played in a room the size of a regular classroom.
Materials needed	None
Preparation	None

Instructions

1. Ask for a volunteer to be "it" and have them stand near the wall at one end of the room.
2. Have the group line up facing "it," standing at least 12-15 feet away.
3. "It" turns their back to the group and says "Green light." Group members can then begin moving forward with the goal of tagging "it."
4. At any time, "it" can say "Red light," signaling that everyone must stop moving forward. "It" must wait a second after saying "Red light," then turn to look at the group. If "it" sees someone still moving forward, that person has to start over again at the far wall. ("It" may be tempted to turn around while saying "Red light," which does not give people enough time to freeze. To avoid this problem, you can have "it" say "Red light 1, 2" before turning around.)
5. "It" then turns back to the wall and says "Green light."
6. The game continues in this way until someone is able to tag "it." That person becomes the new "it" and the exercise begins again.

Processing suggestions

- Watch the different strategies that people use to overtake "it." Some people run as fast as they can, getting closer to "it" but generally finding it harder to freeze quickly enough. Others move slowly and surely, decreasing the risk of getting caught moving but also making little progress toward the goal. What strategies did people use? Which strategies were successful?
- Which strategy most closely resembles the way the group goes about its work?
- How did "it" feel when the group was closing in? Did "it" change strategy or play differently at that point?
- How does the group react when they feel that things are creeping up on them?
- This exercise also can raise issues about how people relate to authority.

Variation – Red Light, Green Light with Poses

Instructions

1. In this version, instead of saying "Red light," "it" calls out a pose—such as "Frog 1, 2," "Statue of Liberty 1, 2," or "Karate master 1, 2." In addition to freezing, the participants must also assume the pose before "it" turns around. "It" must always include the count of "1, 2" before turning around so that people have time to do this. When "it" sees someone who is either still moving or not in the pose, that person has to start over.

Additional processing suggestions

- How do people deal with additional demands made on them?

- How did people interpret the poses? Everyone has a different style, and people may interpret the same message differently. One person's "frog" may not look at all like a frog to another person.
- Did differing interpretations lead to any conflict between "it" and the other players? How was the conflict dealt with?

Relay Race

Goals	Interconnection, Group introspection
Time	10-20 minutes (not including processing)
Physical contact	None
Physical challenges	Requires the ability to run.
Number of participants	8-50
Space requirements	Open floor space in a large room
Materials needed	For each team, a marker or other object to use as a baton
Preparation	None

Instructions

1. Divide the group into two or more teams. (If the group is smaller than eight people, you can have one team that will race against the clock.)
2. Ask the teams to line up against the wall in the order that they will race.
3. Give the first runner on each team the object that the team will use as a baton.
4. When you give the signal, the first person on each team runs to the opposite wall, touches the wall, then runs back and passes the baton to the next person on their team. Each person who receives the baton must have one foot touching the wall until they have the baton in their hand.
5. This continues until the last person from each team has raced the final leg of the relay. The first team to finish is the winner.

Processing suggestions

- Although the exercise creates the illusion that each person is racing against someone from another team, success is really determined by how long it takes the team as a whole to run the race. It is the interaction between team members that is crucial to the team's speed, but each person is very important.
- You can relate this exercise to the importance of getting a job done on time, especially if the group is working toward a deadline.
- You can also use the exercise to start a discussion about being coordinated in the group's work, or about each person doing their piece of a job.
- Watch to see how each team deals with the strengths and weaknesses of its members.

Variation – Relay Chain

Materials needed	None

Instructions

1. Divide the group into two or more teams. (If the group is smaller than eight people, you can have one team that will race against the clock.)
2. Have each team divide itself in half, and the halves go to walls or boundaries opposite each other. If a team has an odd number of members, the larger half should be at the wall where the race will begin.
3. Ask the teams to line up in the order that they will race.
4. The first person on one side for each team races to the other side and joins hands or links elbows with the first person from their team on that side.
5. The two then run together and add the next team member to their chain.
6. This continues until the whole team is on the chain and has run the last leg of the race together.

7. If the chain breaks during the race, the group must return to the wall where they picked up the most recent member, reform their chain, and run that leg of the race over again.

Additional processing suggestions

- You can use the exercise to talk about building a movement—bringing people along with you both physically, as in the exercise, and also in terms of ideas, beliefs, values, and mission.
- You can relate the exercise to issues of leadership, organizing, and support. Working alone, you may get the job done, but are people with you? And are they coming freely, or do you have to drag them along?

Variation – Napkin Race

Additional goals	Focus, Surfacing group dynamics
Physical challenges	Must be able to move from one side of the room to the other.
Number of participants	No more than 20
Materials needed	A paper napkin for each team

Instructions

1. Follow steps 1 and 2 for RELAY RACE.
2. Give the lead person on each team a paper napkin.
3. When you say "Go," the lead people place their napkins on their heads and start moving toward the finish line. The object is to get there without the napkin falling. Players cannot use anything to hold the napkin in place. If it falls off, the person has to go back to the starting point and try again.
4. As soon as a teammate crosses the finish line, the next person (who must have one foot touching the wall) places the napkin on their head and starts across.
5. The exercise continues until one team gets everyone over the finish line.

Additional processing suggestions

- This exercise helps the group understand the importance of proceeding with caution while trying to make as much forward progress as possible. The team that wins has to move quickly enough to beat the other team, but slowly enough so that the napkin does not fall off. This is a helpful illustration of the dilemmas involved in numerous activities. For example, anyone who is teaching or training needs to cover a certain amount of material, but at a pace that will be understandable to all the students.
- Why did the winning team win? What strategies did they use?
- The exercise illustrates the importance of taking cues from those around you, since the runner must rely on facial and verbal cues from others to know if the napkin is about to fall off. How did teammates communicate with one another?
- Once people made it across, were they engaged in helping others cross? Did people spend time encouraging their own teammates or discouraging the other team?

Additional Variations

You can vary NAPKIN RACE in many ways by using different objects that make movement across the room more challenging. Some examples are a book, a plastic spoon in the mouth with an object in the spoon, coins on the back of the hand or elbow, or a piece of candy on the top of one foot. Each variation creates different possibilities for processing.

Simon Says

Goal	Leadership
Time	5-10 minutes for one round (not including processing)
Physical contact	None
Physical challenges	Minimal
Number of participants	Generally 8 to 25, but can also be used with large groups and fixed seating.
Space requirements	Generally, open floor space
Materials needed	None
Preparation	None

Instructions

1. Ask for a volunteer to be "Simon" and have that person stand facing the group.
2. Simon's task is to give a series of commands to do things that can be done standing in place. When a command is preceded by "Simon says" (such as "Simon says scratch your head"), the group should follow it. But when the leader does not say, "Simon says," people should not follow the command and anyone who does is out. When giving the commands, Simon should always demonstrate the action but does not necessarily have to say what it is. For example: "Simon says tap your elbow. ... Simon says do this."
3. The object of the exercise is for Simon to get everyone out.

Processing suggestions

- What strategies worked best for the leader? Did the strategies involve any questionable practices?
- What strategies worked best for the participants?
- The exercise opens up many areas of processing regarding leadership. Do people follow what leaders say or what they do? Do leaders sometimes say one thing and do another? The exercise illustrates the incongruity of a leader who is trying to fool and eliminate the followers.
- Are there forces or people in your life trying to get you "out"?
- The exercise illustrates both verbal and nonverbal communication. Which was more powerful and effective?
- Rules don't cover all the possibilities. You may need to strategize and be subtle in trying to accomplish your goals.
- People have automatic responses, things we are "hard-wired" to do. Did the exercise illustrate this?

Variation – Rolling Simon Says Times *X*

Number of participants	8 to 20

Instructions

1. Have the group stand in a circle.
2. Ask for a volunteer to be the first Simon.
3. The rules are the same as for SIMON SAYS except that each person takes a turn being Simon for a specified number of commands, usually 4 to 6. In other words, during their turn at leadership, each person has a certain number of tries to get at least one member of the group out.
4. After each Simon's turn is up, move clockwise around the circle until everyone has had a turn at being Simon.
5. When each new Simon begins, anybody who was out with the last Simon rejoins the exercise.

Additional processing suggestions

- Discuss the need for everyone to take leadership. How does leadership flow in this group, in this school, in this community, in this society?
- Different styles of leadership can flow through a group.
- What are the most effective strategies used by different leaders?
- How do individuals respond differently when they have the opportunity to lead? Do they take it on, or throw it away?
- What did it feel like to lead? What did you do with the opportunity to lead? Did you take risks or hold back? Why?

Variation – Rolling Simon Says Timed

Number of participants	8 to 20
Materials needed	A watch or clock that counts seconds

Instructions

1. Proceed as for ROLLING SIMON SAYS TIMES *X*, except that instead of a specific number of commands each Simon has a specified amount of time (such as 45 seconds) to try getting people out.

Additional processing suggestions

- We only have so much time to get the job done, so we need to use it wisely.
- Time constraints and other stresses can affect our ability to function effectively. Some people work well under stress, and others don't.

Variation – Dueling Simon Says

Number of participants	Generally 8-25, but can also be used with very large groups.
Space requirements	Can work with fixed seating or theater seating.
Preparation	Prepare two people to be the leaders; they can be facilitators or members of the group. They should be people who can do what the exercise requires without letting the group know that they are essentially giving a scripted performance. It is recommended that the two leaders rehearse ahead of time.

Instructions

1. The leaders stand in front of the group or audience and ask everyone to stand up (if this is practical).
2. Leader 1 explains the instructions for SIMON SAYS, and tells the group that the two leaders are going to pass the leadership of this exercise back and forth.
3. Leader 1 gives several commands, preceded or not by "Simon says," and the group follows along.
4. Leader 1 then defers to Leader 2, who begins giving commands.
5. At some point, Leader 1 interrupts, saying that Leader 2 isn't doing a good job. Leader 1 starts giving commands and telling the group to follow.
6. Leader 2 objects and insists that Leader 1 is not playing fair or not doing the exercise correctly.
7. Both leaders continue giving commands, trying to get the group to follow them. Most likely the group will become confused and not know whom to follow.
8. After a few moments of confusion, the leaders together give the command, "Simon says sit down" (or something else appropriate if the audience is already seated

Additional processing suggestions

- When those in positions of leadership or authority cannot come together or are not consistent in their approach, there may be mixed messages that result in no one following anyone.
- How did people respond when the leadership became confused?
- How many people stopped playing?

- In what situations do you see similar forms of leadership?
- What can be done to change this dysfunction?
- How do you make choices when drawn in two directions?
- How is it possible to listen to conflicting points of view?

Slide by Slide

Goals	Planning, Organizing, Interconnection, Group problem solving, Surfacing group dynamics
Time	10-15 minutes (not including processing)
Physical contact	Some contact as people change places
Physical challenges	Must be able to move from block to block
Number of participants	8-14
Space requirements	Open floor space
Materials needed	Masking tape and sticky notes
Preparation	See "Setting Up the Grid."

Setting Up the Grid

Block out a grid on the floor with masking tape. The grid should have one more square than there are players. Number the squares in the grid consecutively, but only up to the number of players.

For 8 players, set up the floor like this:

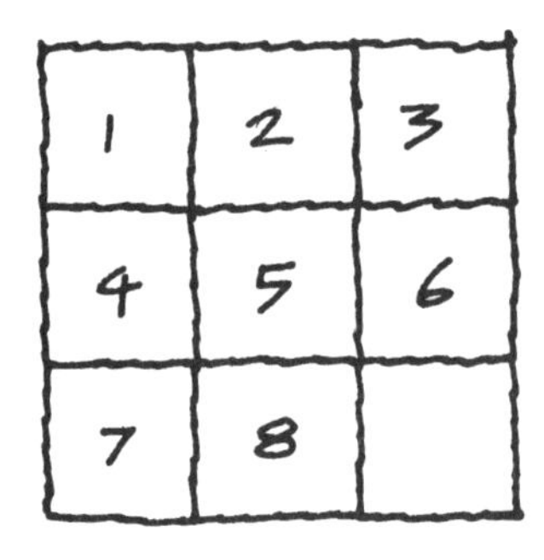

For 9 or 10 players, set up like this:

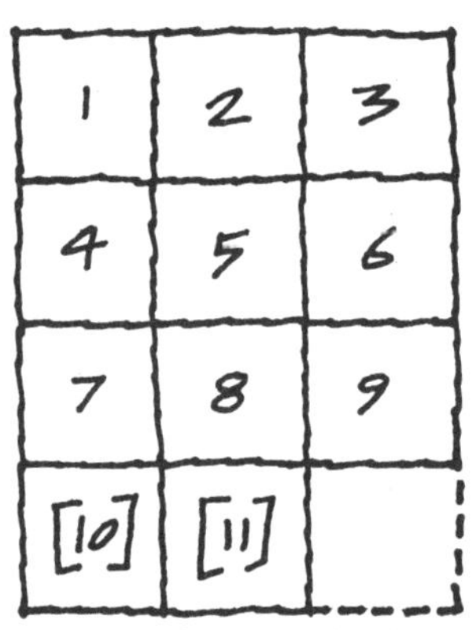

For 11 players, add the last block.

For 12 or 13 players, set up like this:

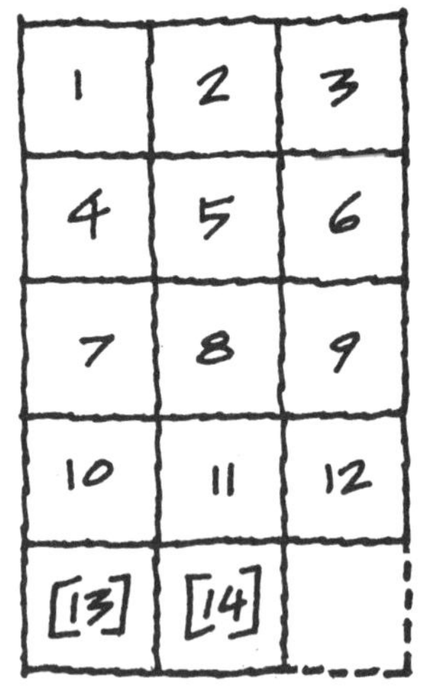

For 14 players, add the last block.

Instructions

1. Give each player a piece of paper with a number that corresponds to one of the numbered blocks.
2. Tell each person to stand in a block that has a different number from the number the person is holding.
3. The group's task is to rearrange themselves so that everyone is standing in the block corresponding to their number.
4. The rules for movement are:
   - Only one person can be in a block at a time.
   - A person can move only into an empty space.

- Only vertical and horizontal movements are allowed; people cannot move diagonally. (Some players may have seen the handheld puzzles with moving tiles. The movements in this exercise are the same.)

5. The exercise ends when everyone is lined up in order.

Processing suggestions

- How was the goal reached?
- Did certain people take on leadership positions?
- Did the group plan ahead of time what they were going to do, or did they just start moving?
- This exercise illustrates the tension between individual goals and group goals. Were players more concerned about getting to their own space or making sure that everyone was in the right space?
- This exercise demonstrates the effect that individuals have on an entire group or system. As one person moves into the empty square, they open up a space for someone else to move, but they also restrict other people's movements.
- You can also relate people's movements to the adjustments and changes that need to happen in order for goals to be met.
- The exercise works best when the group is able to order their tasks and give each other space.
- How did the group feel about the rules that constrained their movements? For example, the "no diagonal movement" rule makes sense in the tile puzzles, since the puzzles contain no mechanism for diagonal movement. But with human beings, the rule is an artificial barrier to reaching the goal. Is this similar to other situations the group is facing?

Sound-Motion-Go-Around

Goals	Group introspection, Different perspectives
Time	5-10 minutes (not including processing)
Physical contact	None
Physical challenges	Must be able to repeat others' motions.
Number of participants	8-20
Space requirements	Open floor space
Materials needed	None
Preparation	None

Notes:

- This exercise can lead into a discussion about accepting differences.
- You can use either part of the exercise (sound or motion) separately, depending on the needs of the group.

A. Sound

Note: This part of this exercise tends to be high-risk, like all exercises that call on people to make sounds.

Instructions

1. Have everyone stand in a circle. Start the exercise by making a sound; each person in turn repeats the same sound until it has traveled all the way around the circle.
2. Start again by making a sound, but this time tell the group that each person should change the sound as they wish when it is their turn.

B. Motion

Instructions

1. Follow the instructions above using motions rather than sounds.

Processing suggestions

- Notice how people made the same sound or the same motion differently. People have different styles in almost everything they do.
- In a group that is coming together to accomplish something, people need to recognize and be tolerant of each other's differences in style.

Variation – Wave-Go-Around

Physical challenges	Requires the ability to jump.

Note: This variation can be done alone or it can be added to SOUND-MOTION-GO-AROUND as a challenge to a group experienced with that exercise.

Instructions

1. With the group standing in a circle, tell them to pretend a mouse is running around under their heels. Everyone has to lift their heels as the mouse runs by, so that the movement of lifting heels travels around the circle.
2. Next, say that a cat is running around the circle. Everyone has to jump up a bit as the cat passes.
3. Finally, say that a large dog is running around the circle. Jump higher to let the dog go by.

Additional processing suggestions

- This exercise illustrates the need to recognize differences in capacity. Some people just can't jump high enough for a fast-running dog. In the exercise, that doesn't matter. But in this group's work together, sometimes more will be expected than a person is able to do. Can this group be tolerant and supportive and learn to work together despite differences in capacity?
- How did people feel doing the exercise? Were there differences in style or ability?
- Was the group able to keep the mouse/cat/dog unharmed or did it get stepped on? How was it able to do so?
- You can also use the exercise to talk about differences in timing and energy. As the group responded to the running animals, waves of energy rose and fell around the circle. In the same way, in the group's work together there will be high points and low points of group energy. The low points are bound to come. The important thing is to expect them to come, but also expect them to go. However, when someone doesn't share the group's goals, or purposefully acts in a dysfunctional way, that is unacceptable.

Squat Ball

Goals	Surfacing group dynamics, Trust, Focus
Time	5-10 minutes (not including processing)
Physical contact	Feet touching
Physical challenges	Must be able to use your hands to push the ball across the floor and to block it as it comes toward you. This is a highly energetic, fast-paced exercise.
Number of participants	8-15
Space requirements	Open floor space
Materials needed	A medium-size ball, such as a volleyball or a small soccer ball
Preparation	None

Instructions

1. Have the group stand in a circle with their feet roughly shoulder-width apart or a bit wider (all players should have their feet about the same distance apart), with feet touching the feet of the people standing to their right and left.
2. Ask for a volunteer to start the play.
3. The object of the exercise is to get the ball through someone else's legs three times.
4. Players can't block the ball by moving their feet or their knees, but they can use their hands.
5. If the ball goes through a person's legs three times, that person is out. People who are out become ball retrievers.
6. The exercise should proceed at a fast pace with no time-outs. The ball is in play as soon as it is retrieved. As the facilitator you may want to model this by putting the ball through someone's legs just after you have retrieved it, or by trying to distract the group and then putting the ball through people's legs.
7. Call time after 4-5 minutes, or when half the players are out.

Processing suggestions

- What techniques did people use to get others out or to remain in play themselves? Were various tactics fair?
- Did people gang up on others trying to get them out? Are alliances ever made in this group? Do they help or hurt the group? What about in society? Do people align with others to get certain people "out"?
- How did it feel to get out? How did it feel to just watch from the outside? What was people's level of engagement after getting out?
- How did focus and paying attention to the center of the action relate to staying in the game?
- Were people taken by surprise while playing? Were there ways to be better prepared so you wouldn't be caught off guard?
- How does the group deal with being caught off guard in their work?

Support Sequence Circle

Goals	Interconnection, Trust
Time	5 minutes (not including processing)
Physical contact	Holding hands
Physical challenges	Must be able to lean forward or backward
Number of participants	10 to 40
Space requirements	Open floor space
Materials needed	None
Preparation	None

Note: This exercise is difficult and often doesn't work, but in these situations the processing can often be richer and more meaningful than when the exercise is done successfully.

Instructions

1. Have the group stand shoulder-to-shoulder in a circle and hold hands. There must be an even number of people; a facilitator can be part of the circle or not as necessary. With large groups and a single facilitator, it is best if you are not part of the circle but instead stand in the center.
2. Have people go around the circle and alternate saying "In" or "Out."
3. At your count of three, the "Ins" lean toward the center of the circle while the "Outs" lean back.
4. If the circle is stable, the "Ins" and "Outs" can try switching positions. This can be done to a rhythm.

Processing suggestions

- This exercise can illustrate the group's ability to support each other, and what happens when people are not able (or do not choose) to support each other adequately.
- Each individual has a critical part to play and the ultimate success depends on everyone. One person's dysfunction will throw the whole group off.
- For this reason, this can be a useful exercise to do just before the group implements an event or initiative they have been planning.
- The switching-positions element can be discussed in terms of the difficulty of making transitions.

Take a Shot

Goals	Introspection, Surfacing group dynamics
Time	5-10 minutes (not including processing)
Physical contact	None
Physical challenges	Requires the ability to pass a ball and throw it through a hoop.
Number of participants	8-20
Space requirements	Open floor space
Materials needed	A Nerf ball, a basketball hoop, and a radio. Lacking these supplies, you can use a wadded-up ball of paper, a wastebasket, and someone to sing or make music somehow.
Preparation	None

Instructions

1. Have the group stand in a circle around the hoop.
2. Designate one person to be the DJ. This person will turn their back on the rest of the group and play the music, stopping at random intervals.
3. When the music starts, the group passes the ball around the circle to the right.
4. When the music stops, the person who is holding the ball has to shoot. If they miss, they are out; if they make the shot, they stay in the game.
5. The exercise continues until everyone is out except the last person, who is the winner.

Processing suggestions

- This exercise raises issues of how people handle pressure, stress, and risk.
- Ask why people didn't want to get stuck with the ball. The fewer shots they take, the less chance that they will be out. How did people deal with this risk?
- This exercise may produce a lot of stress for participants and it can demonstrate how people handle stress. How did people feel when they missed a shot and when they made a shot?
- How do the issues of pressure, risk-taking, and performance that we see in this exercise relate to the group's work?
- Willingness to "take a shot" at something usually depends on skill level in the required task. For example, those who play basketball may be more willing to take a shot in this exercise. How does this relate to tasks that people have before them in the group and in other aspects of their lives?
- You can emphasize the importance of "taking a shot" at something when the opportunity presents itself, and about people supporting each other as they do this.
- Sometimes people will try to pass the ball off if they have it when the music stops, and this can raise issues of taking responsibility.

Too Much

Goals	Personal problem solving, Surfacing group dynamics
Time	5-10 minutes (not including processing)
Physical contact	None
Physical challenges	Minimal
Number of participants	8-12
Space requirements	Minimal
Materials needed	A 3-ounce or 5-ounce paper cup, a large bowl, water, and a quantity of small, light objects such as dried beans or pebbles
Preparation	Fill the bowl about two-thirds with water; there should be enough water for the cup to be submerged.

Instructions

1. Divide the small objects equally among the players.
2. To begin, float the empty cup on the surface of the water.
3. Each player in turn puts three of their objects into the cup. The person whose objects sink the cup is the loser.

Processing suggestions

- What strategies did people use to try keeping the cup afloat? Which ones were successful?
- Did it matter whether objects were placed in the cup gently or forcefully?
- How did people cope with the increasing challenge as the exercise progressed?
- How did it feel to have to take your turn when the cup seemed ready to sink?
- Processing can also discuss the issue of a person's or a group's capacity to achieve its goals, and how it can be overwhelmed by demands that exceed the capacity.
- How far can we push ourselves until we sink?
- Are we willing to take risks?

Variation – Team Too Much

Number of participants	12-30
Materials needed	Enough materials so that each team has its own cup, bowl, and objects.

Instructions

1. Divide the group into two or three teams.
2. Give each team the materials, including three objects for each participant.
3. Have the teams decide the order in which people will play.
4. When you give the signal, player 1 on each team places their objects in the cup. Alternatively, you can play so that Team A goes first, then Team B, then Team C.
5. Continue in the manner you have chosen until one cup sinks or all of the teams' cups sink.

Additional processing suggestions

- This variation adds the component of competition. What are the dynamics that come out when people are divided into teams?
- How did it feel to sink or not sink the cup for the team? How is this different from when you do something on your own?

Trust Circle

Goals	Trust, Group introspection
Time	10-15 minutes (not including processing)
Physical contact	Extensive
Physical challenges	Requires the ability to fall backwards and to tolerate close contact.
Number of participants	8-20
Space requirements	Open floor space
Materials needed	None
Preparation	None

Note: This is a physically high-risk exercise because there is some danger that someone could fall, and it is emotionally high-risk because the person in the middle is in a vulnerable position. It should be done only with a group that knows each other well and where the trust level is fairly high.

Instructions

1. If there are 16-20 people participating, you divide them into two groups.
2. Have each group stand in a circle so that they are almost shoulder to shoulder.
3. Caution the group that everyone must take this exercise very seriously, remain alert at all times, and do everything they can to be sure the person in the middle does not fall.
4. In each group, one person volunteers to step into the circle. That person crosses their arms across their chest and closes their eyes.
5. The people forming the circle extend their hands, palms forward, ready to hold up the person in the middle.
6. Keeping body straight and feet together, the person in the middle falls back into the hands of those forming the circle.
7. The group then carefully passes the person around the circle. It is helpful to have each group member say the name of the person they are passing around as they catch that person.
8. Anyone who is willing can take a turn being passed around.

Processing suggestions

- This exercise surfaces issues of trust in the group.
- Processing can focus on the importance of the group providing support for each of its members.
- It can also be used to point out the danger of having group members who are not fully invested in the safety or goals of the group.
- How did it feel to be passed around? Was anyone worried they would be dropped? Did people feel safe in the middle? Do people feel safe in this group?

Trust Fall

Goal	Trust
Time	10-15 minutes (not including processing)
Physical contact	Extensive
Physical challenges	Requires the ability to fall backwards and to tolerate both height and close contact.
Number of participants	10-20
Space requirements	Minimal
Materials needed	A sturdy table or other surface
Preparation	Set up the space so that people can easily get onto the table, and be sure that the area used for the exercise is safe.

Note: This is a very high-risk exercise; it should be done only with a group that knows each other well and has a strong degree of trust in each other. Be sensitive to people in the group whose size/weight would present a problem if they volunteer to do the fall.

Instructions

1. Explain what the TRUST FALL is and ask for a volunteer to go first.
2. Have the volunteer stand on the edge of the sturdy table with their back to the group.
3. Have the group stand in two lines extending out from the edge of the table where the volunteer is standing.
4. All the way down the line, the two people facing each other should interlock their arms securely.
5. Tell people that everyone needs to be alert and ready.
6. When you are certain that everyone is ready, give the signal for the volunteer to fall back, into the interlocked arms. Important: make sure to instruct the personal falling that they should keep their arms by their sides tightly. Watch carefully as the volunteer falls.
7. After the fall, be certain that the volunteer is lowered carefully to the ground.
8. Provide the opportunity for others in the group to do the TRUST FALL if they wish, being certain each time that the group is alert and ready.

Processing suggestions

- This exercise shows how safety in the group allows people to take risks they wouldn't normally take. People are dependent on each other to catch them when they fall.
- Talk about how everyone—the person who falls and the people who catch—grows and learns from this experience.
- Who decided to fall? Who chose not to fall? Who went first?
- What motivated people to volunteer for a TRUST FALL?
- For those who did not volunteer, what held them back?
- Did people feel confident that they would not get hurt?
- Did those doing the catching feel confident that they could support the "fallers" adequately?

Web of Connection

Goal	Interconnection
Time	5-10 minutes (not including processing)
Physical contact	None
Physical challenges	Must be able to throw a ball of yarn (though a helper could do this).
Number of participants	10-30
Space requirements	Open floor space. Can also be done seated around a table.
Materials needed	A ball of yarn long enough to create a web connecting everyone in the circle
Preparation	None

Instructions

1. If you have open floor space, have people stand in a circle.
2. The person who begins holds the loose end of the yarn, says the name of someone across the circle, and throws the ball of yarn to that person. (If the group is seated around a table, people can roll the yarn instead of throwing it.)
3. The person who received the yarn says someone else's name and, while holding on to the thread of the yarn, throws (or rolls) the ball of yarn to them. The person with the yarn must throw it to someone who has not received it yet.
4. This continues until everyone in the circle has received the yarn. The last person to receive it throws it back to the person who began.

Processing suggestions

Some points you can raise in processing are:

- The common "threads" that bring together people in this group.
- The network that connects people starts with personal contacts (that is, calling the name of the person you are throwing to).
- Everyone is part of something bigger.
- The group has created an intricate pattern.
- People have, by working together, created something beautiful.

Variation – Warm-Up Web

Instructions

1. You can combine this exercise with a Warm-up Question (see chapter 10), so that people answer the question, then toss the yarn. This differs from the usual format for Warm-up Questions in that you do not proceed around the circle and people don't know when it will be their turn to respond.

Variation – Carry the Web

Additional materials Scissors

Note: This variation is appropriate for a group that is meeting for the only time or the last time.

Instructions

1. Proceed as for WEB OF CONNECTION.
2. When everyone has received the yarn, go around the circle and cut the yarn so that everyone has a piece.

Additional processing suggestions

- People will be taking with them specific things gained from being in the group, such as knowledge, skills, relationships, or understanding of different perspectives. What do people think they will be taking away with them?
- How can we remember what we learned or accomplished in this group?

Who's That There Behind the Curtain?

Goals	Interconnection, Communication
Time	5-10 minutes (not including processing)
Physical contact	None
Physical challenges	None
Number of participants	12-20
Space requirements	Open floor space
Materials needed	A piece of material that cannot be seen through and is large enough to serve as the curtain
Preparation	None

Note: This exercise depends on the group members knowing each others' names, but it can also be used as a lively way to reinforce names with a group that has been getting to know each other.

Instructions

1. This exercise requires two people to hold the curtain. If there is only one facilitator, ask for a volunteer to help.
2. Divide the group into two teams and have the teams sit or stand together on opposite sides of the curtain. Keep the curtain close to the ground so the opposing teams can't see each other's feet. Instruct people to duck down so the other team can't see their heads.
3. Each team decides, without speaking, who should go up to the curtain (still ducking down).
4. When a person from each team is in front of the curtain, drop the curtain quickly.
5. Whoever is the first to say the name of the other person is the winner of that round.
6. Repeat several times.

Processing suggestions

- Who went up in each of the groups? Was there anyone who did not go up to the curtain? Do we want people to know us? Do we put ourselves in a position to get to know people, and for other people to get to know us? It takes courage for someone to step out of their comfort zone to meet new people and challenges, but doing so can be beneficial for the person and for the group.
- Was it difficult for people to say the person's name from the other team, even if they knew their name? Why did some people find this difficult? Often it is difficult to retrieve information on the spot. You may want to use this exercise to talk about the importance of preparation and knowing information ahead of time.
- Did people ever guess the wrong name? What led to this? Sometimes people make assumptions instead of looking at what is in front of them. While this may be easier and quicker than taking the time to look and find out the truth, it often leads to misinformation.
- You can also use this exercise to talk about deepening relationships and connections with people in the group. How well do people in the group know each other?

The Wind Blows

Goals	Interconnection, Leadership
Time	10-15 minutes (not including processing)
Physical contact	None
Physical challenges	Must be able to move around.
Number of participants	The maximum number depends on the number of chairs that can be arranged in one circle. The ideal number is 12-25.
Space requirements	Open floor space
Materials needed	Enough chairs for the group minus one
Preparation	None

Note: This exercise is good for groups that don't know each other well. It functions to mix people around the room and get them to move away from their friends. It can be a good prelude to a PAIRING (p. 237), since it increases the likelihood that, at the end of the exercise, people will not be sitting next to those they usually talk with.

Instructions

1. Arrange the chairs in a circle, with enough chairs for all participants minus one. In most circumstances, the facilitator should participate.
2. Explain that one person will be at the front of the room, and they will say a "wind blows" statement. Give some examples of "wind blows" statements, such as "The wind blows for everyone wearing blue," or "…anyone who has a quarter in their pocket." Keep the tone light; this exercise is not intended to be high-risk.
3. Explain that everyone to whom the statement applies (plus the person who gave the "wind blows" statement) must walk within the circle and find an empty chair to sit in. For example, if you say, "The wind blows for everyone who's wearing sneakers," everyone wearing sneakers gets up and moves around looking for an empty chair, and you also look for an empty chair.
4. The person who is left without a chair then says the next "wind blows" statement. They can say whatever they want, such as "everyone who's been to New York" or "everyone who likes to sing."
5. Explain the rules: There is no running. People looking for an empty chair cannot take the chair directly to their left or to their right, and they can't sit back down in the seat from which they just stood up. Also, explain that "wind blows" statements cannot single people out—they must apply to more than one person. For example, if only one person in the room is wearing flip-flops, you cannot say "The wind blows for everyone wearing flip-flops."
6. Then say the first "wind blows" statement. It should be one that gets a lot of people moving, such as "The wind blows for everyone who brushed their teeth this morning" or even "The wind blows for everyone."
7. Continue for several rounds, then announce that the next round will be the last.

Processing suggestions

- THE WIND BLOWS gives people the experience of being up in front of the group and taking on a leadership role, even if just for a moment. Were people comfortable in that position? Did some people look forward to it and others try to avoid it?
- The exercise gives people the experience of thinking on their feet.
- You can use THE WIND BLOWS to talk about what it's like to feel left out (being the only person without a chair). You might relate this experience to the group's work (such as people being left

out in terms of information or decision-making in schools or other environments) or to the group's dynamics, if certain people in the group are being excluded.

Variation – The Wind Hops, Wind Spins, etc.

Physical challenges	Must be able to perform the specified movement.

Instructions

1. Follow the instructions for THE WIND BLOWS, but use other movements besides walking to get to a different chair, and rename the exercise based on the movement. Some examples are: WIND HOPS, WIND SPINS, BACKWARD WIND BLOWS, HEEL-TO-TOE WIND BLOWS, WIND JUMPS, ONE-EYED WIND BLOWS, SIDEWAYS WIND BLOWS. You can also create variations that involve doing something (for example, shaking someone's hand—THE WIND BLOWS WITH HANDSHAKES) before finding a chair. Be sure to caution people about safety issues and to enforce the rules regarding safety.

Additional processing suggestions

- How was this variation more challenging than regular WIND BLOWS? Are there ways in which it was easier?
- How is this change related to the dynamics in the group?
- What did people learn from this approach?
- Often things become more complex as we go along, but with experience we can rise to the challenge.
- Specific processing points will depend on the movements the group used. For example, for BACKWARD WIND BLOWS, you can point out the importance of vision and seeing the whole picture when moving toward making a decision. Otherwise, there can be chaos and people's ideas can collide.

Variation – The Wind Blows with Words or Questions

Additional goal	Communication
Preparation	Make a list of five or six words or questions related to the group's goals, projects, or issues. Write the list on a flip chart clearly visible to the group. Depending on the goals of the exercise, you may want to include non-English words or nonsense words.

Instructions

1. Play THE WIND BLOWS as usual for several rounds. Then show the group the list of words.
2. Announce that the next person who is left without a seat has to choose a word to speak about or a question to answer for 15–20 seconds. If you are using non-English or nonsense words, explain that it is not necessary to know the meaning of the word to speak about it.
3. Give an example, using a word that is not listed, of what someone might say. For example, if the words listed are "future, graduation, success, career, unknown, plan," you might want to speak about the word "hope." The more articulate and thoughtful your example, the more likely it is that the group will say meaningful and thoughtful things as well. It's also important to speak briefly, modeling the amount of time that others should spend. Ask if there are any questions, and then say the next "wind blows" statement.
4. The next person up front speaks about a word/question, then continues with a "wind blows" statement. If you want to be sure all the words/questions are addressed, have each speaker cross their choice off the list.
5. Continue for several rounds, or until all the words/questions have been addressed. If someone who has already spoken about a word/question is left without a seat in a subsequent round, they can just say "The wind blows..." without choosing another topic to discuss.

Additional processing suggestions

- The addition of words/questions provides a more complex demonstration of leadership. For many people, speaking in front of a group can be difficult, and some people will try hard not to be caught up in front. Others may try to get caught because they want to speak to the group.
- Did having the words/questions change how people felt about being caught without a chair?
- Processing can focus on the content of the answers.
- You can also look at why people chose particular words or questions to respond to. Which were chosen first and last, and why? Were any words or questions avoided? Why?
- Non-English and nonsense words can be used to bring up cultural differences and language barriers in diverse settings.

Variation – The Wind Blows with Charades

Additional goals	Acting, Communication
Materials	Slips of paper, pens/pencils, container for the paper
Preparation	Write words or phrases on slips of paper and place these in an open container. Some can be related to the work the group is doing, while others could be more for fun. Alternatively, you can give everyone a slip of paper and a pen and ask them to write the name of a well-known person (actor, politician, cartoon character, etc.) and place it in the designated container. The person should be famous enough so that everyone in the room is likely to know of them.

Instructions

1. Play THE WIND BLOWS as usual for a few rounds.
2. Announce that the next person left standing must draw out a slip of paper, then do something so that the rest of the group can try to identify what is on the slip of paper. The person standing can speak and do just about anything except say what is written on the paper.
3. The rest of the group has a limited time (one or two minutes) to guess correctly what the person is portraying.
4. Continue for several rounds. (It is not necessary to use all the slips.)

Additional processing suggestions

- If the person acted out a famous person, what elements of the character were used? Were there other elements of that character that would have made it easier for the guessers?
- You can use this exercise to open up a discussion about how well we really know each other. What elements of yourself do you think people would act out if it were your name on the slip of paper? What would you want people to act out, and what would you not want people to act out?
- If words or phrases were acted out, which messages were harder to communicate, and which messages were easier?
- How much was communicated physically versus verbally in this exercise? How much do we pay attention to both means of communication in our everyday lives?

Variation – The Wind Blows with Scenarios

Additional goal	Acting
Materials	Container for questions
Preparation	Write several scenarios that one or two people can act out. Some scenarios can relate to the work the group is doing, while others could be more for fun. The scenarios can use words (for example, a student and a teacher arguing about a bad grade) or be silent (for example, two children enjoying a snow day off from school), or you could have some of each. Write each scenario on a piece of paper and place in an open container.

Instructions

1. Play THE WIND BLOWS as usual for a few rounds.
2. Remove an additional chair from the circle if the scenarios you've written involve two people.
3. Announce that in the next round, whoever is left standing must choose a slip of paper and act out the scenario that is on it. Set a time limit of about a minute for the scenario.
4. If the scenario is silent, you can ask people to guess what it represents
5. Continue for several rounds or until all the scenarios have been acted out.

Additional processing suggestions

- This exercise can be used to look at creativity, spontaneity, or speaking and acting skills. It can show how difficult it is to present on your feet without proper preparation.
- How did people react when they saw the scenario they had to act out? Which were the most difficult and easiest scenes to portray?
- Discuss the content of the scenarios and what they show about the group's work.

Variation – The Wind Blows with Hats

Additional goal	Different perspectives
Preparation	Gather several different types of hats and put them in a bag or a box.

Instructions

1. Play THE WIND BLOWS as usual for a few rounds.
2. Announce that in the next round, whoever is left standing must choose a hat and put it on. That person must then try to envision what type of person might wear that hat (how they might talk, walk, or act), and give the next "wind blows" statement in that persona.
3. Continue for several rounds.

Additional processing suggestions

- This exercise could be used to talk about who takes on what role(s) in the group or who "wears which hat(s)."
- It can be used to look at flexibility, adaptability, or willingness to take risks and try something new.
- It could also be used to look at stereotypes or misconceptions of people based on appearance.
- What hats were easiest/hardest to work with?
- How did it feel playing a different role? How comfortable did you feel in your role?
- What roles do we take on or not take on in this group?
- What stereotypes are most common in society and in this community? How accurate are they or how damaging are they?

More Variations

THE WIND BLOWS is a highly adaptable exercise. You may think of additional variations that would suit your group, or you might "mix and match," combining variations such as WIND BLOWS WITH WORDS and WIND BLOWS WITH HATS.

Yes Game

Goals	Focus, Communication, Interconnection
Time	5-10 minutes (not including processing)
Physical contact	None
Physical challenges	Minimal
Number of participants	8-20
Space requirements	Open floor space
Materials needed	None
Preparation	None

Instructions

1. Have the group stand in a circle.
2. Explain that the goal of this exercise is to keep people *in* the circle, not to get people out.
3. The leader (A) points to someone (B) across the circle. Person B must say "yes." When that happens, person A moves to take the place of person B. Meanwhile, person B—after saying "yes"—points to someone else (C), waits for "yes," and moves to take C's place. C points, and so on. Each person must get a "yes" before moving.
4. A person is out if they move before getting a "yes" reply, or if the person they said "yes" to comes to take their place in the circle before they have moved out of it.
5. If the person being pointed to is slow to respond, the pointer can point to someone else in the circle.

Processing suggestions

- For the group to succeed at doing this exercise, each person has to do a lot: listen, pay attention, hold several details in mind at once, and be aware of several dynamics simultaneously.
- The exercise requires people to ask permission, which can be difficult. It deals with the frustration of having to wait for permission before being able to act.
- It can also raise conflict around being "out" because of what someone else did or didn't do.
- Who got out first? Why?
- Did people get out because of what they did or because of what someone else did?
- How did it feel to be responsible for getting someone else out?
- Was the exercise frustrating? Why?
- Does the group face similar frustrations in their work?

Variation – Yes Game with a Goal

Goal	Group problem solving

Instructions

1. In order to make the exercise cooperative rather than competitive, set a goal for the group to go for a certain number of rounds (one round involves point, "yes," and replacing) with no one being out.

Additional processing suggestions

- Ideally, sharing the same goal invests everyone in the work, eliminates competition, and cuts down on intentional dysfunction.
- Did this exercise work better with a goal than without?

Variation – Long Distance Yes

Instructions

1. With the group standing in a circle, ask everyone to take several steps back. (Determine how many steps based on the size of the room and the size of the group.) Then follow the instructions for the YES GAME.
2. You can introduce a different dynamic by stopping at any point in the exercise and having the group move in or out a specified number of steps.

Additional processing suggestions

- To reach a compromise with the values or ideas of others, sometimes people have to travel some distance.
- For a group to succeed, people must move toward one another and sometimes change their own perspective. It may be more difficult to say yes to another person's ideas if our own perspectives are so far away.
- What role did distance play in this exercise?
- Was it more difficult to determine who was being pointed to?
- How distant are we from one another in this group? in society? What impact does it have?
- Who doesn't get pointed to or most often gets left out in society? How does that affect individuals or groups?

Chapter 17

Work Section Exercises

Once your group has done the Introduction, Name/Warm-up, and Springboard sections of the agenda, they are ready to focus directly on the work for which they are assembled. The exercises for the Work Section of the agenda give groups the opportunity to delve deeply into that work. They provide approaches that help people think in new ways and come at the work of the group from new directions, thus enabling them to generate more creative solutions to the challenges they face.

A few of these exercises, such as BRAINSTORMING and ROLE-PLAYS, are useful techniques in almost any setting and can help groups to reach a variety of goals. In an ongoing group, you may want to use these exercises frequently; for example, you can use BRAINSTORMING to set goals, decide on actions to meet the goals, list the tasks needed for the actions, and anticipate problems that might come up.

Other exercises, such as LIFE LINES or DIVERSITY IN MOTION, are suitable for particular types of groups to reach specific goals; you would probably do them no more than once in the life of a group.

All of these exercises are designed for groups of 20 or fewer. If you are working with a larger number, break into small groups with a facilitator for each.

For a complete discussion of the Work Section, including information about structuring small groups into your agenda, see chapter 4.

Brainstorming

Goals	See "Purposes of BRAINSTORMING."
Time	10-15 minutes, plus up to 45 minutes for processing
Physical contact	None
Physical challenges	None
Number of participants	6 to 20
Space requirements	None
Materials needed	Flip chart paper and a marker
Preparation	None

Purposes of BRAINSTORMING

BRAINSTORMING serves to:

- Release the creative energies of a group and focus those energies on coming up with innovative ways of achieving the group's goals.
- Get people thinking about one or more topics that are relevant to the work at hand or to issues in the group.
- Break down fears and inhibitions.
- Create an environment where ideas stand on their own merit, regardless of who proposed the ideas.
- Force the group to suspend judgment so that everyone feels free to express their ideas.

Rules for BRAINSTORMING

1. Say the first thing that comes to your mind; don't censor your ideas.
2. Even if your idea is similar to something else that's been said, say it anyway. It will keep the cre-

ative energies going.

3. During the Brainstorm, do not give your opinion of any of the ideas that are expressed.
4. Don't get into discussions of any ideas until the Brainstorm is completed.
5. There should be no put-downs of anyone or of any ideas.

Following these rules is critical to the success of BRAINSTORMING. Each time you do a Brainstorm, review the rules before beginning, and don't hesitate to refer back to the rules during the exercise when people need reminders.

Instructions

1. Explain that you will be writing a question or topic on the flip chart, and that you want the group to come up with a lot of ideas about it. Explain that the reason for doing a Brainstorm is to generate a large quantity of ideas; the group will deal with the quality of the ideas after the Brainstorm.
2. Explain the rules.
3. Tell people that you may not be able to keep up, so they should shout out their ideas more than once until you write them down. (Do not ask the group to say their ideas one at a time because this may decrease the power of the exercise.)
3. Write the question or topic on the flip chart and ask the group to come up with ideas that respond to it.
4. Write down everyone's ideas as they come out. It is important to write the ideas where everyone can see them, because seeing the ideas will stimulate further thoughts. Do your best to keep up.
5. Don't end the BRAINSTORMING too quickly. It's OK for the group to be silent for a little while; the tension can create additional ideas. You can encourage more ideas by asking for "one or two more."

Processing suggestions

- Once the Brainstorm is completed, work through the ideas with the group. You may want to start by circling a couple of ideas that may need further clarification and asking the people who contributed those ideas to explain them.
- Then work with the information in such a way as to move the group toward their goals. For example, you could ask the group to eliminate ideas that aren't practical or serious. You could have them categorize the ideas and discuss specific ones in detail. Or you could have the group prioritize the ideas down to the top three or four.
- This part of the session could take up to 45 minutes or longer.

Variation – Brainwarming

Materials needed	Paper and a pen or pencil for each participant

Instructions

1. This exercise is used to augment BRAINSTORMING. Before the spoken Brainstorm, the participants spend a few minutes working with the question or topic on paper and coming up with ideas.

Variation – Brainrace

Instructions

1. This exercise is simply a fast Brainstorm. It follows all the rules and procedures of BRAINSTORMING; the only difference is that the pace is speeded up. Participants are asked to throw out their ideas as fast as possible, and the leader works very fast to keep up. You will usually want to limit the number of responses you take to ten or fifteen, rather than filling an entire flip chart page. This approach is particularly useful with a group that is familiar with BRAINSTORMING, or when you have limited time.

Brave New World

Goals	Group problem solving, Group introspection, Different perspectives
Time	15-30 minutes (not including processing)
Physical contact	None
Physical challenges	Minimal
Number of participants	10-20
Space requirements	Open floor space
Materials needed	A piece of paper for each station, a slip of paper for each participant, tape, and a container from which to draw out the slips
Preparation	Prepare the stations and the slips of paper (see "Setting up Stations"). Place the slips in the container.

Note: This exercise is very high-risk because it exposes who is valued in the group and how. Carefully consider the level of trust in the group before using this exercise.

Setting up Stations

In the space you will be using, establish several stations, which will serve as stops on your group's journey. To set up a station, simply tape up a piece of paper with instructions. For example:

- Pick up medical supplies. Drop off one person.
- Pick up water drums. Drop off two people.

The number of stations will depend on the size of the group and what you are trying to achieve with the exercise. For example, with a group of 10-15 you may want to set up four or five stations and plan to have 2-3 people left at the end.

Then make slips of paper, enough for each participant to have one, with an age, a sex, and an occupation and/or other important characteristics. For example:

- 80-year-old male doctor
- 25-year-old female, mother of two, diagnosed with HIV
- 6-year-old male whose mother has been diagnosed with HIV
- 42-year-old female writer
- 30-year-old male construction worker

Collectively, the slips should represent a cast of characters that will present a challenge to the group during the exercise.

Instructions

1. Have each person in turn draw a slip of paper and read to the group the character description on the slip. For the duration of the exercise, each person assumes the identity of the character on their slip.
2. Inform the group that, due to a cataclysmic disaster, they now are in a vast wasteland and must travel to a safer place to start a new society. On the journey they must stop at each station to pick

up supplies, but a specified number of people must be left behind to make room for the supplies. The group must decide whom to leave based on the character descriptions.

3. Orient the group to the station stops they must make. Then step back and let the group move through the wasteland, making decisions about who is most valuable to the group and who will be left behind. Take note of what strategies they use, but do not give any further help to the group.
4. If you wish to use the exercise to illustrate decision-making under pressure, you can set a time limit for the journey.

Processing suggestions

- Many group dynamics around decision-making and priorities will come out. This exercise will give you a lot to work with in terms of looking at how the group functions.
- What were the strategies or processes that the group used to make decisions? How did these strategies change during the journey?
- Who led the decision-making and why? Does this reflect day-to-day decision-making patterns in the group?
- How did it feel to be left behind and how did it feel to be chosen to remain in the group? What, if anything, did the people who made it through have in common? How does this relate to the group and/or the group's work?
- The exercise can also be used to reflect on how our society prioritizes skills and characteristics (age, money, health, gender, race, etc.), and how people internalize those priorities in their own decision-making.

Communication Continuum

Goal	Communication
Time	10-15 minutes (not including processing)
Physical contact	None
Physical challenges	None
Number of participants	6 to 20
Space requirements	None
Materials	A piece of paper and a pen or pencil for each participant
Preparation	See "Preparing the Continuum."

Note: This exercise is helpful on days when the session will be dedicated to dealing with group issues. It is a high-risk exercise, most appropriate for groups that have been working together for a while.

Preparing the Continuum

1. Draw a horizontal line on the flip chart and place numbers along the line from 1 to 10, so that it represents a scale, or a continuum.
2. On a separate piece of flip chart paper, draw the same continuum, but on this version draw brackets to delineate two zones—the 1 to 5 range and the 6 to 10 range.
3. Under the 1 to 5 range, write "Fights, Fears, Factions."
4. Under the 6 to 10 range, write "Safety, Innovation, Experimentation." Keep this version out of sight until you are ready to process the exercise.

Instructions

1. Give everyone a piece of paper and a pen or pencil.
2. Ask people to think about how well they communicate as a group, then to rate the group's communication from 1 to 10 (with 1 the worst and 10 the best). Ask people to write their answers down and not to share them, so that they do not influence each other's responses. Ask the group to be quiet for a minute while people think and jot down a number.
3. When everyone is ready, ask each person to show you their paper, or tell you their number. Mark each rating on the first continuum (the one without the words).
4. Ask people who gave numbers at the top of the range and at the bottom of the range to say why they gave those numbers.
5. Ask for other comments from the group. This work will often initiate deep discussion about where the group is in its development at this particular moment.
6. Then show the group the second version of the continuum. Explain that often groups with communication in the 1 to 5 range have a lot of fights. Since people don't feel safe to be themselves in the group, there is a lot of fear, and the group tends to break down into subgroups or factions. As communication skills move into the 6 to 10 range, the group creates an atmosphere that is safe for everyone. People then feel free to try new things and experiment, which allows the group to succeed in meeting its goals.
7. Compare these ranges with the continuum that the group has created. Ask if people think they have put the group in the right range. Why or why not?

Processing suggestions

- No additional processing is needed.

Variation – Commitment Continuum

Instructions

1. Follow the instructions for COMMUNICATION CONTINUUM, but have people rate their own commitment to the group, or to the goals of a project. Do not use a second version of the continuum; just lead a discussion based on the original scale.

Diversity in Motion

Goals	Communication, Cultural awareness
Time	30-60 minutes (not including processing)
Physical contact	None
Physical challenges	Minimal
Number of participants	10-40
Space requirements	Open floor space
Materials needed	None
Preparation	Prepare a list of groups that you will call out. See "Naming Groups."

Note: This exercise can be high-risk and is best done with a group that knows each other well or that has come together to work on diversity issues.

Naming Groups

The groups that you call out in the exercise will depend on the composition and the needs of your whole group. Be aware of the risk level for each small group. Some of the suggestions below would be unacceptably high-risk in some groups but low-risk in others.

Here are some suggestions for groups to call out:

People who are female/male, please move together across the room.
People who name themselves African-American, Black, or Caribbean…
People who name themselves Hispanic or Latino…
People who name themselves White, Caucasian, or European…
People who name themselves Asian or Pacific Islander…
People who name themselves Native American or American Indian…
People who were born outside the United States…
People who are gay, lesbian, or bisexual, or who have a family member who is…
People who come from a family where there is alcohol or another addiction…
People who are physically disabled or have a family member who is …
People who are or ever have been unemployed…
People who are in a group that they wish had been called…

You may want to make a point of calling a group that is not represented in the room, so people can consider that fact.

Instructions

1. Have the whole group gather on one side of the room. Then explain the ground rules for this exercise:
   - Listen carefully to those who are speaking.
   - Be respectful at all times. No put-downs.
   - Remember that everything said and done here is confidential, not to be repeated outside of this room.
   - If someone is not following the ground rules, stop the exercise and restate what is unacceptable behavior.
2. Describe how the exercise works.
3. Name the first group that you want to call out. Those who feel they are part of that group should move together to the

other side of the room. However, everyone has the right to pass on their participation; no one has to move if they don't want to.

4. When the new group is assembled, ask them to respond to several questions, which will help them to think about their group and will also give information to those who are not in the group. Everyone has the right to pass on answering the questions. The questions are:
   - What do you want others to know about you?
   - What do you never want to hear again about this group?
   - What makes you proud to be part of this group?
   - What can we do to support you and your group?
5. Then ask the people who are not in the new group if they heard things that surprised them, and if so, what.
6. Give each group some time to ask questions of those in the other group.
7. After the questions (you may not have enough time for everyone's questions to be asked and answered), have those in the new group move back to the other side.
8. Follow this procedure for each group that you call out.

Processing suggestions

- How did it feel when you moved across the room? How did it feel when you didn't move?
- What did you learn about yourself? What did you learn about others, and about the group?
- Were there any surprises for you? What groups were not called that you wanted to be called?
- When we split into separate groups based on certain characteristics, what are the effects on the whole group? Has the feeling in this group changed based on this exercise?
- Does this exercise reflect life in the larger world?
- What have we learned from each other today?
- Is it best to bring out the things that make us different from each other, or to overlook them and focus on our similarities?
- To conclude processing, you can add some comments to summarize this experience.
- Be alert to hurtful or inaccurate comments that may have been made. Acknowledge that this has occurred and try to offer some comfort and support as appropriate.

Freeze Frame Report-Backs

Goals	Communication, Reinforcing information
Time	10-15 minutes (not including processing)
Physical contact	None necessary
Physical challenges	Minimal
Number of participants	10-30
Space requirements	Open floor space
Materials needed	None
Preparation	None

Note: FREEZE FRAMES can bring fun and interaction into report-backs from small groups. For example, if the agenda has included work in small groups to choose the top-priority issue for the group to address, you can have each small group report back their decision by doing a FREEZE FRAME of their priority issue, then explaining what the issue is and why they selected it.

Instructions

1. When you divide the group into small groups to do a specific task, tell them that they are to report the results of their work back to the large group by presenting a FREEZE FRAME, which is a tableau that illustrates what the group wants to say. Each small group should figure out and practice their FREEZE FRAME before presenting to the rest of the group.
2. The small groups proceed one by one with their report-backs, as follows: One member of the group comes to the front of the room and freezes in a pose that they think illustrates the concept. Then other members come to the front in turn and strike poses that add to the scene. Everyone should be facing in the same direction, so that all aspects of the scene are visible to the audience. Once people are frozen, they cannot move, and no talking or sounds are allowed.
3. When everyone in the small group has become a part of the FREEZE FRAME, the rest of the group tries to guess what the FREEZE FRAME represents. After a few guesses, the small group announces the theme of their FREEZE FRAME.

Processing suggestions

- Work with the content of each FREEZE FRAME to make points about what is being illustrated.
- Everyone adds their perspective to create a more complete picture.
- How were those in the audience able to guess what each FREEZE FRAME represented? Was it a particular addition to the FREEZE FRAME that clarified the meaning, or did it sometimes take the whole picture?
- This exercise can illustrate the importance of body language in communication.
- How did the group come up with this FREEZE FRAME? Were there other ideas about how to illustrate the concept?
- Did anyone take leadership, or was it more of a group effort?

The Good Show

Goals	Group problem solving, Acting, Organizing, Different perspectives, Surfacing group dynamics
Time	20-30 minutes (not including processing)
Physical contact	Minimal
Physical challenges	Minimal
Number of participants	10-30
Space requirements	Open floor space
Materials needed	None
Preparation	Prepare a list of five or six elements to be included in the skits. See "Choosing the Elements."

Choosing the Elements

THE GOOD SHOW is an improvisational skit with five or six specific elements that must be included. In choosing the elements, think about your reasons for doing this exercise. What do you want the group to learn or understand? What are the needs of the group that you want them to work with as they create their "GOOD SHOW"?

Ideally the list of elements will include emotions, actions, and characters. For example:

- Someone is happy.
- Someone is enthusiastic.
- Someone is bored.
- Someone feels dispirited.
- Something gets lost.
- There is a misunderstanding.
- A car breaks down.
- Someone learns something.
- Someone takes a stand.
- Someone is criticized.
- Someone is praised.
- Someone speaks French.
- There is an embrace.
- There is a police officer.
- There is a child.
- There is a parent.
- There is a storekeeper.

To get at a particular issue in the group, you can specify elements that will raise that issue—for example, "someone is leaving" or "something is stolen."

Instructions

1. Divide the group into two or more small groups.
2. Give each group the same list of elements and tell them to create a skit that includes all of the elements and that is entertaining for the rest of the group to watch. If it suits your purposes, you can place time limits on the work: for example, five minutes to prepare the show and three minutes to present it.

3. Send each group off to a separate space and give them a few minutes to prepare.
4. When you call time, have the groups come back and present their skits to each other.

Processing suggestions

- After each group presents its skit, ask the audience if the group met the criteria—did the skit include all of the elements and was it entertaining?
- How did different groups working with the same elements create very different products? Did some groups focus on certain elements more than others? Why, and what was the effect on the audience?
- If you set time limits, discuss how the group has limited time to achieve its goals and get its message across. Efficiency is important.
- If you included specific elements in order to raise group issues, discuss the issues as they were represented in the shows and as they play out in the group. For example, if the group is experiencing a loss, skits that included something being lost will allow for exploration of how people relate to loss.

Variation – The Musical Good Show

Note: This exercise can be used as a warm-up for a group that is creating musical numbers to perform.

Instructions

Here are three ways to create "musical good shows":

A. Add a song, rap, or musical performance to the list of elements.
B. Instead of a skit, the show must be a song with the required elements included in the lyrics or the performance of the song.
C. Instead of a skit, the show must be a musical performance with group members contributing according to a list of elements that define certain roles. In addition to content elements as in THE GOOD SHOW, the list of elements might also include:
   - Someone uses their mouth to make a beat.
   - Someone uses high-pitched sounds.
   - Someone slaps one of their body parts.
   - Two people must perform the words.
   - Someone uses their foot or feet.
   - Someone claps.

Additional processing suggestions

- What worked about the musical element in THE GOOD SHOW? What didn't work? Which elements should we keep when we create our musical piece?
- How was music used to convey the messages of the show? What messages were communicated?

Group Collage

Goals	Group problem solving, Creativity, Visual arts
Time	20-30 minutes (not including processing)
Physical contact	None
Physical challenges	Minimal
Number of participants	12-30
Space requirements	Space for people to spread out as they work
Materials needed	Poster board, markers, scissors, glue or tape, magazines and newspapers with pictures
Preparation	Decide on the topic(s) that the small groups will work on.

Note: This exercise involves the whole group in a creative activity. It also allows the group to explore an issue or topic in a nonverbal, visual, and imaginative way.

Instructions

1. Break the group into working groups of four to six people.
2. The task for each small group is to create a collage that expresses their feelings about a particular topic related to the work of the group. You can give the whole group the same topic, or give a different topic to each small group.

Processing suggestions

- Have each group present their collage and ask for comments about each one.
- In your own comments, you may want to draw explicit parallels with the work of the group, or it may seem more appropriate to let the creations speak for themselves.
- What decision-making process did the groups go through? How did they decide which images to include?
- Was there clear leadership, or was the leadership diffused throughout the group? Was there a plan or did the collage come together spontaneously? Were everyone's voices heard? How were disagreements resolved?
- What were people thinking about as they created their collage?
- Was it hard to represent the topic on paper? Was it hard to find images in the media that related to the topic?

Variation – Group Drawing

Materials needed	Poster board and markers or other materials to draw with

Instructions

1. This exercise is the same as GROUP COLLAGE, except that the group is asked to create a drawing.

Additional processing suggestions

- How did the group decide how to represent their feelings about the topic through drawing? How did the group decide who would draw what, and how it would be arranged on the paper?
- Sometimes people will choose not to draw because they doubt their skill. Did anyone choose not to draw? Why? It is important to be able to express yourself without judgment—your own or others.

Group Poem

Goals	Group introspection, Creativity
Time	15-30 minutes
Physical contact	None
Physical challenges	Minimal
Number of participants	8-30
Space requirements	Minimal
Materials needed	A piece of paper, a pencil, and a writing surface for each member of the group
Preparation	Write some simple lines to use as an example for the group. See "Poem Pieces."

Note: GROUP POEM can work well at any point in a group's process, but it can be a particularly good way to wrap up a group's work together by letting people reflect on what they have accomplished and share their thoughts with the rest of the group in a creative way.

Poem Pieces

We worked together and in small groups
We jumped through quite a lot of hoops
And in the end we did it!

Roses are red. Violets are blue.
This project was cool, and the group is, too.

Instructions

1. Give each group member a piece of paper and a pencil.
2. Tell them that their task is to write a few lines about the group or about the work/project they have accomplished. (With a larger group, stress that they should write only a couple of lines.) Their lines do not have to rhyme, and they can be as simple or as complex as the writer wants.
3. Read your example(s) of some simple lines.
4. Tell the group the ground rules: No put-downs are allowed. Nobody's name should be used in the poems. People can submit their poems anonymously.
5. Give the group a couple of minutes to work independently on their lines.
6. Call time and collect all the papers.
7. Put the papers in random order, and read the "group poem" back to the group. If a contribution breaks the guidelines by including names or put-downs, do not read it.
8. After the meeting, you may want to type up the poem and give copies to the group at a later date.

Processing suggestions

- A lengthy process is probably not necessary, unless put-downs or a great deal of negativity surfaced in the poem. Generally it will be enough to briefly summarize what you heard in the poem.

Info Flow

Goals	Creativity, Reinforcing information, Group introspection
Time	30 minutes—more or less, depending on the size of the group (not including processing)
Physical contact	None
Physical challenges	None
Number of participants	10-20
Space requirements	Open floor space
Materials needed	None
Preparation	See "What Info?"

What Info?

Prepare copies of the information for group members to "flow" on. This could be specific information or content that the group has been learning. It could also be a concept that you want the group to think about (for example, "You should buy certain products in order to be thin, happy, and popular.").

Groups can all have the same information, or each group can have something different.

Instructions

1. Break the group into small groups of 3-4 people.
2. Distribute copies of the information you have prepared.
3. Give each group 5-10 minutes to come up with a lyrical presentation (song, rap, poetry, spoken word) about the information.
4. Bring the groups back together and have them present to each other.

Processing suggestions

- What were some effective techniques in these presentations for conveying information?
- Discuss the ways in which content can be enhanced by coming at it through creative channels, using the arts to get messages across and voices heard.
- You can talk about being media savvy. How do the media get messages across through song, jingles, or music?
- Were the groups' presentations similar or different?
- How did the groups come up with their ideas?
- How did the groups tailor the format of their presentations to best reach their audience?
- If the group is preparing to present information to an outside audience, did they learn things from the presentations that they did not know before?

Info Pictionary

Goals	Group problem solving, Reinforcing information
Time	15-20 minutes (not including processing)
Physical contact	None
Physical challenges	Minimal
Number of participants	10-20
Space requirements	Minimal
Materials needed	6-20 index cards, markers, and flip chart paper
Preparation	Write on each index card a piece of information that you want the group to review. If you don't have a flip chart stand, post several pieces of the flip chart paper.

Note: This exercise can be used to review any information that the group has worked with previously.

Instructions

1. Divide the group into two teams and indicate which team will go first.
2. Have each team decide who will draw first for that team.
3. The first person to draw chooses a card and has 30 seconds to draw on the flip chart paper a picture that conveys the information on the card. (If the information is very complex, you can allow 60 seconds.) In that same time frame, while the person is drawing, the rest of the team tries to guess what the information is. A correct guess earns one point.
4. If the team does not guess correctly in the allotted time, the other team has a chance to guess and earn the point.
5. The teams alternate until all the index cards have been used.

Processing suggestions

- Discuss the images and symbols that were used to represent the information. Do they tell us anything about what the information means to us?
- Did this graphic representation help to reinforce the information? Do people feel this helped them remember the information? Was it confusing?
- How did the teams work together to solve the problems?

Inside Me Drawings

Goals	Personal introspection, Communication, Different perspectives, Interconnection
Time	20-30 minutes (not including processing)
Physical contact	None
Physical challenges	Drawing on a large sheet of paper
Number of participants	8-15
Space requirements	Enough room for people to spread out their paper, and wall space to hang up the drawings
Materials needed	Drawing materials, masking tape, and a sheet of flip chart paper for each participant, including the facilitators
Preparation	None

Instructions

1. Give each participant (including the facilitators) a sheet of flip chart paper and some drawing materials.
2. Ask people to spread out so that everyone has room to draw.
3. The instructions are to draw a figure representing yourself, and inside the figure to write or visually represent the following elements:
   in the head—what you think about
   in the hands—what you like to do with your hands
   in the heart—what you love
   in the stomach—what you like to eat
   in the feet—where you'vc been
4. Have everyone hang up their drawings.
5. Then, depending on your reasons for doing this exercise, choose one of these approaches:
   a. Have the group spend a fixed amount of time in silence looking at everyone's drawings.
   b. Do a version of GROUP-UPS (p. 290) related to the drawings. For example: "Everyone who likes burritos, like Daniella, come stand by her picture."

Processing suggestions

- How much do we really know about each other? There is a lot to learn about a person, and it takes effort to try to get to know someone beneath the surface.
- How do we learn what is in people's hearts and minds? We often make assumptions about people based on what they say and how they behave that prove to be wrong once we get to know them on a deeper level.
- How do we communicate to others about ourselves? How do we choose what to share about ourselves, and what to keep hidden?
- Do you want people to know a true, authentic "you," or are you more concerned about presenting the best "you"?
- What surprised you about what others put in their drawings?
- Did anything that you wrote about yourself surprise you? If you had done this drawing in the past (one, five, or ten years ago), what would have been the same and what would have changed? If you do this in the future, what will be different?
- Are any two drawings the same? Each of us is unique, though we may have a lot in common.

Life Lines

Goal	Introspection
Time	At least 30 minutes (not including processing)
Physical contact	None
Physical challenges	Minimal
Number of participants	8-20
Space requirements	Minimal, except that participants need space to create their LIFE LINES.
Materials needed	Two sheets of flip chart paper for each group member, and colored markers
Preparation	None

Note: This is a very high-risk exercise that should be used only with groups that know each other and have a fairly high degree of trust.

Instructions

1. Ask people to sit quietly for a few moments and reflect on the significant events in their lives, beginning with the important events in their childhood and continuing to the present.
2. Give each person two sheets of flip chart paper and some markers. On the first sheet, people should list their significant life events in chronological order (listing only those events that they are comfortable sharing with others). Give the group a few minutes to complete this task.
3. Then ask them to create their LIFE LINES on the second sheets, using symbols and drawings (no text) to depict their life experiences, leading up to their being in this group at this time. Allow approximately ten minutes for this task.
4. At the end of that time, assign pairs and have people discuss their LIFE LINES with their partners. Tell people that what they share and how much they share is up to them. If there is enough trust in the group, have people share their LIFE LINES with the entire group instead of in pairs. Tell people that they can pass if they want to. Note that this approach will add a significant amount of time to the exercise.

Processing suggestions

- This exercise can be a powerful group-builder when it is used to foster an appreciation for the many different routes people have taken that have all led to participation in this group at this time.
- What are some obstacles people have overcome to be here?
- What are some experiences that have helped lead people to this place?
- How have people's paths been similar? How have they been different?
- How was the experience of creating the LIFE LINE? Was it difficult? Did things come up that surprised you?
- What was it like to experience your partner's life through this exercise?

Variation – Life Maps

Preparation	Decide on four or five areas that you want people to use as the focus points on their LIFE MAPS. (See "Focus Points.") Write the areas on the flip chart.

Focus Points

The LIFE MAPS exercise focuses on a few areas of experience that you want group members to pay attention to. These areas could be very broad, or they could be quite specific, but they should be related to the work you are doing or an issue you want to bring up. For example, if the focus is on school issues, the LIFE MAP areas could lead people to think about school experiences they have had. As another example, if the group is planning an event, you could ask people to think about different aspects of similar events they have been part of.

Instructions

1. Describe the focus points for the LIFE MAPS.
2. Proceed as for LIFE LINES.

Quiz-A-Rama

Goals	Group problem solving, Surfacing group dynamics, Reinforcing information
Time	15-20 minutes (not including processing)
Physical contact	None
Physical challenges	Minimal
Number of participants	8-20
Space requirements	Minimal
Materials needed	Approximately 20 index cards, tape, pen or marker
Preparation	See "Cards on the Wall."

Note: One way this exercise can be used is to provide a way to reflect on their time together for a long-term group that is coming to an end.

Note: One facilitator should be the "host" while the other is the "judge."

Cards on the Wall

1. Decide on four or five categories for questions that are related to the work of the group. For example, if you are using this exercise as a way to prepare for an upcoming meeting, categories could be the goals for the meeting, items for the agenda, or logistical considerations.
2. Write approximately 20 questions, with a roughly equal number for each category. The questions should vary in difficulty, since they will be assigned different point values. For example, "Name two goals for the event" might be worth 200 points, and "Name everyone on the clean-up team" might be worth 500.
3. Write each question on an index card. On the other side of the card, write the number of points the question is worth, based on its difficulty.
4. Tape the cards to the wall arranged by category and in order by point value within each category. Cards should be question-side down.

Instructions

1. Divide the group into three or four teams, with 3-5 players per team.
2. Have each team choose a person to report their answers.
3. Each team in turn chooses a category and level of difficulty and tries to answer the question they have chosen. If they answer correctly, they keep the card and get the points, and choose another question card. If they answer incorrectly, the other teams have a chance to try for the points, either in order or according to who calls out the answer first. The team with the most points wins.

Processing suggestions

- This exercise can help the group to see how focused and prepared they are in the categories that were tested. Processing can make points about being prepared and building skills in these areas.
- Since people worked together in teams, processing can look at teamwork issues and dynamics.

Role-Plays

Goals	Dependent on your goals for the session
Time	10 minutes for preparation, then 10-15 minutes for each small group's presentation and processing. If you have more than two or three small groups, Role-Plays can take up a large portion of your meeting time, and you might want to have some small groups do a different activity while some prepare Role-Plays.
Physical contact	None required
Physical challenges	None
Number of participants	10 to 30
Space requirements	Space for the small groups to prepare their Role-Plays simultaneously, and space for the whole group to watch the Role-Plays
Materials	None required
Preparation	See "Three Ways to Do ROLE-PLAYS" and decide on your approach.

Three Ways to Do ROLE-PLAYS

Role-Plays can be useful tools for getting a group to delve into an issue or to prepare for a situation they are facing. Here are three approaches to setting up a Role-Play:

A. Before the session, write out some scenarios that revolve around issues you want the group to deal with. Two or three sentences are usually enough to provide the necessary information in a scenario. When you are writing the scenarios, try to imagine how they will play out. Your goal is to create scenarios that will allow both the issues and some possible solutions to emerge. If you want the whole group to take part in the Role-Plays, be sure that you have enough scenarios with enough characters.

B. If your work for the day will include BRAINSTORMING (p. 385) or a WORDSTORM (p. 413), have the group dig more deeply into the subjects discussed by following up with a Role-Play. Assign each small group one word or concept from the Brainstorm or WORDSTORM discussion and ask them to create a Role-Play that builds on it.

C. Give the group simple instructions for the subject of a Role-Play, without spelling out details. Examples are: "Do a Role-Play of this group at its best and this group at its worst," or "Show a good way and a bad way of dealing with a conflict at our event."

Instructions

1. Divide people into small groups of 3-6.
2. Give each small group a scenario, a word or concept, or some instructions.
3. Give the small groups 5-10 minutes to create and practice their Role-Plays. If possible, have each group prepare in a separate room or area.
4. Bring the small groups back together and have each present its Role-Play for the whole group. Process each Role-Play after it is presented.

Processing suggestions

What the group learns from processing the Role-Plays is often the most important part of the exercise. Try to bring as many voices as possible into the discussion.

- Have the actors stay in front of the group when they complete their Role-Play. Ask them questions, and encourage the rest of the group to ask questions about what they have seen.
- Ask questions of the audience about their responses to what happened in the Role-Play.

The Speech Game

Goals	Preparation for giving speeches, Interconnection, Leadership
Time	10-15 minutes (not including processing)
Physical contact	None
Physical challenges	Must be able to move around.
Number of participants	Maximum number depends on the number of chairs that can be arranged in one circle. Ideally 12-25.
Space requirements	Open floor space
Materials	Enough chairs for the group minus one
Preparation	Think about the first WIND BLOWS statement to begin the exercise. It should be one that gets a lot of people moving.

Note: This exercise is a good way to begin preparing people to give speeches. Inexperienced speakers often concentrate on mastering the words in their speech and do not consider how to let their feelings about what they are saying come through. THE SPEECH GAME deals with the importance of having feeling behind your words by providing an entertaining way to practice deliberately using emotion while giving a short speech.

Instructions

1. Draw a line down the middle of the flip chart to create two columns.
2. Remind the group of the rules for BRAINSTORMING (p. 385).
3. Have people Brainstorm a list of 10-12 topics (any topics are fine) and write them in column 1.
4. Have people Brainstorm a list of 10-12 emotions and write them in column 2.
5. Tell the group that you will be playing THE WIND BLOWS (p. 377) with a twist: The person who is left without a seat must choose one topic and one emotion from the lists, then give a 30-second speech on the topic while using the emotion. After the speech, the person says, "The wind blows …."
6. Give an example (perhaps by asking the group to call out a topic and an emotion for you to use).
7. You can either have each person announce the topic and the emotion they will use, or have them keep it secret and ask the group to guess which ones the person chose.
8. If you wish, you can eliminate each topic and emotion from the lists once they have been used.
9. If someone who has already had a turn is left without a seat in a subsequent round, they can just say, "The wind blows..." without choosing another topic to speak about.
10. Continue until everyone has had a turn or until all the topics have been used.

Processing suggestions

- Discuss the importance of conveying feelings to those who are listening to a speech. Which feelings were most difficult to convey?
- How could listeners tell if the emotions were genuine?
- What techniques did speakers use that were effective in conveying emotion?
- What techniques were "over the top"?
- Did some speakers talk about the feeling without conveying the feeling (for example, by saying, "I'm angry!" but not seeming to be angry)?

Stand and Deliver

Goals	Personal introspection, Different perspectives
Time	15-25 minutes (not including processing)
Physical contact	None
Physical challenges	Minimal
Number of participants	8-40
Space requirements	Open floor space
Materials needed	Marker, tape, and four or five large pieces of paper
Preparation	See "Setting It Up."

Setting It Up

- Prepare four signs on the large pieces of paper as follows: "Strongly Agree," "Agree," "Disagree," "Strongly Disagree." Then post one sign in each corner of the room. Depending on your goals for the session, you could also make and post a sign saying "No Opinion."
- Prepare a series of statements (three or four are usually enough) to be read to the group. The statements should reflect the issues that bear on the group's purpose and work. For example, in a drug prevention group, you may want to use the statement "Drinking once in a while is OK." In a group that is working to address issues of absenteeism in a school, you could use the statement "The school day should start and end one hour later."

Instructions

1. Tell people that you are going to read a statement, and that everyone should go and stand under the sign that corresponds most closely to their view on the subject.
2. Read the first statement to the group and give people a few moments to gather under the sign they choose.
3. Tell people to discuss among themselves in their groups why they chose that opinion.
4. Ask for comments from members of the four groups, proceeding around the room in a logical order.
5. Ask if anyone would like to switch groups. If someone does switch, ask them to tell the whole group what changed their mind.
6. Follow the same procedure for the rest of the statements.

Processing suggestions

- This exercise is a good way to help people sort out their thoughts and feelings about certain issues. You can look at some of the following questions in processing:
- Are there varied opinions among people in the same group?
- Which issues found people holding the strongest opinions?
- Which issues had the most people changing their minds?
- What caused people to change their minds—was it emotion or logic?
- If the group is polarized around issues that affect their work, what steps can be taken?

Take a Seat

Goals	Different perspectives, Organizing, Surfacing group dynamics, Group problem solving
Time	10-20 minutes (not including processing)
Physical contact	Most participants will have a lot of contact.
Physical challenges	Must be able to squeeze onto chairs with several other people.
Number of participants	8-15
Space requirements	Open floor space
Materials needed	A chair (preferably without arms) for each person in the group
Preparation	Line up the chairs in a row, making sure they are right next to each other.

Note: This exercise can be used to illustrate societal dynamics that involve unequal distribution of resources or power, as well as issues of racism and classism.

Instructions

1. Ask everyone to take a seat.
2. Tell two people to stand up. Take their chairs away and give both of the chairs to one other person (Person 1). Choose who gets the chairs based on some arbitrary characteristic (such as the color they are wearing, how tall they are, how dressed up they are, etc.), and state the criterion to the group.
3. Tell those without chairs that they must sit down, sharing chairs with others (but not with Person 1).
4. After they accomplish this, take another chair away from someone and give it to Person 1. Tell Person 1 to feel free to stretch out and get comfortable. The person who lost their chair must find a chair to share.
5. Repeat this, so that Person 1 has five chairs.
6. Then pull away an additional chair from the group and choose someone (Person 2) to have that chair to themselves.
7. Tell the rest of the group to fit on the rest of the chairs.
8. Continue with this process of giving chairs to Person 1, and let it play out until the entire group (except for the two "special" people) has to fit on one chair or until people act out or give up. Be watchful about safety issues as people try to fit onto fewer and fewer chairs.
9. You can add a dynamic aspect to the game by treating people differently based on their "status" in the exercise, and by giving compliments, imposing consequences, and adding commentary. For example: Be encouraging, kind, solicitous, and complimentary toward Person 1 and Person 2. With the rest of the group, be distant and stern. Tell them that people who do not fit themselves onto the chairs will have to clean up after the meeting. Tell them they are not trying hard enough and warn them to be careful, not to break the chairs, etc. It is important to stay in the role of being serious or stern. If group members start to question, simply tell them that this is how it works, and they need to follow instructions.

Processing suggestions

- What do the chairs represent? (money, resources, power)
- Who do the people represent (Person 1, Person 2, the rest with fewer and fewer chairs)? What are their races, classes, genders, etc.?
- What did the facilitator represent? ("the system," institutions, policies)
- Did group members question the facilitator? How do people question systems of inequality?

- Ask Person 1 how it felt to have so many chairs to relax in. Were there more chairs than Person 1 could use?
- Ask Person 2 how it felt to have a chair and to be comfortable while others had less and less to share. How did it feel to be in between the person with too many chairs and the people without enough?
- Ask the rest of the group what it was like to have everyone fighting over too few chairs. How did people respond to the situation (arguing, giving up, fitting in, helping some people and not others)?
- Did the group question the facilitator or accept the rules as given? Does this happen in society? What happens when people question the rules?

Visualization

Goal	Introspection
Time	5-10 minutes (not including processing)
Physical contact	None
Physical challenges	Minimal
Number of participants	No maximum number
Space requirements	Minimal
Materials needed	None
Preparation	Decide on the subject for the Visualization; it can be anything that will help the group make progress toward its goals. Write out the Visualization, either as a detailed script or as an outline with the main points you want to cover. It should be short—no more than three or four minutes when slowly read out loud. See Appendix D: Creating Visualizations.

Note: Visualization can help people let go of their customary patterns of thinking and break through into new ways of thinking. This exercise allows people to reflect quietly on a subject, then to share their thoughts as they wish. It can be particularly useful at the beginning of a group undertaking, to help create an understanding of the potential outcomes, or at the end, to help people reflect on what has occurred.

Note: Visualization is a high-risk exercise. Participants are not required to share anything with others, but they are asked to let go of defenses and allow thoughts and feelings to come. For many people, this can be threatening. The exercise will work in most groups; however, in some groups it may be challenging to overcome people's resistance.

Instructions

1. In the group, tell people to find a comfortable position that they can stay in for several minutes. If there is room, people could sprawl on the floor if they wish. However, everyone needs to be in their own space—no heads on laps, etc.
2. Once everyone is comfortable, ask them to close their eyes and to keep them closed for the duration of the exercise. Tell group members that they do not have to participate, but they must be quiet to allow those who do participate to have the experience. Tell them that it is important to stay awake, listen, and focus on the voice of the facilitator. However, if the Visualization is making someone uncomfortable, they should feel free to let their mind go in the direction it wants.
3. Spend a few minutes helping people to relax. Tell them to be aware of the steadiness of their breath—not to change their breathing, but simply to focus awareness on it.
4. Then begin reading the Visualization you have prepared. Speak slowly and pause frequently to give people time to focus on what you have said.
5. When you finish, tell people they can keep their eyes closed until they are ready to return their awareness to the group. Everyone should remain silent until you begin processing.
6. When most people have opened their eyes, state this quietly to the group and invite those who

still have their eyes closed to rejoin the group.

Processing suggestions

- Ask people to share, if they wish, what they experienced during the Visualization. Particular questions and areas of discussion will depend upon the subject of the Visualization.

The Wind Blows for Practice

Goals	Reinforcing information, Interconnection, Leadership
Time	10-15 minutes (not including processing)
Physical contact	None
Physical challenges	Must be able to move around.
Number of participants	The maximum number depends on the number of chairs that can be arranged in one circle. The ideal number is 12-25.
Space requirements	Open floor space
Materials needed	Enough chairs for the group minus one, a container for questions
Preparation	Write on slips of paper several questions about the material that you want the group to review, and place the slips in an open container. Write the correct responses on papers that can be posted for people to see.

Note: This is a variation of THE WIND BLOWS (p. 413), best used with groups that are familiar with that exercise. It is helpful for meetings at which people need to remember specific material, especially if they need practice in presenting the material orally. It should be used after the group has been working with the material and they know it fairly well.

Instructions

1. Arrange the chairs in a circle, with enough chairs for all participants minus one. In most circumstances, the facilitator should participate.
2. Play THE WIND BLOWS as usual for several rounds.
3. Announce that the next person who is left without a seat has to choose a question from the question box.
4. That person answers the question.
5. Ask the group if the response is complete and accurate. Discuss briefly, then post the response you have written.
6. The person standing then continues with THE WIND BLOWS.
7. The next person chooses from the remaining questions, and so on, until all the questions have been answered. If someone who has already answered a question is left without a seat in a subsequent round, they can just say "The wind blows..." without choosing another question.

Processing suggestions

- Processing can focus on the group's assessment of how well prepared they are with the material.

Variation – The Wind Blows with Scenarios

Additional goal	Acting
Preparation	Write several scenarios that one or two people can act out. Some scenarios can relate to the work the group is doing, while others could be more for fun. The scenarios can use words (for example, a student and a teacher arguing about a bad grade) or be silent (for example, two children enjoying a snow day off from school), or you could have some of each. Write each scenario on a piece of paper and place in an open container.

Instructions

1. Play THE WIND BLOWS as usual for a few rounds.
2. Remove an additional chair from the circle if the scenarios you've written involve two people.

3. Announce that in the next round, whoever is left standing must choose a slip of paper and act out the scenario that is on it. Set a time limit of about a minute on the scenario.
4. If the scenario is silent, you can ask people to guess what it represents.
5. Continue for several rounds or until all the scenarios have been acted out.

Additional processing suggestions

- This exercise can be used to look at creativity, spontaneity, or speaking and acting skills. It can show how difficult it is to present on your feet without proper preparation.
- How did people react when they saw the scenario they had to act out? Which were the most difficult and the easiest scenes to portray?
- Discuss the content of the scenarios and what they show about the group's work.

Wordstorm

Goals	See "Purposes of WORDSTORMING"
Time	5-10 minutes, plus up to 25 minutes for processing
Physical contact	None
Physical challenges	None
Number of participants	6 to 20
Space requirements	None
Materials needed	Flip chart paper and a marker
Preparation	See "Choosing the Word."

Purposes of WORDSTORMING

WORDSTORMING is like BRAINSTORMING, except that it deals with ideas and feelings around a particular word or concept, whereas BRAINSTORMING elicits ideas or solutions to a question or problem. WORDSTORMING is an associative process that:

- Gets people thinking in a nonlinear way about one or more topics that are relevant to the work at hand or to issues in the group.
- Breaks down fears and inhibitions.
- Allows a group to create its own process of reflection.
- Creates a landscape of concepts that you can use to facilitate and broaden discussion.

Choosing the Word

Your choice of the word to use in a process of free association depends upon the group, the issues it is working with, your goals for the session, and your assessment of the risk level that you think is appropriate for the group. If you are working with an unformed group, the word you choose is likely to be straightforward. For example, in a training session on smoking prevention, you can do a WORDSTORM on "Smoke" or "Smoking."

In contrast, if you are using a WORDSTORM to work on a group-dynamics issue with a formed group, your choice needs to be more subtle. For example, if the group is having a problem regarding lack of trust, you could do a WORDSTORM on "Trust," but this direct plunge into the issue may have a chilling effect on people's ability and willingness to engage freely in the process. Instead, you could do a WORDSTORM on "Friendship." In this way, you are helping the group to reflect on an issue that is intimately related to trust, and processing will bring out the importance of people being able to trust each other.

Rules for WORDSTORMING

1. Say the first words that come to your mind; don't censor your ideas.
2. Even if your word is similar to something else that's been said, say it anyway.
3. During the WORDSTORM, do not give your opinion of any of the words that are expressed.
4. Don't get into discussions of any words until the WORDSTORM is completed.
5. There should be no put-downs of anyone or of the words that people contribute.

Following these rules is critical to the success of the WORDSTORM, so don't hesitate to refer back to the rules during the exercise and to ensure that the rules are followed throughout. Each time you do a WORDSTORM, review the rules before beginning.

Instructions

1. Tell the group that you are going to put a word on the flip chart, and that you want people to call out any words that come to their minds when they see the word.
2. Explain the rules (see "Rules for WORDSTORMING").
3. Write the word at the top of the flip chart paper.
4. Write down people's responses as fast as you can. (It's OK if people say words that relate to other words that come out in the WORDSTORM more than to the original word.)
5. Continue until the group has no more words to offer or when the page is full.

Processing suggestions

Look over the words and lead a discussion about what this list of words tells you. For example, circle a word and ask who said it and why they offered that word. Ask if others agree about how the words are related. Circle a few more words. Draw lines showing the connections that people are making between words and concepts, and ask people to suggest connections. You can also ask questions like:

- Are there any words up here that seem unusual to you?
- Which words really mean [the original word] to you?
- Which words show the positive side of [the original word]?
- Which words show the negative side?

Variation – Word Race

Instructions

1. This is a fast-lane WORDSTORM, following the rules and procedures of a WORDSTORM at a faster pace. Write down just 10-15 responses rather than filling the entire page with words. This approach is particularly useful with a group that is familiar with WORDSTORMS, or when you have limited time.

Variation – Picture Storm

Instructions

1. This exercise functions in the same way as a WORDSTORM, except that the focus is a picture that you put up, rather than a word.

Variation – Double Wordstorm

Additional materials	Another piece of flip chart paper
Preparation	Choose two words related to the group's work and to each other.

Note: This exercise is useful for generating discussions about how ideas or issues relate to each other.

Instructions

1. Write one of the words on the each piece of flip chart paper.
2. Do a WORDSTORM on the first word.
3. Do a WORDSTORM on the second word.

Additional processing suggestion

- Challenge group members to connect words to both original WORDSTORM words.

Variation – Double/Triple Word Race

Instructions

1. Do a WORD RACE, but with two or three words on the same page, using related words or concepts.

Variation – Relay Wordstorm

Time	10-15 minutes (not including processing)
Physical challenges	Minimal
Materials needed	Two pieces of flip chart paper and two markers
Preparation	Choose two words related to the work of the group or to issues that you want the group to discuss. Print each word clearly in large letters on a piece of flip chart paper. Hang the papers one or two feet apart on the wall.

Note: Depending on your goals, you could set the exercise up as a competition between teams, or you could set a time limit per individual or per team.

Instructions

1. Divide the group into two teams, standing in lines at the other end of the room from the flip chart paper (or seated on opposite sides of a table).
2. Give a marker to the first person in line for each team.
3. When you give the signal, the first member of each team walks to their team's paper and writes a word that is related to the original word.
4. The player then walks back to their team and passes the marker to the next person. Each person in turn adds a word related to the original word, continuing until everyone has added a word.
5. Depending on the size of the group and how long you want the exercise to run, you can continue adding words through a second or third round.

Additional processing suggestions

- You can look at aspects of the exercise such as how it feels to think under pressure, how teams work together for a common goal, and how individual contributions come together to make a whole.
- If the exercise was set up as a competition, how did this change the nature of the WORDSTORM?

World Party

Goals	Introspection, Communication, Different perspectives, Cultural awareness
Time	15 to 20 minutes (not including processing)
Physical contact	None
Physical challenges	None
Number of participants	10-20
Space requirements	Open floor space
Materials needed	Plain adhesive labels (one for each participant) that are the right size to place on people's foreheads. Optionally, refreshments and party decorations.
Preparation	See "Preparing the Party."

Preparing the Party

- On each sticker, write a phrase that characterizes a kind of person. For example, stickers could say "middle-aged homeless man," "high school English teacher," "elderly priest," "Latino grandmother," "Asian high school student," "head of a large corporation," "teen mother of two," "ex-convict." Use types that represent a range of cultural and class stereotypes.
- You may also want to set up the meeting room for a party, with refreshments and/or decorations. Having refreshments, in particular, will help the exercise to succeed.

Instructions

1. Put a label on each person's forehead, without letting people see their own labels.
2. Instruct people that they are to interact with everyone based on what they see on the labels. They are not to spend time trying to find out what their own labels say. Then let the "party" begin.
3. Stop the party after a suitable period of time (perhaps 5 to 15 minutes), but tell people not to look at their labels yet.

Processing suggestions

- The first part of the processing should take place as soon as the exercise ends and before people look at their own labels. Ask people what they think their labels might say, based on how they were treated during the party.
- Then have people remove their labels and read them. Discuss what stereotypes people were acting on. What are the positive and negative associations with different labels/groups of people? Who was treated hurtfully, and why? Who was treated well, and why?
- You might want to do the processing in a structured way, as follows: Go around the circle, with each person first saying how they were treated and what they think their label says, then looking at the label. The group discusses that label/stereotype before moving on to the next person.

Variation – Attitude Party

Preparation	Prepare as for WORLD PARTY, except write an emotion on each label.

Instructions

1. Follow the instructions for WORLD PARTY, except tell the group that they are to act toward each person according to the emotion they read on the label. For example, if someone is labeled "Anger," everyone interacts with that person in an angry way.

Additional processing suggestions

- Processing can look at the ways in which people evoke certain responses in others. For example, how does a person connected with the feeling "Hope" bring out hope in others?
- You can also discuss the different ways the same emotion can be expressed. For example, if a person has the label "Joy," were there a variety of ways that they saw others acting with joy?

Variation – Task Party

Additional materials	Materials to create a puzzle (or some other task)
Preparation	See "Setting It Up."

Setting It Up

- Prepare a label for each participant. Create the labels strategically, thinking about each person. You may want to consider the roles that group members usually take and then give them labels for opposite or very dissimilar roles. For example, someone who is not a leader in the group might have the label, "I have great ideas," whereas a consistent leader could have the label, "No one ever listens to me." Other suggestions are: "Laugh at everything I say," "I am a leader," "Nothing I say makes sense," "I'm weird," "I'm smart," "Nobody likes me," etc.
- Make a list with each person's name and the corresponding label.
- Instead of a holding a "party," decide on a task for the group to do. One suggestion is putting together a puzzle.
- To make the puzzle, use a sheet of flip chart paper or poster board. Draw a complex squiggle and also, if you wish, write a word or phrase on the paper within the scribbles (something that is relevant to the group and its work). Then cut up the paper into as many pieces as there will be participants. You can make the puzzle more or less difficult depending on what your goals are for the exercise.

Instructions

1. Place the appropriate label on each participant's forehead without letting people see what their own labels say.
2. Give each person a piece of the puzzle (or assign the group their task).
3. Tell the group that they are to work together to complete the puzzle or task, but that they must react and behave toward each other as the label indicates. For example, if someone is labeled as a leader, everyone must listen to that person respectfully. The group then goes about solving the puzzle or completing their task.

Additional processing suggestions

- This exercise can be used to demonstrate how behavior is a two-way process. People behave toward others using pre-conceived labels and stereotypes, and those people in turn will act in ways that either fulfill or challenge the stereotype or label. For example, those who are treated as leaders may display leadership; those who are treated as outcasts may become disinvested in or turn away from the group's goals.
- You can use this exercise to start a discussion on societal dynamics of race, class, and other differences.
- You may want to bring up the point that people replay roles in groups that are similar to the roles they play in their families of origin or other parts of life, and that it is important to try on new roles in this group.

- How did it feel to be treated like your label? Did you fight it or go with it?
- In a formed group, you can discuss what roles people play in the group, and how the members' behavior may reinforce or challenge the roles and behaviors seen in the group.
- How difficult is it to play a different role once people think of you a certain way?

Chapter 18

Evaluation Exercises

This chapter describes several methods for asking group members to evaluate a session. See pages 48-50 for information about the procedure and processing for evaluations and why it's important to do them. Here are two important reminders from that chapter about the role of the facilitator:

- Participate in the evaluation as a member of the group, but in go-around evaluation, ask for a volunteer to begin.
- Listen respectfully and with an open mind to everyone's evaluation. If group members give negative evaluations, don't discuss, argue, or become defensive.

Why bother?

If you are thinking of skipping the evaluation, look for your reason here:

- *Everyone's had a chance to express themselves; there's no need to go around the circle again.* If there's little left to say, the evaluation will be brief, and there's no way to tell in advance what value it will bring to the group.
- *This meeting did not go well, but I know what went wrong. I don't need to hear about it from everyone.* Actually, you might be surprised at what people say. Some will focus on the positive, which should help you feel better. But more importantly, if people are holding negative feelings about the meeting, everyone is better served if these feelings are given a safe and sanctioned outlet. The evaluation surfaces and disperses the negativity, allowing people to leave with a feeling of closure. For an ongoing group, the evaluation lets people come to subsequent meetings with a much cleaner slate.
- *Everyone seems to like these meetings, but there's one person who puts out negativity all the time. Why give him another forum?* The negative person will get to hear that others do not share his negativity. Others will have a context in which to place his negativity, which will tend to reduce its influence.
- *The group is too big.* No group is too big for a GROUP SHOUT, GROUP WHISPER, or GROUP THOUGHT Evaluation.
- *The agenda is packed. There's not enough time.* If you limit comments, a GROUP SHOUT or GROUP WHISPER Evaluation can be done in less than two minutes.
- *We've run out of time!* Unless people have a train to catch, you can do a GROUP SHOUT or GROUP WHISPER Evaluation with no comments in about 30 seconds.
- *This was a great meeting. Let's end on a high note and let everyone go home.* Better yet, let everyone take a few seconds to express their appreciation of the meeting. The evaluation lets people testify to the value of the group, and thus it sets the stage for more productive work in the future. And it will make people feel even better to hear the various ways that the meeting met everyone's needs.

Written Evaluations

Written evaluations are sometimes a valuable supplement to verbal evaluations because they allow you to gather detailed information in a permanent form. They are especially important in large groups, where individual verbal evaluations are not possible, and in one-time groups, where people may be reluctant to speak frankly in an unfamiliar setting. The evaluations should be anonymous, and you should encourage people to be candid.

See Appendix A for the evaluation form that we use at many sessions.

If you plan to ask for written evaluations, be sure to allow time in your agenda and to have enough pens or pencils available.

Other Exercises for Evaluation

The exercises in this chapter all serve the purpose of evaluating a particular meeting or group session. Some exercises in other chapters of this book, however, are useful tools for helping the group to evaluate a particular piece of its work or to bring closure to a program cycle or to the group itself when it is ending. Check out these exercises:

BACK-TO-BACK FEEDBACK	p. 186
GROUP POEM	p. 397
GROUP SCULPTURE	p. 198
PICTURE WALL	p. 205
QUIZ-A-RAMA	p. 403

Evaluation Scales

Time	15-60 seconds per participant
Physical contact	None
Physical challenges	None
Number of participants	Up to 20
Space requirements	None

Note: This is the standard evaluation, which gives you the most information from each group member.

Instructions

1. Going around the circle, each person rates the meeting or event on a scale from 1 to 10, with 1 being the worst and 10 being the best, and makes a comment to explain the rating. Both parts of the evaluation (rating and comment) are optional.

Variations

You can use any other scale you can think of in place of the 1 to 10 scale, such as: A to F, 1 to 100, or having people give the meeting a thumbs up, thumbs down, or somewhere in between.

Evaluation Comparisons

Time	15-60 seconds per participant
Physical contact	None
Physical challenges	None
Number of participants	Up to 20
Space requirements	None

Instructions

1. Going around the circle, each person rates the meeting by comparing it to something that you have specified—for example, "If this meeting were a sandwich, what kind would it be and why?" or "If this meeting were a weather forecast, what would it be and why?"

Note: This type of evaluation tends to be more fun than it is substantive. Some group members may go into great detail about their favorite kind of sandwich, but you may not find out much about how the meeting went. The weather forecast version tends to give you the best information.

Group Shout Evaluation

Time	1-2 minutes
Physical contact	None
Physical challenges	None
Number of participants	No maximum number
Space requirements	None. Can be used with theater seating.

Instructions

1. Ask the group to think about how they rate the meeting on a scale of 1 to 10, with 1 being the worst and 10 being the best.
2. Tell them that on the count of 3 everyone will shout out their rating at the same time.
3. Listen carefully to the numbers and try to report back what you heard. (For example, "I heard a lot of 8's and 9's, as well as a couple of 5's.") You may need to have the group shout a few times to get everyone participating and to really hear the numbers.
4. Ask for a few comments from participants.

Variation – Group Whisper Evaluation

Instructions

1. Follow the instructions for GROUP SHOUT EVALUATION except that instead of shouting, people whisper the number that they choose to evaluate the meeting.

Group Stretch Evaluation

Time	15-60 seconds per participant
Physical contact	None
Physical challenges	Minimal
Number of participants	Up to 20
Space requirements	Open floor space

Instructions

1. Going around the circle, each person does a stretch (touching toes, rolling shoulders, reaching arms up, etc.) that represents their thoughts and feelings about the meeting. After the stretch, the person says why and how the stretch reflected the meeting.

Group Thought Evaluation

Time	2-5 minutes, depending on how many comments you take
Physical contact	Possibly holding hands
Physical challenges	None
Number of participants	No maximum number
Space requirements	None. Can be used in rooms with theater seating.

Note: This exercise is useful when you want to create a quieter and more thoughtful ending experience.

Instructions

1. In a small group, you can ask that people hold hands.
2. Tell the group that there will be a quiet moment while each person thinks about how they rate the meeting on a scale of 1 to 10.
3. Take a few comments from people who evaluated at different levels.

Stand-Up Evaluation

Time	2-5 minutes, depending on how many comments you take
Physical contact	None
Physical challenges	None
Number of participants	No maximum number
Space requirements	None

Instructions

1. Ask people to think about how they rate the meeting on a scale of 1 to 10, with 1 being the worst and 10 being the best.
2. Then ask those who rate the meeting as 10 to stand up.
3. Ask if one person from that group will say a few words about why they are giving the meeting that rating.
4. Continue through the numbers until everyone has had a chance to stand up.

Appendices

- A Written Evaluation Form
- B Adapting Interactive Exercises for Physical Limitations
- C Words for Word Association
- D Creating Visualizations

Appendix A: Written Evaluation Form

Written evaluations are sometimes a valuable supplement to verbal evaluations because they allow you to gather detailed information in a permanent form. They are especially important in large groups, where individual verbal evaluations are not possible, and in one-time groups, where people may be reluctant to speak frankly in an unfamiliar setting. The evaluations should be anonymous, and you should encourage people to be candid.

An effective written evaluation gives participants a framework for thinking about the meeting and thus helps to provide good feedback to the facilitator about how people experienced the meeting and how it could be improved. The form in this appendix tries to meet those goals.

This form asks for date and location, but you should adapt or change the heading to provide the information that will be most useful to you. In a school setting, for example, you may want to keep track of the class period in which the session took place.

If you plan to ask for written evaluations, be sure to allow time in your agenda and to have enough pens or pencils available.

For information about verbal evaluations, see chapters 4 and 18.

Meeting Evaluation

Date ________________ Topic ________________________________

1. The best thing about this session was:

2. The worst thing about this session was:

3. If you could change something about the session, what would you change?

4. Circle all the words that describe the session.

interesting	boring	fun	stiff	confusing	informative
dull	lively	challenging	unhelpful	helpful	
disturbing	difficult	tiring	mediocre	useful	

5. Are there other words or comments that you want to add?

6. Rate this session on the following scale and use the back of this page, if you wish, to comment on your rating.

10	9	8	7	6	5	4	3	2	1
Great			Good			Fair			Poor

Appendix B: Adapting Interactive Exercises for Physical Limitations

As much as possible, try to include all members of the group in all aspects of the Interactive Meeting Format. If a group member has a physical limitation that makes participation in an exercise difficult, think carefully about which exercises to use in your agendas and about how you can adapt exercises to minimize or eliminate the difficulty. When you run the exercises, do it without calling attention to the adaptations.

With so many exercises and so many kinds of physical limitations that people in a group might be dealing with, it's not possible for us to suggest adaptations for all situations. Instead, our goals are to raise awareness about the importance of including all group members and to prompt you to think about how to be as inclusive as possible through your choice of exercises and through appropriate adaptations.

This appendix does not specifically deal with issues related to learning or emotions that pose challenges to full participation, but be aware that exercises can be adapted for these situations, too.

Adapting and Creating Exercises

This book contains dozens of variations of exercises, and many of these were created to meet a particular need of a group. Similarly, exercises can be adapted to meet the needs of group members who are dealing with various kinds of limitations. See chapter 4—especially "Keep Your Designs Fresh" (p. 60) and "Create Your Own Exercises" (p. 61)—to help you start thinking about how to adapt and create exercises.

Here are two examples of familiar exercises adapted for different situations:

THE WIND BLOWS (p. 377)
This exercise involves people walking quickly to find a new seat, but you can adapt it for a group in which someone is in a wheelchair. Before the group begins, set up the room as follows: For each member of the group (including the facilitators if they will participate in the exercise), make a square on the floor with masking tape. Each square should be large enough to accommodate a wheelchair, and the squares should be arranged in the horseshoe shape that we recommend for meetings. When people arrive for the meeting, they should place their chairs/wheelchairs in the squares.

When it is time for the exercise to begin, ask the group members who are not in wheelchairs to move their chairs out of the way and to stand in the squares. The number of available squares must equal the number of participants minus one; use masking tape to place an X in any extra squares. Tell the group the rules and emphasize that people need to move cautiously. Refer to "moving" rather than "walking" or "running" so that everyone is fully included. Then proceed as usual with the exercise, except that people must occupy a square rather than sit in a chair.

TRUST FALL (p. 373)
This exercise, in which members of the group volunteer to fall back into others' interlocked arms, would seem to exclude those who are unable to do the fall as well as those who do not have enough strength to catch. However, you can adapt the exercise by having the volunteer fall back onto a blanket that others are holding securely. Those with insufficient arm strength can be part of the experience by holding some part of the blanket, or at least by touching it.

Assigning Do-Able Roles

Many exercises ask for one or more participants to take on special roles, and in some cases these roles involve abilities that make it possible for people with physical limitations to take part in the exercise. Two examples are:

WHO'S THAT THERE BEHIND THE CURTAIN? (p. 376)
Two people are needed to hold and drop the curtain. This role would suit a person who could not kneel or squat. In processing, include the role and perceptions of the curtain-holders as well as of the people on either side of the curtain.

HOSPITAL TAG WITH A HEALER (p. 271)
This is an excellent opportunity for a person with movement limitations to take a central role in an exercise as the "healer."

Watching Carefully

In some cases, all that is required to make an exercise work well for everyone is your careful observation. For example, if you want to do CONCENTRIC CIRCLES (p. 190) with a group in which someone has a mobility issue, as the group counts off by 2s notice whether that person is a "1" or a "2." Then make that person's group the outer circle, which doesn't move. If more than one person has a mobility issue, before the group counts off try to determine by observation if those with mobility issues will be in the same group. If not, you will have to ask someone to switch places.

In-Your-Chair Exercises

Chapter 13 contains more than 30 exercises that do not require much movement. In addition, many exercises in other chapters are typically done while people are seated, or could be done this way. Remember also that any exercise can be changed and adapted to keep it fresh for the group; by making small changes to exercises that the group has already done, you not only keep the exercises fun for the group, but also provide new processing points that may be even more appropriate to the group's situation.

It's important, however, not to repeatedly confine the group as a whole to exercises that do not require much movement. Keep thinking about adapting exercises and assigning do-able roles so that the group can have a variety of experiences.

Scenario: An Adaptation of THE HUMAN KNOT

Tony was the facilitator for a youth group. In planning the group's meetings, he had to be aware of the physical limitations of a group member, Lorraine, who was born with one arm that was half the size of the other.

Tony strove to plan each meeting so that there was an environment of safety and full participation, without drawing attention to the adaptations that were necessary to include Lorraine. She made it clear at the beginning that she was willing to not participate sometimes due to her disability, but Tony felt that frequent nonparticipation would eventually isolate her from the group.

He wanted to use the HUMAN KNOT to build trust and cooperation in the group and to make points on leadership and teamwork, so he thought of an adaptation. He obtained yarn in a variety of colors and gave each person a length of yarn. People then did the exercise in the usual way except that, instead of holding hands, each person held on to their own piece of yarn and to someone else's piece of yarn. The different colors helped people to identify each other as they worked to unravel their knot.

The exercise served its function of demonstrating the importance of group cooperation and trust. In addition, it allowed Lorraine to begin trusting the group. Tony saw how it helped her to open up more as the group worked together.

Appendix C: Words for Word Association

The Word Association Contest (p. 254) requires a large number of words for participants to respond to. This appendix contains lists of words that you could use for the exercise.

The words are categorized as low-, medium-, and high-risk, in an attempt to describe how people in general would react to them on an emotional level. However, the actual risk level for any word depends on the group. Before choosing the words you will use, be sure they reflect the level of risk that you want the group to experience. In most cases, you will simply use low-risk words; include words that could be high-risk in your group only to serve a particular goal that you are working toward.

Within these categories, words are presented randomly.

Low-Risk Words

history
fortune
clouds
baseball
toes
travel
progress
notebook
street
movies
morning
music
lake
honesty
winter
flower
dance
beginning
hours
tuna fish
carnival
toast
fun
trees
Boston
energy
sleep
winter
situation
English
youth
trailer
rug
poster
silence
glasses
paper towels
11 o'clock
newspaper
schedule
mystery
society
boat
blanket
cooperation
sports
beach
trucks
dreams
past
birthday
comedy
communication
ice cream
simple
cold
forest
information
help
mayor
Internet
country
crowd
date
competition
geography
apples
teens
chair
toothpaste
novel
running
clocks
lunch
upside down
computer
cheeseburger
hat
yesterday
noise
painting
pizza
elbows
broccoli
order
respect
sky
rules
California
solution
food
growth
together
clean
park
salvation
authority
bulletin board
cafeteria
grass
cookies
enthusiasm
chimney
Santa Claus
story
power
rock 'n' roll
farmer
saxophone
meeting
corn
Pepsi
singing
tomorrow
stairs
wisdom
learning
boxes
cafeteria
Saturday
plastic
light
empowerment
theater

Medium-Risk Words

money
religion
love
justice
graduation
problem
country
freedom
science
teacher
honesty
communism
biology
life
city
mathematics
arguments
conquest
heartbeat

risk
escape
projects
authority
order
voting
homework
church
courage
rent
school
books
car
child
government
fear
hope
relationship
doctor

travel
confusion
legs
success
feminism
isolation
work
lawyer
website
complication
romance
peace
student
oppression
anger
responsibility
revolution
community
achievement

High-Risk Words

crime
drugs
home
sex
war
racism
soldier
future
college
family
classism
judge

holidays
violence
blood
blind
condom
rescue
homophobia
prisoner
babies
beer
suicide
girls

jail
death
sexism
police
motherhood
fascism
alcohol
suffering
boys
AIDS

Appendix D: Creating Visualizations

VISUALIZATION is an exercise that provides the time, the peace, and the structure for people to think about issues, experiences, hopes, or dreams that are relevant to the group's goals. It is an excellent exercise to prepare for work or discussion of group issues. The specific content of each Visualization that you write will depend on what you are trying to achieve with it, but this appendix provides some guidelines. Be sure, also, to read the description of the exercise on page 409.

Before leading a group through a Visualization, write out what you plan to say, either word-for-word or using bullet points. Every Visualization exercise includes three parts: getting relaxed, the Visualization itself, and coming back. If you wish, you can do the first and last of these parts in the same way every time.

Getting Relaxed

This simply involves helping people to prepare themselves to enter into the content of the Visualization. Here is an example:

> Close your eyes and become aware of your breathing. Don't try to change your breath; just be aware of it. With every out breath, let more tension flow out of your body. You don't have to do anything right now except to become aware of your breathing, relax, and listen. …
>
> Let your whole head relax. Roll your head from side to side and feel the tension go out of your neck. …
>
> With each breath, feel the tension leaving you. Let your shoulders relax. Let the relaxation travel down your arms and into your fingers. Curl up your fingers tight, then relax them and let the tension flow out of them. …
>
> Relax your legs. Wiggle your toes, and then relax your feet. …
>
> Throughout this exercise, remain in this relaxed feeling. With your mind and heart open, just let the thoughts and feelings come. Don't get stuck in judging yourself or anyone else. Just let the feelings be there. …

The Visualization Itself

One type of Visualization focuses on reality and brings participants on a journey through the past or to a different environment. For example:

- Participants take a reflective journey through a time period such as the past year, the years of high school, or the time since the group began meeting.
- Group members move through an event that all were involved in.
- Students in one kind of school (such as urban, suburban, rural, small, or large) visualize being in a different kind of school.
- People visualize being part of a real culture that is different from their own.

This type of Visualization provides participants with a deeper understanding of a particular context, which could be a context they are a part of or one they have never experienced. Write these Visualizations in the form of a story with a beginning, middle, and end, with questions along the way. For example, the Visualization would move from the beginning of the year through to the end, or from entering a building, through various rooms and/or experiences, to leaving the building. Choose two or three key points to focus on. For these points, pause to ask a question or two, such as "What did it feel like?" or "What were you thinking?" You can also pose more general reflective questions, such as "What ideas did you come in with? Have those ideas proved true, or not?"

Another type of Visualization asks people to imagine something that does not exist, or does not yet exist, such as their ideal school, work environment, department store, or party. In these Visualizations, you want to engage people's senses by asking questions such as "What does it look like? … smell like? …sound like?" Ask the group to form images of the people in this ideal environment: "Who is there? …What are they doing?" You can ask the participants to place themselves in the environment and to explore what it feels like to be there.

In both types, less is more. Too many points to think about can overwhelm the listeners and make it difficult for them to relax and let images come to them. You should include some questions and specifics, but not too many.

Here is an example of the center of a Visualization exercise regarding the ideal school:

> Now begin to form a picture of a school you would like to go to—your ideal school. … What does the building look like on the outside? … Picture yourself entering the building. What do you see? How does it feel? … Walk through the hallways and look into the classrooms. What stands out to you? … Walk to the cafeteria. What are the smells as you enter? … Picture the students in the cafeteria, the halls, the classrooms. What are they like? … What sounds do you hear throughout the building? … Now come into a classroom and find a seat. What is going on in the class with the teacher and the students? How do you feel being there? … What makes this school such a good place to be?

Coming Back

To end the experience of the Visualization, you need to give people time to return mentally and emotionally. It's particularly important to relieve the anxiety that some people will feel about when to open their eyes. Here's an example of this section:

> Now remain silent and keep your eyes closed for another few moments, as you take some deep, relaxing breaths. These memories and thoughts are part of you; let them slowly sink to the back of your consciousness. …
>
> Take your time with this process. Keep your eyes closed until you are ready to return your awareness to the group. I'll let you know when most people have rejoined the group and it is time to end the exercise.